"This is a magnificent, creative, scholarly—indeed a noble—book and one that should be in every investment library and on every practitioner's desk. Like a good doctor, the author diagnoses a serious illness, and then provides a prescription for how to alleviate it."

—Victor Niederhoffer, Chief Speculator,
Manchester Investments

"Professor Damodaran systematically destroys the great myths of investment management, attacking each in turn with remorseless logic. He shows how many 'systems' for successful investing actually lose money, even though investors themselves are sometimes unaware of this. He shows too that hope and good intentions are no substitute for information and analysis. Before you make your next investment, read this book."

—Morgen Witzel, Editor-in-Chief,
Corporate Finance Review

"A necessary part of a serious investor's toolkit. Dissecting investment myths is terribly important for the long-term investor. This book is an enjoyable and systematic attack on long-held investment beliefs. A true etymology of investment folklore that clinically tests out popularly held beliefs. A cautionary book for the serious investor."

—Satya Pradhuman, Vice President,
Small Cap Research Department,
Merrill Lynch & Co.

INVESTMENT FABLES

FT Prentice Hall
FINANCIAL TIMES

In an increasingly competitive world, it is quality
of thinking that gives an edge—an idea that opens new
doors, a technique that solves a problem, or an insight
that simply helps make sense of it all.

We work with leading authors in the various arenas
of business and finance to bring cutting-edge thinking
and best learning practice to a global market.

It is our goal to create world-class print publications
and electronic products that give readers
knowledge and understanding which can then be
applied, whether studying or at work.

To find out more about our business
products, you can visit us at www.ft-ph.com

Pearson
Education

INVESTMENT FABLES

EXPOSING THE MYTHS

OF "CAN'T MISS"

INVESTMENT STRATEGIES

ASWATH DAMODARAN
WWW.DAMODARAN.COM

An imprint of PEARSON Education
London • New York • San Francisco • Toronto • Sydney
Tokyo • Singapore • Hong Kong • Cape Town • Madrid •
Paris • Milan • Munich • Amsterdam

Library of Congress Cataloging-in-Publication Data

Damodaran, Aswath.
   Investment fables : exposing the myths of "can't miss" investment strategies /
Aswath Damodaran.
      p. cm. — (Financial Times Prentice Hall books)
   Includes bibliographical references and index.
   ISBN 0-13-140312-5
   1. Investment analysis.   2. Investments.   I. Title.   II. Series.

HG4529.D358 2004
332.6—dc22

2004040413

Editorial/production supervision: *Nicholas Radhuber*
Executive editor: *Tim Moore*
Editorial assistant: *Richard Winkler*
Marketing manager: *Alexis R. Heydt-Long*
Manufacturing buyer: *Maura Zaldivar*
Cover design director: *Jerry Votta*
Cover design: *Anthony Gemmellaro*
Art director: *Gail Cocker-Bogusz*

© 2004 Pearson Education, Inc.
Publishing as Financial Times Prentice Hall
Upper Saddle River, New Jersey 07458

Financial Times Prentice Hall books are widely used by corporations and
government agencies for training, marketing, and resale.

**Prentice Hall offers excellent discounts on this book when ordered in quantity for bulk
purchases or special sales. For more information, please contact:
U.S. Corporate and Government Sales
1-800-382-3419
corpsales@pearsontechgroup.com**

**For sales outside of the U.S., please contact:
International Sales
1-317-581-3793
international@pearsontechgroup.com**

Company and product names mentioned herein are the trademarks
or registered trademarks of their respective owners.

Printed in the United States of America

3rd Printing

ISBN 0-13-140312-5

Pearson Education LTD.
Pearson Education Australia PTY, Limited
Pearson Education Singapore, Pte. Ltd.
Pearson Education North Asia Ltd.
Pearson Education Canada, Ltd.
Pearson Educación de Mexico, S.A. de C.V.
Pearson Education—Japan
Pearson Education Malaysia, Pte. Ltd.

*To my father, who showed me the power of ideas,
and to my mother, who taught me the value of common sense.*

FINANCIAL TIMES PRENTICE HALL BOOKS

For more information, please go to www.ft-ph.com

Business and Technology

Sarv Devaraj and Rajiv Kohli
    The IT Payoff: Measuring the Business Value of Information Technology Investments

Nicholas D. Evans
    Business Innovation and Disruptive Technology: Harnessing the Power of Breakthrough Technology…for Competitive Advantage

Nicholas D. Evans
    Consumer Gadgets: 50 Ways to Have Fun and Simplify Your Life with Today's Technology…and Tomorrow's

Faisal Hoque
    The Alignment Effect: How to Get Real Business Value Out of Technology

Economics

David Dranove
    What's Your Life Worth? Health Care Rationing…Who Lives? Who Dies? Who Decides?

John C. Edmunds
    Brave New Wealthy World: Winning the Struggle for World Prosperity

Jonathan Wight
    Saving Adam Smith: A Tale of Wealth, Transformation, and Virtue

Entrepreneurship

Oren Fuerst and Uri Geiger
    From Concept to Wall Street: A Complete Guide to Entrepreneurship and Venture Capital

David Gladstone and Laura Gladstone
    Venture Capital Handbook: An Entrepreneur's Guide to Raising Venture Capital, Revised and Updated

Thomas K. McKnight
    Will It Fly? How to Know if Your New Business Idea Has Wings… Before You Take the Leap

Erica Orloff and Kathy Levinson, Ph.D.
    The 60-Second Commute: A Guide to Your 24/7 Home Office Life

Jeff Saperstein and Daniel Rouach
    Creating Regional Wealth in the Innovation Economy: Models, Perspectives, and Best Practices

Stephen Spinelli, Jr., Robert M. Rosenberg, and Sue Birley
    Franchising: Pathway to Wealth Creation

CONTENTS

Chapter 7   GROW, BABY, GROW!: THE GROWTH STORY   197

Chapter 8   THE WORST IS BEHIND YOU: THE CONTRARIAN STORY   233

Chapter 11 A SURE THING: NO RISK AND SURE PROFITS 353

Chapter 12 IT'S ALL UPSIDE: THE MOMENTUM STORY 391

INVESTMENT FABLES:
TALL TALES
ABOUT STOCKS

As investors, you have all been on the receiving end of sales pitches from brokers, friends and investment advisors about stocks that they claim will deliver spectacular returns. These stories not only sound persuasive and reasonable but are also backed up by evidence—anecdotal, in some cases, and statistical, in others—that the strategies work. When you try to implement them for your investments, though, you seldom can match their success on paper. All too often, you end up with buyer's remorse, poorer for the experience and promising yourselves that you will not fall for the allure of these stories again. All too often, you forget the lessons of past mistakes and are easy prey for the next big stock story.

While there are literally hundreds of schemes to beat the market in circulation, they are all variants of about a dozen basic themes that have been around for as long as there have been stocks to buy and sell. These broad themes are modified, given new names and marketed as new and different investment strategies by salespeople to a new generation of investors. There must be something in these stories that appeals to investor instincts and to human weaknesses—greed, fear and hubris, to name but three—to give them the staying power that they do. This book is an exploration of the appeal of these stories, why so many investors fall for them and fail with them, and what it may take to win with each of them.

As you will see, with each story, there is a kernel of truth that makes it believable and a base in financial theory that allows proponents to claim to have a solid rationale. Each chapter begins with an examination of the basis for each investment story and the theory that would justify its adoption. Why bother with the theory? Not only will it give you perspective on what makes each story work, but it will also allow you to identify potential weaknesses with the story.

If you have been on the receiving end of one of these investment stories, you probably have also been told of studies that back them up and you are offered evidence of their potency. It should come as no surprise, given the source, that most of these studies give you only a portion of the truth. As you will see in this book, every investment strategy ever devised has succeeded for some periods and with some stocks, but the complete picture requires an assessment of whether it works over long periods and with a wide cross section of stocks. That is why you will see a review of the existing empirical evidence, drawn from both believers and skeptics, on each strategy and some of the potential problems with each.

With every investment strategy, investors also grapple with the question of what adopting that strategy will mean in terms of investment choices. If you adopt a strategy of buying "low" PE stocks, you have to judge what represents a low PE ratio and what types of stocks have low PE ratios. If you believe that your best investments are in small companies, you have to decide how to measure the size of companies—sales, market capitalization, etc.—and what level would represent a small company. You will be presented with rules of thumb, that a PE of 8 is cheap or that a company with a market capitalization less than $100 million is small, but these rules of thumb can be dangerous as markets themselves change over time. To provide a frame of reference, this book examines the distribution of various measures—PE, price-to-book ratio and market capitalization, to name a few—across the entire market. This should then allow you to get a sense of differences across the market and to develop portfolio standards.

The best test of any strategy is to apply it to the market and to peruse the portfolio that you would have ended up with as a result of following it. This book attempts to do this with each of the broad strategies examined, and you can ask yourself whether you would be comfortable investing in the stocks that make up this portfolio. If you are not, it is a warning sign that this strategy may not be appropriate for you. If you are a careful investor, putting this portfolio under a microscope will allow you to study the strategy for weaknesses and examine what you can do to minimize the damage.

It is worth emphasizing what this book is about and what it does not try to do. It is not about promoting or debunking investment strategies, since there are plenty of analysts and brokers who do the former and lots of cynics, many from academia, who do the latter. But it is about providing a full picture of each investment strategy so that you can make your own judgments about what works and what does not. It is not about answering every investment question that has ever been asked; no one can have the foresight to do this. But it is about providing you with the ammunition to ask the right questions when confronted with promoters of these strategies. It is not a book for pessimists who are convinced that picking stocks is an exercise in futility, but it is a book for optimists who want to figure out how to make active strategies pay off and how to use them prudently. It is not about things you cannot and should not do while investing, but it is about things you can and should do as an investor to improve your odds for success.

As long as there have been financial markets, there have been mountebanks and frauds luring investors into get-rich schemes that ultimately fail. In the aftermath of these failings, you are often tempted to turn to the courts and to governments to protect you from yourself. The best antidote, though, to an unscrupulous sales pitch about "stocks that cannot lose" or to a "get rich quickly" scheme is a skeptical and informed investor. I hope this book helps you become one.

1 INTRODUCTION

Investing is full of stories that sound good when they are told but don't hold up under close scrutiny. Consider a few: Buy stock in good companies and the returns will surely follow. Buy after bad news. Buy after good news. Stocks always win in the long term. Follow the insiders. Buy stocks with big dividends. Buy stocks that have gone down the most. Go with stocks that have gone up the most. What makes these stories alluring is that there is a kernel of truth to each one of these stories but none of them is foolproof. You will examine these and other investment sales pitches in this book, consider the potential downside with each, and study how you might be able to modify each one to reduce downside risk.

THE POWER OF THE STORY

Human beings are much more likely to be swayed by good stories than they are by graphs and numbers. The most effective sales pitches to investors tell a compelling story, backed up by anecdotal evidence. But what makes a story compelling in the first place? Investment stories are convincing not only because they are told well but also because they draw on several common factors:

- Most good investment stories appeal to a fundamental component of human nature, whether it be greed, hope, fear or envy. In fact, what often sets apart successful investment salespeople from unsuccessful ones is their uncanny ability to gauge an investor's weak spots and create a story to take advantage of them.

1

■ Good investment stories are also backed up by the evidence, at least as presented by the storyteller. As you will see in this book, though, the evidence may only tell part of the story and much of what is presented as incontrovertible proof of the efficacy of an investment strategy falls apart on closer examination.

In each chapter that follows, you will see the rationale that allows the stories presented in this book to resonate with investors. As you read these sections, you will undoubtedly remember variants of these stories told by your broker, investment advisor or neighbor.

CATEGORIZING INVESTMENT STORIES

Investment stories come in all forms. Some are designed to appeal to investors who do not like to take risks, and they generally talk about low-risk ways to play the stock market. Others are oriented toward risk seekers who want to get rich quickly; these stories emphasize the potential upside and hardly ever talk about risk. Still others are structured for those who believe that you can get something for nothing if you are smarter or better prepared than others in the market. Finally, there are stories for the optimists who believe that you always win in the long term. In this section, you will get a preview of the stories that are examined in detail in the coming chapters.

STORIES FOR THE RISK AVERSE

Some investors are born risk averse, whereas others become risk averse because of circumstances—an insecure job or impending retirement can make you far more concerned about losing money. Still others are scared into risk aversion by an extended bear market. Whatever the reason for the risk aversion, the investment stories that sell the best to these investors emphasize low-risk strategies while promising much higher returns than they are making currently on their safe investments.

High Dividend Stocks.   Risk-averse investors generally prefer the safety of government or high-grade corporate bonds to the riskiness of stocks. They feel more secure with bonds, knowing that they can count on these bonds delivering income in the form of coupons while they hold them and that the principal invested in these bonds is intact. To attract these investors to stocks, you have to try to offer them comparable income and safety, while also providing them a premium for taking the additional risk. Stocks that pay high dividends are attractive to risk-averse investors because they resemble bonds in terms of generating income, with the added bonus of price appreciation. The dividends on some stocks are higher than the coupons earned on safe bonds, and while the principal invested in stocks is not protected in the same way that the principal invested in bonds is, the risk can be alleviated if the company paying the dividend is large and has substantial assets.

Stocks with Low Price-Earnings Ratios.   Stocks that trade at low multiples of earnings have historically been viewed as both cheap and as safe equity investments. While you can see why a stock that trades at 5 times earnings is considered cheap, why would it be classified as safe? The presumption is that the firm will continue to make these earnings in the long term and that this earnings power should provide a floor on the price. In fact, value investors like Ben Graham have long argued that buying stocks with low PE ratios is a low-risk, high-return strategy. For investors who are concerned about the risk in equities, this strategy seems to offer a low-risk way of entering the stock market.

Stocks That Trade at Less Than Book Value.   A close relative of the low PE stock in the cheap stock family is the stock that trades at below book value. To some investors, the book value of a stock is not only the accountant's measure of how much the equity in a firm is worth but is also a more reliable measure of a stock's worth than the market price, which is set by investors swayed by fads and fancies. Thus, a stock that trades at less than book value is viewed as an undervalued stock. To some risk-averse investors, who believe that book value is equivalent to liquidation value, stocks that trade at below book value also come with what they see as backup insurance. If the stock price does not go up, the firm should be able to liquidate its assets and deliver the (higher) book value.

Stable Earnings Companies. For many investors, the risk of investing in the equity of a company is tied to uncertainty about the company's capacity to earn money in the future. Even the best-run companies can have earnings that are volatile and unpredictable. Consequently, if you could invest in a company that has stable and predictable earnings, you could essentially combine the benefits of stock ownership with the reliability of bonds. How would a company achieve this earnings stability? It could do so by diversifying into multiple businesses or countries and becoming a conglomerate or multinational; bad times in one business or country would then be offset by good times in another, leading to more stable earnings over time. It could draw on a variety of products now available in financial markets—futures, options and other derivatives—to protect itself against interest rate, currency or commodity price risk and thus make its earnings more predictable. In its least benign form, the earnings stability can be purely cosmetic, created by accounting ploys and sleight of hand.

STORIES FOR THE RISK SEEKER

In buoyant markets, investors often seek out risk, hoping to make high returns to compensate. Not surprisingly, they are not interested in stocks that look like bonds. Instead, they want to find companies that provide the best upside potential even though they might be risky. The investment stories that work best for them are the ones that emphasize risks, but present them as a chance to make a killing (upside risk) rather than as a danger (downside risk).

Great Companies. Buy good companies, you are told, and the returns will follow. While the definition of good can vary from investor to investor and from investment publication to publication, most definitions of good companies revolve around financial yardsticks. Companies that earn high accounting rates of return and have done well for their stockholders in the past usually qualify. In recent years, a new category has been created with good defined more broadly to include social benefits. A good company with this broader definition would be one that does well for its stockholders, employees, customers and society at the same time. The rationale for investing in these companies is that the superior management of these companies will find ways to turn threats into opportunities, leading to dual benefits—higher returns and lower risk.

Growth Stocks. If you put your money into the companies with the highest earnings growth in the market, you are playing the segment of the market that is most likely to have an exponential payoff (or meltdown). While growth stocks do not offer much in terms of dividends, usually trade at high multiples of earnings, and are usually risky, risk-seeking investors are not fazed by any of these concerns. They buy stocks for price appreciation rather than dividends, and their view is that the high earnings multiples will only translate into even higher prices as the earnings grow over time. To the skeptic's question of what happens if the growth does not manifest itself, these investors will respond that they have the skill to pick the right companies—companies that have found the key to sustainable, long term growth.

Loser Stocks. Stocks that have fallen dramatically in the recent past offer interesting opportunities for investors who are willing to take risk. While these companies generally have serious problems—some have incompetent management, others have too much debt and still others have made strategic missteps—the argument used to justify investing in them is that they have fallen so much that they cannot fall much more. Risk-seeking investors, who believe that markets have overreacted to bad news and pushed prices down too far, buy these stocks hoping that stock prices bounce back.

Hidden Bargains. To the bargain hunters, the best stocks to buy are the ones that few other investors are aware of. In a market like the United States, in which thousands of professional money managers and analysts track stocks, this may seem like a tall order, but there are thousands of stocks in smaller companies that are neither tracked by analysts nor held by institutions. The ranks of these ignored stocks are swelled each year by initial public offerings that bring new firms into the marketplace. The hope of finding the next great growth company—a Microsoft or a Cisco—before anyone else does drives many risk-seeking investors to forage through these smaller, less followed segments of the market, looking for young and promising companies. In fact, some investors with more funds at their disposal try to get in even earlier in the process by being venture capitalists and private equity investors in small, private businesses. If they pick the right businesses to invest in, they can cash out when these businesses eventually go public.

STORIES FOR THE GREEDY

In any listing of human vices, greed usually finds itself somewhere near the top. Philosophers and priests have inveighed against greed through the ages, but it is also the fuel that drives financial markets. The demand for stocks would be limited in a world where investors were not greedy for higher returns. Not surprisingly, those selling investment stories have also recognized that even a subtle appeal to the greed of investors is sufficient to get them interested. The investment stories that play to greed share a common theme: they allow you to believe that you can get something for nothing.

Get on the Fast Track. Growth companies can be good investments in the long term, but it usually takes a long time for a small firm to grow into a big one. For impatient investors who want their payoff now, the wait can seem endless. Some firms accelerate the growth process by acquiring other companies, in their own and in other businesses. By paying for these acquisitions with new stock issues, these firms can speed the process even further. Investors are attracted to these companies for two reasons: The first is that they are usually the newsmakers in any market; acquisitions attract a great deal of press attention. The second is that the limitations of acquisition accounting often make these firms look much better than their peer group; in fact, with the right accounting treatment the growth can be made to look close to costless.[1] Investors play both sides of the acquisition game, with some buying acquisitive companies, hoping to ride their growth to high payoffs, and others trying to invest in potential target companies, hoping to gain a share of the premium paid on the acquisitions.

No Money Down, No Risk, Big Profits.   Every investor dreams of finding the investment equivalent of a free lunch: an investment with no risk and high returns (at least relative to what you could have earned on a bona fide riskless investment like a government bond). For these "arbitrage" opportunities to exist, you have to find two identical investments that are priced differently at the same time by markets and a guarantee that the prices will converge over time. Not surprisingly, these pure arbitrage opportunities are rare and are most likely to exist in futures and options markets. Even in those markets, they are accessible only to a few investors with low transactions costs and superior execution capabilities. You are far more likely to find near-arbitrage opportunities, in which two assets that are not quite identical trade at different prices, and speculative arbitrage, which is more speculation than arbitrage. Since there is no guarantee of price convergence, these investments will remain risky even to the most sophisticated investors and become even riskier when a significant portion of the investment comes from borrowing.

Go with the Flow: Momentum Strategies.   To some investors, a low-risk and high-return strategy is to buy stocks that are going up and to go along for the ride. Implicit in this strategy is the assumption that there is significant momentum in stock prices: stocks that go up will continue to go up and stocks that go down will continue to go down. Chartists and technical analysts have used chart patterns—trend lines, support lines and resistance lines, to name but three—for decades to both decipher the trend and, just as importantly, to get advance notice of a shift in the trend. After all, the momentum that brought you profits can very quickly turn against you. In recent years, momentum investors have also expanded their analysis to include trading volume. A stock that surges on high trading volume has both price and volume momentum and is considered a better investment than one that goes up on low trading volume.

STORIES FOR THE HOPEFUL

No matter how poor their past investment choices have been, some investors seem all too willing to forget the past and to try yet again to find a way of beating the average investor. For some, the hope for success rests on finding and following the right investment experts, investing in the stocks they pick. For others, the hope comes from an almost religious belief that stocks always win in the long term and that all you need to succeed is patience.

Just Follow the Experts. There is no shortage of experts, self-anointed or otherwise, in financial markets. There are equity research analysts, touting their superior access to information and management, making recommendations on which stocks to buy and sell. You have insiders at firms, from chief executive officers to board members, acting as cheerleaders in public but telling us far more about what they really think about their companies when they buy and sell stock in them. There are investment newsletters and advisory services, too many to keep track of, each claiming to have found the secret formula for great stock picking. For some investors, who are confused by the cacophony of contradictory views on markets and the volume of news about stocks, these experts offer welcome solace by taking on the responsibility of picking the right stocks.

Stocks Always Win in the Long Term.   It has almost become conventional wisdom in the United States that the stock market may have a bad year or even a string of bad years but that stocks always win in the long term. Take any 10-year period in market history, you will be told, and stocks have done better than government bonds or bills. If you buy into this reasoning and you have a long time horizon, you would put all of your money in stocks since they will earn more for you than less risky alternatives over long periods. Of course, you can augment your returns if you can invest in stocks only in the good years and avoid them in the bad years. There are dozens of indicators, from the winner of the Super Bowl to the level of interest rates, that claim to tell you when to get into stocks and when to get out. The payoff to timing markets correctly is so large that everyone who invests in the stock markets, individual or institution, tries to do it at one time or another.

DECONSTRUCTING AN INVESTMENT STORY

Every investment story outlined in this book has been around for decades. Part of the reason is that each story has a kernel of truth in it. Consider, for example, the rationale for buying stocks that trade at low multiples of earnings. They are more likely to be cheap, you will be told. This makes sense to investors, not only because it is intuitive, but also because it is often backed up by evidence. Over the last seven decades, for instance, a portfolio of stocks with low PE ratios would have outperformed a portfolio of stocks with high PE ratios by almost 7% a year. Given the claims and counterclaims that make investing so confusing, it is important that you take each story apart methodically, looking at both its strong and weak points. In this section, the steps in the process that will be adopted in each chapter to analyze each story are laid out.

I. THEORETICAL ROOTS: ISOLATING THE KERNEL OF TRUTH

Most investment storytellers claim to have contempt for theorists. They believe that theory is for academics and other ivory tower residents, who do not have to make investment choices for a living. The irony is that every investment story that has survived in the long term has done so because it is firmly rooted in financial theory. After all, you can use a valuation model to illustrate why stocks that trade at low multiples of earnings may be cheap and why companies with good management should trade at much higher values.

You will begin by examining the theoretical foundations for every story in this book. For instance, if your sales pitch is that stocks that have gone up the most in the past are more likely to continue going up—the classic momentum story— what types of assumptions would you have to make about investors and markets for this to happen? While this may seem like a diversion, there are three reasons why understanding the underlying theory is useful:

- Even if you think that you have discovered the ultimate investment strategy, you should be curious about what makes the strategy work. This will allow you to modify and adjust the strategy as the world changes. For instance, if you believe that stocks exhibit price momentum because investors learn slowly about new information, you may have to modify the strategy to reflect the fact that news reaches investors far more quickly today than it did a decade ago or earlier.

- No investment strategy works all the time. Understanding the theory will help you determine the periods when a strategy is most likely to work and when it is most likely to fail. If you view stocks with high dividends as an attractive alternative to bonds, for instance, the attraction should get even stronger in periods when interest rates on bonds are low.

■ Every strategy also has its weak spots. By beginning with the theory and working forward, you can identify what you as an investor need to worry about most with each investment story and what you might be able to control to reflect your concerns. For instance, using a valuation model to assess the price-earnings ratio will lead you very quickly to the two primary concerns that you should have when investing in stocks with low PE ratios: that they will not have much growth in earnings to offer and that they may be very risky.

If you lack a quantitative bent, rest assured that the theory needed to illustrate the investment stories is simple.

II. LOOKING AT THE EVIDENCE: GETTING THE FULL PICTURE

The sheer magnitude of data that you have available on financial markets going back a century can be both a boon and a bane to investors. On the one hand, having the data available allows you to test almost any investment proposition that you want to. On the other hand, if you wanted to push a point of view, such as the notion that high growth companies are better investments than low growth companies, you can find backing for this view in some periods of market history and with some stocks. Given that almost all evidence that is presented for or against investment strategies comes with some bias, each of the chapters in this book attempts to do the following:

■ *Look at the viability of each strategy in the long term across the broadest cross section of stocks*. Rather than look at small subsamples of stocks over arbitrary time periods, you will look at all stocks listed in the United

States over the longest period for which data is available. Thus, to examine whether stocks that trade at a discount on book value are, on average, good investments over time, you will look at the returns an investor would have earned on all stocks with this characteristic from 1926 to the present. As you will see, some highly touted strategies do break down when they are exposed to this level of scrutiny.

■ *Look at subperiods of history to see when the strategy has succeeded and when it has failed.* Every strategy in this book has good periods, during which it has generated substantial returns, and bad periods, when it has failed. If you adopt an investment strategy of buying stocks with low price-earnings ratios, you will find that there are some subperiods in history in which this strategy does much better than others. By taking a closer look at market conditions—interest rates and GDP growth, for example—during these periods, you may be able to fine-tune your strategy and make it more effective.

■ *Put the returns from the strategy under a microscope to see if they can be explained by chance.* Strategies that are built around holding stocks deliver volatile returns, beating the market by large amounts in some years and underperforming badly in others. Consequently, you have to be careful how you read the final results of your analysis. For instance, if you do find that stocks in small companies deliver 2% more in returns each year, on average, than larger companies, over a ten-year period, it is possible that this extra return can be explained purely by chance. Luckily, there are statistical tests that allow you to assess whether this is the case.

As a final note, every strategy examined in this book has been tested before by both advocates and skeptics of the strategy. While some of these studies are dated, you can get a fuller picture of whether a strategy works by looking at these different points of view.[2]

III. CRUNCHING THE NUMBERS:
DEVELOPING A FRAME OF REFERENCE

Investment strategies are often based upon rules of thumb—8 times earnings is cheap, a stock that trades at a PE that is less than its expected growth rate is cheap, etc.—and these rules have wide appeal among investors. After all, with more than 7000 listed stocks traded in the United States, investors are faced with an overwhelming amount of information. With this information overload, any rule that makes life simpler is welcomed. While there may be good reasons to adopt rules of thumb when investing, there are costs associated with using them as well:

- *Rules of thumb developed in a market can quickly become outmoded as market conditions change or in a different market.* Consider, for instance, the rule of thumb that stocks trading at less than 8 times earnings are cheap. While this may have made sense when the rule was developed in the 1960s, about half of all stocks in the United States traded at less than 8 times earnings in 1981 (making it too loose a definition of cheap) and less than 10% of all stocks did so in 1997 (making it too tight a definition in that year).
- *Rules of thumb are no substitute for the whole picture.* Investors who use rules of thumb as a substitute for the whole picture can sometimes miss useful and important information that they could have used to better their strategies.

But how can you consolidate and make sense of the information that is available on so many different stocks? With each investment strategy, you will be presented with how the measures used in that strategy varied across the market at the time this book was written. For instance, you will look at the distribution of earnings growth across companies in the United States—how many companies in the market have earnings growth greater than 25%, between 20% and 25% etc.—when you analyze a strategy of buying high growth companies. Since these values will undoubtedly change in the months and years to come, the numbers will be updated and provided to readers on the web site for the book.

To get a true sense of an investment strategy and whether you would want to adopt it, you should also take a look at the portfolio of stocks that would emerge from this strategy. With each strategy in this book, you will do this looking across all of your investment choices at the time. If your strategy is to invest in low PE stocks, for instance, you will see the portfolio of the 100 stocks that had the lowest PE ratios in the United States at the end of 2002. There are at least two reasons for doing this:

- *Beyond anecdotal evidence:* By going beyond the anecdotal evidence, you will get a fuller picture of both the strengths and weaknesses of each strategy. You will find, for instance, that the typical low PE stock is not a mature, safe company (as is often claimed by its proponents) but a small, risky company that you have never heard of before.
- *Risk testing:* For an investment strategy to work for you, you have to be comfortable with the portfolio that emerges with that strategy. The only way you can see if this is true is by looking at the list of stocks that would qualify as good stocks with each strategy.

IV. More to the Story: Probing for Weaknesses

Every investment story has its strong points and its weak ones. While you can rest assured that you will be given a detailed analysis of the strengths, proponents of the strategy almost never talk about its weaknesses. To use an investment strategy effectively, though, you need to be just as informed about its limitations as you are about its potential promise.

Toward the end of every chapter in this book, you will examine everything that can potentially go wrong with each strategy, using the portfolio that emerges from that strategy as your basis. Consider, for instance, the 100 stocks with the lowest PE ratios that would have been your portfolio with a low PE strategy. If one of the concerns you have is that low PE companies are riskier than the rest of the market, you can compare the riskiness of the portfolio of low PE stocks to the riskiness of the rest of the market and examine how many stocks you will lose in your portfolio if you want to avoid the riskiest stocks in the market (in the top quartile, for example).

If you have multiple concerns about a strategy and you eliminate stocks from your portfolio as a result of each concern, you may very well find yourself with very few stocks left in your final portfolio. In the process, though, you will learn about where each strategy breaks down.

V. Lessons for Investors

If the message you take away from this book is that you cannot succeed with any investment strategy, it will have failed in its mission. Each strategy has potential for success if it matches your risk preferences and time horizon and if you are careful about how you use it. At the end of every chapter, the lessons of the chapter—positive as well as negative—are summarized and presented as a series of screens that you can adopt to increase your odds of success. Consider, for instance, a strategy of investing in companies with low price-earnings ratios. After presenting the perils associated with this strategy—low PE ratio companies can have unsustainable earnings, low growth and high risk—you will consider a series of screens that you can use to construct a portfolio of low PE stocks with sustainable earnings, reasonable growth and limited exposure to risk. The portfolio that emerges using these screens is presented at the end of each chapter. You should not consider this investment advice, since stock prices and fundamentals will have changed by the time you read this book. Instead, you should view this as an ongoing process that you can use to find the best stocks for you in any market at any time.

CONCLUSION

Investment stories have been around for as long as we have had financial markets and they show remarkable longevity. The same stories are recycled with each generation of investors and presented as new and different by their proponents. The stories that are examined in the chapters to come have been laid out and categorized by the human emotion that makes each one so compelling; some stories appeal to the fearful (risk averse), others to the hopeful and still others to the greedy. The process used in each chapter to examine each of the investment stories is also laid out, starting with the story, followed by the theoretical foundations and the evidence of its effectiveness (or lack thereof) and closing with its potential weaknesses (and ways of protecting yourself against them).

ENDNOTES

1. With pooling accounting, which was legal until very recently, companies that used stock to acquire other companies were not required to show the cost of their acquisitions in their financial statements. Instead, they were allowed to show just the book value of the assets of the acquired companies.

2. The other studies are referenced in the footnotes of each chapter. If you are interested, you can trace the source articles and read them.

2

HIGH DIVIDEND STOCKS:
BONDS WITH PRICE
APPRECIATION?

SAM'S LOST DIVIDENDS

Once upon a time, there lived a happy and carefree retiree named Sam. Sam was in good health and thoroughly enjoyed having nothing to do. His only regret was that his hard-earned money was invested in treasury bonds, earning a measly rate of 3% a year. One day, Sam's friend, Joe, who liked to offer unsolicited investment advice, suggested that Sam take his money out of bonds and invest in stocks. When Sam demurred, saying that he did not like to take risk and that he needed the cash income from his bonds, Joe gave him a list of 10 companies that paid high dividends. "Buy these stocks," he said, "and you will get the best of both worlds: the income of a bond and the upside potential of stocks." Sam did so and was rewarded for a while with a portfolio of stocks that delivered a dividend yield of 5%, leaving him a happy person.

Barely a year later, troubles started when Sam did not receive the dividend check from one of his companies. When he called the company, he was told that they had run into financial trouble and were suspending dividend payments. Sam, to his surprise, found out that even companies that have paid dividends for decades are not legally obligated to keep paying them. Sam also found that four of the companies in his portfolio called themselves real estate investment trusts, though he was not quite sure what they did. He found out soon enough, when the entire real investment trust sector dropped 30% in the course of a week, pulling down the value of his portfolio. Much as he tried to tell himself that it was only a paper loss and that he could continue to receive dividends, he felt uncomfortable with the knowledge that he had less savings now than when he started with his portfolio. Finally, Sam also noticed that the remaining six stocks in his portfolio reported little or no earnings growth from period to period. By the end of the third year, his portfolio had dropped in value and the dividend yield had declined to 2.5%. Chastened by his losses, Sam sold his stocks and put his money back into bonds. And he never listened to Joe again.

Moral of the story: High dividends do not a bond make.

If you are an investor who abhors risk, you probably prefer to invest your money in treasury bonds or safe corporate bonds, rather than stocks, because bonds offer a guaranteed income stream in the form of coupons. The tradeoff is that bonds have limited potential for price appreciation. A bond's price may increase as interest rates go down, but most of the money you make on your investment must come from the coupons you receive over the bond's life. Notwithstanding your aversion to risk, you may sometimes be induced to invest in stocks by what seems like an unbeatable combination—a stock that delivers dividends that are comparable to the coupons on bonds, with the possibility of price appreciation. In this chapter, you will consider why some stocks pay high dividends, whether such dividends can be compared with the coupons paid on bonds, and the dangers that can sometimes lurk in these stocks.

CORE OF THE STORY

When you buy a stock, your potential return comes from two sources. The first is the dividend that you expect the stock to pay over time, and the second is the expected price appreciation you see in the stock. The dividends you will receive from investing in stocks will generally be lower than what you would have earned as coupons if you had invested the same amount in bonds; this sets up the classic tradeoff between bonds and stocks. You earn much higher current income on a bond, but your potential for price appreciation is much greater with equity. Bonds are less risky but equities offer higher expected returns. But what if you could find stocks that deliver dividends that are comparable to the coupons paid on bonds? Two different arguments are made by those who believe that such stocks are good investments.

- *Optimist Pitch: "You have the best of both worlds"*: In this pitch, you are told that you can get the best of both bond and equity investments when you buy high dividend stocks. Summarizing the pitch: *These are stocks that deliver dividends that are comparable and, in some cases, higher than coupons on bonds. Buy these stocks and you can count on receiving the dividends for the long term. If the stock price goes up, it is an added bonus. If it does not, you still earn more in dividends than you would have earned by investing in bonds.* In fact, this story is bolstered by the fact that many stocks that pay high dividends are safer, larger companies for which the potential risk is low.

■ *Pessimist Pitch: "Defensive investments":* This is the pitch that gains resonance in bear markets. In an environment in which investors have seen their equity portfolios wither as the stock market declines, stocks that pay high dividends offer solace. Summarizing this argument: *Even though these stocks may lose value like other stocks, investors holding on to them can still count on receiving the dividends.* In fact, during crises, a general flight to safety occurs across all markets. While it manifests itself immediately as a shift from stocks to government bonds, it also shows up within equity markets as investors shift from higher-risk stocks (often high growth companies that pay no or little dividends) to low-risk stocks (often stable companies that pay high dividends).

These sales pitches have the most appeal to investors who are not only risk averse but also count on their portfolios to deliver a steady stream of income. It should come as no surprise that older investors, often retired, are the most receptive audience.

THEORETICAL ROOTS: DIVIDENDS AND VALUE

Can paying more in dividends make a company a more attractive investment? There is a surprising degree of disagreement about the answer to this question in corporate financial theory. One of the most widely circulated propositions in corporate finance—the Miller-Modigliani theorem—states that dividends are neutral and cannot affect returns.[1] How, you might wonder, is this possible? When a company pays more in dividends every year, say, 4% of the stock price rather than the 2% it pays currently, does that not increase the total return? Not in a Miller-Modigliani world. In this world, the expected price appreciation on this stock will drop by exactly the same amount as the dividend increase, say, from 10% to 8%, leaving you with a total return of 12%. While there remain numerous adherents to this view, there are theorists who disagree by noting that a firm may signal its confidence in its future earnings by increasing dividends. Accordingly, stock prices will increase when dividends are increased and drop when dividends are cut. To complete the discussion, still others argue that dividends expose investors to higher taxes and thus should reduce value. Thus, dividends can increase, decrease or have no effect on value, depending upon which of these three arguments you subscribe to.

DIVIDENDS DO NOT MATTER: THE MILLER-MODIGLIANI THEOREM

The basis of the argument that dividends don't matter is simple. Firms that pay more dividends will offer less price appreciation and deliver the same total return to stockholders. This is because a firm's value comes from the investments it makes—plant, equipment and other real assets, for example—and whether these investments deliver high or low returns. If a firm that pays more in dividends can issue new shares in the market, raise equity, and take exactly the same investments it would have made if it had not paid the dividend, its overall value should be unaffected by its dividend policy. After all, the assets it owns and the earnings it generates are the same whether it pays a large dividend or not.

You, as an investor, will also need to be indifferent between receiving dividends and capital gains for this proposition to hold. After all, if you are taxed at a higher rate on dividends than on capital gains, you will be less happy with the higher dividends, even though your total returns will be the same, simply because you will have to pay more in taxes. For dividends to not matter, you either have to pay no taxes or pay the same taxes on dividends and capital gains.

The assumptions needed to arrive at the proposition that dividends do not affect value may seem so restrictive that you will be tempted to reject it without testing it; after all, it is not costless to issue new stock and dividends, and capital gains and dividends have historically not been taxed at the same rate. That would be a mistake, however, because the theory does contain a valuable message for investors: *A firm that invests in poor projects that make substandard returns cannot hope to increase its value to investors by just offering them higher dividends. Alternatively, a firm with great investments may be able to sustain its value even if it does not pay any dividends.*

DIVIDENDS ARE BAD: THE TAX ARGUMENT

Dividends have historically been treated less favorably than capital gains by the tax authorities in the United States. For much of the last century, dividends have been treated as ordinary income and taxed at rates much higher than price appreciation, which has been treated and taxed as capital gains. Consequently, dividend payments create a tax disadvantage for investors and should reduce the returns to stockholders after personal taxes. Stockholders should respond by reducing the stock prices of the firms making these payments, relative to firms that do not pay dividends. In this scenario, firms will be better off either retaining the money they would have paid out as dividends or repurchasing stock.

The double taxation of dividends—once at the corporate level and once at the investor level—has not been addressed directly in U.S. tax law until very recently,[2] but it has been dealt with in other countries in a couple of ways. In some countries, like Britain, individual investors are allowed a tax credit for the corporate taxes paid on cash flows paid to them as dividends. In other countries, like Germany, the portion of the earnings paid out as dividends is taxed at a lower rate than the portion reinvested in the firm.

In 2003, in a landmark change for investors in the United States, the tax rate on dividends was reduced to 15%, as was the tax rate for capital gains. For the first time in almost a century, investors will no longer be taxed at a higher rate on dividends than on capital gains. You should keep this in mind as you look at the historical evidence on dividend paying stocks in the sections to come, which suggests that high dividend paying stocks earn higher pre-tax returns than low dividend paying or non-dividend paying stocks. If that higher return was being demanded by investors as compensation for the tax disadvantage associated with dividends, it may very well disappear in the years to come. Furthermore, high tax rate individuals who have tended to avoid high dividend paying stocks in the past may find them attractive in the future.

DIVIDENDS ARE GOOD: THE CLIENTELE AND SIGNALING STORIES

Notwithstanding the historical tax disadvantages, many firms continue to pay dividends, and investors in these firms typically view such payments favorably. There are some academics and practitioners who argue that dividends are good and can increase firm value; these people provide at least three reasons.

- *Some investors like dividends.* These investors may not be paying much in taxes and consequently do not care about the tax disadvantage associated with dividends. Or they might need and value the cash flow generated by the dividend payment. Why do they not sell stock to raise the cash they need? The transactions costs and the difficulty of breaking up small holdings[3] and selling unit shares may make selling small amounts of stock infeasible. Given the vast diversity of individual and institutional investors in the market, it is not surprising that, over time, stockholders tend to invest in firms whose dividend policies match their preferences. Stockholders in high tax brackets who did not need the cash flow from dividend payments tended to invest in companies that pay low or no dividends. By contrast, stockholders in low tax brackets who need the cash from dividend payments usually invested in companies with high dividends. This clustering of stockholders in companies with dividend policies that matched their preferences is called the *clientele effect* and may explain why some companies not only pay dividends but increase them over time.

■ *Markets view dividends as signals.* Financial markets examine every action a firm takes for implications for the future. When firms announce changes in dividend policy, they are conveying information to markets, whether they intend to or not. By increasing dividends, firms commit to paying these dividends in the long term. Their willingness to make this commitment indicates to investors that they believe they have the capacity to generate these cash flows in the long term. This positive signal should therefore lead investors to increase the stock price. Decreasing dividends is a negative signal, largely because firms are reluctant to cut dividends. Thus, when a firm takes this action, markets see it as an indication that this firm is in substantial and long-term financial trouble. Consequently, such actions lead to a drop in stock prices.

■ *Some managers cannot be trusted with cash.* Not all companies have good investments and competent management. If a firm's investment prospects are poor and its managers are not viewed as careful custodians of stockholder wealth, paying dividends will reduce the cash available to them and thus the likelihood of wasteful investments.

LOOKING AT THE EVIDENCE

Over the last few decades, researchers have explored whether buying stocks based upon their dividend payments is a good strategy. Some of these studies look at the broad question of whether stocks with higher dividend yields deliver higher total returns. If the dividend story holds up, you would expect stocks with high dividend yields to also earn high returns. Others take a more focused approach of looking at only those stocks that have the highest dividend yields. One example is the Dow Dogs strategy, whereby you buy the 10 stocks in the Dow 30 that have the highest dividend yields. In recent years, a third strategy of buying stocks that have the biggest increases in dividends (rather than the highest dividends) has also been tested. In this section, the empirical evidence that has accumulated on all of these fronts is presented.

DO HIGHER YIELD STOCKS EARN HIGHER RETURNS?

The dividend yield is usually computed by dividing the dividends per share by the current stock price. Thus, it is defined to be

$$\text{Dividend Yield} = \text{Annual Dividends per share} / \text{Current Stock Price}$$

However, there are variations in how the annual dividends per share are computed, leading to different estimates of the dividend yield for the same stock. Some people use the dividends paid in the last financial year, others use dividends paid over the last four quarters and some use expected dividends per share over the next financial year. If higher dividends make stocks more attractive investments, stocks with higher dividend yields should generate higher returns than stocks with lower dividend yields.

Over the last four decades, researchers have tried to examine whether higher dividend yield stocks are superior investments. The simplest way to test this hypothesis is to create portfolios of stocks according to their dividend yields and examine returns on these portfolios over long periods. In Figure 2.1, the average annual returns—these include price appreciation and dividend yields—are computed on ten portfolios created according to dividend yields at the begin-

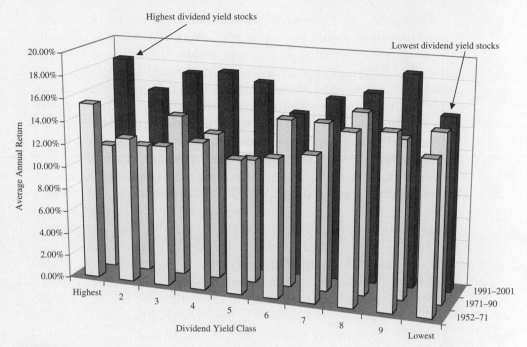

FIGURE 2.1

Returns on Dividend Yield Classes: 1952–2001

Data from Ken French at Dartmouth. The stocks were categorized into classes according to the dividend yields at the beginning of each year, and the annual returns in the following year were calculated. This figure represents the average annual return over the period.

ning of every year from 1952 to 2001. Looking at subperiods, you see that the highest dividend yield portfolio earned an annual return of about 16% between 1952 and 1971, about 3% more than the returns on the lowest dividend yield portfolio. During this period, the lowest returns were earned by the firms in the intermediate dividend yield classes. Between 1971 and 1990, the lowest dividend yield stocks earned a higher annual return than the highest dividend yield stocks. Between 1991 and 2001, the advantage shifts back to higher dividend yield stocks. Over the entire period, higher dividend yield stocks generate a slightly higher annual return than did lower dividend yield stocks.

What are you to make of this shifting in advantage across periods? First, you should consider the volatility a cautionary note. A strategy of investing in high dividend yield stocks would have delivered mixed results over the subperiods, working well in some periods and not in others. Second, you could look at the periods during which high dividend yield stocks did best and try to find common factors that may help you fine-tune this strategy. For instance, high dividend stocks may behave much like bonds in periods of high inflation and rising interest rates and lose value. This would explain why they underperformed the rest of the market between 1971 and 1990.

In a test of whether high dividend stocks are good defensive investments, you can see whether high-dividend-paying stocks hold up better than non-dividend-paying stocks during bear markets. Using data from 1927 to 2001, the returns on highest dividend yield stocks (top 20%) were compared to returns on the lowest dividend yield stocks (bottom 20%) in bull market years (when total market return exceeded 10%), bear market years (when total market return was negative) and neutral years (when total market return was between 0% and 10%). The results are summarized in Figure 2.2.

There is little evidence for the claim that high dividend stocks are better defensive investments, especially in bear markets. Between 1927 and 2001, high dividend yield stocks actually did worse than did low dividend yield stocks during bear markets.

THE DIVIDEND DOGS

An extreme version of a high dividend portfolio is the strategy of investing in the "Dow Dogs," the ten stocks with the highest dividend yields in the Dow 30. Proponents of this strategy claim that they generate high returns from it, but they base this claim on a comparison of the returns that they would have made on the strategy to what they would have made investing in the Dow 30. For instance, a web site dedicated to this strategy (dogsofthedow.com) claims that you would have earned 17.7% a year from 1973 to 2002 investing in the 10 highest dividend yield stocks in the Dow, a much higher return than the 11.9% you would have made on the rest of the Dow.

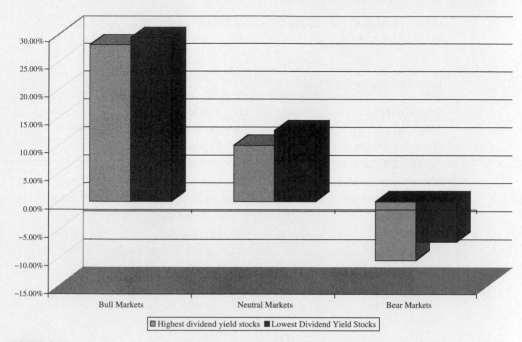

30.00%
25.00%
20.00%
15.00%
10.00%
5.00%
0.00%
-5.00%
-10.00%
-15.00%

Bull Markets   Neutral Markets   Bear Markets

☐ Highest dividend yield stocks ■ Lowest Dividend Yield Stocks

FIGURE 2.2
Are High Dividend Yield Stocks Better Defensive Investments?

Data from French. These are the average annual returns on high dividend yield and low dividend yield stocks in bull market years (stocks up more than 10%), neutral market years (stocks up between 0% and 10%) and bear market years (stocks down for the year).

Not only is this comparison an extraordinarily narrow one—after all, there are several thousands stocks that are not part of the Dow—but it can be misleading. Many of the Dow Dog stocks are riskier than the rest of the Dow 30 stocks, and the higher returns they make could be just compensation for the higher risk. In addition, any investor investing in these stocks over the periods covered (the sixties and the seventies) would have faced a substantial tax liability from the high dividends. It should come as no surprise that those studies that do control for the risk differences and factor in the tax effects conclude that the superior performance of the Dow Dog stocks is a mirage.[4]

Perhaps, the best test of a strategy is to look at the stocks that would be picked on the basis of the strategy and ask yourself whether you would be comfortable with these stocks.

After ranking the Dow 30 stocks by dividend yield, in May 2003, the stocks listed in Table 2.1 emerged as the Dow Dogs:

TABLE 2.1   Dow Dogs: May 2003

COMPANY	PRICE	YIELD
Altria	42.31	6.05%
General Motors	33.26	6.01%
Eastman Kodak	30.28	5.94%
SBC Communications	25.15	4.49%
JP Morgan Chase	30.9	4.40%
AT&T	19.25	3.90%
DuPont	40.99	3.42%
Honeywell	24.47	3.06%
ExxonMobil	35.98	2.78%
General Electric	27.64	2.75%

As an investor considering this portfolio, you should ask yourself the following questions:

1. Would you want your entire wealth to be invested in only ten stocks, two of which are telecom companies? From the standpoint of spreading your risks and diversifying, this does not seem prudent.
2. Why would 10 of the most highly followed stocks in the world be so seriously misvalued by investors? In other words, why are other investors not seeing the same opportunities that you do in these stocks?
3. Many of the stocks on this list have at least one big concern weighing them down: Altria (formerly Philip Morris) has tobacco lawsuits, and J.P. Morgan Chase faced legal problems associated with Enron. Will these companies continue to pay their dividends if these concerns turn into financial liabilities?

You may very well conclude that the reward is worth the risk, but that should not be a conclusion made in haste and without analysis.

DIVIDEND INCREASES

In a different version of the dividend story, stocks that have increased their dividends over time are viewed as better investments than stocks for which dividends have been stagnant or gone down. There are two ways in which this proposition has been tested. The first set of studies has examined the stock price reaction when a company announces an increase or a cut in dividends. The consensus from this research is that stock prices increase when dividends are increased and drop when dividends are cut. Figure 2.3 looks at what happens to stock prices of companies that announce dividend increases and decreases.[5]

When dividends are cut, stock prices drop by about 4.5% on average, whereas stock prices increase about 1% on average

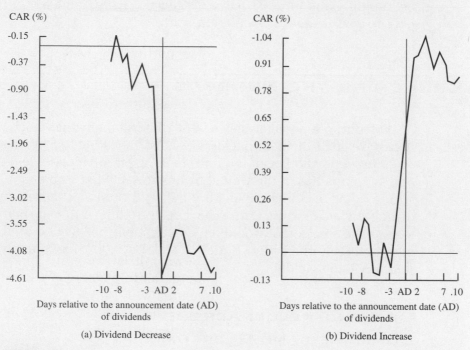

(a) Dividend Decrease

(b) Dividend Increase

FIGURE 2.3

Stock Price Reaction to Dividend Changes: U.S. Companies

Source study: Aharony and Swary. They looked at hundreds of dividend announcements made by firms in the 1970s in this study.

on the announcement of a dividend increase. The asymmetry between the two responses can be explained by the fact that far more firms increase dividends than decrease dividends in a typical year.

The second set of studies documents the longer-term returns on portfolios constructed of companies that increase their dividends the most. Here, the results are mixed. After the initial price jolt created by the dividend increase, there is some evidence of continued price increases[6] for a few weeks after the announcement but the price increase is modest. In other words, buying stocks that have boosted dividends recently does not deliver higher returns in the long term.

It is worth emphasizing again that all of the evidence presented in this section reflects the tax law as it used to be. Equalizing the tax rate on dividends in line with the tax rate on capital gains in 2003 has changed the game, and we will have to revisit the evidence again soon.

CRUNCHING THE NUMBERS

For purposes of analysis, accept the argument that stocks that have high dividend yields are good investments. In this section, you will begin by first looking at dividend yields across companies in the United States to see what would constitute a low or a high dividend yield, and then at changes in dividend yields for the entire market over time. You will then look at the stocks that would have been identified as potential investments in the United States in October 2002, based upon their dividend yields.

DIVIDEND YIELDS: ACROSS COMPANIES AND OVER TIME

What is a typical dividend yield for a company and how has it changed over time? It is worth answering this question before you consider investment strategies based upon it. In Figure 2.4, the distribution of dividend yields on companies that pay dividends in the United States in October 2002 is presented.

The first and perhaps most interesting statistic is the number of companies that do not pay dividends. Of the 7100 companies in the sample, 5173 did not pay dividends. The second is the variation in dividend yields among the companies that pay dividends. While the average dividend yield across stocks that pay dividends is about 3.32%, this number is pushed upward by the presence of a few companies that have very high dividend yields (8% or more). A more meaningful statistic is the median dividend yield among dividend paying stocks, which is 2.54%.

Much has been said about how dividends paid by U.S. stocks have decreased over time. In Figure 2.5, the dividend yield for U.S. stocks from 1960 to 2001 is reported.

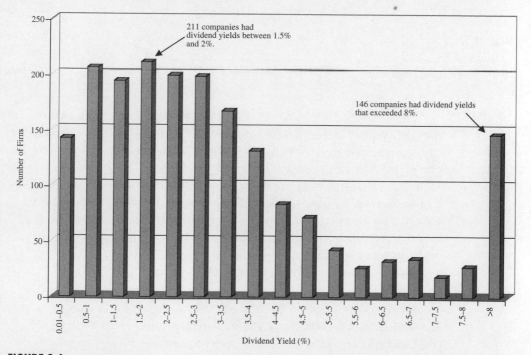

FIGURE 2.4
Dividend Yields across U.S. Stocks

Data from Value Line. The dividend yield for each stock is the annual dividends per share over the last four quarters divided by the stock price at the time of the analysis.

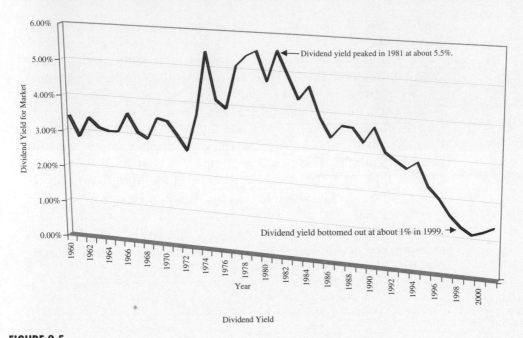

FIGURE 2.5
Dividend Yields in the United States: 1960–2001
Data from Bloomberg. This is the average dividend yield across all U.S. stocks at the end of every year from 1960 to 2001.

The dividend yield for U.S. stocks dropped from 3%–4% in the 1950s to 1%–2% in the late 1990s. Even with the drop in stock prices from 1999 to 2002, the dividend yield remained low at 1.37% at the end of 2001.

One important aspect of corporate behavior is missed when you focus on dividends alone. During the 1980s and 1990s, companies increasingly turned to stock buybacks as a way of returning cash to stockholders. In Figure 2.6, the aggregate dividends paid and aggregate stock buybacks for U.S. firms from 1989 to 1998 is reported.

Note that almost as much cash was returned in the form of stock buybacks in 1998 as was paid out in dividends that year. Since this represents a quantum leap over buybacks 10 years prior, adding it to the dividend yield to come up with a consolidated measure of cash returned to stockholders may provide you with a more reasonable measure of cash payouts than looking at just the dividend yield.

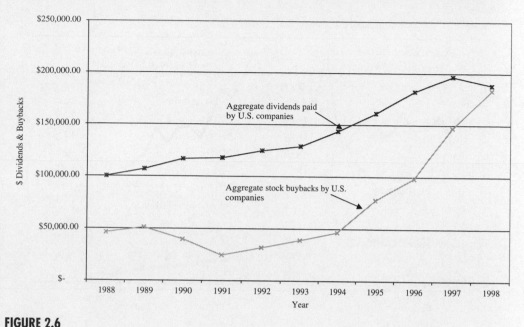

FIGURE 2.6

Stock Buybacks and Dividends: Aggregate for U.S. Firms: 1989–98

Data from Compustat. The stock buybacks and dividends represent the aggregate dollar values across all U.S. companies.

SECTOR DIFFERENCES IN DIVIDEND POLICY

There are clear differences in dividend policy across sectors. In some sectors such as banking and utilities, it has long been customary for firms to pay out large dividends relative both to earnings (dividend payout ratios) and to market value (dividend yields). In other sectors, such as technology, firms have traditionally paid out little or no dividends. In Table 2.2, the five sectors with the highest and lowest dividend yields in the United States in October 2002 are listed.

These differences across sectors matter for two reasons. First, what constitutes a high or low dividend yield may depend upon the sector. Thus, a dividend yield of 2% may be viewed as a low yield for an electric utility but would be a high yield for a software firm. Second, picking the stocks that have the highest dividend yields in the market will result in a portfolio that is overweighted in financial service, utility and real estate investment trusts (REIT) stocks. While this is not

TABLE 2.2   Sectors with High and Low Dividend Yields: October 2002

LOWEST DIVIDEND PAYING SECTORS		HIGHEST DIVIDEND PAYING SECTORS	
INDUSTRY	AVERAGE YIELD	INDUSTRY	AVERAGE YIELD
Biotechnology	0.00%	Bank	2.22%
E-Commerce	0.00%	Petroleum	2.41%
Internet	0.00%	Maritime	2.61%
Semiconductor Cap Eq	0.00%	Water Utility	2.69%
Telecom. Equipment	0.00%	Chemical (Basic)	2.99%
Educational Services	0.02%	Electric Utility	4.11%
Cable TV	0.04%	Natural Gas	4.40%
Wireless Networking	0.06%	Tobacco	5.48%
Information Services	0.07%	Investment Cos	6.30%
Computer Software	0.07%	R.E.I.T.	6.63%

necessarily a negative, investors have to be aware of this fact when they construct these portfolios.

As noted earlier in this chapter, different dividend policies attract different investors. Not surprisingly, investors who buy stocks in high dividend paying sectors tend to view more dividends as a good thing and to reward companies that pay higher dividends. The same cannot be said about investors who buy technology or biotechnology stocks.

Why do some sectors pay more in dividends than others? While part of the reason may lie in the history of these sectors, a great deal of the differences in dividend policy can be explained by differences in fundamentals. Sectors with higher growth potential and more volatile earnings tend to pay less in dividends, especially relative to market value. Firms in these sectors often have to reinvest their earnings to grow and are also wary of paying out dividends that they may not be able to sustain. Sectors with more stable income and less growth potential tend to pay more dividends. Real estate investment trusts offer a special case since they are required by statute to pay 95% of their earnings in dividends.[7]

A PORTFOLIO OF HIGH DIVIDEND STOCKS

The best way to understand what a portfolio driven by high dividend yields would look like is to construct one and then analyze its characteristics. Looking across the 7100 U.S. companies for which information was available in October 2002, you can develop a list of the 100 companies with the highest dividend yields. The portfolio is presented in Table 2.3. Given the discussion about differences in dividend policy across sectors, it should come as no surprise that a few sectors are disproportionately represented in this sector. Real estate investment trusts represent 40% of the stocks in the portfolio with utilities (electric and gas) and financial service firms (banks, investment companies and insurance) represent about 20% each.

Another striking aspect of this table is the magnitude of the dividend yields. Many of these stocks have dividend yields in excess of 10%. Since the treasury bond rate was about 4% in October 2002 and investment grade corporate bonds were yielding in the 5%–6% range, you can see the allure of these stocks to investors in search of high cash yields on their investments. It is worth noting, however, that the dividends represent dividends paid over the last financial year whereas the stock price is the current price. The price will therefore reflect more updated information about the firm. If bad news has come out about the firm recently, the price will have dropped and the resulting dividend yield will be high. This is especially so for the stocks with dividend yields of 20% or higher. Investors should exercise due diligence by examining more recent news releases before they buy these stocks.

MORE TO THE STORY

There are three key considerations that you have to take into account in adopting a high dividend strategy. The first is that some stocks with high dividend yields may be paying

TABLE 2.3 Stocks with the Highest Dividend Yields in the United States: October 2002

Company Name	Industry Name	Dividend Yield	Company Name	Industry Name	Dividend Yield
Koger Equity Inc	R. E. I. T	8.87%	AmeriGas Partners	Natural Gas (Distrib.)	9.54%
Telsp Celular Participacoes	Telcom. Services	8.91%	RFS Hotel Investors	R. E. I. T	9.56%
Equity Inns Inc	Hotel/Gaming	8.92%	Sizeler Prop Inv	R. E. I. T	9.58%
Plains All American Pipeline L	Oilfield Services/Equip.	8.96%	Chateau Cmntys Inc	R. E. I. T	9.61%
Apartment Invt & Mgmt Co	R. E. I. T	9.00%	Crown American Rlty	R. E. I. T	9.61%
Arden Rlty Group	R. E. I. T	9.02%	R.J. Reynolds Tobacco	Tobacco	9.65%
Entertainment Pptys	R. E. I. T	9.07%	Redwood Trust Inc	R. E. I. T	9.71%
DNP Select Inc Fund	Investment Co.	9.08%	Heritage Propane	Oilfield Services/Equip.	9.83%
Glenborough Rlty Trust	R. E. I. T	9.11%	U.S. Restaurant Ppptys	R. E. I. T	9.83%
National Health Rlty Inc	Medical Services	9.17%	Mid-Amer Apt Cmntys	R. E. I. T	9.98%
Great Northern Iron Ore	Steel (General)	9.18%	Aberdeen Asia-Pac Fd	Investment Co	10.00%
EPCOS AG	Electronics	9.19%	San Juan Basin Rlty	Natural Gas (Diversified)	10.00%
Rameo-Gershenson Pptys	R. E. I. T	9.20%	Crescent Real Est	R. E. I. T	10.01%
National Health Invs Inc	R. E. I. T	9.23%	JDN Realty Corp	R. E. I. T	10.14%
Tanger Factory OUtlet	R. E. I. T	9.26%	Ferrellgas Partners L P	Natural Gas (Distrib.)	10.16%
Star Financial Inc	R. E. I. T	9.27%	British Airways ADR	Air Transport	10.22%
PICO Hldgs Inc	Insurance (Prop/Casualty)	9.30%	Kratmont Realty Trust	R. E. I. T	10.32%
Town & Ctry Tr	R. E. I. T	9.33%	CMS Energy Corp	Electric Util (Central)	10.36%
Kilroy Rlty Corp	R. E. I. T	9.38%	TCW Conv. Sec. Fund	Investment Co	10.37%
AMLI Res. Prop Tr	R. E. I. T	9.39%	Allied Capital Corp	Financial Sves (Div)	10.39%
Great Lakes REIT	R. E. I. T	9.39%	Plum Creek Timber	Paper & Forest Products	10.49%
First Indl Rlty Tr Inc	R. E. I. T	9.41%	Gables Residential Tr	R. E. I. T	10.60%
Public Serv Enterprise	Electric Utility (East)	9.43%	American First Apt Inv L P	Investment Co	10.66%
OGE Energy	Electric Util. (Central)	9.47%	Permian Basin Rty Tr	R. E. I. T	10.90%
New Plan Excel Rlty	R. E. I. T	9.49%	Summit Pptys Inc	R. E. I. T	11.05%
Mission West Pptys	R. E. I. T	9.51%	Gilmcher Tlty Trust	R. E. I. T	11.08%

TABLE 2.3 Stocks with the Highest Dividend Yields in the United States: October 2002 (continued)

Company Name	Industry Name	Dividend Yield	Company Name	Industry Name	Dividend Yield
Highwood Pptys Inc	R. E. I. T.	11.25%	Cornerstone Realty	R. E. I. T.	15.09%
Nationwide Health Pptys Inc	R. E. I. T.	11.36%	AmeriservFinl Inc	Bank	15.25%
Alliant Energy	Electric Util. (Central)	11.65%	Airlese Ltd	Trucking/Transp. Leasing	15.39%
Royce Value Trust	Investment Co.	11.72%	Annaly Mortgage Mgmt.	R. E. I. T.	16.19%
MicroFinancial Inc	Financial Svcs. (Div.)	11.77%	Gabelli Equity	Investment Co.	16.22%
Allegheny Technologies	Metals & Mining (Div.)	11.85%	NovaStar Financial	R. E. I. T.	16.42%
Books-A-Million	Retail (Special Lines)	11.95%	Associated Estates	R. E. I. T.	16.56%
Westar Energy	Electric Util. (Central)	11.96%	NorthWestern Corp	Electric Util. (Central)	17.28%
Williams Coal Sm Gs	Natural Gas (Diversified)	12.00%	Fila Hldgs S P A ADR	Shoe	17.62%
Vector Group Ltd	Tobacco	12.19%	Bovar Inc	Environmental	18.00%
Liberty All-Star	Investment Co.	12.21%	Aquila	Electric Util. (Central)	19.18%
Nordic Amer Tanker Shp	Maritime	12.39%	Terra Nitrogen	Chemical (Specialty)	19.28%
ACM Income Fund	Investment Co.	12.48%	Scheid Vineyards	Food Processing	19.69%
ABN Amro Holdings	Bank (Foreign)	12.67%	Scott's Liquid Gold Inc	Toiletries/Cosmetics	20.83%
TECO Energy	Electric Utility (East)	12.77%	Apex MortgageCapital	Financial Svcs. (Div.)	23.01%
Advanced Tobacco Products	Tobacco	12.82%	Cookson Group PLC	Machinery	23.93%
Thornburg Mtg	R. E. I. T.	12.83%	General Chem Group	Chemical (Basic)	25.00%
Amer Elec Power	Electric Util. (Central)	13.06%	AES Corp	Power	26.32%
Sharp Corportion	Electronics	13.07%	Etz Lavud Ltd	Diversified Co.	26.32%
Post Pptys Inc	R. E. I. T.	13.12%	Capstead Mtg Corp	R. E. I. T.	29.04%
American Cap Strategies	Financial Svcs. (Div.)	13.63%	Harbor Global Co LTD	R. E. I. T.	32.31%
MICROWAVE FILTER	Electronics	13.86%	Telefonica de Argentina SA	Telecom. Services	32.56%
MFA Mortgage	R. E. I. T.	14.45%	Dynegy Inc 'A'	Natural Gas (Diversified)	37.04%
Knightsbridge Tankers	Maritime	15.00%			

much more in dividends than they can afford. It is only a matter of time, then, before the dividends are cut. The second is that any firm that pays a substantial portion of its earnings as dividends is reinvesting less and can therefore expect to grow at a much lower rate in the future. Thus, you often have to trade off higher dividend yields for lower earnings growth in the future. The third is that you as an investor may have a much greater tax cost on this strategy, since dividends were taxed at a higher rate than capital gains until recently.

UNSUSTAINABLE DIVIDENDS

While investors may buy stocks that pay high dividends as substitutes for bonds, there is one significant difference. A conventional bond offers a promised coupon; in other words, when you buy a bond with a coupon rate of 8%, the issuer contractually promises to pay $80 a year for the lifetime of the bond. While issuers can default, they cannot arbitrarily decide to reduce this payment. In contrast, a company does not contractually promise to maintain or increase its dividends. Thus, a company that pays a $2 dividend this year can reduce the dividend or even eliminate it if it so chooses. While investors may view this action with disappointment and sell the stock (causing the price to drop), they cannot force the company to pay dividends.

What are the implications for investors? A stock with a high dividend may be an attractive investment, but only if the dividends can be sustained. How do you know whether dividends are sustainable? There are three approaches. The first and simplest one compares dividends to earnings in the most recent period to see if too much is being paid out. The second approach modifies the first one to allow for the fact that earnings are volatile. It compares dividends paid to normalized or average earnings over time to make the same judgment. The third approach tries to measure how much the company could have paid in dividends, allowing for the reality that companies often cannot pay out their entire earnings in dividends when they have to reinvest to grow.

Comparisons to Actual or Normalized Earnings. The first and simplest approach to evaluating the sustainability of dividends is to compare the dividends paid in the most recent period to the earnings in the period. The ratio of dividends to earnings is the payout ratio. Figure 2.7 presents the distribution of dividend payout ratios in the most recent financial year for U.S. stocks in October 2002.

A firm that has a dividend payout ratio greater than 100% paid out more than its earnings as dividends, at least in the most recent financial year. If the firm's earnings do not recover promptly, this payout is clearly unsustainable for the long term and can have significant accounting and economic consequences. From an accounting standpoint, this action will reduce the book value of equity in the firm. From an economic standpoint, the firm is not only not reinvesting in the business but is also reducing its asset base, thus reducing its capacity to grow in the future.

While avoiding firms that pay out more than they earn as dividends may be an obvious strategy, you could impose

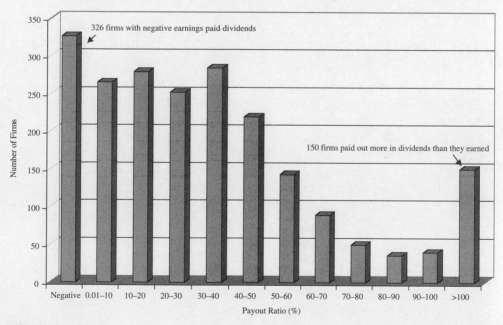

FIGURE 2.7

Dividend Payout Ratios: U.S. Stocks in October 2002

Data from Value Line. The payout ratio is the dollar dividend paid out as a percent of the net income. If the net income is negative, the payout ratio cannot be calculated.

tighter constraints. For instance, some conservative investors and financial advisors suggest that you avoid firms that pay out more than a certain percent of their earnings—two-thirds (or a payout ratio of 67%) is a commonly used rule of thumb. While these constraints are usually arbitrary, they reflect the fact that earnings are volatile and that dividends in firms that pay out more than the cutoff payout ratio are at risk.

Revisit the sample of the 100 companies with the highest dividend yields (from Table 2.3) and compare annual dividends to trailing earnings—earnings in the most recent four quarters. Figure 2.8 summarizes the findings.

Of the 100 firms in the portfolio, 57 had dividends that exceeded their earnings over the last four quarters and 12 paid dividends even though they had losses for the year.

Some analysts would accuse you of being excessively cautious in your analysis. They would argue that trailing

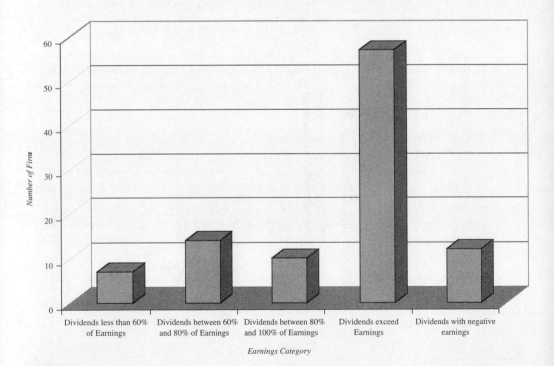

FIGURE 2.8
Dividends vs. Earnings
Data from Value Line. The dividends for each company were compared to the earnings for the company.

12-month earnings are depressed because of poor overall economic growth and that you should be comparing dividends to earnings in a normal year or sustainable earnings. One simple modification they would recommend is looking at average earnings over some past period, say, five years. While you can accept the logic of the argument, this is a conservative investment strategy and it seems prudent to use the toughest test that you can for deciding whether dividends are sustainable.

Returning to the list, it is quite clear that using the cutoff of 67% for the payout ratio would prune the portfolio down to about 15 firms. Even using a liberal cutoff point of 80% for the dividend payout ratio prunes the portfolio down to only 21 companies, which are listed in Table 2.4.

TABLE 2.4   Firms with High Dividend Yields and Payout Ratios Below 80%

COMPANY	ANNUAL DIVIDENDS PER SHARE	TRAILING 12-MONTH EPS	PAYOUT RATIO
MicroFinancial Inc	$0.20	$1.26	15.87%
Telesp Celular	$0.15	$0.90	16.67%
Dynegy Inc 'A'	$0.30	$1.46	20.55%
AES Corp	$0.25	$1.17	21.37%
El Paso Corp	$0.87	$2.93	29.69%
Mission West Properties	$0.96	$2.52	38.10%
Koger Equity Inc	$1.40	$2.94	47.62%
R.J. Reynolds Tobacco	$3.80	$6.32	60.13%
TECO Energy	$1.42	$2.31	61.47%
Advanced Tobacco	$0.05	$0.08	62.50%
Apex Mortgage Capital	$2.00	$3.11	64.31%
Permian Basin Rty Tr	$0.56	$0.85	65.88%
Williams Coal Sm Gs	$0.88	$1.33	66.17%
Public Serv Enterprise	$2.16	$3.20	67.50%
Allegheny Energy	$1.72	$2.51	68.53%
CMS Energy Corp	$0.72	$1.04	69.23%
MFA Mortgage	$1.12	$1.58	70.89%
Aquila Inc	$0.70	$0.95	73.68%
UIL Holdings	$2.88	$3.77	76.39%
NorthWestern Corp	$1.27	$1.62	78.40%
Redwood Trust Inc	$2.52	$3.18	79.25%

Even within this sample, there are some warning signals that should be heeded. First, consider the numerous energy companies that make the list. Since this portfolio was constructed in the aftermath of the accounting debacle at Enron, the possibility that the stated earnings at these firms may also be contaminated is one reason why stock prices are depressed. If the earnings at these companies are overstated, their dividends will have to be cut in future periods. Second, note that a couple of tobacco companies also make the list. For these firms, the specter of large judgments in lawsuits overhangs the earnings; a few such judgments may very well result in the elimination or reduction of dividends. Note, though, that you are not arguing that these stocks should be avoided but that you need to do your homework before buying these stocks. In practical terms, you would need to examine the financial statements of the energy companies on this list to see if there are signs of Enronitis—the hiding of liabilities or mysterious (and unsustainable) earnings. You may very well conclude that the market's fears are misplaced and that these stocks are good investments. With tobacco companies, you will need to do a similar analysis on potential tobacco liabilities.

Comparisons to Potential Dividends.   While comparing dividends to earnings may provide a simple way of measuring whether dividends are sustainable, it is not a complete test for two reasons.

- *Earnings are not cash flows.* Accountants measure earnings by subtracting accounting expenses from revenues. To the extent that some of these expenses are noncash expenses (depreciation and amortization, for instance) and because accrual accounting (which is what is used in corporate accounting statements) does not always yield the same results as cash accounting, accounting earnings can be very different from cash flows.
- *Firms may have reinvestment needs.* Even if earnings roughly approximate cash flows, firms may not be able to pay them out in dividends. This is because firms

often have to reinvest to maintain assets and these capital investments (which do not show up in income statements when they are made) will reduce cash flows.

For dividends to be truly sustainable, the cash flows left over after capital expenditures have to be greater than the dividends.

How can you measure the cash flows available for dividends? One measure is the "free cash flow to equity" method, which measures cash left over after reinvestment needs are met. To measure the cash flow to equity, you begin with the net income and make the following adjustments:

- You add back noncash accounting expenses such as depreciation and amortization.
- You subtract capital expenditures since they represent a cash drain on the firm. While some analysts draw a distinction between nondiscretionary and discretionary capital expenditures, you should consider all such expenditures in computing free cash flows to equity.
- You will subtract the change in noncash working capital to arrive at the cash flow. Thus, an increase in working capital (inventory or accounts receivable, for instance) will reduce cash flows, whereas a decrease in working capital will increase cash flows. Making this adjustment essentially converts accrual earnings to cash earnings.
- You will subtract the net cash flow resulting from debt. Debt repayments represent cash outflows, whereas new debt represents cash inflows. The difference between the two should affect your cash flow to equity.

Free Cash Flow to Equity (FCFE) = Net Income + Depreciation and Amortization − Capital Expenditures − Change in Noncash Working Capital − (Debt Repayments − New Debt Issues)

Note that the net cash flow from debt can be positive if debt issues exceed debt repayments. Conservative analysts who do not want dividends to be funded by net debt issues often compute a conservative version of free cash flow to equity, which ignores net debt cash flows:

Conservative FCFE = Net Income +
Depreciation and Amortization – Capital Expenditures –
Change in Noncash Working Capital

While you can compute the FCFE by using information in the income statement and the balance sheet, you can also obtain it from the statement of cash flows.

How would the 21 firms that had payout ratios less than 80% in Table 2.4 look if you compared dividends to FCFE? To answer this question, the FCFE was computed with the conservative approach (not factoring in new debt issues). Table 2.5 summarizes the findings.

The real estate investment trusts and tobacco companies look even better on the question of dividend sustainability when dividends are compared to free cash flows to equity. R.J. Reynolds, for instance, has free cash flows to equity of $10.75 per share and pays out $3.80 in dividends, suggesting a large buffer for dividend payments. Concerns about lawsuits and legislation may still sway you in your final investment decision. The biggest divergence between earnings per share and FCFE shows up with the energy firms. All of the energy firms have substantially lower free cash flows to equity than earnings per share; five of them have negative free cash flows to equity. Since FCFE represent cash available for dividends, how, you might wonder, can they afford to pay the dividends that they do? In the late 1990s, energy firms borrowed money (on and off the books) and made equity issues to fund dividend payments. As a result, they became highly leveraged. The conclusion you would draw is that these firms cannot sustain these dividends. This is also true, albeit to a lesser degree, for Telesp Celular.

Low Growth

As a firm increases the dividends it pays to stockholders, it is reinvesting less of its earnings back into its business. In the long term, this has to translate into lower growth in earnings

TABLE 2.5 Dividends versus FCFE for Firms with Payout Ratio < 80%

COMPANY	DPS	EPS	FCFE/SHARE
MicroFinancial Inc	$0.20	$1.26	$2.25
Telesp Celular Participacoes	$0.15	$0.90	$0.14
Dynegy Inc 'A'	$0.30	$1.46	−$2.67
AES Corp	$0.25	$1.17	−$3.17
El Paso Corp	$0.87	$2.93	−$7.17
Mission West Pptys	$0.96	$2.52	$3.31
Koger Equity Inc	$1.40	$2.94	$3.12
R.J. Reynolds Tobacco	$3.80	$6.32	$10.75
TECO Energy	$1.42	$2.31	−$2.47
Advanced Tobacco Products	$0.05	$0.08	$0.08
Apex Mortgage Capital	$2.00	$3.11	$3.11
Permian Basin Rty Tr	$0.56	$0.85	$1.05
Williams Coal Sm Gs	$0.88	$1.33	$1.33
Public Serv. Enterprise	$2.16	$3.20	−$4.24
Allegheny Energy	$1.72	$2.51	$1.36
CMS Energy Corp	$0.72	$1.04	−$4.46
MFA Mortgage	$1.12	$1.58	$1.63
Aquila Inc	$0.70	$0.95	−$1.23
UIL Holdings	$2.88	$3.77	$7.22
NorthWestern Corp	$1.27	$1.62	$2.54
Redwood Trust Inc	$2.52	$3.18	$2.98

per share.[8] In fact, the long-term sustainable growth rate in earnings per share for a firm can be written as a function of its payout ratio and the quality of its investments (measured by its return on equity):

Expected Long-Term Growth Rate in earnings per share =
(1 − Payout Ratio) (Return on Equity)

To illustrate, a firm that pays out 40% of its earnings as dividends and earns a 20% return on equity can expect to see its earnings per share grow 12% a year in the long term.

Expected growth rate in earnings per share =
(1 − .40) (.20) = .12 or 12%

Investors who invest in companies that pay high dividends have to accept a tradeoff. These firms will generally have much lower expected growth rates in earnings.

Consider again the sample of high dividend paying stocks in Table 2.5 that have sustainable dividends—the firms that have dividends that exceed free cash flows to equity were eliminated. In Table 2.6, the sustainable growth rates in these firms are estimated and compared to analyst estimates of expected growth.

The fundamental growth rates are low for every one of the firms, partly because these firms have high payout ratios and partly because of low returns on equity on their investments. For those firms for which analyst estimates of growth are available, the expected growth rates in earnings per share over the next 5 years are low. In fact, if you require firms to have expected fundamental growth rates of 3% or higher, the only three firms that make the final cut are two real estate investment trusts—Mission West Properties and Koger Equity—and one tobacco firm, Advanced Tobacco. In summary, screening firms for

TABLE 2.6 Fundamental and Analyst Estimates of Growth for Firms with Sustainable Dividends

COMPANY	ROE	PAYOUT RATIO	EXPECTED GROWTH	ANALYST ESTIMATE OF 5-YEAR GROWTH
MicroFinancial Inc	1.71%	15.87%	1.44%	NA
Mission West Pptys	6.55%	38.10%	4.05%	NA
Koger Equity Inc	7.66%	47.62%	4.01%	NA
R.J. Reynolds Tobacco	2.81%	60.13%	1.12%	5.50%
Advanced Tobacco	10.53%	62.50%	3.95%	NA
Apex Mortgage Capital	4.53%	64.31%	1.62%	NA
Permian Basin Rty Tr	4.16%	65.88%	1.42%	NA
Williams Coal Sm Gs	5.44%	66.17%	1.84%	NA
Allegheny Energy	−1.25%	68.53%	−0.39%	3.00%
MFA Mortgage	3.38%	70.89%	0.98%	NA
UIL Holdings	1.81%	76.39%	0.43%	3.80%
NorthWestern Corp	3.74%	78.40%	0.81%	2.70%
Redwood Trust Inc	5.35%	79.25%	1.11%	NA

sustainability of dividends and for reasonable growth rates in earnings reduces the original sample of 100 firms to 3 firms.

TAXES

As has often been said, the only two things that are certain in life are taxes and death. While investors may get a chance to pause and admire the pretax returns they make on their investment portfolios, they can spend only the returns that they have left after taxes. Strategies that yield attractive pretax returns can generate substandard after-tax returns.

How big a drag are taxes on investment returns? An examination of the returns on the U.S. stock market and on government bonds shows that stocks have generated much higher returns than treasury bills or bonds. Thus, $100 invested in stocks in 1928 would have grown to $125,599, by the end of 2001, significantly higher than what your portfolio would have been worth if invested in T bills ($1,713) or T bonds ($3,587). This is impressive but it is also before taxes and transactions costs. For the moment, consider the effect of taxes on these returns. Assume that the investor buying these stocks faced a tax rate of 35% on dividends and 20% on capital gains over this period. To compute the effect of taxes on returns, you do have to consider how often this investor trades. If you assume that he turns over his entire portfolio at the end of each year, he would have to pay taxes on both dividends and the price appreciation each year. Figure 2.9 shows the effect on the portfolio value over the period and the effect of taxes on the ending portfolio.

Note that introducing taxes into returns reduced the ending value of the portfolio by more than two-thirds: from $125,598 to $39,623.

If taxes affect all investments, you may wonder why its effect is emphasized with a high dividend strategy. While the taxes on capital gains can be deferred by not trading on your winners, the taxes on dividends have to be paid each period that you receive dividends. Thus, a strategy of investing in stocks that have higher dividend yields than average will result in less flexibility when it comes to tax timing and more

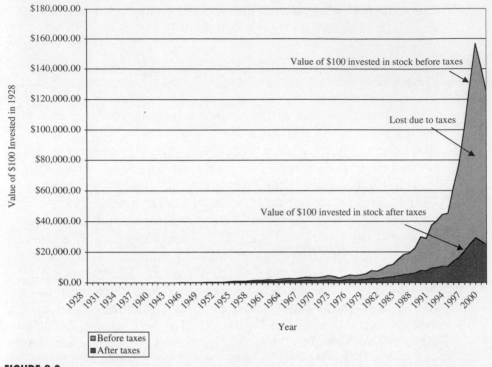

FIGURE 2.9
Value of $100 Invested in Stocks: Before and After Taxes

Data from Federal Reserve. The graph measures the cumulated value of $100 invested in stock in 1928, including dividends and price appreciation.

taxes, at least relative to investing in low dividend yield stocks for the long term. Figure 2.10 illustrates this for an investor by contrasting the performance of a portfolio with a dividend yield half that of the market each year to one with twice the dividend yield, keeping the total returns constant.[9]

Note that the portfolio of stocks with half the dividend yield of the market has an ending value of just over $30,000 in 2001, whereas one with a dividend yield twice that of the market has an ending value of roughly half that amount. An investor interested in building up a portfolio over time may find that much of the "excess return" analysts claim to find with high dividend yield portfolios may be dissipated by the higher tax liabilities created.

Did this tax liability make a strategy of buying stocks that pay high dividends a poor one for an investor who faced high tax

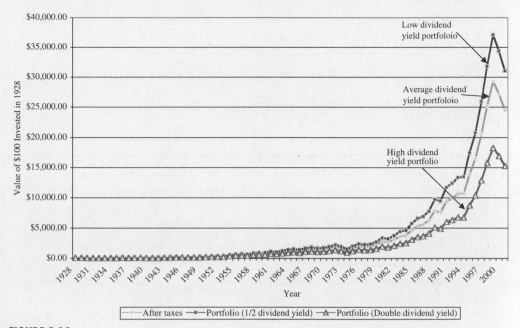

FIGURE 2.10

Value of $100 Invested in Stocks in 1928 and Dividend Yields

Data from Federal Reserve. The graphs represent the cumulated value of $100 invested in 1928 in each of three portfolios (high dividend yield, average dividend yield and low dividend yield).

rates? Not necessarily, for two reasons. The first is that the return may still have been higher after you paid the additional taxes on this strategy. The second is that different parts of the same investor's portfolio were treated differently for tax purposes. Even a high-tax-rate investor was allowed to accumulate funds in pension plans and delay or defer taxes until retirement. Investing your pension plan in high dividend paying stocks then would have given you the benefits of the strategy without the tax costs.

One of the perils of looking at the past is that you can miss significant changes in the world. Much of what has been said in this section about the tax disadvantages of dividends may now truly be history since new tax legislation, signed into law in May 2003, reduced the tax rate on dividends to 15% and set it equal to the tax rate on capital gains. The tax disadvantage of dividends has clearly been much reduced if not eliminated. This will not only affect the values of dividend paying stocks but it will also change the way many companies view dividends. In the early part of 2003, technology firms like Microsoft and Oracle, which had never paid dividends, announced that they would start paying dividends.

LESSONS FOR INVESTORS

Consider the lessons of this chapter. Stocks that pay high dividends have historically delivered higher returns than the rest of the market, and stocks that increase dividends see their stock prices go up. On the other hand, stocks that pay high dividends grow earnings far more slowly (thus delivering less in price appreciation) and are often unable to sustain dividends in the long term. The last section demonstrates the attrition in a high dividend portfolio once you begin to ask questions about the sustainability of dividends and expected growth rates. You began with a sample of the 100 companies that had the highest dividend yields, but you eliminated 79 of these firms either because they had negative earnings or because their dividend payout ratios exceeded 80%. Of the remaining 21 firms, 8 firms were eliminated because they had negative free cash flows to equity or because their dividends exceeded their free cash flows to equity. Of the 13 firms left, only 3 had expected growth rates greater than 3%.

Looking at the process, you would have been better served if you had not begun the process by looking at the highest dividend yield paying stocks and instead looked for stocks that met multiple criteria—high dividends, sustainable earnings and reasonable growth rates in earnings per share—across all traded stocks. For instance, you could screen all U.S. stocks for those stocks that have the following characteristics:

■ *Dividend yields that exceed the treasury bond rate:* The treasury bond rate offers a useful measure for comparison since it represents what you would earn on a riskless investment. If you can buy stocks that deliver dividend yields that exceed this rate and you can keep earning these dividends forever, you would not even need price appreciation on the stock to break even on the investments.

■ *Dividend payout ratios that are less than a cutoff:* Earlier in the chapter, fairly arbitrary cutoffs ranging from 67% to 80% were considered. The idea behind this constraint is to eliminate firms that are paying out more in dividends than they can sustain.

■ *Reasonable expected growth in earnings per share:* If you want price appreciation in addition to high dividends, the companies you invest in have to be able to grow earnings. Though it is unrealistic to expect high dividend yield stocks to grow earnings in the double digits, you can require earnings growth that matches overall growth in the economy.

In October 2002, you could screen for firms with dividend yields that exceed 4% (the treasury bond rate at the time of the analysis), dividend payout ratios less than 60%, dividends less than FCFE and expected growth rate in EPS over the next five years greater than 4%. Since real estate investment trusts are structured so differently from other firms, you should eliminate them from the sample as well. The resulting portfolio of 30 companies is presented in the appendix to this chapter.

This portfolio is much more diverse in terms of industries represented than the original sample of 100 firms with the highest dividend yields. While the average dividend yield on the portfolio is lower than the original portfolio, the dividends are much more sustainable and the firms do have some growth potential.

CONCLUSION

Stocks that pay high dividends seem to offer an unbeatable combination of continuing income (dividends) and potential price appreciation. Their allure increases in bear markets as equities decline in value. The empirical evidence also seems to provide some support for the proposition that stocks with higher dividend yields generate higher returns for investors over the long term.

What are the potential dangers of investing in stocks with high dividends? The first is that dividends, unlike coupons on bonds, are not promised cash flows. A dividend that is too high, relative to the earnings and cash flows generated by a firm, is unsustainable and will have to be cut sooner rather than later. Finally, high dividend payouts often translate into low expected growth rates in earnings.

In summary, a strategy of buying high dividend stocks historically has made the most sense for investors with low tax rates or for investments that are tax exempt, like pension funds. With the changes in the tax law, more investors may find this strategy attractive. If you adopt such a strategy, you should screen high dividend paying stocks for sustainability (by looking at dividend payout ratios and free cash flows to equity) and reasonable earnings growth.

ENDNOTES

1. Miller, M. and F. Modigliani, 1961, *Dividend Policy, Growth and the Valuation of Shares*, Journal of Business, v34, 411–433.

2. In early 2003, President Bush presented tax reform that essentially exempted all dividends from personal taxes.

3. Consider a stockholder who owns 100 shares trading at $20 per share, on which she receives a dividend of $0.50 per share. If the firm did not pay a dividend, the stockholder would have to sell 2.5 shares of stock to raise the $50 that would have come from the dividend.

4. McQueen, G., K. Shields and S. R. Thorley, 1997, *Does the Dow-10 Investment Strategy beat the Dow statistically and economically?* Financial Analysts Journal, July/August, 66–72. This study examined this strategy and concluded that while the raw returns from buying the top dividend paying stocks is higher than the rest of the index, adjusting for risk

and taxes eliminates all of the excess return. A study by Hirschey (Hirschey, M., 2000, *The "Dogs of the Dow" Myth*, Financial Review, v35, 1–15.) in 2000 also indicates that there are no excess returns from this strategy after you adjust for risk.

5. Aharony, J., and I. Swary, 1981, *Quarterly Dividends and Earnings Announcements and Stockholders' Returns: An Empirical Analysis*, Journal of Finance, v36, 1–12.

6. Michaely, R., R. H. Thaler and K. L. Womack, 1995, *Price Reactions to Dividend Initiations and Omissions: Overreaction or Drift?* Journal of Finance, v50, 573–608. This study looked at returns on stocks that increase dividends in the months after the dividend increase and concludes that stocks that increase dividends continue to do well, whereas stocks that decrease dividends are poor investments.

7. Real estate investment trusts do not have to pay corporate taxes but they are required to pay high dividends.

8. You can still maintain high growth in net income by issuing new equity, but this action will increase the number of shares outstanding.

9. To provide an example, the average dividend yield across all stocks in 1996 was 3.20% and the total return was 23.82%. The half-dividend yield portfolio was estimated to have a dividend yield of 1.60% and a price appreciation of 22.22% for a total return of 23.82%. The double-dividend yield portfolio had a dividend yield of 6.40% and a price appreciation of 17.42% for a total return of 23.82%.

FIRMS THAT PASS THE DIVIDEND SCREENS: OCTOBER 2002

Stocks with Dividend Yields > 4%, Dividend Payout Ratios < 60%, Dividends < FCFE and Expected EPS Growth > 4%

COMPANY NAME	INDUSTRY	STOCK PRICE	DIVIDEND PER SHARE	DIVIDEND YIELD	DIVIDEND PAYOUT	FCFE/ SHARE	ESTIMATED EPS GROWTH
Alexander & Baldwin	MARITIME	$23.37	$0.90	4.11%	54.01%	$1.08	9.00%
AmSouth Bancorp	BANK	$19.86	$0.88	4.39%	58.10%	$1.64	8.00%
Arch Chemicals	CHEMSPEC	$17.15	$0.80	4.68%	0.00%	$0.82	5.00%
Banco Santander ADR	EUROPEAN	$6.06	$0.29	5.30%	52.89%	$0.47	10.50%
Bay St Bancorp	BANK	$19.01	$0.88	4.64%	19.89%	$1.29	8.00%
Books-A-Million	RETAILSP	$3.26	$0.41	11.95%	0.00%	$0.48	12.00%
Citizens Banking	BANK	$23.41	$1.14	4.75%	52.65%	$2.12	8.00%
Cleco Corp	UTILCENT	$12.20	$0.90	7.97%	56.77%	$2.01	6.50%
Colonial BncGrp 'A'	BANK	$12.05	$0.52	4.29%	43.71%	$1.20	9.00%
Comerica Inc	BANKMID	$42.10	$1.92	4.82%	37.31%	$3.61	9.50%
Commonwealth Industries	MINING	$5.90	$0.20	4.44%	52.52%	$0.48	15.00%
Electronic Data Sys	SOFTWARE	$13.72	$0.60	4.38%	25.13%	$3.09	13.00%
Equity Inns Inc	HOTELGAM	$5.23	$0.52	8.92%	0.00%	$0.67	5.00%
FirstEnergy Corp	UTILCENT	$30.13	$1.50	5.70%	55.94%	$2.88	9.00%
FirstMerit Corp	BANKMID	$22.16	$1.00	4.73%	48.96%	$2.00	9.50%
Goodrich Corp	DEFENSE	$16.74	$0.80	4.51%	37.12%	$2.85	7.00%
Goodyear Tire	TIRE	$9.18	$0.48	5.85%	0.00%	$0.79	34.00%
May Dept Stores	RETAIL	$24.60	$0.95	4.04%	42.07%	$1.63	5.00%
Merchants Bancshares Inc	BANK	$22.08	$0.96	4.24%	34.85%	$2.12	10.00%
MicroFinancial Inc	FINANCL	$2.09	$0.20	11.77%	14.88%	$2.26	7.50%
NICOR Inc	GASDISTR	$29.61	$1.84	6.63%	57.81%	$2.26	7.00%
Petroleo Brasileiro ADR	OILINTEG	$12.25	$0.52	5.47%	48.75%	$0.89	10.00%
Philip Morris	TOBACCO	$42.65	$2.56	6.63%	55.71%	$4.64	9.00%
Provident Bankshares	BANK	$22.39	$0.86	4.10%	45.85%	$1.80	9.50%
Quaker Chemical	CHEMSPEC	$19.55	$0.84	4.34%	54.49%	$1.31	8.00%

Stocks with dividend yields>4%, dividend payout ratios < 60%, dividends < FCFE and expected EPS growth > 4% (continued)

COMPANY NAME	INDUSTRY	STOCK PRICE	DIVIDEND PER SHARE	DIVIDEND YIELD	DIVIDEND PAYOUT	FCFE/ SHARE	ESTIMATED EPS GROWTH
Snap-on Inc.	MACHINE	$26.00	$0.96	4.07%	52.11%	$2.13	4.50%
Standex Int'l	DIVERSIF	$19.72	$0.84	4.43%	49.54%	$1.92	9.50%
Tasty Baking	FOODPROC	$11.59	$0.48	4.33%	52.09%	$0.80	8.00%
Tupperware Corp.	HOUSEPRD	$15.95	$0.88	5.23%	54.26%	$1.42	7.50%
Westar Energy	UTILCENT	$10.47	$1.20	11.96%	-216.34%	$5.59	16.00%

3

THIS STOCK IS SO CHEAP! THE LOW PRICE-EARNINGS STORY

GRAHAM'S DISCIPLE

Jeremy was a value investor, and he had disdain for investors who chased growth stocks and paid exorbitant prices for them. Reading Forbes one day, Jeremy was excited to see the results of an academic study that showed that you could beat the market by buying stocks with low price-earnings ratios, an approach highly favored by other value investors. Getting on Yahoo! Finance, Jeremy looked for stocks that traded at price-earnings ratios less than 8 (a number he had heard on CNBC was a good rule of thumb to use for low PE stocks) and was surprised to find dozens. Not having the money to invest in all of them, he picked the first 20 stocks and bought them.

In the year after his investments, instead of the steady stream of great returns that the academic study had promised, Jeremy found himself badly trailing the market. All his friends who had bought technology stocks were doing much better than he, and they mocked him. Taking a closer look at his depleted portfolio, Jeremy found that instead of the safe, solid companies that he had expected to hold, many of his companies were small risky companies with wide swings in earnings. He also discovered that the stocks he picked were unusually prone to reporting accounting irregularities and scandals. Disillusioned, Jeremy decided that value investing was not all it was made out to be and shifted all of his money into a high growth mutual fund.

Moral: A stock that trades at a low PE is not always cheap, and the long term can be a long time coming.

For decades investors have used price-earnings ratios (PEs) as a measure of how expensive or cheap a stock is. A stock that trades at a low multiple of earnings is often characterized as cheap, and investment advisors and analysts have developed rules of thumb over time. Some analysts use absolute measures—for instance, stocks that trade at less than 8 times earnings are considered cheap—whereas other analysts use relative measures, for example, stocks that trade at less than half the price-earnings ratio of the market are cheap. In some cases, the comparison is to the market, and in other cases it is to the sector in which the firm operates.

In this chapter, you consider whether price-earnings ratios are good indicators of value and whether a strategy of buying stocks with low price-earnings ratios generates high returns. As you will see, a stock with a low price-earnings ratio may not be undervalued and strategies that focus on just price-earnings ratios may fail because they ignore the growth potential and risk in a firm. A firm that trades at a low price-earnings ratio because it has little or no prospects for growth in the future and is exposed to a great deal of risk is not a bargain.

CORE OF THE STORY

How do you determine that a stock is cheap? You could look at the price of a stock; but stock prices can be easily altered by changing the number of shares outstanding. You can halve your stock price (roughly) with a two-for-one stock split (by which you double the number of shares), but the stock does not get any cheaper. While some investors may fall for the pitch that a stock that trades for pennies is cheap, most investors are wary enough to see the trap. Dividing the price by the earnings is one way of leveling the playing field so that high-priced and low-priced stocks can be compared. The use of low PE ratios in investment strategies is widespread, and several justifications are offered for the practice:

- *Value investors buy low PE stocks.* Investors in the value investing school have historically measured value by using the price-earnings ratio. Thus, when comparing across stocks, value investors view a stock that trades at five times earnings as cheaper than one that trades at ten times earnings.
- *A low PE stock is an attractive alternative to investing in bonds.* For those investors who prefer to compare what they make on stocks to what they can make on bonds, there is another reason for looking for stocks with low price-earnings ratios. The earnings yield (which is the inverse of the price-earnings ratio, that is, the earnings per share divided by the current stock price) on these stocks is usually high relative to the yield on bonds. To illustrate, a stock with a PE ratio of 8 has an earnings yield of 12.5%, which may provide an attractive alternative to treasury bonds yielding only 4%.
- *Stocks that trade at low PE ratios relative to their peer group must be mispriced.* Since price-earnings ratios vary across sectors, with stocks in some sectors consistently trading at lower PE ratios than stocks in other sectors, you could judge the value of a stock by comparing its PE ratio to the average PE ratio of stocks in the sector in which the firm operates. Thus, a technology stock that trades at 15 times earnings may be considered cheap because the average PE ratio for technology stocks is 22, whereas an electric utility that trades at 10 times earnings can be viewed as expensive because the average PE ratio for utilities is only 7.

THEORETICAL ROOTS: DETERMINANTS OF PE RATIO

Investors have always used earnings multiples to judge investments. The simplicity and intuitive appeal of the price-earnings (PE) ratio makes it an attractive choice in applications ranging from pricing initial public offerings to making judgments on investments, but the PE ratio is related to a firm's fundamentals. As you will see in this section, a low PE ratio by itself does not indicate an undervalued stock.

WHAT IS THE PE RATIO?

The price-earnings ratio is the ratio obtained by dividing the market price per share by the earnings per share over a period.

$$PE = \frac{\text{Market Price per share}}{\text{Earnings per share}}$$

The PE ratio is usually estimated with the current price per share in the numerator and the earnings per share in the denominator.

The biggest problem with PE ratios is the variations on earnings per share used in computing the multiple. The most common measure of the PE ratio divides the current price by the earnings per share in the most recent financial year; this yields the *current PE*. Other people prefer to compute a more updated measure of earnings per share by adding up the earnings per share in each of the last four quarters and dividing the price by this measure of earnings per share, using it to compute a *trailing PE ratio*. Some analysts go even further and use expected earnings per share in the next financial year in the denominator and compute a *forward PE ratio*. Earnings per share can also be computed before or after extraordinary items and based upon actual shares outstanding (primary) or all shares that will be outstanding if managers exercise the options that they have been granted (fully diluted). In other words, you should not be surprised to see different PE ratios reported for the same firm at the same point by different sources. In addition, you should be specific about your definition of a PE ratio if you decide to construct an investment strategy that revolves around its value.

A PRIMER ON ACCOUNTING EARNINGS

Before you look at whether the price-earnings ratio can be used as a measure of the cheapness of a stock, you do need to consider how earnings are measured in financial statements. Accountants use the income statement to provide information about a firm's operating activities over a specific period. In this section, you will examine the principles underlying earnings measurement in accounting and the methods by which they are put into practice.

Two primary principles underlie the measurement of accounting earnings and profitability. The first is the principle of *accrual accounting.* In accrual accounting, the revenue from selling a good or service is recognized in the period in which the good is sold or the service is performed (in whole or substantially). A corresponding effort is made on the expense side to match[1] expenses to revenues. This is in contrast to cash accounting, whereby revenues are recognized when payment is received and expenses are recorded when they are paid. As a consequence, a firm may report high accrual earnings but its cash earnings may be substantially lower (or even negative), or the reverse can apply.

The second principle is the *categorization of expenses into operating, financing and capital expenses.* Operating expenses are expenses that, at least in theory, provide benefits only for the current period; the cost of labor and materials expended to create products that are sold in the current period is a good example. Financing expenses are expenses arising from the nonequity financing used to raise capital for the business; the most common example is interest expenses. Capital expenses are expenses that are expected to generate benefits over multiple periods; for instance, the cost of buying land and buildings is treated as a capital expense.

Operating expenses are subtracted from revenues in the current period to arrive at a measure of operating earnings from the firm. Financing expenses are subtracted from operating earnings to estimate earnings to equity investors or net income. Capital expenses are written off over their useful life (in terms of generating benefits) as depreciation or amortization. Figure 3.1 breaks down a typical income statement.

Income Statement

Gross revenues from sale of products or services	Revenues
Expenses associated with generating revenues. Included in these expenses is the depreciation and amortization of capital expenses from prior years	−Operating Expenses
Operating income for the period	= Operating Income
Expenses associated with borrowing and other financing	− Financial Expenses
Taxes due on taxable income	− Taxes
Earnings to common & preferred equity for current period	= Net Income Before Extraordinary Items
Profits and losses not associated with operations	− (+) Extraordinary Losses (Profits)
Profits or losses associated with changes in accounting rules	− Income Changes Associated with Accounting Changes
Dividends paid to preferred stockholders	− Preferred Dividends
	= Net Income to Common Stockholders

FIGURE 3.1

Income Statement

This is the general format for all income statements. There are variations on this format across different types of businesses.

While the principles governing the measurement of earnings are straightforward, firms do have discretion on a number of different elements, such as the following:

■ *Revenue recognition:* When firms sell products that generate revenues over multiple years, conservative firms spread revenues over time but aggressive firms may show revenues in the initial year. Microsoft, for exam-

ple, has had a history of being conservative in its re-
cording of revenues from its program updates (Windows
98, Windows 2000, etc.). On the other hand, telecommunication firms, in their zeal to pump up revenue
growth, in the late 1990s were often aggressive in re-
cording revenues early.

■ *Operating versus capital expenses:* Some expenses fall
in a gray area between operating and capital expenses.
Consider the expenses incurred by a cable company to
attract new subscribers. Companies that are more aggressive could legitimately argue that the benefits of
these new subscribers will be felt over many years and
spread these expenses over time. At the same time, conservative companies will expense the entire amount in
the year in which the expense is incurred.

■ *Depreciation and amortization:* While capital expenses
are written off over time as depreciation or amortization
charges, firms continue to have discretion in how much
and how quickly they depreciate assets, at least for reporting purposes. Here again, more aggressive firms can
report higher earnings by adopting depreciation and
amortization schedules that result in smaller charges
against earnings.

The bottom line, though, is that while the same accounting standards may apply to all firms, the fidelity to these standards can vary across firms, making it difficult to compare
earnings (and price-earnings ratios) across firms. If you are
not careful, you can very easily conclude that firms that are
more aggressive in measuring earnings are cheaper than firms
that are more conservative. The problem gets worse when you
are comparing the earnings of firms in different markets—
Japan, Germany and the United States, for example—with different accounting standards.

DETERMINANTS OF PE RATIOS

The simplest model for valuing a stock is to assume that
the value of the stock is the present value of the expected future dividends. Since equity in publicly traded firms could

potentially last forever, this present value can be computed fairly simply if you assume that the dividends paid by a firm will grow at a constant rate forever. In this model, which is called the Gordon Growth Model, the value of equity can be written as:

$$\text{Value per share today} = \frac{\text{Expected Dividend per share next year}}{\text{Cost of Equity} - \text{Expected Growth Rate}}$$

The cost of equity is the rate of return that investors in the stock require, given its risk. As a simple example, consider investing in stock in Consolidated Edison, the utility that serves much of New York city. The stock is expected to pay a dividend of $2.20 per share next year (out of expected earnings per share of $3.30), the cost of equity for the firm is 8%, and the expected growth rate in perpetuity is 3%. The value per share can be written as:

$$\text{Value per share of Con Ed} = \frac{\$2.20}{(.08 - .03)} = \$44.00 \text{ per share}$$

Generations of students in valuation classes have looked at this model and some of them have thrown up their hands in despair. How, they wonder, can you value firms like Microsoft that do not pay dividends? And what you do when the expected growth rate is higher than the cost of equity, rendering the value negative? There are simple answers to both questions. The first is that a growth rate that can be maintained forever cannot be greater than the growth rate of the economy. Thus, an expected growth rate that is 15% would be incompatible with this model; in fact, the expected growth rate has to be less than the 4%–5% that even the most optimistic forecasters believe that the economy (U.S. or global) can grow at in the long term.[2] The second is that firms that are growing at these stable growth rates should have cash available to return to their stockholders; most firms that pay no dividends do so because they have to reinvest in their businesses to generate high growth.

To get from this model for value to one for the price-earnings ratio, you will divide both sides of the equation by the expected earnings per share next year. When you do, you obtain the discounted cash flow equation specifying the forward PE ratio for a stable growth firm.

$$\frac{\text{Value per share today}}{\text{Expected EPS next year}} = \text{Forward PE} =$$

$$\frac{\text{Expected Dividend per share} / \text{Expected EPS}}{\text{Cost of Equity} - \text{Expected Growth Rate}}$$

$$= \frac{\text{Expected Payout Ratio}}{(\text{Cost of Equity} - \text{Expected Growth Rate})}$$

To illustrate with Con Ed, using the numbers from the previous paragraph, you get the following:

Forward PE for Con Ed = ($2.20 / $3.30) / (.08 − .04) = 16.67

The PE ratio will increase as the expected growth rate increases; higher growth firms should have higher PE ratios, which makes intuitive sense. The PE ratio will be lower if the firm is a high-risk firm and has a high cost of equity. Finally, the PE ratio will increase as the payout ratio increases, for any given growth rate. In other words, firms that are more efficient about generating growth (by earning a higher return on equity) will trade at higher multiples of earnings.

The price-earnings ratio for a high growth firm can also be related to fundamentals. When you work through the algebra, which is more tedious than difficult, the variables that determine the price-earnings ratio remain the same: the risk of the company, the expected growth rate and the payout ratio, with the only difference being that these variables have to be estimated separately for each growth phase.[3] In the special case in which you expect a stock to grow at a high rate for the next few years and grow at a stable rate after that, you would estimate the payout ratio, cost of equity and expected growth rate in the high growth period and the stable growth period. This approach is general enough to be applied to any firm, even one that is not paying dividends right now

Looking at the determinants of price-earnings ratios, you can clearly see that a low price-earnings ratio, by itself, signifies little. If you expect low growth in earnings (or even negative growth) and there is high risk in a firm's earnings, you should pay a low multiple of earnings for the firm. For a firm to be undervalued, you need to get a mismatch: a low price-earnings ratio without the stigma of high risk or poor growth. Later in this chapter, you will examine a portfolio of low PE stocks to see if you can separate the firms that have low PE ratios and are fairly valued or even overvalued from firms that have low PE ratios that may be attractive investments.

LOOKING AT THE EVIDENCE

Do portfolios of stocks with low price-earnings ratios out-perform the market? The answer to this question is central to this chapter, and you will look at the performance of stocks with low PE ratios over the last few decades in this section.

BEN GRAHAM AND VALUE SCREENING

Many value investors claim to trace their antecedents to Ben Graham and to use the book *Security Analysis* that he co-authored with David Dodd, in 1934 as their investment bible.[4] It was in the first edition of this book that Ben Graham put his mind to converting his views on markets to specific screens that could be used to find undervalued stocks. While the numbers in the screens did change slightly from edition to edition, they preserved their original form and are summarized below:

1. Earnings-to-price ratio that is double the AAA bond yield
2. PE of the stock less than 40% of the average PE for all stocks over the last five years
3. Dividend yield greater than two-thirds of the AAA corporate bond yield
4. Price less than two-thirds of tangible book value[5]
5. Price less than two-thirds of net current asset value (NCAV), where net current asset value is defined as liquid current assets including cash minus current liabilities

6. Debt-equity ratio (book value) less than 1
7. Current assets greater than twice current liabilities
8. Debt less than twice net current assets
9. Historical growth in EPS (over last 10 years) greater than 7%
10. No more than two years of declining earnings over the previous ten years

Note that the first screen is a price-earnings ratio screen. Only stocks with low price-earnings ratios would have a chance of passing this screen. It is interesting that many of the remaining screens are designed to eliminate those stocks that have low PE ratios for the wrong reasons: low growth and high risk.

How well do Ben Graham's screens work when it comes to picking stocks? Henry Oppenheimer studied the portfolios obtained from these screens from 1974 to 1981 and concluded that you could have made an annual return well in excess of the market.[6] Academics have tested individual screens—low PE ratios and high dividend yields to name two—in recent years and have found that they deliver higher returns. Mark Hulbert, who evaluates the performance of investment newsletters, found newsletters that professed to follow Graham did much better than other newsletters. The only jarring note is that an attempt to convert the screens into a mutual fund that would deliver high returns did fail. In the 1970s, an investor named James Rea was convinced enough of the value of these screens that he founded a fund called the Rea-Graham fund, which would invest in stocks on the basis of the Graham screens. While it had some initial successes, the fund floundered during the 1980s and early 1990s and was ranked in the bottom quartile for performance.

LOW PE STOCKS VERSUS THE REST OF THE MARKET

Studies that have looked at the relationship between PE ratios and excess returns have consistently found that stocks with low PE ratios earn significantly higher returns than stocks with high PE ratios over long time horizons. Since some of the research is more than two decades old and the results vary widely depending upon the sampling period, it might be best to review the raw data and look at the longest period for which data is available.

In Figure 3.2, you begin by looking at the annual returns that would have been earned by U.S. stocks categorized into ten classes according to PE ratios from 1952 to 2001. The stocks were categorized by PE ratios at the start of each year, and the total return, inclusive of dividends and price appreciation, was computed for each of the ten portfolios over the year.

On average, the stocks in the lowest PE ratio classes earned almost twice the returns of the stocks in the highest PE ratio classes. To examine how sensitive these conclusions were to how the portfolios were constructed, you can look at

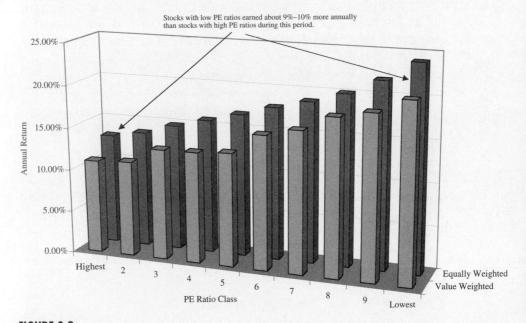

FIGURE 3.2

PE Ratios and Stock Returns: 1952–2001

Data from Fama/French. Stocks in the United States were categorized by PE ratios at the beginning of each year from 1952 to 2001, and returns were computed for each portfolio in the following year.

two constructs. In the first, equally weighted portfolios were created, and an equal amount of money was put into each firm in each portfolio. In the second, more was invested in the firms with higher market value and less in the smaller firms to create value-weighted portfolios. The results were slightly more favorable with the equally weighted portfolio, with the lowest PE ratio stocks earning an average annual return of 24.11% and the highest PE ratio stocks earning 13.03%. With the value-weighted portfolios, the corresponding numbers were 20.85% and 11%, respectively. In both cases, though, low PE stocks clearly outperformed high PE stocks as investments.

To examine whether there are differences in subperiods, let's look at the annual returns from 1952 to 1971, 1972 to 1990, and 1991 to 2001 for stocks in each PE ratio portfolio in Figure 3.3. Again, the portfolios were created on the basis of PE ratios at the beginning of each year, and returns were measured over the course of the year.

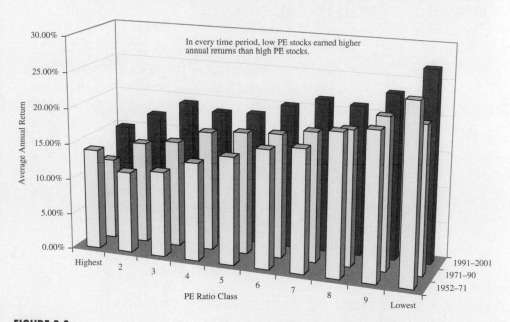

FIGURE 3.3

Returns on PE Ratio Classes: 1952–2001

Data from Fama/French. The annual returns are computed for stocks in different PE ratio classes for subperiods of history.

Firms in the lowest PE ratio class earned 10% more each year than the stocks in the high PE class between 1952 and 1971, about 9% more each year between 1971 and 1990, and about 12% more each year between 1991 and 2001. In other words, there is no visible decline in the returns earned by low PE stocks in recent years.

Thus, the evidence is overwhelming that low PE stocks earn higher returns than high PE stocks over long periods. Those studies that adjust for differences in risk across stocks confirm that low PE stocks continue to earn higher returns after adjusting for risk. Since the portfolios examined in the last section were constructed only with stocks listed in the United States, it is also worth noting that the excess returns earned by low PE ratio stocks also show up in other international markets.

CRUNCHING THE NUMBERS

Earlier in this chapter, reference was made to a rule of thumb that a stock that trades at a PE ratio less than 8 is cheap. While there are numerous benchmarks such as these in the market, you should be wary of these numbers. Many of them are outdated and have no basis in fact. In this section, you will begin by looking at the distribution of PE ratios across the market to get a sense of what would constitute a high, low or average PE ratio. You will then follow up by looking at how PE ratios vary across different sectors and also how they have changed over time. Finally, you will construct a portfolio of stocks with the lowest PE ratios in the market, with the intention of examining it more closely for potential flaws in the strategy.

PE RATIOS ACROSS THE MARKET

While there are numerous rules of thumb when it comes to PE ratios, it is impossible to assess whether they make sense without looking at how PE ratios vary across stocks in the market. Figure 3.4 presents the distribution of PE ratios for all U.S. stocks in October 2002. The current PE, trailing PE and forward PE ratios are all presented in this figure.

Looking at this distribution, you can see that while there are a large number of companies with PE ratios between 8 and 20, there are also a significant number of companies with PE ratios well in excess of 100. Some of these companies are high growth companies that trade at high prices relative to current earnings because investors expect their earnings to grow substantially in the future. Some of these companies are cyclical companies whose earnings have dropped as a consequence of a recession. Since investors expect their earnings to bounce back as the economy recovers, the price-earnings ratio is high. At the other extreme are companies whose PE ratios are 12 or less. In October 2002, these firms would be considered cheap if you looked at just the PE ratio. A final point about

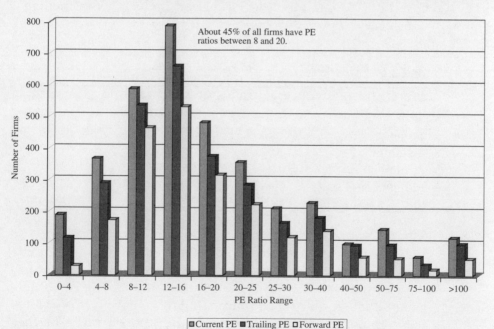

FIGURE 3.4

PE Ratios Across the Market: October 2002

Data from Value Line. The number of firms in the United States that fall within each PE ratio class for stocks is reported.

these PE ratios relates to companies for which the PE ratio could not be computed because earnings per share were negative. In the sample, which included 7102 companies, 3489 companies had negative earnings in the most recent financial year and current PE ratios could not be computed for them. With trailing and forward earnings, you continue to lose about 40% of the overall sample for the same reason.

The fact that PE ratios cannot be less than zero but can take on very high values has consequences when you compute statistics. The average PE ratio, which is computed by averaging across all companies, will be pushed up by the extreme high values. A far more meaningful statistic would be the median PE; half of all companies will have PE ratios less than this value, and half of all companies will have PE ratios that are higher than this value. Table 3.1 summarizes statistics on both measures of the price-earnings ratio, starting with the mean and the standard deviation and including the median, 10th and 90th percentile values.

TABLE 3.1 Summary Statistics: PE Ratios for U.S. Stocks

	CURRENT PE	TRAILING PE	FORWARD PE
Mean	31.08	30.99	23.44
Median	15.30	15.00	14.99
Minimum	0.01	0.01	0.90
Maximum	7103.00	6589.00	1081.00
90th percentile	69.02	53.74	36.86
10th percentile	4.22	5.69	7.94

Looking at all three measures of the PE ratio, you see that the average is consistently higher than the median, reflecting the fact that PE ratios can be very high numbers but cannot be less than zero. It is not surprising that analysts wishing to sell you stocks often use the pitch that the PE ratio for the stock is below the average for the industry. An effective retort would be to ask them whether the PE ratio for the stock is less than the median for the industry.

PE RATIOS ACROSS SECTORS

Price-earnings ratio can vary widely across sectors, and what comprises a low PE ratio in one sector can be a high PE ratio in another. In Table 3.2, the ten sectors with the lowest and the highest average PE ratios (current) in the United States in October 2002 are listed.

TABLE 3.2 Highest and Lowest PE Ratio Sectors

INDUSTRY NAME	AVERAGE PE	INDUSTRY NAME	AVERAGE PE
Power	6.94	Newspaper	41.14
Steel (Integrated)	7.98	Entertainment	41.43
Homebuilding	9.46	Telecom. Services	43.14
Electric Utility	10.18	Precision Instrument	44.17
Auto Parts	10.75	Semiconductor	47.10
Tobacco	10.82	Publishing	49.06
Insurance (Life)	10.90	E-Commerce	50.32
Apparel	11.18	Cable TV	53.49
Home Appliance	11.70	Wireless Networking	60.49
Thrift	11.97	Chemical (Basic)	60.76

What are the reasons for the vast divergences in PE ratios across sectors? The fundamentals that were outlined earlier as the determinants of PE—growth, risk and payout (return on equity)—provide the explanation. In general, the sectors with the lowest PE ratios offer not only the lowest expected growth but also have low returns on equity. The sectors with the highest PE ratios offer higher expected growth and higher returns on equity, albeit with more risk. Table 3.3 contrasts measures of growth, risk and return on equity for the two groups: the ten sectors with the highest PE ratios and the ten with the lowest.

In estimating return on capital and return on equity, the averages over the last five years were used to overcome the depressed earnings (and returns on equity) caused by the recession in 2002. Note that the lowest PE sectors have lower projected growth in earnings and revenues and lower project returns than those in the highest PE sectors.

TABLE 3.3 Comparisons on Fundamentals: High PE vs. Low PE Sectors

| | Risk Measures | | Expected Growth in | | Returns | |
	Beta	Standard Deviation	EPS—Next 5 Years	Revenues—Next 5 Years	ROIC[a]	ROE[a]
Low PE sectors	0.61	0.48	11.61%	5.56%	7.64%	9.30%
High PE sectors	1.76	0.84	17.01%	7.65%	14.66%	16.50%

[a] *ROIC: Return on invested capital; ROE = Return on equity.*

PE RATIO ACROSS TIME

A PE ratio of 12 can be considered low in today's market but it would have been high in the equity market of 1981. As PE ratios change over time, the criteria for what constitutes a low or a high PE will also change. Consequently, the average PE ratio for all stocks in the United States is examined in Figure 3.5.

Note that the PE ratios have varied significantly over time, reaching a low of about 7 in 1975 and climbing to a high of 33 at the market peak in 1999.

What causes PE ratios to change over time? The very same factors that determine the PE ratios of individual companies—cash flows, growth and cost of equity—also determine the PE ratios for individual companies. PE ratios were low in the mid-1970s because economic growth was dragged down by the oil

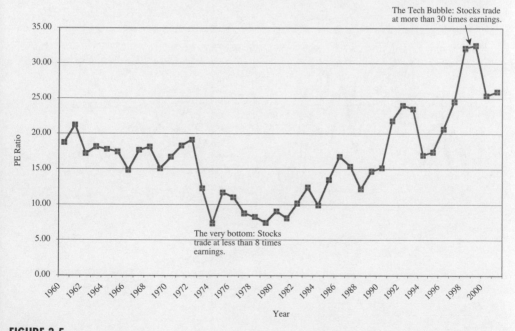

FIGURE 3.5

PE Ratio for S&P: 1960–2001

Data from Bloomberg. This is the average PE ratio across all U.S. stocks at the end of each year from 1960 to 2002.

embargo and subsequent inflation in the United States and because nominal interest rates were high. In fact, the period between 1975 and 1981 when PE ratios remained low represents a period when government bond rates in the United States reach double digits for the first time in history. The decline in interest rates in the 1990s accompanied by rapid economic growth and higher productivity in the 1990s contributed to making PE ratios in that decade much higher.

As PE ratios change over time, the determination of what constitutes a low PE will also change. In Figure 3.6, you examine the PE ratios that would have represented the 5th, 10th and 25th percentile of all stocks listed on the New York Stock Exchange every year from 1951 to 2001.

In 1975, the low point for PE ratios for U.S. stocks, 5% of all stocks had PE ratios less than 2.18, 10% of all stocks had PE ratios less than 2.64, and 25% of all stocks had PE ratios

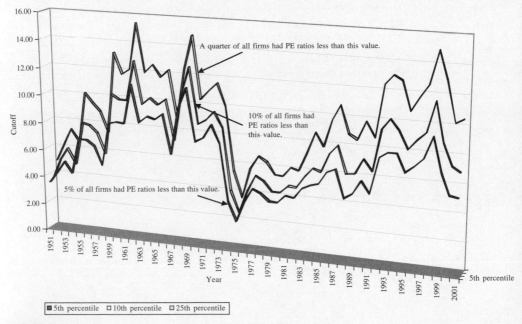

FIGURE 3.6

PE Ratio: Cutoffs over Time

Data from Fama/French. The 5th, 10th, and 25th percentile of PE ratios across all U.S. stocks is reported for each year.

less than 3.56. In contrast, in 1998, 5% of stocks had PE ratios less than 9.42, 10% had PE ratios less than 11.64, and 25% had PE ratios less than 14.88. This is why a rule of thumb (e.g., PE less than 8 is cheap!) has to be taken with a grain of salt. While it would have been factual in 1998, it would not have been so in 1975, since more than half of all stocks traded at PE ratios lower than 8 in that year.

A Low PE Portfolio

If you decided to adopt a strategy of buying low PE stocks, what would your portfolio look like? The only way to answer this question is to create such a portfolio. Assume you begin with the all listed U.S. stocks and screen for the stocks with the lowest PE ratios. You have three measures of the PE ratio for each company: the PE based upon earnings in the most recent financial year (current PE), the PE based upon earnings in the most recent four quarters (trailing PE), and the PE based upon expected earnings in the next financial year (forward PE). Each measure has its adherents, and there is information in each. Erring on the side of conservatism, you can look for stocks that have PE ratios less than 10 on all three measures. The resulting portfolio in October 2002 is presented in Table 3.4.

Taking a closer look at the portfolio, you will see that 116 stocks in the market (out of an overall sample of 7000+ companies) met the criteria of having current, trailing and forward price earnings ratios all less than 10. The portfolio is fairly diversified, though utility and financial service stocks are disproportionately represented.

MORE TO THE STORY

Given the high returns that low PE ratio stocks earn, should you rush out and buy such stocks? While such a portfolio may include a number of undervalued companies, it may also contain other less desirable companies for several

TABLE 3.4 Stocks with PE Ratios Less Than 10: United States—October 2002

Company Name	Industry	Current PE	Trailing PE	Forward PE	Company Name	Industry	Current PE	Trailing PE	Forward PE
Acclaim Entertainment	ENT TECH	7.45	3.88	5.73	Kroger Co	GROCERY	9.70	9.70	7.87
AES Corp	POWER	0.70	0.70	1.31	Lafarge No America	CEMENT	8.59	7.53	7.70
Aftermarket Tech	AUTO-OEM	8.14	6.44	6.29	LandAmerica Finl Group	FINANCL	6.29	5.79	6.52
Allegheny Energy	UTILEAST	1.22	1.74	2.68	Lennar Corp	HOMEBILD	8.54	7.98	6.65
Allied Waste	ENVIRONM	6.93	6.81	6.57	M.D.C. Holdings	HOMEBILD	6.22	6.27	6.15
Allmerica Financial	INSPRPTY	2.57	4.91	3.23	Magna Int'l 'A'	AUTO-OEM	8.51	8.42	8.52
Amer Axle	AUTO-OEM	9.53	7.59	7.31	Marathon Oil Corp	OILINTEG	5.12	8.07	9.41
Aquila Inc	UTILCENT	2.83	5.55	6.81	May Dept Stores	RETAIL	9.60	9.60	9.80
Argosy Gaming	HOTELGAM	8.18	6.30	7.16	McDermott Int'l	DIVERSIF	5.69	5.69	3.59
Ashland Inc	OILINTEG	4.27	8.76	7.59	Metro One Telecom	INDUSRV	8.02	7.91	3.94
Astoria Financial	THRIFT	9.66	9.66	7.88	MGIC Investment	FINANCL	6.96	6.81	6.34
Bally Total Fitness	RECREATE	2.75	2.84	3.01	MicroFinancial Inc	FINANCL	1.34	1.34	3.17
Beverly Enterprises	MEDSERV	4.75	4.84	4.30	Mirant Corp	POWER	0.68	0.77	1.33
Building Materials	BUILDSUP	6.16	6.16	7.02	Nash Finch Co	FOODWHOL	7.52	6.00	5.73
CAE Inc	DEFENSE	5.76	5.76	6.60	Nationwide Fin'l	INSLIFE	8.02	8.20	7.77
Calpine Corp	POWER	1.16	1.40	2.31	Nautilus Group Inc	RETAILSP	7.17	5.49	5.18
Can. Imperial Bank	BANKCAN	7.62	7.62	8.55	New Century Financial	FINANCL	9.94	4.21	3.44
Centex Corp	HOMEBILD	7.02	6.80	5.61	Petroleo Brasileiro ADR	OILINTEG	2.97	2.97	3.23
Chromcraft Revington	FURNITUR	7.11	7.47	6.84	Petroleum Geo ADR	OILFIELD	3.15	3.65	2.35
Cleco Corp	UTILCENT	7.34	6.81	7.87	Philip Morris	TOBACCO	9.59	8.58	9.17
CMS Energy Corp	UTILCENT	5.92	6.90	5.48	Pinnacle West Capital	UTILWEST	6.67	6.67	8.23
CryoLife Inc	MEDSUPPL	6.01	6.01	4.19	PMI Group	INSPRPTY	8.71	8.71	7.29
Del Monte Foods	FOODPROC	8.23	8.23	8.47	PNM Resources	UTILWEST	4.97	6.60	9.60
Dixie Group	TEXTILE	0.00	9.33	6.22	Precision Castparts	DEFENSE	5.44	5.41	6.55
Dominion Homes Inc	HOMEBILD	7.14	5.04	5.55	Public Serv Enterprise	UTILEAST	5.62	6.49	6.01

Company	Code			
Downey Financial	THRIFT	8.46	9.14	9.76
DPL Inc	UTILCENT	8.34	8.34	9.22
Duke Energy	UTILEAST	7.78	8.27	7.65
Dura Automotive 'A'	AUTO-OEM	5.99	5.90	3.62
Dynegy Inc 'A'	GASDIVRS	0.46	0.56	3.87
El Paso Electric	UTILWEST	8.17	8.17	9.43
Electronic Data Sys	SOFTWARE	5.84	5.14	4.37
ENDESA ADR	FGNEUTIL	8.13	9.77	8.01
ePlus Inc	INTERNET	7.70	7.87	7.80
Federated Dept Stores	RETAIL	9.62	9.05	8.63
Fidelity Nat'l Fin'l	FINANCL	9.09	7.26	6.48
First Amer Corp	FINANCL	9.03	8.11	9.55
FirstFed Fin'l-CA	THRIFT	8.90	8.96	9.28
Fleming Cos	FOODWHOL	2.47	2.47	2.23
Flowserve Corp	MACHINE	8.78	6.88	5.31
Foot Locker	RETAILSP	9.48	8.94	8.53
Gadzooks Inc	RETAILSP	7.58	6.74	7.02
Geneseo Inc	SHOE	7.15	7.61	9.02
Gerber Scientific	INSTRMNT	9.29	9.29	5.69
Goodrich Corp	DEFENSE	5.92	5.92	6.78
Greater Bay Bancorp	BANK	8.24	6.33	6.45
Green Mountain Pwr	UTILEAST	7.78	7.78	9.43
Group 1 Automotive	RETAILSP	8.89	8.89	6.93
Gulfmark Offshore	MARITIME	7.09	9.88	8.78
Handleman Co	RECREATE	5.87	5.78	5.74
Haverty Furniture	RETAILSP	9.70	8.40	9.45
Pulte Homes	HOMEBILD	8.49	7.10	6.20
Quaker Fabric	TEXTILE	9.16	7.23	7.34
Quanta Services	INDUSRV	1.89	1.89	4.21
R.J. Reynolds Tobacco	TOBACCO	8.03	5.99	5.65
Radian Group Inc	FINANCL	9.39	8.46	7.80
Radiologix Inc	MEDSERV	7.35	6.67	7.77
Republic Bancorp Inc KY Cl A	BANK	9.87	8.64	9.09
Ryland Group	HOMEBILD	7.21	6.26	6.87
Salton Inc	HOUSEPRD	2.76	2.76	6.52
Sears Roebuck	RETAIL	7.77	7.13	4.69
Shaw Group	METALFAB	8.90	6.31	5.84
Sola Int'l	MEDSUPPL	6.95	7.27	9.23
Sprint Corp	TELESERV	8.47	8.47	8.85
Stillwater Mining	GOLDSILV	3.25	3.25	5.28
SUPERVALU INC	FOODWHOL	9.02	8.19	7.03
TECO Energy	UTILEAST	5.71	5.71	5.79
Telefonos de Mexico ADR	TELEFGN	8.04	8.04	8.03
Toll Brothers	HOMEBILD	6.51	6.18	6.66
Tommy Hilfiger	APPAREL	5.76	6.67	5.50
Trans World Entertain	RETAILSP	7.50	7.50	7.52
Triumph Group Inc	INSTRMNT	8.41	8.92	7.94
TXU Corp	UTILCENT	3.58	3.19	2.70
Tyco Int'l Ltd	DIVERSIF	5.01	5.00	7.52
UIL Holdings	UTILEAST	7.08	7.88	8.35
United Rentals	MACHINE	3.96	3.96	3.11
Universal Amern Finl Corp	INSLIFE	8.99	9.76	8.31

(continued)

TABLE 3.4 Stocks with PE Ratios Less Than 10: United States — October 2002 (*Continued*)

COMPANY NAME	INDUSTRY	CURRENT PE	TRAILING PE	FORWARD PE
HEALTHSOUTH Corp	MEDSERV	4.41	4.41	3.84
Helen of Troy Ltd	COSMETIC	9.01	9.01	7.27
Household Int'l	FINANCL	6.59	7.06	4.52
Imperial Chem ADR	CHEMDIV	7.01	7.01	8.97
InterTAN Inc	RETAILSP	9.00	9.00	8.59
KB Home	HOMEBILD	8.51	7.13	6.32
Universal Corp	TOBACCO	8.35	8.35	8.62
URS Corp	INDUSRV	7.37	6.24	7.37
Warrantech Corp	INDUSRV	7.59	5.61	3.00
Westar Energy	UTILGENT	0.00	3.34	9.43
Westpoint Stevens	TEXTILE	0.00	5.29	1.60
Whirlpool Corp	APPLIANC	8.41	7.49	7.13
World Acceptance	FINANCL	6.45	6.10	6.98

reasons. First, not all earnings are of equal quality. In recent years, some firms have used accounting sleight of hand and one-time income to report higher earnings. You would expect these firms to trade at lower price-earnings ratios than other firms. Second, even if the earnings are not skewed by accounting choices, the earnings can be volatile and the low PE ratio may reflect this higher risk associated with investing in a stock. Third, a low PE ratio can also indicate that a firm's growth prospects have run out. Consequently, it could be a poor investment.

RISK AND PE RATIOS

In the earlier section, you compared the returns of stocks with low price-earnings ratios to other stocks in the market over a long period and concluded that low PE stocks do earn higher returns on average. It is possible, however, that these stocks are riskier than average and that the extra return is just fair compensation for the additional risk. The simplest measure of risk you could consider is stock price volatility, measured with a standard deviation in stock prices over a prior period. Consider the portfolio of low PE stocks that you constructed at the end of the last section. The standard deviation in stock prices was computed for each stock in the portfolio. In Figure 3.7, the average standard deviation for the low PE portfolio is compared with the standard deviation of all stocks in the market for a three-year and a five-year period.

Surprisingly, the lowest PE stocks, are, on average, less volatile than the highest PE stocks, though some stocks in the low PE portfolio are more volatile than average.

Some studies try to control for risk by estimating excess returns that adjust for risk. To do so, though, they have to use a risk-and-return model, which measures the risk in investments and evaluates their expected returns, given the measured risk. For instance, some researchers have used the capital asset pricing model and estimated the betas of low PE and high PE portfolios. They come to the same conclusion that the analyses that do not adjust for risk come to: that low

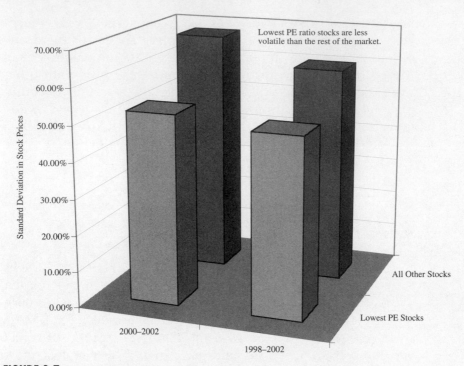

FIGURE 3.7
Standard Deviation in Stock Prices

Data from Value Line. The average annualized standard deviation in weekly stock prices over three and five years is reported.

PE ratio stocks earn much higher returns, after adjusting for beta risk, than do high PE ratio stocks. Consequently, the beta was computed for each of the stocks in the low PE portfolio, and the average was contrasted for the portfolio with the average for all other stocks, as shown in Figure 3.8.

On this measure of risk as well, the low PE ratio portfolio fares well, with the average beta of low PE stocks being lower than the average PE for the rest of the market.

While the average beta and standard deviation of the low PE portfolio is lower than the average for the rest of the market, it is still prudent to screen stocks in the portfolio for risk. You could, for instance, eliminate all firms that would fall in the top quintile of listed stocks in terms of risk, beta or standard deviation. Looking at stocks listed in October 2002, this would have yielded cutoff values of 1.25 for beta and 80% for standard deviation. Removing firms with betas greater than

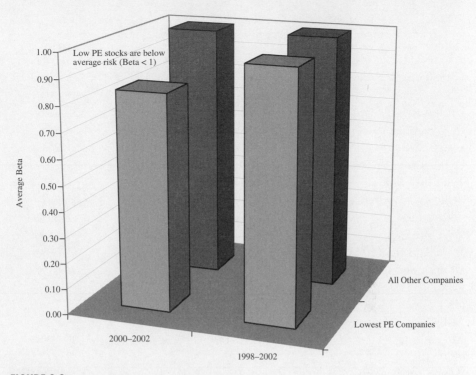

FIGURE 3.8
Betas of Low PE Ratio Companies
Data from Value Line. This is the average beta (computed over 5 years of weekly returns) across stocks in the portfolio.

1.25 or standard deviations that exceed 80% from the sample reduces the number of stocks in the portfolio from 115 to 91. Table 3.5 lists the 24 firms removed as a result of failing the risk screen.

TABLE 3.5 Firms Removed from Low PE Portfolio: Risk Test

COMPANY NAME	INDUSTRY	BETA	STANDARD DEVIATION
Beverly Enterprises	Medserv	1.27	75.58%
Allmerica Financial	Insprpty	1.31	49.50%
Precision Castparts	Defense	1.33	52.58%
Federated Dept Stores	Retail	1.34	46.00%
Telefonos de Mexico ADR	Telefgn	1.4	43.74%

(continued)

TABLE 3.5 Firms Removed from Low PE Portfolio: Risk Test *(Continued)*

COMPANY NAME	INDUSTRY	BETA	STANDARD DEVIATION
Petroleum Geo ADR	Oilfield	1.4	74.49%
Shaw Group	Metalfab	1.44	69.20%
United Rentals	Machine	1.68	58.13%
Flowserve Corp	Machine	1.71	54.84%
InterTAN Inc	Retailsp	1.73	61.29%
Dynegy Inc 'A'	Gasdivrs	1.78	77.24%
Tyco Int'l Ltd	Diversif	1.87	60.57%
Stillwater Mining	Goldsilv	1.87	65.61%
Salton Inc	Houseprd	2.05	73.57%
CryoLife Inc	Medsuppl	−0.34	81.08%
Dura Automotive 'A'	Auto-oem	2.35	81.56%
Quanta Services	Indusrv	2.48	82.67%
Calpine Corp	Power	1.95	85.18%
Metro One Telecom	Indusrv	1.74	86.70%
AES Corp	Power	2.26	89.64%
Aftermarket Tech	Auto-oem	1.02	100.83%
ePlus Inc	Internet	1.57	113.77%
Westpoint Stevens	Textile	0.74	126.22%
Acclaim Entertainment	Ent tech	3.33	237.57%

Note that firms are required to pass both risk tests. Thus, firms that have betas less than 1.25 (such as Westpoint Stevens) but standard deviations greater than 80% are eliminated from the portfolio.

LOW GROWTH AND PE RATIOS

One reason for a low PE ratio for a stock would be low expected growth. Many low PE ratio companies are in mature businesses for which the potential for growth is minimal. If you invest in stocks with low PE ratios, you run the risk of holding stocks with anemic or even negative growth rates. As an investor, therefore, you have to consider whether the tradeoff of a lower PE ratio for lower growth works in your favor.

As with risk, growth can be measured in many ways. You could look at growth in earnings over the last few quarters or years, but that would be backward looking. There are stocks whose earnings have stagnated over the last few years that may be ripe for high growth, just as there are stocks whose earnings have gone up sharply in the last few years that have little or no expected growth in the future. It is to avoid this peering into the past that investors often prefer to focus on expected growth in earnings in the future. Estimates of this growth rate are available for different forecast periods from analysts and are often averaged and summarized (across analysts) by services such as I/B/E/S or Zacks. The average past and expected growth rates in earnings per share for firms in the low PE portfolio are computed and compared in Figure 3.9 to the same statistics for the rest of the market in October 2002.

The earnings of the lowest PE ratio stocks have grown faster than the earnings of other stocks if you look back in

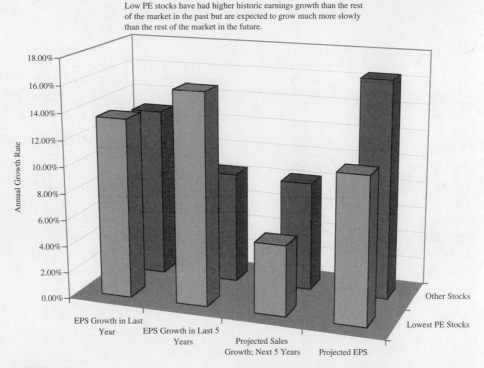

FIGURE 3.9

Growth Rates: Lowest PE Stocks vs. Other Stocks

Data from Value Line. The projected sales and EPS growth for the next five years comes from analyst forecasts.

time (one year or five years). However, the projected growth in both sales and earnings is much lower for the low PE ratio stocks, indicating that this may be a potential problem with the portfolio and a partial explanation for why these stocks trade at lower values. Consequently, you should consider screening the portfolio of low PE stocks for those with low or negative growth rates. Introducing a minimum expected growth rate of 10% in expected earnings reduces the sample of low PE stocks by 52 firms. A minimum expected growth rate of 5% would reduce the sample by 27 firms. If you believe that analyst estimates tend to be too optimistic and introduce an additional constraint that historical growth in earnings would also have to exceed 5%, you would lose another 18 firms from the sample. Table 3.6 summarizes the 41 firms that are eliminated by introduction of a dual growth constraint—a historical earnings per share growth rate that exceeds 5% and analyst projected earnings per share growth greater than 5%.

TABLE 3.6 Firms Removed from Low PE Portfolio: Growth Test

COMPANY NAME	TICKER SYMBOL	PROJECTED EPS GROWTH	EPS GROWTH— LAST 5 YEARS
REMOVED BECAUSE PROJECTED GROWTH LESS THAN OR EQUAL TO 5%			
Aquila Inc	ILA	–10.00%	7.00%
CMS Energy Corp	CMS	–4.00%	–0.50%
PNM Resources	PNM	–1.50%	11.50%
UIL Holdings	UIL	–1.00%	4.00%
Trans World Entertain	TWMC	–0.50%	0.00%
Stillwater Mining	SWC	0.50%	0.00%
Allegheny Energy	AYE	1.00%	8.50%
Allmerica Financial	AFC	1.00%	11.50%
Marathon Oil Corp	MRO	1.00%	28.00%
Imperial Chem ADR	ICI	1.50%	–3.50%
Pinnacle West Capital	PNW	2.00%	9.00%
El Paso Electric	EE	2.50%	15.50%
Salton Inc	SFP	2.50%	72.50%
Calpine Corp	CPN	3.50%	0.00%
Sprint Corp	FON	3.50%	0.00%
Ashland Inc	ASH	3.50%	14.50%
Universal Corp	UVV	3.50%	15.50%

Company Name	Ticker Symbol	Projected EPS Growth	EPS Growth— Last 5 Years
REMOVED BECAUSE PROJECTED GROWTH LESS THAN OR EQUAL TO 5%			
Westpoint Stevens	WXS	4.00%	0.00%
ENDESA ADR	ELE	4.00%	1.00%
Quanta Services	PWR	4.50%	0.00%
TECO Energy	TE	4.50%	4.50%
Lafarge No. America	LAF	4.50%	17.50%
Del Monte Foods	DLM	5.00%	0.00%
May Dept. Stores	MAY	5.00%	6.00%
Tommy Hilfiger	TOM	5.00%	15.00%
Precision Castparts	PCP	5.00%	20.50%
AES Corp	AES	5.00%	28.50%
REMOVED BECAUSE HISTORICAL GROWTH LESS THAN OR EQUAL TO 5%			
Westar Energy	WR	16.00%	–25.50%
Green Mountain Pwr	GMP	20.50%	–19.50%
Petroleum Geo ADR	PGO	15.00%	–14.50%
Beverly Enterprises	BEV	9.50%	–12.50%
Gerber Scientific	GRB	14.00%	–9.50%
Quaker Fabric	QFAB	18.17%	–5.50%
Sola Int'l	SOL	6.00%	–3.50%
Nash Finch Co	NAFC	17.50%	–3.50%
Aftermarket Tech	ATAC	8.50%	2.00%
TXU Corp	TXU	9.50%	2.00%
Electronic Data Sys	EDS	13.00%	2.50%
Chromcraft Revington	CRC	13.00%	4.00%
Gadzooks Inc	GADZ	18.33%	5.00%

EARNINGS QUALITY AND PE RATIOS

With their focus on earnings per share, PE ratios put you at the mercy of the accountants who measure these earnings. If you assumed that accountants make mistakes but that they work within established accounting standards to estimate earnings without bias, you would be able to use PE ratios without qualms. In the aftermath of the accounting scandals of recent years, you could argue that accounting earnings are susceptible to manipulation. If earnings are high not because of a firm's operating efficiency but because of one-time items such as gains from divestiture or questionable items such as income from pension funds, you should discount these earnings more (leading to lower PE ratios).

How can you screen stocks to eliminate those with questionable earnings? It is difficult to do, since you learn of troubles after they occur. You could, however, look for clues that have historically accompanied earnings manipulation. One would be frequent earnings restatements by firms, especially when such restatements disproportionately reduce earnings.[7] Another would be the repeated use of one-time charges to reduce earnings. For example, Xerox had large one-time charges that reduced or eliminated earnings every single financial year during the 1990s. A third is a disconnect between revenue growth and earnings growth. While it is entirely possible for firms to report high earnings growth when revenue growth is low for a year or two, it is difficult to see how any firms can continue to grow earnings 20% a year, year after year, if their revenues growth is only 5% a year.

LESSONS FOR INVESTORS

The primary lesson of this chapter is that firms that have low price-earnings ratios may be neither undervalued nor good investments. If you combine that with the fact that the primary culprits for low PE ratios are low growth and high risk, it is clear that you want a portfolio of stocks with low PE ratios, high-quality earnings with potential for growth and low risk. The key then becomes coming up with the screens that will allow you to bring all of these needs into the portfolio.

(a) *Low PE ratios:* There are two decisions you need to make here. The first is the measure of PE that you will be using. Not only do you have to decide whether you will use current, trailing or forward PE, but you will also have to choose whether you want to use primary or diluted earnings. The second decision you have to make is on what cutoff you will use for a low PE ratio.

In other words, will you pick all stocks with PE ratios less than 12 or only those with PE ratios less than 8? As noted earlier in the chapter, what constitutes a low PE ratio is relative. In other words, a PE ratio of 12 is low in a market in which the median PE is 25 but will be high in a market where the median PE is 7. To scale your choices to the level of the market, you can use the 10th or 20th percentile as the cutoff for a low PE ratio; which one you pick will depend upon how stringent your other screens are and how many stocks you would like to have in your final portfolio.

(b) *Low risk:* Here again, you have two judgments to make. The first is the measure of risk that you will use to screen firms. The standard deviation in stock prices and betas were used as screens in the last section, but there are other quantitative measures of risk that you could also consider. You could use the debt-equity ratio to measure the risk from financial leverage. In addition, there are qualitative measures of risk. Standard and Poor's, for instance, assigns stocks a letter grade that resembles the ratings they assign corporate bonds. An A-rated equity, by S&P's measure, is much safer than a BBB-rated equity. The second is the level of risk at which you will screen out stocks. With standard deviation, for instance, will you screen out all stocks that have standard deviations that exceed the median or average for the market or will you set a lower standard?

(c) *Reasonable expected growth in earnings:* While it is unlikely that you will find companies with low PE ratios and high expected growth rates, you can set a threshold level for growth. You could eliminate all firms, for instance, whose expected growth rate in earnings is less than 5%. How do you come up with this cutoff? You could look at the entire market and use the median or average growth rate of the market as an index.

(d) *Quality of earnings:* This is perhaps the toughest and most time-intensive test to meet. To do it right, you would need to examine the financial statements of each of the firms that make it through the prior screens in detail, and over several years. If you want simpler tests, you could eliminate firms for which you have doubts about earnings quality. For instance, you could remove firms that have the following:

- Repeatedly restated earnings over the last few years: These can be a sign of underlying accounting problems at firms.
- Grown through acquisitions rather than internal investments: Companies that grow through acquisitions are much more likely to have one-time charges (like restructuring expenses) and noncash charges (such as goodwill amortization) that make current earnings less reliable.
- Significant option grants or profits from one-time deals: One-time profits complicate the search for "normalized earnings," and large option grants can make forecasting per share numbers very difficult.

Taking into account these screens, stocks that passed the following screens were considered in October 2002:

- PE ratios (current, trailing and forward) less than 12 (the 20th percentile at the time of the screening).
- Betas that are less than 1 and standard deviations in stock prices over the last five years of less than 60% (which was the median standard deviation across all traded stocks). To control for the fact that some of these firms may have too much debt, any firms that had debt that exceeded 60% of their book capital were eliminated.
- Expected growth in earnings per share (from analyst estimates) over the next five years greater than 5% and historical growth rates in earnings per share (over the last five years) that exceed 5%.

In addition, any firms that had restated earnings[8] over the previous five years or that had more than two large[9] restructuring charges over the previous five years were eliminated. The resulting portfolio of 27 stocks is summarized in the ap-

pendix at the end of this chapter. The portfolio is well diversified and comes from 23 different industries, as defined by
Value Line.

CONCLUSION

The conventional wisdom is that low PE stocks are cheap
and represent good value. That is backed up by empirical evidence that shows low PE stocks earning healthy premiums
over high PE stocks. If you relate price-earnings ratios back to
fundamentals, however, low PE ratios can also be indicative of
high risk and low future growth rates. In this chapter, we
made this linkage explicit by creating a portfolio of low PE
stocks and eliminating those stocks that fail the risk and
growth tests. Of the 115 stocks that had trailing, current and
forward PE ratios that were less than 10, more than 60% of the
sample would have been removed because they had above-
average risk or below-average growth.

In summary, a strategy of investing in stocks just based
upon their low price-earnings ratios can be dangerous. A more
nuanced strategy of investing in low PE ratio stocks with reasonable growth and below-average risk offers more promise,
but only if you are a long-term investor.

ENDNOTES

1. If a cost (such as an administrative cost) cannot be easily
   linked with a particular revenues, it is usually recognized as
   an expense in the period in which it is consumed.

2. If this sounds high, it is because it is stated in nominal terms.
   In real terms, the growth rate is only 2%–2.5%.

3. If you are interested, you can look up the determinants of the
   PE ratio for a high growth firm in Damodaran, A., *Investment
   Valuation*, John Wiley and Sons.

4. Graham, B., and D. Dodd, 1934, *Security Analysis*. McGraw Hill.

5. Tangible book value is computed by subtracting the value of intangible assets such as goodwill from the total book value.

6. Oppenheimer, H. R., 1984, *A Test of Ben Graham's Stock Selection Criteria* (September/October): v40(5), 68–74.

7. When firms restate earnings, they have to file an amended financial statement with the Securities and Exchange Commission (SEC). One easy way of finding firms that have done repeated restatements is to examine the SEC filings data online and to count the number of restatements over a period (three to five years).

8. When a company restates earnings, it has to file an amended 10K with the SEC. The SEC web site was checked for the number of amended 10Ks over the last five years for any firms that passed the PE, growth and risk screens.

9. A large charge is one that exceeded 20% of the precharge income of the firm. Thus, for a firm with $1 billion in precharge income, a restructuring charge that is greater than $200 million would have been viewed as a large charge.

Appendix:
Companies That Pass PE Tests in the United States: October 2002

Company Name	Identification Ticker	Industry	PE Ratios Current PE	Trailing PE	Forward PE	Risk Measures Beta	Std. Dev'n	Debt/ Capital	EPS Growth Growth— Last 5 Years	Projected Growth: Next 5 Years	Options as % of Shares
Washington Federal	WFSL	Thrift	11.22	10.90	10.89	0.90	32.84%	0.00%	7.50%	11.50%	0.00%
CEC Entertainment	CEC	Restaurant	10.28	11.30	9.65	0.90	38.87%	13.36%	65.00%	17.00%	2.57%
Magna Int'l 'A'	MGA	Auto Parts	8.77	9.30	8.44	0.90	27.78%	24.01%	9.50%	10.50%	17.21%
Bank of Nova Scotia	BNS.TO	Bank (Canadian)	10.65	10.80	10.05	0.90	24.71%	29.40%	15.00%	10.00%	1.68%
Centex Construction	CXP	Cement & Aggregates	9.87	10.90	9.04	0.75	38.04%	29.89%	20.50%	8.50%	0.38%
Zions Bancorp	ZION	Bank	11.46	11.60	10.83	0.95	31.70%	30.94%	15.00%	11.50%	1.07%
Nat'l Bank of Canada	NA.TO	Bank (Canadian)	10.09	11.50	9.38	0.80	22.60%	31.25%	13.00%	9.50%	0.48%
V.F. Corp	VFC	Apparel	11.03	11.20	10.72	0.90	35.17%	31.76%	6.50%	8.50%	3.11%
Right Management	RMCI	Human Resources	8.97	9.30	8.69	0.60	53.97%	35.38%	9.00%	23.50%	9.19%
Tredegar Corp	TG	Chemical (Specialty)	9.46	11.40	8.64	0.80	43.01%	35.63%	16.50%	14.00%	1.90%
Ryan's Family	RYAN	Restaurant	9.00	9.70	8.70	0.75	34.50%	35.97%	15.00%	14.00%	3.53%
Loews Corp	LTR	Financial Svcs. (Div.)	8.12	10.60	6.71	0.90	37.83%	39.40%	5.50%	8.00%	0.00%
Building Materials	BMHC	Retail Building Supply	7.66	7.60	7.25	0.85	39.13%	40.80%	7.50%	8.00%	0.85%
Ameron Int'l	AMN	Building Materials	7.23	7.10	6.78	0.75	33.63%	42.33%	14.50%	5.00%	3.18%
IHOP Corp	IHP	Restaurant	10.86	12.00	9.87	0.85	32.28%	43.17%	15.00%	12.00%	1.77%
Universal Forest	UFPI	Building Materials	9.60	9.80	8.46	0.75	32.67%	43.28%	14.00%	12.00%	2.91%
TBC Corp	TBCC	Tire & Rubber	9.88	9.90	9.29	0.85	45.08%	43.84%	7.00%	10.00%	1.84%
Haverty Furniture	HVT	Retail (Special Lines)	10.57	10.20	9.70	0.85	51.68%	45.48%	17.50%	14.00%	2.39%
Brown Shoe	BWS	Shoe	9.52	10.90	9.05	0.75	51.55%	45.73%	9.00%	8.00%	1.97%
Philip Morris	MO	Tobacco	9.02	9.10	8.94	0.65	36.31%	50.60%	10.50%	9.00%	0.00%
Smithfield Foods	SFD	Food Processing	11.77	11.00	9.93	0.90	39.34%	52.06%	26.00%	10.00%	2.15%
Sealed Air	SEE	Packaging	7.17	7.00	6.93	0.75	53.38%	52.12%	5.50%	15.00%	0.00%
SUPERVALU INC	SVU	Food Wholesalers	8.21	8.70	7.31	0.75	37.58%	54.11%	8.00%	10.00%	0.81%

(continued)

Companies That Pass PE Tests in the United States: October 2002 (Continued)

| Identification | | | PE Ratios | | | Risk Measures | | | EPS Growth | | Options |
Company Name	Ticker	Industry	Current PE	Trailing PE	Forward PE	Beta	Std. Dev'n	Debt/Capital	Growth—Last 5 Years	Projected Growth: Next 5 Years	As % of Shares
Duke Energy	DUK	Electric Utility (East)	8.79	11.00	8.48	0.70	36.49%	55.13%	6.00%	7.50%	0.70%
Safeway Inc	SWY	Grocery	8.16	8.90	7.75	0.75	31.68%	55.68%	25.00%	12.00%	1.97%
Hovnanian Enterpr	HOV	Homebuilding	8.19	10.40	8.45	0.95	52.20%	57.91%	22.00%	22.50%	3.70%
CAE Inc	CAE.TO	Aerospace/Defense	8.92	7.50	6.86	0.75	59.44%	59.97%	17.50%	12.00%	1.17%

4

LESS THAN BOOK VALUE?
WHAT A BARGAIN!

Helga, a psychologist, had always wanted to be an accountant. She bemoaned the fact that her discipline was subjective and lacked precision, and wished that she could work in a field where there were clear rules and principles. One day, she read an article in the *Wall Street Journal* on Global Telecom, whose stock, the report said, was trading at half its book value. From her limited knowledge of accounting, Helga knew that book value represented the accountant's estimate of what the equity in the bank was worth. "If a stock is trading at less than book value, it must be cheap," she exclaimed, as she invested heavily in the stock.

Convinced that she was secure in her investment, Helga waited for the stock price to move up to the book value of equity. Instead, it moved down. When she took a closer look at Global Telecom, she learned that its management had a terrible reputation and that it had either lost money or made very little every year for the last 10 years. Helga still kept her faith in the accounting value, convinced that, at worst, someone would buy the firm for the book value. At the end of the year, her hopes were dashed. The accountants announced that they were writing down the book value of the equity to reflect poor investments that the firm had made in the past. The stock price no longer was lower than the book value, but the book value had come down to the price rather than the other way around. Helga never yearned to be an accountant again.

Moral: The book value is an opinion and not a fact.

The book value of equity is the accountant's measure of what equity in a firm is worth. While the credibility of accountants has declined over the last few years, many investors continue to believe that accountants provide not only a more conservative but also a more realistic measure of what equity is truly worth than do financial markets, which these investors view as subject to irrational mood swings. A logical consequence of this view is that stocks that trade at substantially less than book value are undervalued and those that trade at more than book value are overvalued. As you will see in this chapter, while this may sometimes be true, there are many stocks that deserve to trade at less than book value because they have made poor investments, high risk, or both.

CORE OF THE STORY

The notion that stocks that trade at less than book value are undervalued has been around for decades. It has been used as a value screen by investors and portfolio managers. Services that track mutual funds (Morningstar, Value Line and Lipper) have used it as their basis for categorizing funds into value and growth funds—value funds invest in stocks with low price-to-book value (PBV) ratios and growth funds in stocks with high price-to-book-value ratios. As with PE ratios, rules of thumb abound—stocks that trade at less than book value are undervalued, whereas stocks that trade at more than twice book value are overvalued.

Why does this story carry so much weight with investors? There are several reasons; two are considered below:

- *Markets are less reliable than accountants when it comes to estimating value.* If you believe that markets are both volatile and irrational, and combine this with a trust in the inherently conservative nature of accounting estimates of value, it follows logically that you would put more weight on accounting estimate of values (book value) than on market estimates of the same (market value). Thus, when a firm trades at less than book value, you will be inclined to believe that it is markets that have a mistaken estimate of value rather than accountants.

■ *Book value is liquidation value.* In addition to the trust that some investors have in accountants' estimates of value, there is also the embedded belief that a firm, if liquidated, would fetch its book value. If this is the case, proponents argue, a stock that trades at less than book value is a bargain to someone who can liquidate its assets and pay off its debt As investors, you can piggyback on such investors and gain as the stock price approaches book value.

THEORETICAL ROOTS:
PRICE TO BOOK RATIOS
AND FUNDAMENTALS

In Chapter 3, you examined the variables that affect the price-earnings ratio by going back to a simple valuation model and deriving the determinants of the multiple. You will follow the same path with price-to-book ratios. You will begin again with the definition of the price-to-book ratio (and any variants thereof) and then evaluate the variables that may cause some companies to have high price-to-book ratios and others to have low price-to-book ratios.

DEFINING THE PRICE-TO-BOOK RATIO

The price-to-book ratio is the ratio obtained by dividing the market price per share by the book value of equity per share at a point in time.

$$PBV = \text{Price to Book} = \frac{\text{Market Price per share}}{\text{Book Value of Equity per share}}$$

The price-to-book ratio is usually estimated with the current price per share in the numerator and the book value per share in the denominator. The book value per share is the book value of equity divided by the number of shares outstanding. There are far fewer variants of price-to-book ratios than there are in price-earnings ratios. It is true that you can still compute book value of equity per share based upon the actual number of shares outstanding (primary book value per share) or upon potential shares outstanding, assuming that options get exercised (diluted book value per share). However, you do not have the variants on current, trailing and forward values as you did for the price-earnings ratio. It is conventional to use as updated a measure of book value of equity per share as you can get. If firms report earnings annually, this will be based upon the equity in the last annual report. If firms report on a quarterly basis, you can use the equity from the most recent quarterly balance sheet.

How Accountants Measure Book Value

To understand book value, you should start with the *balance sheet*, shown in Figure 4.1, which summarizes the assets owned by a firm, the value of these assets and the mix of financing, debt and equity used to finance these assets at a given time.

What is an asset? An asset is any resource that has the potential to either generate future cash inflows or reduce future cash outflows. While that is a general definition broad enough to cover almost any kind of asset, accountants add a caveat that for a resource to be an asset, a firm has to have acquired it in a previous transaction and be able to quantify future benefits with reasonable precision. The accounting view of asset value is to a great extent grounded in the notion of *historical*

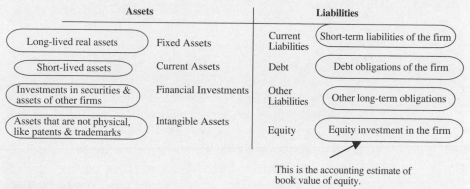

FIGURE 4.1
The Balance Sheet

While this is the conventional format for balance sheets in the United States, there are mild variations in how balance sheets are set up elsewhere in the globe. In parts of Asia, the assets are shown on the right-hand side and liabilities on the left-hand side. German companies consolidate pension fund assets and liabilities in corporate balance sheets.

cost, which is the original cost of the asset, adjusted upward for improvements made to the asset since purchase and downward for the loss in value associated with the aging of the asset. This historical cost is called the *book value.* This is especially true of fixed assets, such as land, building and equipment. While accountants are more amenable to revaluing current assets, such as inventory and accounts receivable, and some marketable securities at current market values (a process called marking to market), the book value of all assets on a balance sheet often will bear little or no resemblance to their market value.

Since assets are valued according to historical cost, the liabilities suffer from the same absence of updating. Thus, the debt shown on a firm's balance sheet represents the original amount borrowed from banks or bondholders, rather than an updated market value. What about the book value of equity? The value of equity shown on the balance sheet reflects the original proceeds received by the firm when it issued the equity, augmented by any earnings made since (or reduced by any losses) and reduced by any dividends paid out during the period. While these three items go into what you can call the book value of equity, a few other items also affect this estimate.

1. When companies buy back stock for short periods with the intent of reissuing the stock or using it to cover option exercises, they are allowed to show the repurchased stock as *treasury stock,* which reduces the book value of equity. Firms are not allowed to keep treasury stock on the books for extended periods and must reduce their book value of equity by the value of repurchased stock in the case of stock buybacks. Since these buybacks occur at the current market price, they can result in significant reductions in the book value of equity.

2. Firms that have significant losses over extended periods or carry out massive stock buybacks can end up with negative book values of equity.

3. If a firm has a substantial amount invested in marketable securities, any unrealized gain or loss in marketable securities that are classified as available-for-sale is shown as an increase or decrease in the book value of equity in the balance sheet.

As part of their financial statements, firms provide a summary of changes in shareholders' equity during the period, where all the changes that occurred to the accounting (book value) measure of equity value are summarized.

As with earnings, firms can influence the book value of their assets by their decisions on whether to expense or capitalize items; when items are expensed they do not show up as assets. Even when an expense is capitalized, the choice of depreciation method can affect an asset's book value; firms that use accelerated depreciation—whereby more depreciation is claimed in the early years and less in the later years—will report lower book values for assets. Firms can have an even bigger impact on the book value of equity when they take restructuring or one-time charges. In summary, any investment approach based upon book value of equity has to grapple with these issues, and the price-to-book ratio may not be a good indicator of value for many companies.

DETERMINANTS OF PBV RATIOS

Consider again the model presented in the last chapter for valuing a stock in a firm in which the dividends paid will grow at a constant rate forever. In this model, the value of equity can be written as:

$$\text{Value per share today} = \frac{\text{Expected Dividend per share next year}}{\text{Cost of Equity} - \text{Expected Growth Rate}}$$

To get from this model for value per share to one for the price-to-book ratio, you will divide both sides of the equation by the book value of equity per share today. When you do, you obtain the discounted cash flow equation specifying the price-to-book ratio for a stable growth firm.

$$\frac{\text{Value per share today}}{\text{Book Value of Equity today}} = \text{PBV} = \frac{\dfrac{\text{Expected Dividend per share}}{\text{Book Value of Equity per share today}}}{\text{Cost of Equity} - \text{Expected Growth Rate}}$$

$$= \frac{\dfrac{\text{Expected Dividend per share}}{\text{Expected EPS next year}} \times \dfrac{\text{Expected EPS next year}}{\text{Book Value of Equity per share today}}}{\text{Cost of Equity} - \text{Expected Growth Rate}}$$

$$= \frac{\text{Expected Payout Ratio} \times \text{Return on Equity}}{(\text{Cost of Equity} - \text{Expected Growth Rate})}$$

Consider again the example of Con Ed introduced in the last chapter. Recapping the facts, the stock is expected to pay a dividend of $2.20 per share next year out of expected earnings per share of $3.30, the cost of equity is 8%, and the expected growth rate in perpetuity is 3%. In addition, assume that the book value of equity per share currently is $33. You can estimate the price-to-book ratio for Con Ed:

Price-to-Book Ratio for Con Ed

$$= \frac{\text{Expected Payout Ratio} \times \text{Return on Equity}}{(\text{Cost of Equity} - \text{Expected Growth Rate})}$$

$$= \frac{(2.20 / 3.30) \times (3.30 / 33)}{(.08 - .03)} = 1.33$$

The PBV will increase as the expected growth rate increases; higher growth firms should have higher PBV ratios, which makes intuitive sense. The price-to-book ratio will be lower if the firm is a high-risk firm and has a high cost of equity. The price-to-book ratio will increase as the payout ratio increases, for any given growth rate; firms that are more efficient about generating growth (by earning a higher return on equity) will trade at higher multiples of book value. In fact, substituting in the equation for payout into this equation:

$$\text{Payout Ratio} = 1 - g \;/\; \text{Return on Equity}$$

$$\text{Price-to-Book Ratio} \;=\; \frac{(1 - g \,/\, \text{Return on Equity}) \times \text{Return on Equity}}{(\text{Cost of Equity} - g)}$$

$$=\; \frac{(\text{Return on Equity} - g)}{(\text{Cost of Equity} - g)}$$

The key determinant of price-to-book ratios is the difference between a firm's return on equity and its cost of equity. Firms that are expected to consistently earn less on their investments (return on equity) than you would require them to earn given their risk (cost of equity) should trade at less than book value.

As noted in the last chapter, this analysis can be easily extended to cover a firm in high growth. The equation will become more complicated but the determinants of price-to-book ratios remain the same: return on equity, expected growth, payout ratios and cost of equity. A company whose stock is trading at a discount on its book value is not necessarily cheap. In particular, you should expect companies that have low returns on equity, high-risk and low growth potential to trade at low price-to-book ratios. If you want to find undervalued companies then, you have to find mismatches—low or average risk companies that trade at low price-to-book ratios while maintaining reasonable returns on equity.

LOOKING AT THE EVIDENCE

Some investors argue that stocks that trade at low price-book-value ratios are undervalued, and several studies seem to back a strategy of buying such stocks. You will begin by looking at the relationship between returns and price-to-book ratios across long periods in the United States and extend the analysis to consider other markets.

EVIDENCE FROM THE UNITED STATES

The simplest way to test whether low price-to-book stocks are good investments is to look at the returns that these stocks earn relative to other stocks in the market. An examination of stock returns in the United States between 1973 and 1984 found that the strategy of picking stocks with high book/price ratios (low price-book values) would have yielded an excess return of 4.5% a year.[1] In another analysis of stock returns between 1963 and 1990, firms were classified on the basis of price-to-book ratios into 12 portfolios. Firms in the highest price-to-book value class earned an average monthly return of 0.30%, while firms in the lowest price to book value class earned an average monthly return of 1.83% for the 1963–1990 period.[2]

This research was updated to consider how well a strategy of buying low price-to-book-value stocks would have done in from 1991 to 2001 and compared these returns to returns in earlier periods. To make the comparison, we computed the annual returns on ten portfolios created from price-to-book ratios at the end of the previous year. The results are summarized in Figure 4.2.

In each of the three subperiods that you looked at stock returns, the lowest price-to-book stocks earned higher returns than the stocks with higher price-to-book ratios. In the 1927–1960 period, the difference in annual returns between the lowest price-to-book stock portfolio and the highest was 3.48%. In the 1961–1990 subperiod, the difference in returns

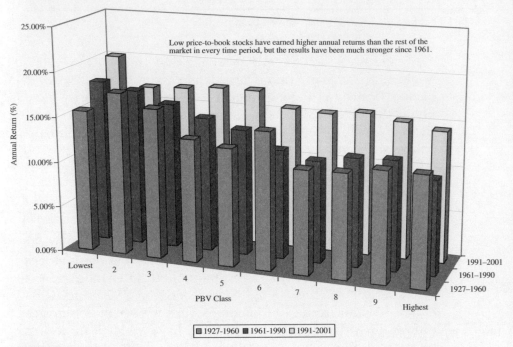

FIGURE 4.2

PBV Classes and Returns: 1927—2001

Data from Fama/French. The stocks were categorized by the ratio of price to book value at the beginning of each year, and the annual returns were measured over the next year. The average annual return across each period is reported.

between these two portfolios expanded to 7.57%. In the 1991–2001 period, the lowest price-to-book stocks continued to earn a premium of 5.72% over the highest price-to-book stocks. Thus, the higher returns earned by low price-to-book stocks have persisted over long periods.

As noted with price-earnings ratios though, these findings should not be taken as an indication that low price-to-book ratio stocks earn higher returns than higher price-to-book stocks in every period. Figure 4.3 reports on the difference between the lowest price-to-book and highest price-to-book portfolio, by year, from 1927 to 2001.

While low price-to-book stocks have outperformed high price-to-book stocks on average, there have been extended

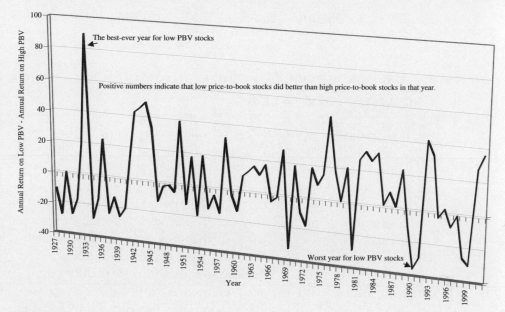

FIGURE 4.3

Lowest vs. Highest Price-to-Book Stocks: 1927–2001

From Fama/French. This is the difference between the annual return on the lowest PBV stocks (bottom 10%) and the highest PBV stocks (top 10%).

periods when they have underperformed as well. In fact, looking at the time periods when low price-to-book stocks have performed best—early in the 1930s, during World War II, in the late 1970s and early in the 1990s—you can draw the conclusion that low price-to-book stocks perform best when the overall market is in the doldrums, reflecting their status as defensive stocks.

A concern in investing is transactions costs. One study examined the question of whether low price-to-book stocks generate excess returns after transactions costs.[3] This study found that after adjusting for 1.0% transaction costs and annual rebalancing, investors would have outperformed the market by 4.82% over the 1963–1988 period if they had invested in small firms with low price-to-book ratios. The optimal time period for rebalancing these portfolios, where the payoff to updating exceeded the transactions costs, was two years.

EVIDENCE FROM OUTSIDE THE UNITED STATES

The finding that low price-to-book stocks earn higher returns than high price-to-book stocks over extended periods is not unique to the United States. An analysis in 1991 found that the book-to-market ratio had a strong role in explaining the cross section of average returns on Japanese stocks.[4] Extending the evaluation of price-book-value ratios across other international markets, stocks with low price-book-value ratios earned excess returns in every market that was examined between 1981 and 1992.[5] The annualized estimates of the return differential earned by stocks with low price-book-value ratios, over the market index, in each of the markets studied is listed in Table 4.1.

TABLE 4.1   Return Premia for Low Price-to-Book Portfolio by Country

COUNTRY	ADDED RETURN TO LOW P/BV PORTFOLIO
France	3.26%
Germany	1.39%
Switzerland	1.17%
United Kingdom	1.09%
Japan	3.43%
United States	1.06%
Europe	1.30%
Global	1.88%

Extending this analysis to emerging markets, a study of Korean stocks uncovered the same relationship between low price-to-book stocks and high returns.[6]

Thus, a strategy of buying low price-to-book value stocks seems to hold much promise. Why don't more investors use it then, you might ask? You will consider some of the possible problems with this strategy in the next section and look at screens that can be added on to remove these problems.

CRUNCHING THE NUMBERS

In this section, you will begin by looking at the distribution of price-to-book ratios across companies in the United States and then consider differences in price-to-book ratios across sectors. Finally, you will generate a portfolio of stocks that have the lowest price-to-book ratios in the market, with the intention of taking a closer look at these stocks in the next section.

DISTRIBUTION OF PRICE-TO-BOOK RATIOS ACROSS THE MARKET

To get a sense of what constitutes a high, low or average price-to-book value ratio, we computed the ratio for every firm listed in the United States. Figure 4.4 summarizes the distribution of price-to-book ratios in October 2002.

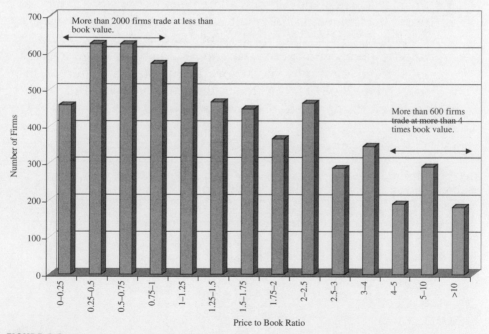

FIGURE 4.4

Price-to-Book Ratios: U.S. Companies, October 2002

Data from Value Line. The number of firms in the U.S. market that trade in each price-to-book ratio class is reported.

The average price-to-book ratio across all U.S. stocks in October 2002 was 3.05, but this number is skewed by the presence of about 600 firms that trade at price-to-book ratios that exceed 4. A more meaningful measure is the median price-to-book ratio of 1.30; roughly half of all U.S. firms trade at price-to-book ratios that are less than this value.

Another point worth making about price-to-book ratios is that there are firms with negative book values of equity—the result of continuously losing money—where price-to-book ratios cannot be computed. In this sample of 7102 firms, there were 1229 firms where this occurred. In contrast, though, 2045 firms had negative earnings and PE ratios could not be computed for them.

PRICE-TO-BOOK RATIOS BY SECTOR

Price-to-book ratios vary widely across different sectors of the market. In some sectors, a large percent of stocks trade at below book value. In others, it is not uncommon to see stocks trading at 5 to 10 times book value. To examine differences in price-to-book ratios across sectors, we computed the average price-to-book ratio by sector for all firms in the United States in October 2002. Table 4.2 lists the ten sectors with the highest and lowest price-to-book ratios.

TABLE 4.2 Sectors with the Highest and Lowest Price-to-Book Ratios

LOWEST PRICE-TO-BOOK SECTORS		HIGHEST PRICE-TO-BOOK SECTORS	
INDUSTRY NAME	PRICE-TO-BOOK	INDUSTRY NAME	PRICE-TO-BOOK
Power	0.30	Biotechnology	4.27
Investment Co. (Foreign)	0.63	Educational Services	4.50
Maritime	0.74	Trucking/Transp. Leasing	4.51
Entertainment	0.83	Information Services	4.83
Electric Utility (West)	0.86	Pharmacy Services	4.84
Steel (Integrated)	0.87	Drug	5.84
R.E.I.T.	0.89	Medical Supplies	5.85
Foreign Telecom.	0.94	Beverage (Alcoholic)	6.04
Textile	0.98	Beverage (Soft Drink)	6.67
Tire & Rubber	0.99	Household Products	7.99

Why are there such large differences across sectors? The answer lies in the earlier analysis of the fundamentals that determine price-to-book ratios. In particular, you should expect that companies with high risk, low growth and, most importantly, low returns on equity to trade at low price-to-book ratios. In Table 4.3, the average returns on equity, expected growth rates and market debt to capital ratios for the ten sectors with the highest and lowest price-to-book ratios are presented.

TABLE 4.3 Fundamentals of Low Price-to-Book vs. High Price-to-Book Sectors

	ROE	BETA	DEBT TO CAPITAL	EXPECTED GROWTH RATE
Low PBV sectors	1.90%	0.93	50.99%	12.28%
High PBV sectors	13.16%	0.89	10.33%	20.13%

The results conform to expectations. The sectors with the lowest price-to-book ratios have average returns on equity well below those of the sectors with the highest price-to-book ratios, are exposed to more risk (especially financial leverage), and have much lower projected growth rates. In other words, there are good reasons why there are large differences in price-to-book ratios across sectors.

There is one more point that needs to be made about price-to-book ratios. Since book values are based upon accounting judgments, it should come as no surprise that the highest price-to-book ratios are in sectors in which the most important assets are kept off the books. In particular, the expensing of research and development expenses at biotechnology and drug companies results in book values being understated at these firms. For beverage and household product companies, the most important asset is often brand name, which is both intangible and not reflected in balance sheets. This, in turn, may explain why these companies report high returns on equity and trade at high price-to-book ratios.

A LOW PRICE-TO-BOOK PORTFOLIO

If you picked the stocks that trade at the lowest price-to-book ratios in the market, what would you portfolio look like? In answer to this question, all listed stocks in the United

TABLE 4.4 Stocks with the Lowest Price-to-Book Ratios: United States, October 2002

COMPANY NAME	PRICE/BV	COMPANY NAME	PRICE/BV
SpectraSite Hldgs Inc	0.01	Digital Lightwave	0.33
WorldCom Inc	0.01	Net Perceptions Inc	0.32
Vina Technologies Inc	0.18	PECO II Inc	0.16
Jupiter Media Metrix Inc	0.11	Ventiv Health Inc	0.26
Metawave Communications Corp	0.08	Lexent Inc	0.35
Beacon Power Corp	0.20	Travis Boats & Motors Inc	0.14
DDi Corp	0.07	AES Corp	0.09
Mississippi Chem Corp	0.05	NMS Communications Corp	0.24
Sorrento Networks Corp	0.14	EOTT Energy Partners-LP	0.26
BackWeb Technologies Ltd	0.14	Ceres Group Inc	0.28
Leap Wireless Intl Inc	0.02	ACT Teleconferencing	0.37
SBA Communications Corp	0.02	Atlas Air Inc	0.14
TranSwitch Corp	0.10	MetaSolv Inc	0.26
iBasis Inc	0.14	Management Network Grp Inc.	0.35
Alamosa Hldgs Inc	0.05	Sapient Corp	0.37
UbiquiTel Inc	0.13	Electroglas Inc	0.15
Inktomi Corp	0.09	SatCon Technology	0.38
Cylink Corp	0.31	KANA Software Inc	0.36
ATS Medical	0.10	Pegasus Communications	0.29
T/R Systems Inc	0.20	SIPEX Corp	0.22
AHL Services	0.09	Factory 2-U Stores Inc	0.21
724 Solutions Inc	0.16	Aspen Technology Inc	0.24
Gilat Satellite	0.05	America West Hldg	0.08
Critical Path	0.35	Mail-Well Inc	0.28
Petroleum Geo ADR	0.05	Pantry Inc	0.26
Genaissance Pharmaceuticals	0.19	Armstrong Holdings	0.07
Synavant Inc	0.16	Mirant Corp	0.08
Evergreen Solar Inc	0.12	Ditech Communications Corp	0.23
Therma-Wave Inc	0.08	eBenX Inc	0.37
Corvis Corp	0.27	Analysts Int'l	0.35
Finisar Corp	0.13	Quovadx Inc	0.27
Airspan Networks Inc	0.15	Aclara Biosciences Inc	0.37
Seitel Inc	0.07	Metalink Ltd	0.34
i2 Technologies	0.23	Value City Dept Strs	0.28
Mobility Electronics Inc	0.37	QuickLogic Corp	0.34
Time Warner Telecom Inc	0.09	Corning Inc	0.26
Vascular Solutions Inc	0.28	Artesyn Technologies Inc	0.28
Optical Communication Prods	0.39	Digi Int'l	0.35
Allegiance Telecom	0.15	MicroFinancial Inc	0.20
SMTC Corp	0.14	Calpine Corp	0.28
Dynegy Inc 'A'	0.06	EXFO Electro-Optical Engr	0.25
Charter Communications Inc	0.15	MasTec Inc	0.30
Lucent Technologies	0.24	Hypercom Corp	0.37
U.S. Energy Sys Inc	0.31	Champion Enterprises	0.39
Braun Consulting Inc	0.32	Tesoro Petroleum	0.15
Latitude Communications Inc	0.24	Hawk Corp	0.32
AXT Inc	0.13	Spectrian Corp	0.24
Digital Generation Sys	0.34	Trenwick Group Ltd	0.35
Titanium Metals	0.10	GlobespanVirata Inc	0.26
Pemstar Inc	0.22	Spartan Stores Inc	0.22

Company Name	Price/BV	Company Name	Price/BV
SonicWALL Inc	0.35	TTM Technologies Inc	0.42
Discovery Partners Intl Inc	0.40	Oglebay Norton Co	0.42
Integrated Silicon Solution	0.37	Standard Management Corp	0.43
Quanta Services	0.15	Chart Industries	0.43
REMEC Inc	0.40	Technology Solutions	0.43
eXcelon Corp	0.39	Tweeter Home	0.43
CyberOptics	0.32	Captaris Inc	0.43
Olympic Steel Inc	0.28	Net2Phone Inc	0.44
McDermott Int'l	0.29	Resonate Inc	0.44
Qwest Communic	0.12	Chartered Semiconductor Mfg	0.44
Metris Cos	0.15	Massey Energy	0.44
Trans World Entertain	0.28	Oregon Steel Mills	0.44
DiamondCluster Intl Inc	0.26	Caliper Technologies Corp	0.44
Dixie Group	0.37	Pinnacle Entertainment Inc	0.44
Sierra Wireless Inc	0.36	Proxim Corp Cl A	0.44
FPIC Insurance	0.37	Innotrac Corp	0.44
Alcatel ADR	0.20	R.J. Reynolds Tobacco	0.44
Park-Ohio	0.33	SportsLine.com Inc	0.45
Aquila Inc	0.26	Sonus Networks Inc	0.45
Integrated Elect Svcs	0.28	Stolt-Nielsen ADR	0.45
AAR Corp	0.40	JNI Corp	0.45
Milacron Inc	0.33	Point 360	0.45
HEALTHSOUTH Corp	0.38	Books-A-Million	0.45
Hi/fn Inc	0.38	Cirrus Logic	0.45
MPS Group	0.35	Zygo Corp	0.46
Three-Five Sys	0.37	Edge Petroleum	0.46
Sierra Pacific Res	0.32	Fleming Cos	0.46
Allegheny Energy	0.20	Goodyear Tire	0.47
Advanced Micro Dev	0.34	Callon Pete Co	0.47
Applica Inc	0.39	PDI Inc	0.47
United Rentals	0.35	IMCO Recycling	0.47
Cont'l Airlines	0.27	Chesapeake Corp	0.47
Bally Total Fitness	0.39	Docent Inc	0.47
AmeriCredit Corp	0.37	Salton Inc	0.47
Gentiva Health Services Inc	0.32	DigitalThink Inc	0.48
Allmerica Financial	0.18	RSA Security	0.49
Sea Containers Ltd 'A'	0.37	Deltagen Inc	0.49
Avnet Inc	0.30	Applied Extrusion Tech	0.49
Dura Automotive 'A'	0.36	Vignette Corp	0.49
Westar Energy	0.39	Marimba Inc	0.49
Delta Air Lines	0.28	TELUS Corp	0.49
Carpenter Technology	0.38	Arris Group Inc	0.50
TXU Corp	0.38	MSC.Software	0.50
Integrated Information Sys	0.22	answerthink inc	0.50
Click Commerce Inc	0.25	Ascential Software	0.50
G't Atlantic & Pacific	0.41	CNH Global NV	0.50
XETA Corp	0.41	Maxtor Corp	0.50
Interface Inc 'A'	0.41		
RWD Technologies	0.41		
Descartes Sys Group Inc	0.42		

States in October 2002 that had a traded price available for them and positive book values of equity were examined. The price-to-book ratios were computed for each of the firms in this sample of 5883 firms, The 195 firms that trade at less than 50% of their book value of equity are listed in Table 4.4.

MORE TO THE STORY

There are stocks that trade at low prices, relative to book value, that are not undervalued. As noted earlier in the chapter, low price-to-book ratios can be attributed to high risk or low returns on equity. In this section, you will consider the characteristics of the stocks in the low price-to-book portfolio and examine potential problems for investment strategies.

HIGH-RISK STOCKS

Is it possible that the higher returns earned by low price-to-book stocks can be explained by the fact that they are riskier than average? Some of the studies referenced in the last section attempted to test for this hypothesis by computing returns adjusted for risk: excess returns. The earlier ones did so by estimating the betas and returns after adjusting for differences in betas for low price-to-book stocks and concluded that these stocks still made excess returns. Thus, stocks with low price-to-book value ratios earn excess returns relative to high price-to-book stocks if you use conventional measures of risk and return.

In recent years, other researchers have argued that these conventional measures of risk are imperfect and incomplete. Low price-book-value ratios may operate as a measure of risk, since firms with prices well below book value are more likely to be in financial trouble and go out of business. Investors therefore have to evaluate whether the additional returns made by such firms justifies the additional risk taken by investing in them.

In Figure 4.5, compare how stocks in the low price-to-book ratio portfolio constructed at the end of the last section measure up against the rest of the market on three measures of risk.

- *Beta:* Beta operates as a standardized measure of how a stock moves with the market. A beta greater than 1 indicates a stock with above-average risk.
- *Standard deviation in stock prices over the past three years:* Unlike beta, which measures how a stock moves with the market, the standard deviation is a measure of stock price volatility.
- *Ratio of total debt to book value of capital:* This is computed by dividing the total book value debt (short term

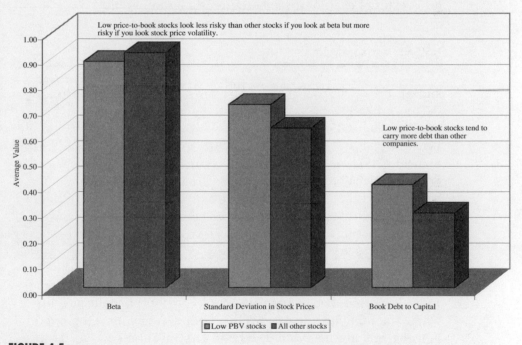

FIGURE 4.5

Low PBV versus Other Stocks

Data from Value Line. The averages are reported for the low price-to-book portfolio and the market on three variables: the beta and standard deviation estimated over three years and the ratio of book debt to book capital.

and long term) by the book value of both debt and equity (capital). It is a measure of how much a firm owes and is of importance if you are concerned about distress and bankruptcy.

Low price-to-book stocks do not look excessively risky on a beta basis since the average beta across these stocks is slightly lower than the average beta across all other stocks. They do look more risky than other stocks on the two other measures of risk: stock price volatility and debt-to-capital ratios.

To screen the low price-to-book portfolios and remove stocks with excessive risk exposure, you can screen the stocks on all three measures of risk, using different levels of the measure for screens. The number of stocks that you will lose as a result of each of these screens is listed in Table 4.5.

TABLE 4.5 Stocks Screened for Risk

SCREEN	NUMBER OF FIRMS THAT FAIL SCREEN
Beta less than 1	162
Beta less than 1.25	129
Beta less than 1.5	93
Standard deviation less than 60%	169
Standard deviation less than 70%	152
Standard deviation less than 80%	127
Debt ratio less than 50%	61
Debt ratio less than 60%	47
Debt ratio less than 70%	21

A large number of the 195 stocks in the portfolio are lost when the standard deviation and beta screens are employed. Fewer firms are lost with a debt-to-capital ratio screen. If you adopt a composite risk measure that includes all three screens—stocks with betas that are less than 1.5, standard deviations in stock prices that are lower than 80% and debt to capital ratios smaller than 70%—the number of stocks in the low price-to-book portfolio drops to 51 stocks.

LOW-PRICED STOCKS

Stocks that trade at low price-to-book ratios often do so because their stock prices have dropped precipitously. It should come as no surprise that a large number of low price-to-book ratio stocks trade at very low prices and that many trade at less than a dollar per share. Why would this matter? The transactions costs associated with buying stocks that trade at low prices is often much higher than average or high-priced stocks for three reasons:

a. The brokerage costs associated with buying stocks is generally a fixed cost for even lots (lots of 100 shares), and this cost will increase as a percent of the investment as stock prices drop. If you trade through a broker who charges you $30 for an even lot trade, the brokerage commission would increase from .3% of your investment if you were buying 100 shares at $100 per share; to 3% if you were buying 100 shares at $10 per share; to 30% if you were buying 100 shares at $1 per share. Institutional and individual investors may be able to negotiate a reduction in brokerage costs as they increase the number of shares they buy, but the costs will still increase as stock prices drop.

b. As stock prices drop below a certain level, institutional investors will often abandon a stock. This will reduce the liquidity in the stock and increase the price impact that you have when you trade a stock. You will push up the stock price as you buy and down as you sell, even with small trades.

c. The spread between the bid price (at which you can sell the stock) and the ask price (at which you can buy) tends to become a larger percent of the stock price as the price drops. The loss of liquidity as investors flee the stock exacerbates the problem.

How big are the transactions costs associated with buying low-priced stock? If you consider all three components of the cost—the commissions, the bid-ask spread and the price impact—the total costs can easily exceed 25% of your investment for stock trading at less than $1 and 15% for stock trading at less than $2. Since you can spread these costs out over time, the drag on your returns will be smaller the longer your time horizon. An investor with a 10-year horizon, for instance, will be able to spread the cost over 10 years, making a 25% up-front cost into a 2.5% cost per year.

The portfolio of low price-to-book stocks is examined in Figure 4.6, with stocks categorized according to price levels,

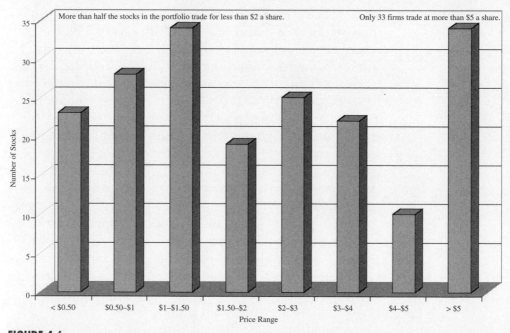

FIGURE 4.6

Price per Share: Low PBV Portfolio

Data from Value Line. Many institutional investors avoid stocks that trade at less than $5 per share because the transactions costs are so high. The number of stocks that trade in each price range is reported.

and the number of stocks that trade at different price levels is reported.

Note that 50 stocks, roughly a quarter of the entire portfolio, trade at less than a dollar a share and another 50 stocks trade at between $1 and $2. If you invested in this portfolio, you would face substantial transactions costs and it is likely that these costs will wipe out any advantages to this strategy, at least in the short term.

It does make sense to screen the stocks in this portfolio for stock price levels. In Table 4.6, the number of companies that would survive a variety of price screens in the low price-to-book portfolio are listed.

TABLE 4.6   Price-Level Screens and Low Price-to-Book Stocks

SCREEN	NUMBER OF FIRMS THAT FAIL SCREEN
Price greater than $10	186
Price greater than $5	160
Price greater than $2	104

Which of these screens should you adopt? Your screens will have to become stricter (higher stock price minimums) as your time horizon becomes shorter. Assuming a five-year time horizon, you should use at least a $2 minimum price screen. Consolidating this screen with the risk screens in the last section, the portfolio of 195 stocks that you began the analysis with would have dropped to 39 firms.

POOR PROJECTS: LOW RETURN ON EQUITY

The most significant limitation of a strategy of buying low price-to-book-value stocks is that the low book value multiples may be well deserved if companies earn and are expected to continue earning low returns on equity. In fact, the relationship between price-to-book-value ratios and returns on equity was considered earlier in this chapter. Stocks with low returns on equity should trade at low price-to-book value ratios. In summary, then, as an investor you would want stocks with low price-to-book ratios that also had reasonable (if not high) returns on equity and limited exposure to risk.

Considering the low price-to-book portfolio of 195 stocks again, we examined the returns on equity at these companies in the most recent year. Figure 4.7 presents the distribution of returns on equity across these stocks.

It is quite clear that a large number of stocks in this portfolio are coming off a woeful earnings year. In fact, 143 of the 198 firms had negative returns on equity, and 71 of these

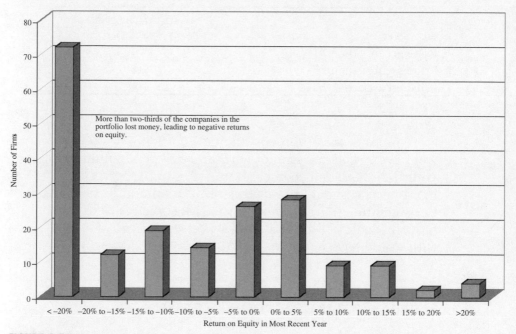

More than two-thirds of the companies in the portfolio lost money, leading to negative returns on equity.

Return on Equity in Most Recent Year

FIGURE 4.7
ROE for Low Price-to-Book Stocks

Data from Value Line. The return on equity for each company is computed by dividing the net income over the most recent four quarters by the book value of equity at the beginning of the year.

firms had returns on equity that were –20% or worse. If you compare the returns on equity on these firms to the average return on equity (of about 10%) for the entire U.S. market, only 15 firms in the sample did better than average. It is true that one year's return on equity can be misleading, especially when the most recent financial year (2001) was a recession year. You could have looked at average returns on equity over the last five years, but it is unlikely to change the overall conclusion. Stocks with low price-to-book ratios trade at the levels they do because they have low or negative returns on equity.

Any investor interested in a low price-to-book strategy would be well served applying a return-on-equity test to the portfolio. Table 4.7 summarizes the number of stocks that would have made the cut with a number of return-on-equity screens.

TABLE 4.7 Return-on-Equity Screens and Low Price-to-Book Stocks

SCREEN	NUMBER OF FIRMS THAT FAIL SCREEN
ROE greater than 0%	143
ROE greater than 5%	171
ROE greater than 10%	180

If you require a minimum return on equity of 10% in conjunction with the minimum price constraint ($2) and eliminate firms that are excessively risky (beta >1.5; standard deviation > 80%, or debt to capital ratios that exceed 70%), you are left with only 7 firms from the original sample of 195 firms. These firms are listed in Table 4.8.

Even among these 7 firms, there are potential red flags. With R.J. Reynolds, it takes the form of potential liabilities in lawsuits associated with tobacco; with the energy companies, it is the overhang of accounting scandals (at other energy companies such as Enron).

TABLE 4.8 Low Price-to-Book Stocks That Meet Price Level, Growth and ROE Tests

Company Name	Price	PBV	ROE	Beta	Standard Deviation	Debt/ Capital
R.J. Reynolds Tobacco	$42.20	0.44	7.41%	0.70	44.01%	17.26%
McDermott Int'l	$ 3.16	0.29	5.06%	1.25	74.42%	28.69%
Healthsouth Corp	$ 4.72	0.38	8.59%	1.25	67.81%	44.36%
Bally Total Fitness	$ 6.92	0.39	13.67%	1.20	48.64%	56.47%
Allegheny Energy	$ 5.86	0.20	11.77%	0.80	40.56%	64.05%
Westar Energy	$10.47	0.39	11.79%	0.50	0.00%	64.87%
MicroFinancial Inc	$ 2.09	0.20	14.74%	0.75	46.20%	65.20%

LESSONS FOR INVESTORS

If low price-to-book-value ratio stocks are riskier than average or have lower returns on equity, a more discerning strategy would require you to find mismatches—stocks with low price-to-book ratios, low risk and high returns on equity. If you used debt ratios as a proxy for default risk and the accounting return on equity in the last year as the proxy for the returns that will be earned on equity in the future, you would expect companies with low price-to-book value ratios, low default risk and high return on equity to be undervalued.

This proposition was partially tested as follows: All NYSE stocks from 1981 to 1990 were screened according to both price-book-value ratios and returns on equity at the end of each year. Two portfolios were created: an undervalued portfolio that each year had low price-book-value ratios (in bottom quartile of all stocks) and high returns on equity (in top quartile of all stocks); and an overvalued portfolio that each year had high price-book-value ratios (in top quartile of all stocks) and low returns on equity (in bottom quartile of all stocks). Returns on each portfolio were then estimated for the following year. Table 4.9 summarizes returns on these two portfolios for each year from 1982 to 1991.

TABLE 4.9   Returns on Mismatched Portfolios: Price-to-Book and ROE

YEAR	UNDERVALUED PORTFOLIO	OVERVALUED PORTFOLIO	S&P 500
1982	37.64%	14.64%	40.35%
1983	34.89%	3.07%	0.68%
1984	20.52%	−28.82%	15.43%
1985	46.55%	30.22%	30.97%
1986	33.61%	0.60%	24.44%
1987	−8.80%	−0.56%	−2.69%
1988	23.52%	7.21%	9.67%
1989	37.50%	16.55%	18.11%
1990	−26.71%	−10.98%	6.18%
1991	74.22%	28.76%	31.74%
1982–91	*25.60%*	*10.61%*	*17.49%*

The undervalued portfolios significantly outperformed the overvalued portfolios in 8 out of 10 years, earning an average of 14.99% more per year between 1982 and 1991, and also had an average return significantly higher than the S&P 500. While default risk was not considered in this test, you could easily add it as a third variable in the screening process.

Going back over the entire sample of stocks, you constructed a series of screens to devise a portfolio that meets multiple criteria in October 2002:

Step 1: Only stocks with price-to-book ratios that were less than 0.80 were considered. This screen is a little looser than the one used to get the 195 stocks in the previous section, but it allows you to use tighter screens for risk and return on equity.

Step 2: To control for risk, all firms that have betas greater than 1.5 or debt to capital ratios (in market value terms) that exceeded 70% were eliminated. The market value test was adopted instead of the book value test because it is a stricter test for these stocks for which the market value of equity is less than the book value of equity. Screening for stocks with low standard deviations was considered, but relatively few firms were eliminated. Hence, this screen was not included.

Step 3: To control for price level, all firms that trade at prices less than $3 were eliminated. This test again is slightly stricter than the $2 minimum price level test that was used in the last section, but it will reduce the overall transactions costs of the strategy.

Step 4: To screen for a minimum return on equity, all firms that had returns on equity of less than 8% in the most recent financial year were eliminated.

The resulting portfolio of 53 stocks is included in the appendix.

CONCLUSION

Many investors believe that stocks that trade at a discount on their book values are bargains. Their argument is based upon the belief that the book value of equity represents a more reliable measure of what the equity of the firm is worth or that book value is a measure of liquidation value. The empirical evidence seems to back them since low price-to-book-ratio stocks have historically earned much higher returns than the rest of the market. The peril in this strategy is that book value is an accounting measure and that it may have nothing to do with either the value of the assets that the firm possesses or what it will receive in liquidation from these assets. In particular, accounting decisions on depreciation and whether to capitalize or expense an item can have significant effects on book value, as will decisions on buying back stock or taking restructuring charges.

Looking at the fundamentals that determine value, you should expect firms with high risk, poor growth prospects and negative or low returns on equity to trade at low price-to-book ratios. These firms are not undervalued. As an investor, you should therefore be looking for stocks that trade at low prices relative to their book values without the contaminants of high risk or poor returns on projects. This chapter considered how best to accomplish this by screening low price-to-book stocks for risk exposure and project returns. The resulting portfolio should allow investors much of the upside of a low price-to-book strategy while protecting them from some of the downside.

ENDNOTES

1. Rosenberg, B., K. Reid and R. Lanstein, 1985, *Persuasive Evidence of Market Inefficiency*, Journal of Portfolio Management, v11, 9–17.

2. Fama, E. F., and K. R. French, 1992, *The Cross-Section of Expected Returns*, Journal of Finance, v47, 427–466. This study is an examination of the effectiveness of different risk and return models in finance. It found that price-to-book explained more of the variation across stock returns than any other fundamental variable, including market capitalization.

3. Dennis, Patrick, Steven B. Perfect, Karl N. Snow, and Kenneth W. Wiles, 1995, *The Effects of Rebalancing on Size and Book-to-Market Ratio Portfolio Returns,* Financial Analysts Journal, May/June, 47–57.

4. Chan, L. K., Y. Hamao, and J. Lakonishok, 1991, *Fundamentals and Stock Returns in Japan*, Journal of Finance, v46, 1739–1789. They concluded that low price-to-book-value stocks in Japan earned a considerable premium over high price-to-book-value stocks.

5. Capaul, C., I. Rowley and W. F. Sharpe, 1993, *International Value and Growth Stock Returns*, Financial Analysts Journal, v49, 27–36.

6. Mukherji, Sandip, Manjeet S. Dhatt, and Yong H. Kim, 1997, *A Fundamental Analysis of Korean Stock Returns*, Financial Analysts Journal, May/June, v53, 75–80.

Appendix:
Undervalued Stocks with Price-to-Book Screens

Company Name	Ticker Symbol	Price	PBV	ROE	Market Debt Ratio	Beta
Aecon Group Inc	ARE.TO	$4.59	0.74	20.81%	52.11%	0.55
AirNet Systems Inc	ANS	$4.70	0.71	9.49%	38.82%	0.85
Amer. Pacific	APFC	$8.42	0.56	10.95%	41.94%	0.50
Americas Car Mart Inc	CRMT	$13.68	0.72	15.06%	35.46%	0.80
Anangel-American Shipholdings	ASIPF	$5.00	0.46	9.92%	63.89%	0.45
Andersons Inc	ANDE	$12.70	0.68	9.29%	67.81%	0.45
Atl. Tele- Network	ANK	$14.45	0.74	15.61%	10.38%	0.70
Badger Paper Mills Inc	BPMI	$7.24	0.34	18.81%	41.52%	0.75
Building Materials	BMHC	$14.06	0.62	8.78%	50.39%	0.85
California First Natl Bancorp	CFNB	$10.75	0.76	11.96%	56.93%	0.75
Carver Bancorp Inc	CNY	$10.89	0.58	8.60%	0.00%	0.70
Cascades Inc	CAS.TO	$15.32	0.74	13.35%	47.47%	0.80
Chromcraft Revington	CRC	$13.47	0.76	8.73%	0.00%	0.50
CKF Bancorp Inc	CKFB	$18.61	0.75	8.17%	0.00%	0.55
Classic Bancshares	CLAS	$24.49	0.75	10.00%	0.00%	0.40
Clean Harbors	CLHB	$15.80	0.64	12.09%	33.23%	0.55
Cont'l Materials Corp	CUO	$26.10	0.71	13.49%	26.21%	0.50
Department 56 Inc	DFS	$13.51	0.72	10.18%	34.29%	0.95
Everlast Worldwide Inc	EVST	$4.12	0.53	16.37%	33.10%	1.25
Finlay Enterprises Inc	FNLY	$11.96	0.69	12.42%	64.52%	0.95
First Cash Inc	FCFS	$10.05	0.76	10.81%	31.32%	0.65
Hampshire Group Ltd	HAMP	$20.40	0.47	12.58%	22.93%	0.60
Harris Steel	HSG/A.TO	$23.00	0.69	16.52%	2.27%	0.45
Hawthorne Fin'L Corp	HTHR	$28.50	0.78	14.42%	19.82%	0.70
Ilx Inc	ILX	$6.10	0.55	8.65%	65.50%	0.50
Integramed Amer Inc	INMD	$5.83	0.41	20.95%	13.58%	1.05
Jos A Bank Clothiers Inc	JOSB	$22.80	0.72	12.48%	10.83%	0.95

(continued)

125

Undervalued Stocks with Price-to-Book Screens (*Continued*)

Company Name	Ticker Symbol	Price	PBV	ROE	Market Debt Ratio	Beta
Korea Electric ADR	KEP	$8.78	0.66	13.60%	66.44%	1.00
Lakes Entertainment Inc	LACO	$6.03	0.48	14.86%	12.62%	0.85
Logansport Finl Corp	LOGN	$17.00	0.77	8.03%	7.44%	0.45
Maxcor Finl Group Inc	MAXF	$6.09	0.6	30.92%	1.46%	0.90
McGraw-Hill Ryerson Ltd	MHR.TO	$32.00	0.67	12.17%	0.00%	0.50
National Sec Group Inc	NSEC	$14.88	0.68	9.20%	5.30%	0.50
Northwest Pipe Co	NWPX	$14.46	0.78	9.39%	40.70%	0.50
Novamerican Steel	TONS	$6.84	0.51	8.04%	59.92%	0.40
Nutraceutical Intl	NUTR	$9.75	0.49	10.75%	23.32%	0.95
O.I. Corp	OICO	$4.06	0.73	12.65%	0.00%	0.40
Ohio Casualty	OCAS	$13.19	0.64	12.19%	0.00%	0.75
Old Dominion Freight	ODFL	$25.48	0.65	8.71%	33.98%	0.60
Paulson Capital	PLCC	$4.80	0.49	21.24%	0.09%	0.95
PC Mall Inc	MALL	$4.05	0.48	10.19%	9.75%	1.45
Q.E.P. Company Inc	QEPC	$4.06	0.56	8.94%	65.75%	0.60
Racing Champions	RACN	$15.50	0.63	12.84%	23.29%	1.35
Reitmans (Canada) Ltd	RET.TO	$23.50	0.79	11.94%	0.00%	0.45
Seaboard Corp	SEB	$230.00	0.59	10.11%	52.75%	0.65
Sportsmans Guide Inc	SGDE	$7.17	0.56	16.84%	0.04%	0.95
Stackpole Ltd	SKD.TO	$23.05	0.75	9.11%	11.99%	0.75
Stratasys Inc	SSYS	$8.30	0.66	8.02%	5.66%	0.75
Supreme Inds Inc	STS	$4.50	0.72	8.91%	25.87%	0.80
Todd Shipyard Cp Del	TOD	$14.20	0.67	10.63%	0.00%	0.50
Todhunter Int'l	THT	$10.70	0.7	10.13%	51.57%	0.40
Tommy Hilfiger	TOM	$7.28	0.77	8.98%	48.50%	1.30
United Auto Group	UAG	$13.37	0.67	8.67%	65.84%	1.20

5 STABLE EARNINGS, BETTER INVESTMENT?

When you invest in a firm, you are exposed to the risk that the firm's underlying business or businesses may go through rough times and that the earnings and stock price of the firm will reflect these downturns. This will be the case even when a firm dominates its business and the business itself is viewed as a good one. To counter this, some firms diversify into multiple businesses, in the process spreading their risk exposure and reducing the likelihood of sharp downturns in earnings. GE provides a good example in the United States. In recent years, firms have also diversified geographically to reduce their risk from a downturn in the domestic economy. In the 1980s, Coca-Cola used this strategy to deliver higher earnings even in the midst of stagnant growth in the beverage market in the United States. The argument that diversifying reduces risk seems incontestable, but does it follow that investing in diversified companies is a good strategy? Some investors seem to think so.

Some undiversified firms, however, manage to report stable earnings even in the presence of economic turmoil. This stability sometimes comes from using financial derivatives to hedge risk and in some cases, through accounting choices. Do smoother earnings streams translate into higher values? Does the markets treat firms differently depending upon how they smooth out earnings? These are the questions that are addressed in this chapter.

CORE OF THE STORY

Equities are riskier than bonds because equity earnings represent what is left over after everyone else has been paid and thus are volatile. But what if you could make your equity earnings more stable? The stock in your firm should become safer and potentially a better investment. As the argument goes, if you can make returns on stocks in these companies that are comparable to what you would make on stocks in more firms with more volatile earnings, you could argue that you are getting the best of both worlds—high returns and low risk. There are three elements to this story.

- *Stocks with stable earnings are less risky than stocks with volatile earnings*. For this story to work, you have to accept the idea that volatility in equity earnings is a good measure of equity risk. Luckily for those who use this story, that is not a difficult sell. The alternative measures of risk used in finance, such as stock price volatility or betas, are all market-based measures. To those investors who do not trust markets—they feel that markets are subject to mood swings and speculation, for instance—earnings stability or the lack thereof seems to provide a more dependable measure of equity risk.
- *Stocks with more stable earnings generate less volatile returns for stockholders*. According to this argument, firms with stable earnings are less likely to roil markets with earnings announcements that surprise investors. The resulting price stability should make the returns on these stocks much more predictable than returns on the rest of the market, especially if the firm takes advantage of its more stable earnings to pay larger dividends every period.
- *Stocks with more stable earnings tend to be under-priced by markets*. This is perhaps the toughest portion of the argument to sustain. One reason given is that companies with stable earnings are often boring companies that don't make the news and investors in search of fads and stars are not interested in them. As a result, stable earnings companies will be underpriced relative to companies with more volatile histories.

MEASUREMENT OF EARNINGS STABILITY

You have three broad choices when it comes to measuring the stability or volatility of earnings.

■ The first and perhaps most direct measure is to look at the variability in earnings over time. At one extreme, you would have stocks that deliver the same dollar earnings year after year and thus exhibit no volatility in earnings. At the other, you would have companies whose earnings fluctuate wildly from huge profits to large losses, creating high variance in earnings. The problem with this measure is that the variability in dollar earnings will be greater for companies with higher dollar earnings and lower for companies with smaller dollar earnings.

■ To alleviate the bias created when you work with dollar earnings, you could look at the percentage changes in earnings from period to period and look for companies that exhibit low variance in these changes. By doing this, you are shifting away from stable earnings to stable growth rates in earnings. While this measure has statistical appeal, it has a significant problem that it shares with the first measure. It treats increases in earnings and decreases in earnings equivalently when it comes to measuring risk.[1] Generally, investors do not consider increases in earnings as risky; it is declines in earnings that worry them.

■ The third measure of earnings stability focuses only on earnings decreases. A firm that reports higher earnings each year, relative to earnings in the prior year, year after year, would be viewed as safe firm. On the other hand, firms that report increases in earnings in some years and decreases in others would be viewed as risky. In fact, you could construct a measure of variance in earnings that looks at only earning decreases.

Once you have chosen your measure of earnings stability, you have to decide on the earnings number that you will focus on. Here, you have several choices. You can estimate the variance in operating income, which is before interest expenses and nonoperating items. While there are obvious benefits to this, it can be a misleading measure of earnings variability if you are considering the risk associated with buying stock and the firm has substantial debt. When it comes to income to equity investors, you can look at net income, which is the aggregate income left over for equity investors, or you can examine earnings per share, which adjusts for changes in the number of shares outstanding. The advantage of the latter is that it allows you to separate firms that grow their net income by issuing new shares and investing those funds from those that grow earnings by reinvesting internal funds. Other things remaining equal, the latter should be more valuable than the former.

THEORETICAL ROOTS: EARNINGS STABILITY AND VALUE

While it may seem intuitive that companies with more stable earnings should be worth more than otherwise similar companies with volatile earnings, the link between earnings stability and value is weak. In this section, you will begin by considering how having a diversified portfolio can color your views about risk and close by examining whether earnings stability can pay off as higher value for a firm.

DIVERSIFICATION AND RISK

Investors have always been told that putting your eggs in one basket (or all your money in one stock) is a dangerous thing to do. In fact, the argument for diversification is at the core of modern portfolio theory. As Nobel prizewinner, Harry Markowitz, noted in his path-breaking paper on portfolio risk, if stocks do not move in tandem (and they do not), a portfolio's risk can be lower than the risk of the individual stocks that go into it.

If you are a diversified investor, you are concerned primarily about the value of your portfolio and the variance in its value. Consequently, you measure the risk of an investment by looking at how it will change the overall risk of your portfolio. In fact, most risk and return models in finance are built on the premise that the investors who set prices by trading in large quantities are diversified and that only the risk added on by a stock to a diversified portfolio (called nondiversifiable or market risk) is rewarded by the market. What does this have to do with earnings stability and its payoff (or lack thereof)? You could construct a portfolio of 50 firms, each of whose earnings are volatile. If the earnings volatility in these firms comes from factors that are specific to their operations or management, it is entirely possible that the composite earnings to the portfolio will be stable. If this is the case, you as an investor would not discount the value of an individual firm just because the firm's earnings are volatile. Nor would you pay a premium for a firm just because its earnings are stable.

So, when will more stable earnings generate higher value for a firm? The first scenario is one in which the earnings stability translates into lower market risk; in other words, the earnings of the firm serve to stabilize the composite earnings of the portfolio. The second scenario is one in which investors are not well diversified and assess the risk of firms as stand-alone investments rather than as part of a portfolio.

STABLE EARNINGS, RISK AND VALUE

To make a link between stable earnings and value, consider the simple discounted cash flow model that was used in the last two chapters to assess value. In that model, in which dividends grow at a constant rate forever, you can write the value of a stock as:

$$\text{Value per share today} = \frac{\text{Expected Dividend per share next year}}{\text{Cost of Equity} - \text{Expected Growth Rate}}$$

The cost of equity is based upon your assessment of the risk in the equity. For stable earnings to affect value, you would first need to make the risk of the equity a function of earnings stability, with the cost of equity being lower for firms with more stable earnings and higher for firms with volatile earnings. If you follow conventional risk and return models in finance and assume diversified investors, the cost of equity will be higher for firms with more market risk and lower for firms with less. If you adopt these models, you will have to establish that the market risk is higher for firms with more volatile earnings.

Once you link the cost of equity to earnings stability, you can show, other things remaining equal, that firms with more stable earnings for any given level of dividends and growth will be valued more highly. But can you hold other things constant? To have stable earnings, you often have to enter more mature and safer businesses with little or no growth potential. In this case, earnings stability creates a tradeoff between less risk (a lower cost of equity) and lower growth (which lowers the expected growth rate). It is possible that your stock can become less valuable as you make earnings more stable if the value of the growth you give up exceeds value created by becoming a safer firm.

The tradeoff becomes even more negative if you give up growth to have more stable earnings but more stable earnings do not reduce market risk. In this case, the growth rate will decline, the cost of equity will remain unchanged, and your value will decrease as earnings stability increases.

LOOKING AT THE EVIDENCE

There are a number of ways in which firms attempt to make earnings less volatile. Some firms have stable earnings because they are in predictable and safe businesses, with little or no competition. Others seek stable earnings through a strategy of diversifying into multiple businesses, hoping that higher income in some will compensate for lower income in others. In a variation of this theme, firms also diversify geographically, with the intent of balancing higher income from some countries against lower income from others. Still other firms use the wide range of options and futures contracts that are now available to reduce or even eliminate their risk exposure. Finally, there are firms that use accounting devices and choices to smooth out volatile earnings; this phenomenon, called earnings management, acquired quite a following in the 1990s. The consequences of each of these approaches to reducing earnings volatility for stock prices and returns is assessed in this section.

STABLE BUSINESSES
WITH NO COMPETITION

For several decades, utility stocks (phone, water and power companies) were prized by risk-averse investors for their steady earnings and high dividends. In fact, these firms could pay the high dividends that they did because their earnings were so predictable. The reasons for the stable earnings were not difficult to uncover. These stocks were regulated monopolies that provided basic and necessary services. The fact that their products and services were nondiscretionary insulated them from overall economic conditions, and the absence of competition gave them secure revenues. In return for the absence of competition, these firms gave up pricing power to the regulatory authorities.

The key question for investors, though, is not whether utility stocks have more stable earnings than other companies, but whether such stable earnings translate into higher stock returns. A simple way of examining this question is to compare the returns earned by utility stocks to returns earned on the overall market. Figure 5.1 makes this comparison.

The average annual returns on utility stocks are lower than the average annual returns on the overall market, but this comparison may not be fair to utility stocks. After all, they are less risky than the rest of the market, and the returns they earn should be adjusted for risk. Figure 5.1 also compares risk-adjusted returns on utility stocks to the returns on the market. In this comparison, utility stocks perform much better, earning an excess return of about 1.4% a year over the last 50 years. It is worth noting that this result mirrors the findings on high dividend yield stocks (which include a disproportionate number of utility stocks) and many of the caveats about that strategy apply to this one as well. In particular, this

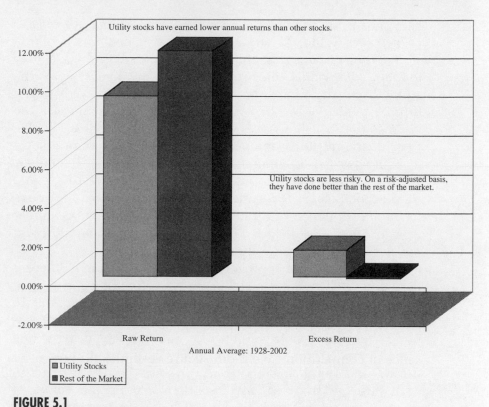

FIGURE 5.1
Utility Stocks vs. the Market

Data from Federal Reserve. The risk-adjusted returns are computed by a comparison of the annual return to the expected return given the betas of these stocks.

strategy would have generated higher tax liabilities and would have required a long time horizon to pay off.

DIVERSIFIED BUSINESS MIX: THE ALLURE OF CONGLOMERATES

Every company, no matter how well run, will be exposed to the risk that the sector it is in can go through hard times. Thus, Intel will be affected by a downturn in the semiconductor business and Microsoft by a decline in the demand for computer software. To insulate against this sector risk, a firm can try to diversify into multiple businesses and become a conglomerate. For the last few decades, strategists have gone back and forth on whether becoming a conglomerate creates or destroys value. In the 1960s and through much of the 1970s, the view was that conglomerates created value, relative to their individual pieces, because you could pool the strengths of the individual firms to create a more powerful firm. A hidden subtext to many of these arguments was the premise that conglomerates were less risky and more valuable than their individual components because they were able to diversify away risk. Financial theorists pointed out the fallacy in this argument by noting that individual investors could have accomplished the same diversification at far lower cost. Later, the argument shifted to one of superior management transferring its skills to poorly managed firms in different businesses and creating often-unnamed synergies.

Researchers have approached this question from a different perspective. They have looked at the question of whether conglomerates trade at a premium or discount to their parts. To make this judgment, they value the pieces of a conglomerate, using the typical multiple at which independent firms in the business trade. Thus, you could break GE down into nine businesses, and value each part based upon what other firms in each business trade at. You can then add up the values of the parts and compare it to the value of the conglomerate. In this comparison, the evidence seems to indicate that conglomerates trade at significant discounts (ranging from 5% to 10%, depending upon the study) to their piecewise values.[2] While one can contest the magnitude of these discounts on estimation grounds—it is difficult to estimate the true earnings of GE Capital, given allocations and other pooled costs—it is clear that some multiple-business firms would be worth more as individual businesses. If conglomerate earnings are more stable than the earnings of stand-alone firms, why is there a conglomerate discount? There are at least two reasons. The first is that a conglomerate is often created by one firm paying large premiums over market value to acquire other publicly traded firms. This overpayment drains more value than the stable earnings may create in value. The second is that conglomerates often suffer from a lack of focus and poor management; divisions of conglomerates underperform their stand-alone competition.

While a conglomerate discount may exist, the question of whether investing in conglomerates generates promising returns for investors still has not been addressed. The overall evidence suggests not, but there may be a silver lining. If you invest in conglomerates that break up into individual pieces through divestitures and spinoffs, you may be able to capture the increase in value as the conglomerate discount disappears. In other words, you stand to make more money when conglomerates break up than when they are built up.

GLOBAL DIVERSIFICATION

An alternative to business diversification (which creates conglomerates) is geographical diversification. By having operations in multiple countries, a firm may be able to offset a decline in business in one country with an increase in another. The net effect should be a reduction in the variability of operating earnings. There is, though, at least one confounding factor at work here that does not apply to business diversification. As your operations spread out over different countries, your earnings will be exposed to foreign currency risk; a U.S. company will find its earnings affected by the strengthening or weakening of the dollar. You can, however, partially protect your earnings from this risk by using futures and options contracts.

Again, there are two basic questions that you need to address in the context of global diversification. The first is whether such diversification results in more stable earnings, and the second is whether investing in globally diversified companies generates higher or lower returns. An examination of Swedish firms that diversify globally concluded that geographical diversification does increase value, unlike industrial diversification.[3] This is consistent with the findings of another study in the United States.[4] The effect is small, though, and investing in a firm that is already globally diversified yields little in terms of excess returns. You would need to invest in companies just before they embark on global diversification to gain any potential benefits.

RISK HEDGERS

A number of external factors, including interest rates, commodity prices and exchange rates, can affect the revenues, earnings and value of a firm. Thus, even the best-managed airline may see its profits decline if oil prices go up. In recent years, firms have been able to hedge a significant portion of this risk, using financial instruments and products. In this section, you will consider two questions. The first relates to whether firms should try to manage this risk. The second looks at the payoff of risk management to investors.

Should Project Risk Be Managed? Firms are exposed to a multitude of macroeconomic risks in their investments. Sometimes shifts in interest rates and exchange rates can augment income and sometimes they can reduce it. Thus, a portion of the variation in earnings over time for any firm can be attributed to these risks. The manager can leave the firm exposed to these risks and assume that its stockholders in the firm will be able to diversify away the risk, or the manager can hedge the risk, using a variety of financial instruments.

To evaluate whether a firm should try to manage or hedge its exposure to this risk, you need to consider three factors. The first is the magnitude of the risk and the impact that it can have on the overall firm's earnings and value. For instance, variation in oil prices may be responsible for 30% of the volatility of earnings for an airline but only 5% of the variation in earnings at a steel company. Since large shifts in earnings can cause serious problems for firms (including defaulting on debt and going bankrupt), firms should be more likely to hedge large risks than small ones. The second factor is the extent to which different investments the firm may have in different parts of the world may result in diversification of some or a great portion of the risk. For instance, Coca-Cola and Citicorp, with operations in dozens of countries, might find that exchange rate movements in some countries that reduce value may be offset by favorable movements in other countries. If firms such as these hedge risk in each country, they will be doing so unnecessarily. The third factor is the degree to which investors in the firm can diversify away the risk on their own by holding portfolios that include stocks that are affected both positively and negatively by exchange rate movements. Firms such as the Home Depot and Boeing, which have a base of well-diversified investors, may find it cheaper not to hedge risk and to allow it to pass through to their investors, who will diversify it away at far less expense.

In addition, you need to consider the cost of managing risk. Hedging risk exposure is cheaper for some types of risk (exchange rate, interest rate) than for others (political risk) and for shorter periods than for longer ones. Other things remaining equal, the greater the cost of hedging risk, the less likely firms will be to hedge. In summary, then, a small, closely held firm considering a large project (relative to the firm's current size) should try to manage project risk. A firm with a diversified investor base, with operations in multiple countries, should be less inclined to manage project risk.

How Do You Manage Project Risk?　Assume now that you are a firm that should be managing project risk and that you are considering the different alternatives available to you to do so. When firms decide to manage risk, they have a variety of choices. They can use futures contracts, forward contracts, and options to manage interest rate, exchange rate and commodity price risk; and they can use insurance products to manage event risk (such as the eventuality of a revolution). They can also manage risk by choosing the financing for the project wisely.

■ The simplest way of hedging some of the risk on a project is to choose financing instruments with cash flows that mirror the cash flows on the project. Thus, Wal-Mart can use a loan denominated in Mexican pesos to finance its retail expansion in Mexico. If the peso depreciates, its assets (the stores in Mexico) will be worth less, but so will its liabilities (the loan), leaving it less affected by the exchange rate movement. Matching financing to the assets can only partially reduce risk, but it is generally a low-cost or no-cost option for risk management. All firms should therefore try to do this as much as they feasibly can.

■ The most widely used products in risk management are futures, forwards, options and swaps. These are generally categorized as derivative products since they derive their value from an underlying asset that is traded. Today, you can buy futures and options contracts to hedge away commodity price risk, currency risk and interest rate risk, to name just a few.

■ The alternative route to risk management is to buy insurance to cover specific event risk. Just as homeowners buy insurance on their house to protect against the eventuality of fire or other damage, companies can buy insurance to protect their assets against possible loss. In fact, it can be argued that, in spite of the attention given to the use of derivatives in risk management, traditional insurance remains the primary vehicle for managing risk. Insurance does not eliminate risk. Rather, it shifts the risk from the firm buying the insurance to the insurance firm selling it, but doing so may provide a benefit to both sides, for a number of reasons. First, the insurance company may be able to create a portfolio of risks, thereby gaining diversification benefits that the self-insured firm itself cannot obtain. Second, the insurance company might acquire the expertise to evaluate risk and thus process claims more efficiently as a consequence of its repeated exposure to that risk. Third, insurance companies might provide other services, such as inspection and safety services, that benefit both sides. While a third party could arguably provide the same service, the insurance company has an incentive to ensure the quality of the service.

The Payoff to Risk Management. Firms can use a variety of products to manage risk, and by doing so, they can reduce the variability in their earnings. But do investors in these firms reap benefits, as a consequence? An evaluation[5] of firms that use foreign currency derivatives to hedge exchange rate risk concluded that they have both smoother earnings and trade at higher values.[6] A subsequent examination suggests that most of the benefit comes from hedging short-term transaction risk and there seems to be little gained from hedging translation exposure (which also affects earnings).[7] Another strand of the research looks at why some firms hedge risk more than others and uncovers interesting factors. Many firms that use derivatives to manage risk often do so to reduce tax liabilities, maintain required investments, and alleviate the fear of financial distress. At the same time, managerial risk aversion also plays a role in whether derivatives get used. Studies indicate that managers are more likely to use derivatives when they hold a larger percent of the outstanding stock in a company.

In summary, the evidence indicates that there is a payoff to managing risk and that firms that manage risk are more highly valued than firms that do not. Two notes of caution are in order, though. The first is that the payoff is a small one and it is unlikely that investors will even notice unless they look closely. The second is that payoff occurs when these firms switch to using the risk management products and not subsequently.

EARNINGS SMOOTHERS

Firms have become particularly adept at meeting and beating analyst estimates of earnings each quarter. While beating earnings estimates can be viewed as a positive development, some firms adopt questionable accounting techniques to accomplish this objective. When valuing these firms, you have to correct operating income for these accounting manipulations.

The Phenomenon of Managed Earnings. In the 1990s, Microsoft and Intel set the pattern for technology firms. In fact, Microsoft beat analyst estimates of earnings in 39 of the 40 quarters during the decade, and Intel posted a record almost as impressive. Other technology firms followed in their footsteps in trying to deliver earnings that were higher than analyst estimates by at least a few pennies. The evidence is overwhelming that the phenomenon is spreading. For an unprecedented 18 quarters in a row from 1996 to 2000, more firms beat consensus earnings estimates than missed them.[8] In another indication of the management of earnings, the gap between the earnings reported by firms to the Internal Revenue Service and that reported to equity investors has been growing over the last decade.

Given that these analyst estimates are expectations, what does this tell you? One possibility is that analysts consistently underestimate earnings and never learn from their mistakes. While this is a possibility, it seems extremely unlikely to persist over an entire decade. The other is that technology firms particularly have far more discretion in how they measure and report earnings and are using this discretion to beat estimates. In particular, the treatment of research expenses as operating expenses gives these firms an advantage when it comes to managing earnings.

Does managing earnings really increase a firm's stock price? It might be possible to beat analysts' estimates quarter after quarter, but are markets as gullible? They are not, and the advent of "whispered earnings estimates" is in reaction to the consistent delivery of earnings that are above expectations. What are whispered earnings? Whispered earnings are implicit earnings estimates that firms like Intel and Microsoft have to beat to surprise the market; these estimates are usually a few cents higher than analyst estimates. For instance, on April 10, 1997, Intel reported earnings of $2.10 per share, higher than analyst estimates of $2.06 per share, but saw its stock price drop 5 points because the whispered earnings estimate had been $2.15. In other words, markets had built into expectations the amount by which Intel had historically beaten earnings estimates.

Techniques for Managing Earnings. How do firms manage earnings? One aspect of good earnings management is the care and nurturing of analyst expectations, a practice that Microsoft perfected during the 1990s. Executives at the firm monitored analyst estimates of earnings and stepped in to lower expectations when they believed that the estimates were too high.[9] Several other techniques are used, and you will consider some of the most common ones in this section. Not all the techniques are harmful to the firm, and some may indeed be considered prudent management.

1. *Plan ahead*. Firms can plan investments and asset sales to keep earnings rising smoothly.

2. *Recognize revenues strategically.* Firms have some leeway as to when revenues have to be recognized. As an example, Microsoft, in 1995, adopted an extremely conservative approach to accounting for revenues from its sale of Windows 95 and chose not to show large chunks of revenues that they were entitled (though not obligated) to show.[10] In fact, by the end of 1996 the firm had accumulated $1.1 billion in unearned revenues that it could borrow on to supplement earnings in weaker quarters.

3. *Book revenues early*. In an opposite phenomenon, firms sometimes ship products during the final days of a weak quarter to distributors and retailers and record the revenues. Consider the case of MicroStrategy, a technology firm that went public in 1998. In the last two quarters of 1999, the firm reported revenue growth of 20% and 27%, respectively, but much of that growth was attributable to large deals announced just days before each quarter ended. In a more elaborate variant of this strategy, two technology firms, both of which need to boost revenues, can enter into a transaction to swap revenues.[11]

4. *Capitalize operating expenses*. Just as with revenue recognition, firms are given some discretion in whether they classify expenses as operating or capital expenses, especially items like software R&D. AOL's practice of capitalizing and writing off the cost of the promotional CDs it provided with magazines, for instance, allowed it to report positive earnings through much of the late 1990s.

5. *Write off restructuring and acquisitions*. A major restructuring charge can result in lower income in the

current period, but it provides two benefits to the firm taking it. Since operating earnings are reported both before and after the restructuring charge, the write-off allows the firm to separate the expense from operations. It also makes beating earnings easier in future quarters. To see how restructuring can boost earnings, consider the case of IBM. By writing off old plants and equipment in the year they are closed, IBM dropped depreciation expenses to 5% of revenue in 1996 from an average of 7% in 1990–1994. The difference, in 1996 revenue, was $1.64 billion, or 18% of the company's $9.02 billion in pretax profit last year. Technology firms have been particularly adept at writing off a large portion of acquisition costs as "in-process R&D" to register increases in earnings in subsequent quarters. A study of 389 firms that wrote off in-process R&D between 1990 and 1996 concluded that these write-offs amounted, on average, to 72% of the purchase price on these acquisitions and increased the acquiring firm's earnings by 22% in the fourth quarter after the acquisition.[12]

6. *Use reserves*. Firms are allowed to build up reserves for bad debts, product returns and other potential losses. Some firms are conservative in their estimates in good years and use the excess reserves that they have built up during these years to smooth out earnings in other years.

7. *Liquidate investments*. Firms with substantial holdings of marketable securities or investments in other firms often have these investments recorded on their books at values well below their market values. Thus, liquidating these investments can result in large capital gains, which can boost income in the period. Technology firms such as Intel have used this route to beat earnings estimates.

Is There a Payoff to Managing Earnings?   Firms generally manage earnings because they believe that they will be rewarded by markets for delivering earnings that are smoother and come in consistently above analyst estimates. As evidence, you can point to the success of firms like Microsoft and Intel and the brutal punishment meted out, especially at technology firms, for firms that do not meet expectations. Many financial managers also seem to believe that investors take earnings numbers at face value and work at delivering bottom lines that reflect this belief. This may explain why any attempts by the Financial Accounting Standards Board (FASB) to change the way earnings are measured are fought with vigor, even when the changes make sense. For instance, any attempts by FASB to value the options granted by these firms to their managers at a fair value and charging them against earnings or to change the way mergers are accounted for have been consistently opposed by technology firms. It may also be in the best interests of the managers of firms to manage earnings. Managers know that they are more likely to be fired when earnings drop significantly, relative to prior periods. Furthermore, there are firms in which managerial compensation is still built around profit targets and meeting these targets can lead to lucrative bonuses.

Whatever the reason for managed earnings, there are questions that you need to answer. The first is whether firms that manage earnings trade at higher multiples of earnings than do otherwise similar firms that do not resort to this practice. A study of the relationship between price-to-book-value ratios and earnings stability concludes that stocks with lower earnings volatility trade at higher values and finds that this is true even when the earnings stability reflects accounting choices rather than operating stability; firms in which earnings are stable but cash flows remain volatile continue to trade at higher values.[13]

CRUNCHING THE NUMBERS

In this section, you will begin by looking at the distribution of earnings volatility across the market. Specifically, you will consider what a high earnings volatility firm would look like and contrast it with a firm with stable earnings. The section is concluded by creating a portfolio of stocks that pass the "stable earnings" test.

EARNINGS VOLATILITY ACROSS THE MARKET

As noted early in the chapter, there is no one accepted measure of earnings volatility. While you could construct statistical measures of volatility—standard deviation or variance in earnings—you would still have to standardize the numbers to make them comparable across firms. After consideration and rejection of a number of different approaches to standardization, the coefficient of variation in earnings, estimated by dividing the standard deviation in earnings between 1997 and 2001 by the absolute value of average earnings during that period, was used to measure earnings volatility.

$$\text{Coefficient of Variation in Earnings} = \frac{\text{Standard Deviation in Earnings}}{\text{Absolute Value of average Earnings over the period}}$$

As an example, consider a firm that had earnings per share of $1.75, $1.00, $2.25 and $3.00 each year for the last four years. The standard deviation across these four values is $0.84, and the average earning per share is $2.00, resulting in a coefficient of variation of 0.42. You are converting the standard deviation in earnings to a standard deviation per dollar of earnings; this firm has a standard deviation of 42 cents per dollar of earnings. Since the average earnings can be negative over the period, you have to use the absolute value of earnings to get a meaningful number.

Since you need a few years of data for the standard deviation to be meaningful, all active publicly traded firms in the United States with at least five years of earnings information available, ending in 2001, were considered as the overall sample. The coefficient of variation in three measures of earnings—earnings before interest, taxes and depreciation (EBITDA), net income and earnings per share—was computed for each firm. Figure 5.2 presents the distribution of values across the market.

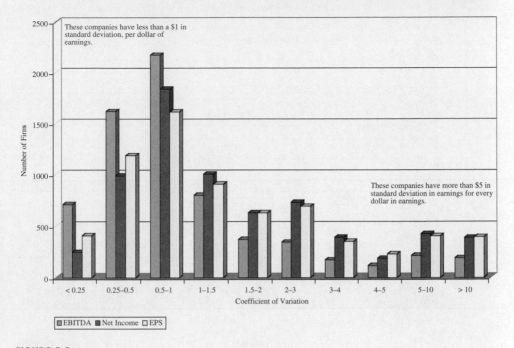

FIGURE 5.2
Coefficient of Variation in Earnings: U.S. Companies in October 2002
Data from Compustat. The coefficient of variation is obtained by dividing the standard deviation in earnings over five years by the average earnings over the period.

Of the 6700 firms that had earnings data for five years or more, about two-thirds of all firms have standard deviations of less than a dollar for every dollar of EBITDA and about half of all firms have standard deviations of less than a dollar for every dollar of net income or EPS. In other words, the volatility in equity earnings (net income and earnings per share) is greater than the volatility in operating income or cash flow.

A more intuitive measure of earnings stability is the number of consecutive years of earnings increases; presumably a firm that has reported increasing earnings every year for the last five years has more predictable (and safer) earnings than a firm whose earnings have gone up and down over the same period. Figure 5.3 presents the number of firms, with earnings per share available for at least five years, that have reported increasing earnings per share every year for the last five years, the last four years and so on.

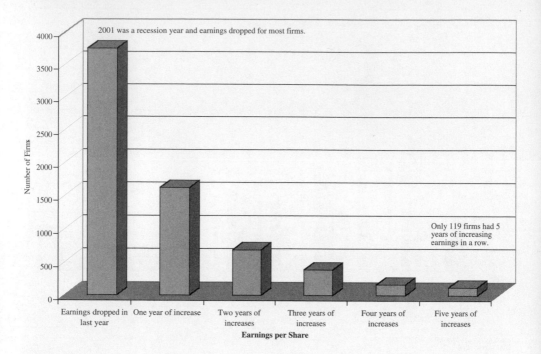

FIGURE 5.3

Consecutive Years of Earnings Increases: U.S. Companies through 2001

Data from Compustat. Looking across all U.S. companies through 2001, you see the number of firms that had reported rising earnings each year over the previous five years, four years, three years, etc.

It should come as no surprise, given that the economy slowed in 2001, that the vast majority of firms reported earnings decreases in 2001. Even in this challenging environment, though, 119 firms reported increasing earnings per share each year for the last five years and 158 firms reported increasing earnings per share each year for the last four years.

A PORTFOLIO OF STABLE EARNINGS COMPANIES

To create a portfolio of stable earnings companies, all firms with at least five years of earnings data were examined and the coefficient of variation in earnings per share for each firm was

TABLE 5.1 Stable Earnings Companies: United States in October 2002

COMPANY NAME	INDUSTRY	COMPANY NAME	INDUSTRY
Progen Industries Ltd	Biological PDS,Ex Diagnstics	Santa Fe Energy Trust	Oil Royalty Traders
Nutraceutical Intl CP	Medicinal Chems,Botanicl PDS	Paychex Inc	Account,Audit,Bookkeep Sves
ASB Financial Corp	Savings Instn,Fed Chartered	BOK Financial Corp	National Commercial Banks
Griffon Corp	Metal Doors,Frames,Mold,Trim	Northern Trust Corp	State Commercial Banks
Arcadis N V	Engineering Services	First State Bancorporation	State Commercial Banks
TPG NV -ADR	Trucking,Courier Svc,Ex Air	Allegiant Bancorp Inc	State Commercial Banks
Leesport Financial Corp	National Commercial Banks	Cash Technologies Inc	Business Services, NEC
Smucker (JM) Co	Can Fruit,Veg,Presrv,Jam,Jel	Home Depot Inc	Lumber & Oth Bldg Matl-Retl
Landauer Inc	Testing Laboratories	Southwest Bancorporation/TX	National Commercial Banks
Corning Natural Gas Corp	Natural Gas Transmis & Distr	Sigma-Aldrich	Biological PDS,Ex Diagnstics
Cintas Corp	Men,Yth,Boys Frnsh,Wrk Clthg	Williams Coal Seam Ryl Trust	Oil Royalty Traders
Horizon Financial Corp/WA	Saving Instn,Not Fed Chart	Hillenbrand Ind-Pre Fasb	Misc Furniture and Fixtures
Wal-Mart Stores	Variety Stores	Realty Income Corp	Real Estate Investment Trust
F & M Bancorp/MD	National Commercial Banks	Cambridge Heart Inc	Electromedical Apparatus
Aquila Inc	Electric & Other Serv Comb	Delta Natural Gas Co Inc	Natural Gas Transmis & Distr
Eastern Amern Natural Gas Tr	Oil Royalty Traders	Firstbank NW Corp/DE	Savings Instn,Fed Chartered
S Y Bancorp Inc	State Commercial Banks	First Natl CP Orangeburg SC	National Commercial Banks
National Penn Bancshares Inc	National Commercial Banks	Voiceflash Networks Inc	Prepackaged Software
Old Republic Intl Corp	Fire, Marine, Casualty Ins	O Reilly Automotive Inc	Auto and Home Supply Stores
Compass Bancshares Inc	National Commercial Banks	Copytele Inc	Computer Peripheral EQ,NEC
Hospitality Properties Trust	Real Estate Investment Trust	American Water Works Inc	Water Supply
Old Second Bancorp Inc/IL	National Commercial Banks	Camco Financial Corp	Savings Instn,Not Fed Chart
Tompkinstrustco Inc	State Commercial Banks	Skyepharma PLC -ADR	Biological PDS,Ex Diagnsties
Dominion Res Black Warrior	Oil Royalty Traders	Family Dollar Stores	Variety Stores
CH Energy Group Inc	Electric & Other Serv Comb	TBC Corp	Motor Veh Parts, Supply-Whsl
Ameren Corp	Electric Services	Midsouth Bancorp Inc	National Commercial Banks
Healthcare Services Group	Sves to Dwellings, Oth Bldgs	Bedford Bancshares Inc	Savings Instn,Fed Chartered
LSB Financial Corp	Savings Instn,Fed Chartered	Pennfed Financial Svcs Inc	Savings Instn,Fed Chartered
Wilmington Trust Corp	State Commercial Banks	Prima Energy Corp	Crude Petroleum & Natural Gs
Harleysville Svgs Finl Corp	Savings Instn,Not Fed Chart	Clarcor Inc	Indl Coml Fans,Blowrs,Oth EQ

(continued)

TABLE 5.1 Stable Earnings Companies: United States in October 2002 (*Continued*)

COMPANY NAME	INDUSTRY	COMPANY NAME	INDUSTRY
Donaldson Co Inc	Indl Coml Fans,Blowrs,Oth EQ	Community First Bankshares	National Commercial Banks
South Jersey Industries	Natural Gas Distribution	Viewcast,Com Inc	Radio,TV Broadcast,Comm EQ
Sempra Energy	Gas & Other Serv Combined	S & T Bancorp Inc	State Commercial Banks
Pacific Capital Bancorp	State Commrcial Banks	R&G Financial Corp -Cl B	State Commercial Banks
Energen Corp	Natural Gas Distribution	Texas Regl Bcshs Inc -Cl A	State Commercial Banks
CVB Financial Corp	State Commercial Banks	Royal Bancshares/PA -Cl A	State Commercial Banks
Raven Industries Inc	Misc Plastics Produts	Amcore Finl Inc	National Commercial Banks
Bunzl Pub Ltd Co -Spon Adr	Paper & Paper Product-Whsl	First Mutual Bancshares Inc	Savings Instn, Not Fed Chart
Alberto-Culver Co -CL B	Retail Stores	Bancorp Conn Inc	Savings Instn, Not Fed Chart
First Merchants Corp	National Commercial Banks	Suffolk Bancorp	National Commercial Banks
NSD Bancorp Inc	State Commercial Banks	Mercantile Bankshares Corp	State Commercial Banks
WPS Resources Corp	Electric & Other Serv Comb	Teleflex Inc	Conglomerates
Webster Finl Corp Waterbury	Savings Instn,Fed Chartered	Public Service Entrp	Electric & Other Serv Comb
FST Finl Corp Ind	National Commercial Banks	Spectrx Inc	Coml Physical, Biologcl Resh
First Long Island Corp	National Commercial Banks	Bostonfed Bancorp Inc	Savings Instn,Fed Chartered
Suntrust Banks Inc	State Commercial Banks	UST Inc	Tobacco Products
Hancock Hldg Co	State Commercial Banks	Allied Capital CP	Misc Business Credit Instn
MAF Bancorp Inc	Savings Instn,Fed Chartered	Mississippi Vy Bancshares	State Commercial Banks
Wesbanco Inc	National Commercial Banks	Roper Industries Inc/DE	Industrial Measurement Instr
First Bancorp P R	Commercial Banks,NEC	Fresh Brands Inc	Groceries & Related PDS-Whsl
Interchange Finl Svcs CP/NJ	State Commercial Banks	Utah Medical Products Inc	Electromedical Apparatus
Norwood Financial Corp	State Commercial Banks	Logansport Financial Corp	Savings Instn,Fed Chartered
Monro Muffler Brake Inc	Auto Repair,Services,Parking	First UTD Corp	National Commercial Banks
Mocon Inc	Meas & Controlling Dev, NEC	Gorman-Rupp Co	Pumps and Pumping Equipment
Synovus Financial CP	National Commercial Banks	Wayne Bancorp Inc/OH	National Commercial Banks
First Fed Cap Corp	Savings Instn,Fed Chartered	New Jersey Resources	Natural Gas Distribution
Bancfirst Corp/OK	State Commercial Banks	FPL Group Inc	Electric Services
First Busey Corp -Cl A	State Commercial Banks	Park National Corp	National Commercial Banks
Teco Energy Inc	Electric & Other Serv Comb	Washington Reit	Real Estate Investment Trust
Affymetrix Inc	Electromedical Apparatus	TTX Co	Transportation Services

computed. In addition to looking for firms with low coefficients of variation in earnings, we imposed two additional tests. The first was that the firm did not report a loss in any of the last five years. The second was that the earnings per share had increased each year for at least the last two years. Incorporating a cap on the coefficient of variation of 0.25 generated a portfolio of 100 companies. This portfolio is presented in Table 5.1.

Taking a closer look at the portfolio, you can see that financial service companies are disproportionately represented, representing about 25% of the stocks in the portfolio.

MORE TO THE STORY

Are stable earnings companies safer investments and, more importantly, better investments than companies with more volatile earnings? To answer these questions, you need to consider four potential weaknesses in a stable earnings company strategy. The first is that companies with stable earnings can still be volatile investments. The second is that companies with stable earnings may offer little growth potential, thus creating a tradeoff between stable earnings and high growth. The third is that companies might use accounting games to make their earnings look more stable. The fourth is that stable earnings companies may be priced right and provide little opportunity for high returns.

STABLE EARNINGS, RISKY INVESTMENT?

A company with stable earnings may not necessarily represent a stable investment, because stock prices are affected by far more than earnings news from the company. Nonearnings news about growth prospects and management changes, macroeconomic news about interest rates and economic growth, and information released by competitors in the same business can all cause stock prices to move even when earnings do not. An investor ultimately measures risk on the basis of stock price movement, and a stock with stable earnings and a volatile price path would still be categorized as risky.

You can look at two stock-price-based measures of risk for the companies in the stable earnings portfolio: the beta, which measures how these stocks move with the market; and the standard deviation in stock prices over the previous five years. To provide a contrast, the differences between the averages for these two measures for the stable earnings portfolio and for the market are examined in Figure 5.4.

Companies with stable earnings are less volatile and have much lower betas, on average, than other companies in the rest of the market. There are, however, a few firms in the sample of stable earnings companies with high betas (greater than 1.25)

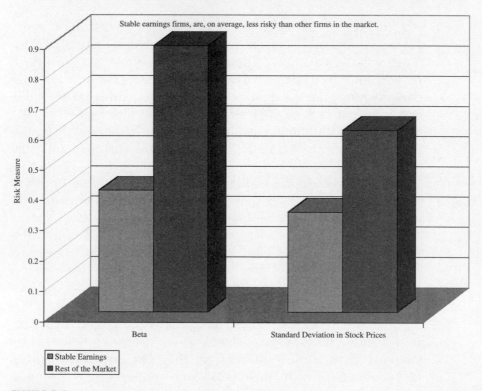

FIGURE 5.4

Stable Earnings versus Rest of Market: Risk Comparison

Data from Value Line: The average beta and standard deviation, estimated over the previous three years, is reported for firms in the stable earnings portfolio and for the rest of the market.

and standard deviations that exceed the average for the market (approximately 60%). If you introduce these risk levels as screens and eliminate firms with stable earnings that have betas exceeding 1.25 or standard deviation exceeding 60%, you lose eight firms out of the initial sample of 100 firms. These firms are listed in Table 5.2.

TABLE 5.2 Stable Earnings Firms that Fail Risk Test

COMPANY NAME	TICKER SYMBOL	BETA 5-YEAR	STD DEV 5-YEAR
Northern Trust Corp	NTRS	1.28	31.4
Home Depot	HD	1.29	36.73
Progen Industries Limited	PGLAF	0.48	62.38
Fresh Choice	SALD	0.62	70.72
SpectRx Inc	SPRX	0.73	70.82
Cambridge Heart Inc	CAMH	1.86	79.28
CopyTele Inc	COPY	1.48	96.29
Affymetrix Inc	AFFX	1.84	97.54

GIVING UP ON GROWTH OPPORTUNITIES

While it is true that lower-risk companies, other things remaining equal, should be worth more than higher-risk companies, it is also true that investors often have to trade off lower risk for lower growth. While it would be unrealistic to expect companies that have stable earnings to also have high growth, you should be wary about companies with stable earnings that report no or very low growth. After all, a stock that delivers the same earnings year after year begins to look like a bond and will be priced as such.

How does the portfolio of stable earnings companies compiled at the end of the last section measure up against the rest of the market when it comes to earnings growth? The average growth in earnings per share and revenues over the last five years and the projected growth in earnings per share (as estimated by analysts) over the next five years for the companies in the portfolio and for the rest of the market were estimated. Figure 5.5 presents the comparison.

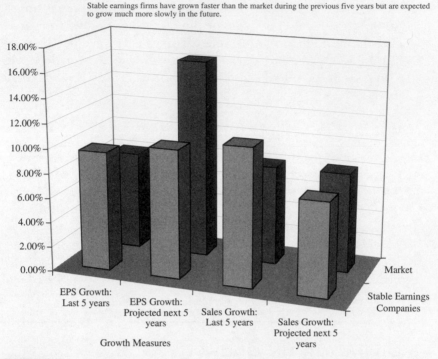

Stable earnings firms have grown faster than the market during the previous five years but are expected to grow much more slowly in the future.

FIGURE 5.5

Stable Earnings Firms vs. Market: Growth

Data from Value Line. The projected growth rates in earnings and sales are from analyst projections.

The stable earnings companies have had higher growth in earnings per share and sales than companies in the rest of the market over the previous five years. However, the projected growth over the next five years is lower in both earnings per share and sales for the stable earnings firms, which suggests that investors do bear a cost when they buy stable earnings companies.

To ensure that the stocks in the portfolio register at least some growth, all firms that had projected growth in earnings per share for the next five years of less than 5% were eliminated. With this screen, you lose 38 firms out of the remaining 92 stocks in the portfolio. With a growth rate screen of 10% or higher in earnings per share for the next five years, you would have eliminated another 20 firms from the sample.

PRICED RIGHT?

Even if you do find a stock with stable earnings and adequate expected growth, there is no guarantee that this stock will be a good investment if it is not priced right. In other words, if you pay a high multiple of earnings because of the earnings stability and growth, you may very well neutralize the advantages that drew you to this stock in the first place.

The price-earnings ratios, using current earnings, for the stocks in the stable earnings portfolio and also the ratio of the PE to the expected growth rate (called the PEG ratio) were computed. Figure 5.6 compares the average PE and PEG ratio

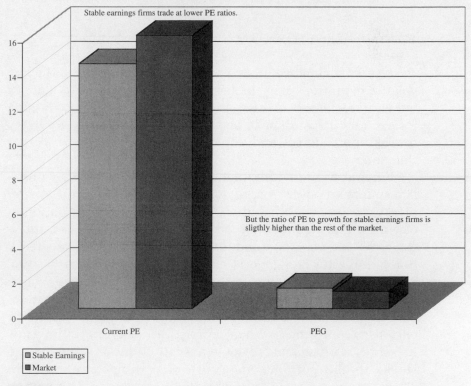

FIGURE 5.6

PE and PEG Ratios: Stable Earnings vs. Rest of the Market

Data from Value Line. The price-earnings ratio is the current price divided by current EPS, and the PEG ratio is the ratio of current PE to expected growth in earnings per share over the next five years.

for the stocks in the stable earnings portfolio and the rest of the market.

The stable earnings firms have slightly lower PE ratios than firms in the rest of the market but trade at higher PEG ratios.

To screen for stocks that may be overpriced, all firms that trade at PE ratios that exceed 15 and PEG ratios greater than 1 were eliminated. If used in conjunction with the risk and growth screens outlined in the earlier parts of this section, the portfolio shrinks to 8 firms. The firms listed in Table 5.3 pass all of the tests: have earnings growth that exceeds 5%, betas less than 1.25, standard deviations less than 60%, PE ratios less than 15 and PEG ratios less than 1.

The firms are primarily utilities and financial service firms.

EARNINGS QUALITY

Firms that manage to report stable earnings while having volatile operations may be using accounting ploys to smooth out earnings. If this is the case, the volatility cannot be hidden forever and investors who buy stocks in these firms are likely to wake up to large (and unpleasant) surprises sooner rather than later.

Since it would be impractical to look at each firm's financial statements over time to detect earnings smoothing, a simpler test was used. In addition to the coefficient of variation in earnings, the coefficient of variation in earnings before interest, taxes, depreciation and amortization (EBITDA) was used. Since the latter is a general measure of operating cash flows, you could argue that firms that report stable earnings while reporting much more volatile cash flows are indulging in accounting sleight of hand and should not be treated as stable earnings companies. When applied to this portfolio, this measure affords some evidence that at least some of the stocks in the portfolio are guilty of earnings management. These are the firms that report high standard deviations in EBITDA while also reporting low standard deviations in earnings per share.

TABLE 5.3 Stable Earnings Firms with Low Risk, Growth Potential and Reasonable Pricing

Company Name	Projected Growth Rate	Current PE	PEG Ratio	Beta 5-Year	Std Dev 5-Year
Prima Energy Corp	23.50%	12.25	0.52	0.53	52.37
First BanCorp PR	14.00%	11.43	0.82	0.44	30.37
R & G Financial Corp	12.00%	10.25	0.85	0.48	40.22
Sempra Energy	7.50%	6.84	0.91	0.66	38.16
Dominion Resources	15.50%	14.35	0.93	0.26	24.61
Public Svc Enter	6.00%	5.62	0.94	0.26	29.94
BOK Financial	15.10%	14.40	0.95	0.53	26.08
Allied Capital Corp	11.00%	10.71	0.97	0.81	31.45

LESSONS FOR INVESTORS

Not all firms that report stable earnings are good investments. At the minimum, you need to consider whether these firms offer any growth potential, whether earnings stability translates into price stability and finally, whether the market is pricing these stocks correctly. It is no bargain to buy a stock with stable earnings, low or no growth, substantial price volatility and a high price-earnings ratio. Reverting to the sample of all firms in the United States, the following screens were used:

- The coefficient of variation in earnings per share has to be in the bottom 10% of the overall sample. You can use alternative measures of earnings stability to make this judgment, still the argument for using earnings per share rather than net income or operating income were presented earlier in the chapter. You can also add on additional screens such as the requirement that earnings have increased every year for the last few years.
- The beta of the stock has to be less than 1.25, and the standard deviation in stock prices over the last three years has to be less than 60%. While it is unlikely that many stable earnings companies will be high risk, there will be some companies for which prices remain volatile even as earnings are stable. The risk screens will eliminate these firms.
- The price-earnings ratio has to be less than 15. Buying a great company at too high a price is no bargain. Consequently, you need to make sure that you are not paying a premium for earnings stability that is not justified.
- The expected growth rate in earnings per share over the next five years has to be 10% or higher. Earnings growth is always a bonus. A company with stable and growing earnings is clearly a better investment than one with stable and stagnant earnings.

The resulting portfolio of 37 companies, compiled from data available in January 2003, is reported in the appendix.

CONCLUSION

Firms that report a steady and stable stream of positive earnings per share are considered by some investors to be good investments because they are safe. Both the theoretical backing and the empirical evidence for this proposition are weak. Firms that pay a large price (on risk management products or acquisitions) to reduce or eliminate risk that investors could have diversified away at no cost are doing a disservice to their stockholders. Stable earnings notwithstanding, you should not expect these firms to be great investments. In this chapter, we considered this issue by first looking at how best to measure earnings volatility. When you construct a portfolio of stocks that have the most stable earnings, other problems show up. The first is that some of these firms, despite their earnings stability, have high stock price volatility and seem risky. The second is that a substantial number of these firms have low or negative growth rates. Finally, many of the remaining firms trade at high PE ratios and do not seem to be bargains at prevailing prices.

ENDNOTES

1. To illustrate, a firm with percentage changes in earnings of +5%, −5% and +5% over three years will be classified as having more stable earnings than a firm that reports percentage changes in earnings of +5%, +15% and +25% over three years.

2. Lang, Larry H. P., and René M. Stulz, 1994, *Tobin's q, corporate diversification, and firm performance*, Journal of Political Economy, v102, 1248–1280.

3. Pramborg, B., *Derivatives Hedging, Geographical Diversification and Firm Value*, Working Paper, Stockholm University.

4. Allayannis, G., J. Ihrig and J. P. Weston, 2001, *Exchange Rate Hedging: Financial versus Operational Strategies*, American Economic Review, v91, 391–395.

5. Allayannis, G., and J. P. Weston, 2000, *Exchange Rate Hedging: Financial versus Operational Strategies*, American Economic Review.

6. To standardize value, Allayannis and Weston looked at the market value as a percent of book value. Companies that hedged foreign currency risk by using derivatives traded at higher market values, relative to book value, than companies that did not.

7. Pramborg, B., 2002, *Derivatives Hedging, Geographical Diversification and Firm Value*, Working Paper, Stockholm University.

8. These estimates are obtained from I/B/E/S, a service that consolidates earnings estimates from analysts.

9. Microsoft preserved its credibility with analysts by also letting them know when their estimates were too low. Firms that are consistently pessimistic in their analyst presentations lose their credibility and consequently their effectiveness in managing earnings.

10. Firms that bought Windows 95 in 1995 also bought the right to upgrades and support in 1996 and 1997. Microsoft could have shown these as revenues in 1995.

11. Forbes magazine carried an article on March 6, 2000, on MicroStrategy; here is an excerpt: "On Oct. 4 MicroStrategy and NCR announced what they described as a $52.5 million licensing and technology agreement. NCR agreed to pay MicroStrategy $27.5 million to license its software. MicroStrategy bought an NCR unit that had been a competitor for what was then $14 million in stock and agreed to pay $11 million cash for a data warehousing system. MicroStrategy reported $17.5 million of the licensing money as revenue in the third quarter, which had closed four days earlier."

12. Only three firms wrote off in-process R&D during the prior decade (1980–89).

13. Barnes, R., 2001, *Earnings Volatility and Market Valuation,* London Business School, Working Paper.

Company Name	Ticker Symbol	Earnings Predictability	Stock Price	Current EPS	Current P/E Ratio	Beta	Standard Deviation	Expected Growth in EPS: Next 5 Years
Ametek Inc	AME	95	$38.49	$2.66	14.47	0.90	33.24%	11.50%
Applebee's Int'l	APPB	100	$23.19	$1.58	14.68	0.95	40.35%	14.50%
Baxter Int'l Inc	BAX	100	$28.00	$2.06	13.59	0.70	32.56%	14.50%
BB&T Corp	BBT	95	$36.99	$2.89	12.80	1.05	27.01%	12.00%
BJ's Wholesale Club	BJ	95	$18.30	$2.09	8.76	0.95	37.65%	12.50%
City National Corp	CYN	95	$43.99	$3.69	11.92	1.00	28.92%	14.50%
Fannie Mae	FNM	100	$64.33	$6.52	9.87	0.95	31.71%	11.00%
First Midwest Bancorp	FMBI	100	$26.71	$1.91	13.98	0.85	19.98%	11.50%
Fortune Brands	FO	90	$46.51	$3.29	14.14	0.90	30.64%	14.50%
Freddie Mac	FRE	100	$59.05	$5.31	11.12	1.00	28.76%	12.00%
Gen'l Electric	GE	100	$24.35	$1.72	14.16	1.30	30.47%	11.00%
Golden West Fin'l	GDW	90	$71.81	$5.98	12.01	0.90	32.21%	16.00%
Horton D.R.	DHI	90	$17.35	$3.10	5.60	1.35	42.39%	17.50%
Household Int'l	HI	100	$27.81	$4.79	5.81	1.45	36.90%	11.50%
IHOP Corp	IHP	100	$24.00	$2.05	11.71	0.80	30.49%	11.50%
Johnson Controls	JCI	95	$80.17	$6.67	12.02	1.00	29.13%	11.00%
Kroger Co	KR	100	$15.45	$1.66	9.31	0.95	31.68%	12.50%
Lincoln Elec Hldgs.	LECO	90	$23.15	$1.86	12.45	0.75	37.04%	11.00%
Magna Int'l 'A'	MGA	95	$56.15	$6.49	8.65	0.90	27.29%	10.50%
Moog Inc 'A'	MOG/A	95	$31.04	$2.67	11.63	0.80	50.50%	10.50%
North Fork Bancorp	NFB	90	$33.74	$2.60	12.98	1.05	26.36%	12.50%
PMI Group	PMI	100	$30.04	$3.97	7.57	1.05	39.16%	12.00%
Polaris Inds	PII	100	$58.60	$4.60	12.74	1.00	33.72%	12.00%
Popular Inc	BPOP	100	$33.80	$2.68	12.61	0.85	29.27%	12.00%
Roslyn Bancorp	RSLN	90	$18.03	$1.85	9.75	1.00	30.14%	14.50%
Ruby Tuesday	RI	95	$17.29	$1.35	12.81	0.80	39.72%	19.00%

(continued)

Stable Earnings, Growth Potential and Low Risk (*Continued*)

Company Name	Ticker Symbol	Earnings Predictability	Stock Price	Current EPS	Current P/E Ratio	Beta	Standard Deviation	Expected Growth in EPS: Next 5 Years
Ryan's Family	RYAN	100	$11.35	$1.16	9.78	0.70	34.86%	11.50%
Safeway Inc	SWY	95	$23.36	$2.57	9.09	0.80	31.50%	12.00%
SouthTrust Corp	SOTR	100	$24.85	$1.89	13.15	1.00	32.02%	11.00%
TCF Financial	TCB	90	$43.69	$3.30	13.24	1.05	28.52%	12.50%
Teleflex Inc	TFX	95	$42.89	$3.13	13.70	0.95	32.89%	10.50%
Universal Forest	UFPI	90	$21.32	$2.08	10.25	0.80	34.15%	12.00%
Washington Federal	WFSL	90	$24.85	$2.32	10.71	0.90	32.91%	11.50%
WellPoint Health Ntwks	WLP	95	$71.16	$4.85	14.67	0.80	29.66%	21.50%
Wendy's Int'l	WEN	95	$27.07	$1.95	13.88	0.60	34.37%	14.50%
Zions Bancorp	ZION	100	$39.35	$3.82	10.30	1.05	31.19%	10.50%

6

IN SEARCH OF EXCELLENCE: ARE GOOD COMPANIES GOOD INVESTMENTS?

PETRA'S SEARCH FOR EXCELLENCE

Petra was an avid reader of management strategy books, and she was convinced that she had found a way to make money on stocks. After all, the strategy books she read often had case studies about the best-managed and the worst-managed companies and the skills (or lack thereof) of the managers in these firms. All she had to do was find the best-run companies in the market and put her money in them and the returns would surely follow. In a stroke of luck, Petra found a listing of the 20 best companies in the United States in *Fortune Magazine* and it was not long before she had all 20 stocks in her portfolio. As she bought the stocks, Petra did notice three things. One was that the stocks traded at lofty multiples of earnings relative to their competitors. The second was that these stocks were widely held by mutual funds and pension funds. The third was that equity research analysts expected these companies to continue to deliver high earnings growth in the future, which Petra took as a good sign.

A year later, Petra was disappointed. While most of the companies in her portfolio were still considered well run and well managed, the stocks had not done well. In fact, she found the market reacting negatively to what she considered good news from these companies; an increase in earnings of 25% was often categorized as bad news because investors were expecting a growth rate of 35%. Worse still, two of the companies in her portfolio fell off their pedestals when their managers were revealed as inept rather than superior. On these two stocks, Petra lost a lot of money. Having learned her lesson, Petra has decided to switch her portfolio to the 20 worst companies in the Unites States for next year.

Motto: When you are considered the best, very good is not good enough.

Buy companies with good products and good management and the investment returns will come. This is a story that you have heard over and over from impeccable sources. Warren Buffett, for instance, has been noted as saying that he buys businesses and not stocks. As with other investment stories, this one resonates because it is both intuitive and reasonable. After all, who can argue with the proposition that well-managed companies should be worth more than poorly managed firms? As you will see in this chapter, the story becomes much more complicated when you frame the question differently. Will you make more money investing in companies that are viewed as well-managed and good companies or in companies that have poor reputations? In this chapter, you will consider the answer and the precautions you need to take when putting this strategy into practice.

CORE OF THE STORY

It seems so intuitive that good companies with superior management should be better investments in the long term that investors often do not need much convincing when they are presented with the argument. Consider some reasons given for buying good companies:

- *History backs you up*. If you look at a portfolio of companies that have done well in the stock market over long periods, you inevitably will find well-managed companies that have succeeded by offering needed products to their customers. Based upon this, some investors and investment advisors argue that you should put your money into companies with good products and management and that you will reap the rewards from this investment over long periods. Better management, you are told, will deliver higher earnings growth over time while finding new investment opportunities for their firms.

■ *Well-managed companies are less risky*. This is a secondary reason that is offered for buying well-managed companies. If one of the risks you face when investing in companies is that managers may make poor or ill-timed decisions that reduce value, this risk should be lower for companies with good management. The combination of higher growth and lower risk should be a winning one over time.

WHAT IS A GOOD COMPANY?

It is difficult to get consensus on what makes for a good company since there are so many dimensions by which you can measure excellence. Many people measure excellence in terms of financial results; good companies earn high returns on their investments and reinvest their funds wisely. Some investors believe that good companies have managers who listen and respond to their stockholders' best interests and that corporate governance is the key. Finally, still others believe that good companies respond not just to stockholders but also to other stakeholders, including their customers, employees and society. Thus, you can have companies that make it on one list and not another. For instance, GE delivered superb financial results under Jack Welch but corporate governance was weak at the company. Conversely, Ben and Jerry's was ranked highly for social responsibility in the 1990s but faced financial disaster during the period.

FINANCIAL PERFORMANCE

The simplest and most direct measure of how good a company is and how well it is run by its management is the firm's financial performance. A well-run company should raise capital as cheaply as it can, husband well the capital that it has to invest, and find worthwhile investments for the capital. In the process, it should enrich investors in the company.

Most measurements of company quality try to measure its success on all of these dimensions. To evaluate the company's success at raising and investing capital, you can look at the return it earns on invested capital and the cost of that capital. The difference between the two is a measure of the excess return that the firm makes and reflects its competitive advantages. In the 1990s, for instance, a dollar measure of this excess return, called economic value added (EVA), acquired a significant following among both managers and consultants. It was defined as follows:

Economic Value Added = (Return on Invested Capital –
Cost of Capital) (Capital Invested)

For instance, the economic value added for a firm with a return on capital of 15%, a cost of capital of 10% and $100 million in capital invested would be:

Economic Value Added = (15% – 10%) (100) = $5 million

A positive economic value added would indicate that a company was earning more than its cost of capital, and the magnitude of the value would indicate how much excess return the firm created over the period. The advantage of this measure over a percentage spread is that it rewards firms that earn high excess returns on large capital investments, which is much more difficult to do.

To estimate the quality of a company's stock as an investment is easier to do. You can measure the return that you would have made from holding the stock over a previous period by adding up the price appreciation and the dividends on the stock, but by itself, this exercise will indicate little, since you have to control for market performance during the period. You will have to compare this return to what you would have made investing in the market on a stock of equivalent risk during the same period. This risk-adjusted return will indicate whether the stock earned more or less than it should have, given what the market did during the period and the riskiness of the stock.

CORPORATE GOVERNANCE

Managers in publicly traded firms often forget that they run these firms for the stockholders and instead view their enterprises as personal fiefdoms. One measure of corporate excellence is the degree to which managers are responsive to stockholders. More responsive firms should be viewed more favorably by markets than less responsive firms.

How can you best measure management responsiveness? Looking at what managers say is close to useless since almost every one of them claims to have to the best interests of stockholders at heart. Nor is it easy to find clues in what managers do. One practical alternative is to look at how the board of directors for a firm is put together and how much power top managers are willing to cede to the board. Some CEOs employ the tactics used by WorldCom and Enron and put together boards of crony directors, with little or no power to oversee what managers are doing. Alternatively, others find groups of well-informed experts who will keep them on their toes and ask them tough questions.

In recent years, *Business Week* has ranked the boards of directors of large U.S. corporations according to a number of criteria. They consider the number of directors on the board, the number of insiders (employees or consultants) on the board, whether the CEO is the chairman of the board, whether the board regularly meets independently without the CEO to assess performance and set compensation and whether directors owned sufficient stock in the firm in making their judgments. For example, in 1997, the best-ranked corporate board was at Campbell Soup, which had only one insider on the board, compensation decisions were made independent of the CEO, and every director was required to buy at least 3000 shares in the firm. The worst-ranked board in 1997 was at Disney, where Michael Eisner packed the board with pliant directors, seven of the seventeen directors were insiders, and the CEO not only chaired the board but also was part of the committee for setting compensation. The *Business Week* list of the best and worst boards in 2002, with reasons for the ranking, is provided in Table 6.1.

TABLE 6.1 Rankings of Boards of Directors in 2002: Business Week

BEST BOARDS	WORST BOARDS
1. *3M:* Only 1 insider on a 9-person board. No directors with business ties to CEO.	1. *Apple:* Conflicts of interest as CEO of Apple sits on boards of companies whose CEOs are on Apple's board.
2. *Apria Healthcare:* Three shareholder activists on board. CEO is not chaiman of board.	2. *Conseco:* Board does not meet without the CEO present.
3. *Colgate Palmolive:* Directors own substantial stock and do not sit on very many other boards.	3. *Dillard's:* Seven directors (including CEO's children) have connections to the company.
4. *GE:* Recently added champion of corporate governance to board. Questions exist about Welch's retirement package.	4. *Gap:* Substantial self-dealing and interlocking directorships.
5. *Home Depot:* Only 2 insiders on 12-member board. Independent directors meet regularly without management.	5. *Kmart:* Passive board as company sinks deeper into trouble.
6. *Intel:* No insiders and has a lead director to act as counterweight to CEO.	6. *Qwest:* No outside director has experience in Qwest's core business.
7. *Johnson & Johnson:* Directors own significant amounts of stock and do not sit on more than four boards.	7. *Tyson Foods:* Of 15 board members, 10 have ties to the company.
8. *Medtronics:* Directors hold regular meetings without CEO.	8. *Xerox:* Too many directors sit on too many boards.
9. *Pfizer:* No executives sit on audit, nominating or compensation committees.	
10. *Texas Instruments:* Directors are well invested in company.	

Source: Business Week

In the aftermath of the corporate scandals of 2002, when investors in many companies discovered that errant boards had allowed CEOs to run loose, other services have woken up to the need to assess corporate governance. Undoubtedly, *Business Week* will have competition as these services devise their own measures of corporate governance at companies.

SOCIAL RESPONSIBILITY

While stockholders have a critical stake in the well-being of firms, other groups are affected by decisions made by managers; employees and customers, for instance, can be affected adversely by decisions that make stockholders better off, and society overall can bear a cost for decisions that enrich stockholders. In fact, proponents of what is called the balanced scorecard have argued that traditional financial analysis gives too much weight to what companies do for their stockholders and too little to what they provide other stakeholders in the firm. A good firm, they argue, does well financially for its stockholders while also generating benefits for employees, customers and society.

If you accept this argument, you are then faced with a practical question of how best to measure these benefits generated for society. While attempts have been made to quantify these benefits, the fact that many of these benefits are qualitative indicates that any measurement of social responsibility will be subjective. In fact, most rankings of firms as corporate citizens are based upon surveys, some of the general public and some of other firms in their peer group. Consider, for instance, how *Fortune* comes up with its widely publicized list of the ten most admired firms each year. The Hay Group, which is the consultant firm that does the rankings, takes the ten largest companies (by revenues) in 58 industries, including large subsidiaries of foreign-owned companies. They then ask 10,000 executives, directors, and securities analysts to select the ten companies they admire most in any industry. They also are asked to rate the companies in their own industries according to eight criteria: innovation, financial soundness, employee talent, use of corporate assets, long-term investment value, social responsibility, quality of management, and quality of products and services. To arrive at each company's final score, which determines its ranking in its industry group, they average the scores that survey respondents gave it on these eight criteria. The ten most admired firms of 2002 are listed in Table 6.2.

TABLE 6.2   Most Admired Firms in 2002: *Fortune Magazine* Survey

RANKING	COMPANY
1	General Electric
2	Southwest Airlines
3	Wal-Mart Stores
4	Microsoft
5	Berkshire Hathaway
6	Home Depot
7	Johnson & Johnson
8	FedEx
9	Citigroup
10	Intel

Source: Fortune Magazine

This list appeared early in 2002. A couple of the firms on the list ran into rough weather during the course of the year—Citigroup for its role in the Enron disaster and GE for some of its financial decisions and Jack Welch's pay packets. It is very likely that one or both firms will not make the 2003 list.

THEORETICAL ROOTS: BUILDING QUALITY INTO VALUE

Companies with good management and superior products should have higher values than companies without these attributes. There are few who would take exception to this statement. In fact, most valuation approaches incorporate these effects into the inputs, and the resulting value reflects these inputs.

INPUTS IN A DCF VALUATION

The value of any firm is a function of the cash flows generated by that firm from its existing investments, the expected growth in these cash flows and the cost of coming up with the capital needed for the investments. There are several places in valuation where you get to reward companies that have good managers and that have made good investment choices:

- The obvious place to start is with current earnings. Firms with good projects and superior managers should report higher earnings from their existing investments. These higher earnings should increase value.
- The growth in earnings for a company is a function of how much the company reinvests in its business and how well it chooses its investments. A firm that is able to find more investment opportunities that generate high returns will have a higher growth rate and a higher value.
- At some point, every company becomes a mature business earning its cost of capital (and nothing more) and growing at rates lower than the economy. A company that makes the right strategic decision and builds up substantial competitive advantages may be able to delay or defer this day of reckoning. The resulting high growth can increase value.
- Finally, companies with good managers may be able to reduce the cost of funding their assets (the cost of capital) by altering the mix of debt and equity and the type of debt they use.

As an example, companies like Microsoft and Wal-Mart are highly regarded because they seem to be able to continue to grow earnings at healthy rates, notwithstanding their sizes. If you consider this the result of superior management, you may value them on the assumption that they will continue to grow and earn high returns. This, in turn, will increase their values.

By incorporating the effects of good management and products into your valuation, you can avoid one of the biggest dangers in valuing firms, which is that storytelling can be used to justify growth rates that are neither reasonable nor sustainable. Thus, you might be told that a dotcom retailer will grow at 60% a year because the online retailing market is huge and that Coca-Cola will grow 20% a year because it has a great brand name. While there is some truth in these stories, a consideration of how these qualitative views translate into the quantitative elements of growth is an essential step toward consistent valuations.

Can different investors consider the same qualitative factors and come to different conclusions about the implications for returns on capital, margins, reinvestment rates, and, consequently, growth? Absolutely. In fact, you would expect differences in opinion about the future and different estimates of value. In a good valuation, the fact that a firm is better managed or has a stronger brand name should be incorporated into the inputs and eventually into value. There is no rationale for adding extra premiums for good management.

EVA AND EXCESS RETURN MODELS

In an earlier section, economic value added was defined as a function of three inputs: the return on invested capital, the cost of capital, and the capital invested in the firm. To see the connection between economic value added and firm value, consider a simple formulation of firm value in terms of the capital invested in existing assets and the excess returns that you expect to make on these assets and new investments in the future:

Firm Value = Capital Invested Currently +
Present Value of Expected EVA in Future Years

The value of a firm is the sum of the capital invested in assets in place and the present value of all future economic value added by the firm.

Consider a firm that has existing assets in which it has capital invested of $100 million. Assume that this firm expects to generate $15 million in after-tax operating income on this investment and that it faces a cost of capital of 10% in perpetuity. You can estimate the economic value added each year by using these inputs:

$$\text{Economic Value Added} = \$15 \text{ million} - .10 \times \$100 \text{ million} = \$5 \text{ million}$$

The value of the firm can be estimated from these inputs by first estimating the present value of expected economic value added over time. Since the $5 million in EVA is expected to last forever and the cost of capital is 10%, the present value (PV) is:

$$\text{Present Value of Economic Value Added} = 5 / .10 = \$50 \text{ million}$$

Adding this to the existing capital of $100 million invested in the firm generates a firm value of $150 million.

$$\text{Value of Firm} = \text{Capital Invested} + \text{PV of Economic Value Added} = 100 + 50 = \$150 \text{ million}$$

The calculations become a little more complicated when you expect the firm to take projects in the future that will generate excess returns, but the basic structure of the valuation will remain intact. The key insight, though, should be that the way you create value as a firm is by generating returns in excess of your cost of capital. Thus, a firm that grows at a substantial rate by taking investments on which it earns its cost of capital will become a larger but not necessarily a more valuable firm. Another way of presenting these results is in terms of market value added (MVA). The market value added, in this case, is the difference between the firm value of $150 million and the capital invested of $100 million, which yields $50 million. This value will be positive only if the return on capital is greater than the cost of capital and will be an increasing function of the spread between the two numbers. Conversely, the number will be negative if the return on capital is less than the cost of capital.

If you conclude that the ultimate payoff to having better management or a superior product or a more effective board of directors is in a higher and more sustainable excess return, you can see that the value of a firm with these characteristics will be higher than the value of an otherwise similar firm without these characteristics.

LOOKING AT THE EVIDENCE

Given the many and often divergent definitions of a good company, it should not be surprising that the evidence also has to be categorized by the definition used. You will begin this section by looking at the evidence on the relationship between the excess returns earned on projects by firms and returns earned on the stocks of these firms. You will follow up by examining whether stronger corporate governance or social consciousness translates into higher stock returns for investors. You will close the section by examining how services that rank companies according to quality, presumably using a combination of factors, do when it comes to finding good investments.

PROJECT QUALITY AND STOCK RETURNS

Will increasing economic value added cause market value to increase? While an increase in economic value added will generally lead to an increase in firm value, it may or may not increase the stock price. This is because the market has built into it its expectations of future economic value added. Thus, a firm like Microsoft is priced on the assumption that it will earn large and increasing economic value added over time.

Whether a firm's market value increases or decreases on the announcement of higher economic value added will depend in large part on what the expected change in economic value added was. For mature firms, for which the market might have expected no increase or even a decrease in economic value added, the announcement of an increase will be good news and cause the market value to increase. For firms that are perceived to have good growth opportunities and are expected to report an increase in economic value added, the market value will decline if the announced increase in economic value added does not measure up to expectations. This should be no surprise to investors, who have recognized this phenomenon with earnings per share for decades; the earnings announcements of firms are judged against expectations, and the earnings surprise is what drives prices.

You would therefore not expect any correlation between the magnitude of the economic value added and stock returns or even between the change in economic value added and stock returns. Stocks that report the biggest increases in economic value added should not necessarily earn high returns for their stockholders.[1] These hypotheses are confirmed by a study done by Richard Bernstein at Merrill Lynch, who examined the relationship between EVA and stock returns.

- A portfolio of the 50 firms that had the highest absolute levels of economic value added earned an annual return on 12.9% between February 1987 and February 1997, while the S&P index returned 13.1% a year over the same period.[2]
- A portfolio of the 50 firms that had the highest growth rates in economic value added over the previous year earned an annual return of 12.8% over the same period.[3]

In short, investing in companies just because they earned large excess returns last year or increased their excess returns the most in the last year is not a winning strategy.

THE PAYOFF TO CORPORATE GOVERNANCE

Are companies with stronger boards of directors and corporate governance principles better investments than firms without these characteristics? While the overall evidence on this question is mixed, it is quite clear that stock prices generally go up when firms move to give their stockholders more power.

Consider first the evidence on the link between the board of directors and value. Research indicates that firms with smaller and more activist boards trade at higher values relative to companies with larger and passive boards. Price Waterhouse, in an examination of corporate governance across countries, conclude that firms in countries with stronger corporate governance trade at a significant premium over companies in countries with weak governance.[4] However, there is little supportive evidence for the proposition that buying stock in companies with stronger corporate governance generates higher returns.

The studies that provide the most promising leads for a strategy of investing in companies on the basis of corporate governance principles are the ones that look at actions that strengthen or weaken corporate governance and the consequence for stock prices. For instance, the stock prices of companies go down when they adopt strict new anti-takeover amendments or change the voting rights on shares to give incumbent managers more voting power, both actions that weaken corporate governance. In contrast, stock prices tend to go up when managers are replaced or when a proxy fight is announced, actions that strengthen corporate governance.

THE PAYOFF TO SOCIAL RESPONSIBILITY

In the last decade, a large number of funds have been created to cater to investors who want to avoid companies that they deem socially irresponsible. While the definition of social responsibility varies from fund to fund, the managers of these funds all argue that investing in "ethical" companies will generate higher returns in the long term. Arrayed against them are others who believe that constraining investment choices will result in lower returns, not higher.

In a finding that is bound to leave both groups dissatisfied, an examination of 103 ethical funds in the United States, U.K.

and Germany from 1990 to 2001 found no significant differences in excess returns between these funds and conventional funds.[5] That is bad news for those investors who had invested in these funds, expecting an economic payoff to social responsibility. It is, however, good news for those investors who invested in these funds for altruistic reasons, fully expecting to pay a price for their social commitment.

BROADER DEFINITIONS OF GOOD COMPANIES

All the research quoted above can be faulted for taking too narrow a view of what constitutes a good company, i.e., that good companies earn excess returns or that they have more effective boards or that they are more socially responsible. You can argue that good companies may have all of these characteristics and that using a richer definition of good companies may yield better results for investors.

Investing in Excellent Companies. Tom Peters, in his widely read book on excellent companies a few years ago, outlined some of the qualities that he believed separated excellent companies from the rest of the market.[6] Without contesting his standards, Michelle Clayman went through the perverse exercise of finding companies that failed on each of the criteria for excellence—a group of unexcellent companies—and contrasting them with a group of excellent companies. Table 6.3 summarizes statistics for both groups.[7]

The excellent companies clearly are in much better financial shape and are more profitable than the unexcellent companies, but are they better investments? Figure 6.1 contrasts the returns these companies would have made versus those of the excellent ones.

The excellent companies may be in better shape financially, but the unexcellent companies would have been much better investments, at least over the time period considered (1981–1985). An investment of $100 in unexcellent companies in 1981 would have grown to $298 by 1986, whereas

TABLE 6.3   Excellent versus Unexcellent Companies: Financial Comparison

	EXCELLENT COMPANIES	UNEXCELLENT COMPANIES
Growth in assets	10.74%	4.77%
Growth in equity	9.37%	3.91%
Return on capital	10.65%	1.68%
Return on equity	12.92%	−15.96%
Net margin	6.40%	1.35%

$100 invested in excellent companies would have grown to only $182. While this study did not control for risk, it does present some evidence that good companies are not necessarily good investments, whereas bad companies can sometimes be excellent investments.

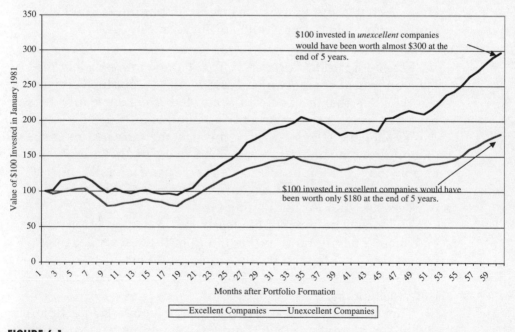

FIGURE 6.1

Excellent vs. Unexcellent Companies

Data from study by Clayman. The figure graphs the value of $100 invested in excellent and unexcellent companies in the 60 months after categorization.

S&P Stock Ratings. Standard and Poor's, the ratings agency, assigns quality ratings to stocks that resemble its bond ratings. Thus, an A-rated stock, according to S&P, is a higher-quality stock than a B+-rated stock; the ratings are based upon financial measures (such as profitability ratios and financial leverage) as well as S&P's subjective ratings of the company. Figure 6.2 summarizes the returns earned by stocks in different ratings classes; the lowest-rated stocks had the highest returns and the highest-rated stocks had the lowest returns.

Again, these findings are not definitive because the higher returns for lower-rated companies may well reflect the higher perceived risk in these companies, but it indicates that investors who bought the highest-ranked stocks, expecting to earn higher returns, would have been sorely disappointed.

***Fortune* Rankings.** An earlier section described how *Fortune Magazine* comes up with its list of most admired companies

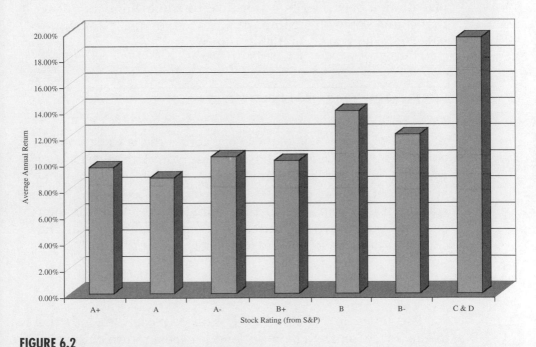

FIGURE 6.2
Annual Returns for S&P Stock Ratings Classes: 1982–91
Data on ratings from S&P. The annual returns are reported for stocks in each ratings class.

each year. In the process, *Fortune* also reports on the scores (from a survey of executives and analysts) for 500 companies. A study looked at the returns that you would have made investing in the 50 most admired and the 50 least admired firms on the *Fortune* list each year from 1983 to 1995. The results are promising. The most admired firms earn a return of 125% in the five years after the portfolios are created, in contrast to the return of 80% earned by the least admired firms. These differences persist even after you adjust for risk and the differences in firm characteristics. The most admired portfolio did better than the least admired portfolio in 8 out of the 11 years in the sample.

These results are in contrast to those obtained from looking at excellent and S&P-rated companies. One possible explanation is that *Fortune* does incorporate more qualitative factors in its rankings, through its survey. These qualitative inputs may be the source of the added value. Whatever the explanation, it does offer hope for investors in high-quality firms that coming up with a composite measure of quality may provide a payoff in terms of higher returns.

CRUNCHING THE NUMBERS

Looking at how companies vary across the market when it comes to excess returns may provide you with insight into what characterizes good companies. You will begin by looking at the distribution of excess returns and economic value added across companies in the United States. You will then consider alternative measures of company quality and the companies that make the list with each measure.

ACROSS THE MARKET

The financial indicator that is most closely tied to the quality of a company's management is excess return earned by the company on its investments, that is, the difference between the return on invested capital and the cost of raising that capital. Embedded in this measure are all aspects of management. The capacity to make good investments is reflected in the return on capital, and the optimal use of the different sources of capital should result in a lower cost of capital.

While a return on capital that exceeds the cost of capital will generate a positive excess return, there are firms that earn huge premiums over the cost of capital. At the other extreme, there are also firms that earn very large negative returns on capital while facing high costs of capital. Figure 6.3 presents the distribution of excess returns earned in 2001 by firms in the United States.

You should note that this represents one year's numbers; The year in this graph is 2001. In this case, the recession during the year affected the earnings (and returns on capital) of many cyclical firms, resulting in negative excess returns for those firms. Notwithstanding this limitation, the divergence between firms in terms of excess returns is striking.

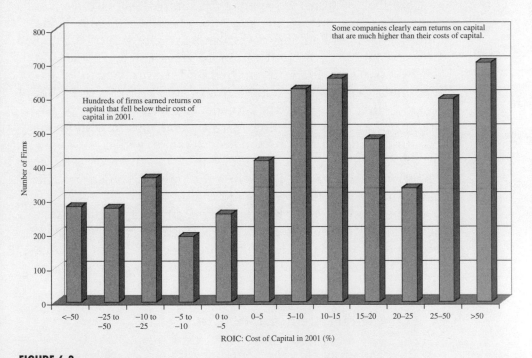

FIGURE 6.3

Excess Return: Distribution across U.S. Stocks in October 2002

Data from Value Line. The excess return is the difference between the return on capital (book value) and the cost of capital during the most recent year.

There are also wide differences in excess returns across sectors. Table 6.4 lists the sectors that generated the most positive and the most negative excess returns in 2001.

A closer look at these sectors provides clues on both the biases and the limitations of the excess return measure. Younger sectors, in which firms are early in the life cycle, such as e-commerce and wireless networking, tend to have very negative excess returns, whereas sectors with significant barriers to entry—brand names with beverages and household products, and patents with drugs, for instance—have the most positive excess returns.

To counterbalance the bias created by looking at excess returns in the most recent year, you can look at more qualitative measures of good companies. Many widely publicized ranking measures such as *Fortune*'s most admired companies were considered and rejected because they cover only a limited number of firms; *Fortune*, for example, ranks only 500 companies. In contrast, the measure chosen, which is Value Line's Timeliness Ranking, covers approximately 1700 companies and has been around for more than three decades. In fact, it has been widely researched and has proven to be exceptionally successful as a predictor of stock returns over that period. Value Line analysts consider a variety of factors, including profitability, earnings growth and earnings momentum, in coming up with its timeliness ranks, which go from 1 for the best (most timely) stocks to 5 for the worst (least timely) stocks. Figure 6.4 presents the number of firms in the Value Line sample that made each ranking.

As you can see from Figure 6.4, roughly half the firms that Value Line follows are categorized as average, having a timeliness ranking of 3. Fewer than 100 firms are assigned the top ranking of 1, and an equivalent number are assigned the worst ranking.

A SUPERIOR COMPANY LIST

The competing measures of company quality make it difficult to construct a portfolio of good companies. You could go with the companies that generated the highest percentage of

TABLE 6.4 Highest and Lowest Excess Return Sectors

INDUSTRY	ROC – COST OF CAPITAL	INDUSTRY	ROC – COST OF CAPITAL
Internet	–32.76%	Beverage (Soft Drink)	13.94%
E-Commerce	–17.78%	Home Appliance	14.10%
Wireless Networking	–11.80%	Medical Supplies	15.42%
Entertainment Tech	–8.07%	Electrical Equipment	15.79%
Telecom Equipment	–8.00%	Semiconductor Cap Eq	16.33%
Insurance (Prop/Casualty)	–7.11%	Beverage (Alcoholic)	17.12%
Investment Co (Foreign)	–6.85%	Petroleum (Integrated)	17.46%
Healthcare Info Systems	–3.77%	Household Products	19.53%
Entertainment	–2.46%	Petroleum (Producing)	19.92%
Manuf Housing/Rec Veh	–1.28%	Toiletries/Cosmetics	20.30%
R.E.I.T.	–1.04%	Tobacco	24.47%
Cable TV	–0.63%	Drug	24.93%

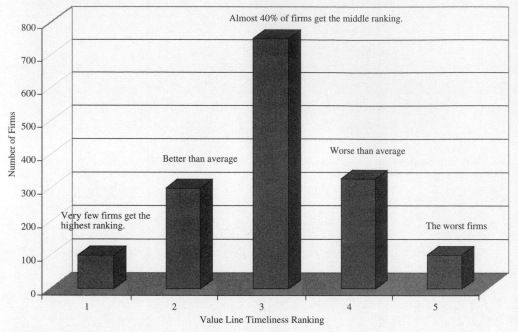

FIGURE 6.4
Value Line Timeliness Ranks
Data from Value Line. This table represents the number of firms that Value Line categorizes in each timeliness class: 1 is best and 5 is worst.

excess returns last year, but you run the risk of creating a portfolio of tiny companies (with substantial risk); note that it is easier for a small firm to earn a 50% return on capital than it is for a larger firm. To counter this, you could go with a portfolio of companies with the highest EVA. Since EVA is a dollar value, this will bias you toward very large companies that generate excess return and there is the danger that you are putting all your weight on financial performance in one year and ignoring qualitative factors.

You can meld the quantitative and the qualitative measures by looking for firms that generated economic value added of at least $50 million in the most recent financial year (which is 2001) while generating excess returns of at least 5% and maintaining a Value Line timeliness ranking of 1. Table 6.5 lists the companies that met all three criteria, and it is the "good company" portfolio that will be put under the microscope in the next section.

TABLE 6.5   Firms with EVA > $50 Million and Timeliness = 1

Company Name	Excess Return	EVA	Company Name	Excess Return	EVA
Dean Foods	5.55%	$280.10	eBay Inc	24.27%	$178.11
MGM Mirage	7.82%	$610.87	Charles River	24.67%	$95.65
Coca-Cola Ent	8.14%	$1,197.72	ITT Industries	24.72%	$550.82
Walter Inds	9.36%	$240.59	Reebok Int'l	25.64%	$171.71
AnnTaylor Stores	10.24%	$71.85	IDEXX Labs	26.40%	$60.88
Nissan ADR	10.73%	$4,323.34	Winn-Dixie	26.94%	$373.02
KB Home	11.04%	$277.90	Moore Corp	27.10%	$114.28
Jo-Ann Stores	11.56%	$50.32	Lincare Holdings	27.41%	$261.41
PepsiAmericas	11.76%	$317.98	Education Mgmt	28.13%	$81.27
Dentsply Int'l	12.03%	$157.27	Bio-Rad Labs 'A'	28.63%	$124.57
Mandalay Resort	12.22%	$410.25	Anheuser-Busch	29.97%	$2,962.04
Moog Inc 'A'	12.48%	$74.22	Procter& Gamble	30.04%	$7,514.72
Constellation Brands	12.92%	$307.04	Williams-Sonoma	32.92%	$160.95
Harrah's	13.10%	$620.06	Fossil Inc	33.43%	$69.25
STERIS Corp	13.22%	$78.21	First Health	35.85%	$186.59
SICOR Inc	14.10%	$58.11	Patterson Dental	36.28%	$132.71
Hovnanian	14.23%	$125.55	Dial Corp	37.71%	$187.70
Quanex Corp	14.53%	$68.36	Sysco Corp	38.59%	$1,218.96
Stericycle Inc	15.95%	$79.68	Forest Labs	40.90%	$414.55
Watts Inds 'A'	16.05%	$58.44	Int'l Game Tech	42.40%	$386.49
Alliant Techsys	16.12%	$228.99	Techne Corp	43.04%	$54.87
Schein (Henry)	16.71%	$125.08	UnitedHealth	43.14%	$1,581.15
PETsMART Inc	18.66%	$98.89	Block (H&R)	45.45%	$845.93

(continued)

TABLE 6.5 Firms with EVA > $50 Million and Timeliness = 1 *(Continued)*

Company Name	Excess Return	EVA	Company Name	Excess Return	EVA
RARE Hospitality	19.39%	$50.68	Winnebago	47.29%	$53.76
Universal Health	19.39%	$292.11	Varian Medical	47.66%	$111.58
Career Education	19.90%	$70.97	Electronic Arts	51.68%	$227.13
Amer Axle	20.10%	$281.46	Ross Stores	53.03%	$267.33
Ball Corp	20.12%	$298.84	Humana Inc	63.67%	$334.55
Lennar Corp	20.52%	$622.60	CDW Computer	64.59%	$248.20
Fisher Scientific	21.89%	$214.53	Chico's FAS	69.61%	$68.17
Dollar General	22.09%	$315.66	Right Mgmt	74.04%	$51.89
Michaels Stores	22.45%	$186.67	Polaris Inds	76.33%	$165.18
AutoZone Inc	23.06%	$480.64	NVR Inc	79.42%	$356.98
Tenet Healthcare	23.14%	$2,197.94	Apollo Group 'A'	171.27%	$183.58
Whole Foods	23.18%	$153.96			
Fortune Brands	23.18%	$705.54			
Express Scripts	23.62%	$236.32			

186

More to the Story

Any investment strategy that is based upon buying well-run, high-quality companies and expecting the growth in earnings in these companies to carry prices higher can be dangerous, since the current price of the company may already reflect the quality of the management and the firm. If the current price is right (and the market is paying a premium for quality), the biggest danger is that the firm will lose its luster over time and that the premium paid will dissipate. If the market is exaggerating the value of quality management, this strategy can lead to poor returns even if the firm delivers its expected growth. It is only when markets underestimate the value of firm quality that this strategy stands a chance of making excess returns.

Failing the Expectations Game

A good company can be a bad investment if it is priced too high. The key to understanding this seeming contradiction is to recognize that, while investing, you are playing the expectations game. If investors expect a company to be superbly managed and price it accordingly, they will have to mark it down if the management happens to be only good (and not superb). By looking at the multiple of earnings that you are paying for a company relative to its peer group, you can measure the expectations that are being built into the price. It is prudent to avoid companies for which expectations have been set too high (multiples are high), even if the company is a good company. Figure 6.5 compares the average PE and price-to-book ratios for the sample of good companies constructed in the last section and the rest of the market.

The market is clearly paying a premium for the companies that were categorized as good, with each of the multiples considered. With current PE, good companies trade at about twice the average for the rest of the market, and with current price to book ratios, they trade at about two and half times the average for the market. The difference is smaller but still significant with trailing PE ratios.

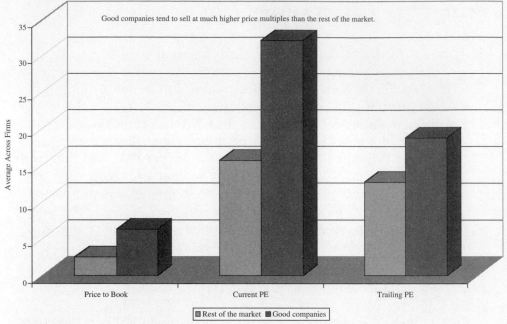

FIGURE 6.5

Pricing Differences: Good Companies vs. Market

Data from Value Line. The average value of each multiple is reported for both the good company port-folio and the rest of the market.

To eliminate companies whose pricing is too rich (high) from your sample of 71 good companies, introduce pricing screens. If companies with price-to-book ratios that exceed 4 or current PE ratios of greater than 25 are removed from the sample, the portfolio declines to the 22 companies listed in Table 6.6.

Imposing tighter screens, a price-to-book screen of 2.5, for example, will reduce the portfolio even further.

REVERTING TO THE "NORM"

Even if good companies are fairly priced, given current performance, you have to consider the possibility that companies change over time. In fact, there is a strong tendency on the part of companies to move toward the average over time.

TABLE 6.6 Good Companies That Pass the Pricing Test

Company Name	Ticker Symbol	Industry	Price-to-Book	Current PE
Kb Home	KBH	Homebild	1.67	8.51
Lennar Corp	LEN	Homebild	2.15	8.54
Amer Axle	AXL	Auto-oem	2.05	9.53
Nissan Motor Adr	NSANY	Auto	2.59	11.26
Walter Inds	WLT	Diversif	1.16	11.85
Reebok Int'l	RBK	Shoe	2.06	14.41
Moog Inc 'A'	MOG/A	Defense	1.75	14.76
Watts Inds 'A'	WTS	Machine	1.83	15.16
Winn-Dixie Stores	WIN	Grocery	2.79	15.46
Constellation Brands	STZ	Alco-bev	2.25	15.56
Hovnanian Enterpr 'A'	HOV	Homebild	2.78	16.41
Fossil Inc	FOSL	Retailsp	3.07	17.42
Rare Hospitality	RARE	Restrnt	2.19	19.60
Fortune Brands	FO	Diversif	3.51	19.69
Humana Inc	HUM	Medserv	1.56	20.08
Quanex Corp	NX	Steel	2.14	20.78
Harrah's Entertain	HET	Hotelgam	3.60	20.99
Mandalay Resort Group	MBG	Hotelgam	2.13	21.13
Sicor Inc	SCRI	Drug	3.53	22.74
Bio-Rad Labs 'A'	BIO	Medsuppl	3.66	23.53
Mgm Mirage	MGG	Hotelgam	2.12	24.02
PepsiAmericas Inc	PAS	Beverage	1.57	24.94

This process is called mean reversion and can be damaging for investors in companies that are considered well above average (as is the case with the portfolio of good companies). If these companies tend toward the average, the pricing is bound to follow.

Screening your portfolio for mean reversion is much more difficult to do than screening for overpricing, but there are two potential screens. The first is a pricing screen. You could buy good companies only if they are priced like average companies. In practical terms, this would imply that you would buy good companies only when they trade at price-earnings or price-to-book ratios that are lower than the average PE or price-to-book ratios for the sectors in which they operate. The second is to buy only companies that have sustained their standing for long periods, with the argument that they must possess strengths that do not dissipate easily. In practical terms, using EVA and Value Line timeliness rankings, you would buy only companies that have maintained a positive EVA exceeding $50 million each year for the last three years and a Value Line timeliness ranking of 1 in each of these years.

To screen the portfolio of good companies for mean reversion, we eliminated companies that traded at current PE ratios that were less than the average current PE for each of their industry groups. Table 6.7 applies the industry average current PE test to the sample of 22 firms that made the general pricing screens.

The four firms that fail the test are highlighted, leaving you with a sample of 18 firms that pass both the pricing and the mean reversion tests.

LESSONS FOR INVESTORS

The most succinct description that can be provided for an effective "good company" strategy is that you want to buy good companies that are not being recognized by the market as such. Given that good companies outperform their peers and have superior financial results, how is it possible to keep them a secret? The answer may lie in the market reaction to short-term events.

First, markets sometimes overreact to disappointing news from good companies, even though the news may not have really have significant long-term value consequences. For instance, assume that Coca-Cola reports lower earnings per share because of foreign currency movements (a stronger dollar reduces the value of foreign earnings) while also reporting strong operating results (higher revenues, more units sold, etc.). If the market price for Coca-Cola drops dramatically, it would represent an overreaction since exchange rate effects

TABLE 6.7 Industry Average Pricing Tests

Company Name	Ticker Symbol	Industry	Current PE	Industry Average Current PE
Kb Home	KBH	Homebild	8.51	13.84
Lennar Corp	LEN	Homebild	8.54	13.84
Amer Axle	AXL	Auto-oem	9.53	16.29
Nissan Motor Adr	NSANY	Auto	11.26	18.83
Walter Inds	WLT	Diversif	11.85	16.43
Reebok Int'l	RBK	Shoe	14.41	23.30
Moog Inc 'A'	MOG/A	Defense	14.76	24.40
Watts Inds 'A'	WTS	Machine	15.16	22.91
Winn-Dixie Stores	**WIN**	**Grocery**	**15.46**	**14.95**
Constellation Brands	STZ	Alco-bev	15.56	23.97
Hovnanian Enterpr	**HOV**	**Homebild**	**16.41**	**13.84**
Fossil Inc	FOSL	Retailsp	17.42	27.63
Rare Hospitality	RARE	Restrnt	19.60	22.77
Fortune Brands	**FO**	**Diversif**	**19.69**	**16.43**
Humana Inc	HUM	Medserv	20.08	32.43
Quanex Corp	NX	Steel	20.78	52.29
Harrah's Entertaln	HET	Hotelgam	20.99	23.59
Mandalay Resort Group	MBG	Hotelgam	21.13	23.59
Sicor Inc	SCRI	Drug	22.74	24.20
Bio-Rad Labs 'A'	BIO	Medsuppl	23.53	27.77
Mgm Mirage	**MGG**	**Hotelgam**	**24.02**	**23.59**
PepsiAmericas Inc	PAS	Beverage	24.94	34.64

tend to smooth out over time. You may be able to buy the stock at a bargain price before it bounces back up.

Second, entire sectors or even markets may be marked down in response to bad news about a few companies in the sector or market. In 2002, for example, all energy companies lost a significant proportion of value because of disastrous happenings at a few of them (Enron and WorldCom). If there are well-managed energy companies in the sector, as there inevitably will be, you may be able to get them at a low price when the sector is down. The same can be said for well-managed and well-run companies in emerging markets that fluctuate as a result of political and economic trouble at the country level. In 2002, for instance, exceptionally well-run Brazilian companies lost 40% to 50% of their value because of Brazil's perceived instability. You could have loaded up your portfolio with these firms and benefited from the bounce back as investors recognized their mistake.

To create a portfolio of well-managed companies that are trading at bargain prices, we impose a series of screens:

1. EVA greater than $50 million in 2001: This screens for companies that meet the financial test of earning excess returns on capital invested in projects.
2. Value Line Timeliness Ranking of 1 or 2 in October 2002: Expanding the ranking to allow firms with a ranking of 2 into the sample is required because only 99 firms have timeliness rankings of 1. This will allow you to make your other screens much more stringent.
3. Price-to-book ratio less than 2.5: This eliminates firms that trade at price-to-book ratios that are substantially higher than the market.
4. PE ratio less than industry average current PE: In addition to finding companies that are reasonably priced, you want to ensure that you have downside protection if your company starts moving toward the average company in the sector in terms of performance.

The resulting portfolio of 61 companies is provided in the appendix.

CONCLUSION

Companies that are well managed and well run should be worth more than companies without these characteristics, but that does not necessarily make them good investments. For a company to be a good investment, you need to buy it at the right price. Much of what was said in this chapter is directed toward putting this into practice.

What constitutes a good company? Given the many dimensions on which you look at firms—financial performance, corporate governance and social consciousness—it is not surprising that different services and entities have widely divergent lists of quality companies. Assuming that you create a composite measure that weights all these factors and comes up with a list of companies, you will need to follow up and screen these companies for reasonable pricing. You will also need to be aware of the long-term tendency of companies to move toward the industry average and protect yourself against this phenomenon.

ENDNOTES

1. Kramer, J. R., and G. Pushner, 1997, *An Empirical Analysis of Economic Value Added as a Proxy for Market Value Added*, Financial Practice and Education, v7, 41–49. This study found that differences in operating income explained differences in market value better than differences in EVA. In 1996, however, O'Byrne, S. F. (*EVA and Market Value*, Journal of Applied Corporate Finance, v9(1), 116-125) found that changes in EVA explained more than 55% of changes in market value over 5-year periods.

2. See *Quantitative Viewpoint*, Merrill Lynch, December 19, 1997.

3. See *Quantitative Viewpoint*, Merrill Lynch, February 3, 1998.

4. Price Waterhouse, *The Opacity Index*, www.pricewaterhouse.com.

5. Bauer, R., K. Koedijk and R. Otten, 2002, *International Evidence on Ethical Mutual Fund Performance and Investment Style*, Working paper, SSRN.

6. Peters, T., 1988, *In Search of Excellence: Lessons from America's Best Run Companies*, Warner Books.

7. Clayman, Michelle, 1994, *Excellence Revisited*, Financial Analysts Journal, May/June, 61–66.

APPENDIX:
GOOD COMPANIES WITH REASONABLE PRICING

Company Name	Ticker Symbol	Industry	EVA	Price-to-Book	Projected Growth Rate	Current PE	Industry Average PE
Omnicare Inc	OCR	DRUGSTOR	$154.81	1.71	19.50%	21.99	57.31
Quanex Corp	NX	STEEL	$68.36	2.14	11.50%	20.78	52.59
Hercules Inc	HPC	CHEMSPEC	$332.42	1.48	8.50%	0.00	23.48
Sunrise Asst. Living	SRZ	MEDSERV	$84.03	1.14	24.00%	9.87	32.42
Korea Electric Adr	KEP	FGNEUTIL	$5,046.16	0.57	7.50%	4.22	26.29
Cendant Corp	CD	FINANCL	$1,225.77	1.67	16.50%	12.12	34.14
Crown Cork	CCK	PACKAGE	$528.85	1.07	23.00%	0.00	21.44
Shopko Stores	SKO	RETAIL	$122.82	0.52	4.00%	12.78	30.08
US Oncology Inc	USON	MEDSERV	$125.38	1.15	14.50%	15.62	32.42
Pacificare Health	PHSY	MEDSERV	$171.78	0.44	2.50%	15.85	32.42
Owens-Illinois	OI	PACKAGE	$636.25	1.02	2.00%	4.88	21.44
Autonation Inc	AN	RETAILSP	$266.62	0.89	17.00%	11.71	27.63
Burlington Coat	BCF	RETAILSP	$90.90	1.16	8.00%	12.55	27.63
Brown Shoe	BWS	SHOE	$58.36	1.11	8.00%	10.02	23.30
Russell Corp	RML	APPAREL	$91.31	1.02	7.50%	12.75	25.87
Pep Boys	PBY	RETAILSP	$117.30	0.87	20.00%	14.84	27.63
Humana Inc	HUM	MEDSERV	$334.55	1.56	21.50%	20.08	32.42
Dress Barn	DBRN	RETAILSP	$63.02	1.88	9.00%	15.78	27.63
Norsk Hydro Adr	NHY	CHEMDIV	$3,107.41	1.16	9.50%	10.98	22.24
PepsiAmericas Inc	PAS	BEVERAGE	$317.98	1.57	19.00%	24.94	34.64
Moog Inc 'A'	MOG/A	DEFENSE	$74.22	1.75	10.50%	14.76	24.40
Ikon Office Solution	IKN	OFFICE	$142.25	0.75	15.00%	14.36	23.62
Reebok Int'l	RBK	SHOE	$171.71	2.06	15.00%	14.41	23.30
Global Imaging Sys	GISX	OFFICE	$60.35	2.13	16.00%	14.92	23.62
Jones Apparel Group	JNY	APPAREL	$340.06	2.14	11.00%	17.30	25.87
Constellation Brands	STZ	ALCO-BEV	$307.04	2.25	16.00%	15.56	23.97
Paxar Corp	PXR	ELECTRNX	$52.04	2.05	12.50%	18.01	26.09

Good Companies with Reasonable Pricing (*Continued*)

Company Name	Ticker Symbol	Industry	EVA	Price-to-Book	Projected Growth Rate	Current PE	Industry Average PE
Universal Forest	UFPI	BUILDING	$64.01	1.32	12.00%	9.23	17.01
Watts Inds 'A'	WTS	MACHINE	$58.44	1.83	14.00%	15.16	22.91
Republic Services	RSG	ENVIRONM	$409.77	1.83	11.00%	15.17	22.75
Dillard's Inc	DDS	RETAIL	$178.60	0.56	16.50%	22.79	30.08
Centex Corp	CTX	HOMEBILD	$444.67	1.27	17.00%	7.02	13.84
Amer Axle	AXL	AUTO-OEM	$281.46	2.05	14.50%	9.53	16.29
Ryland Group	RYL	HOMEBILD	$226.34	1.75	15.50%	7.21	13.84
Ralcorp Holdings	RAH	FOODPROC	$77.16	1.59	15.50%	16.04	21.78
Kerzner Int'l Ltd	KZL	HOTELGAM	$60.64	0.98	9.00%	17.96	23.59
Pulte Homes	PHM	HOMEBILD	$282.63	1.13	15.00%	8.49	13.84
Kb Home	KBH	HOMEBILD	$277.90	1.67	15.00%	8.51	13.84
Lennar Corp	LEN	HOMEBILD	$622.60	2.15	18.50%	8.54	13.84
Coors (Adolph) 'B'	RKY	ALCO-BEV	$250.65	2.36	12.50%	18.74	23.97
Pactiv Corp	PTV	PACKAGE	$395.74	1.60	17.00%	16.38	21.44
Walter Inds	WLT	DIVERSIF	$240.59	1.16	20.00%	11.85	16.43
Int'l Speedway 'A'	ISCA	RECREATE	$131.27	1.88	15.50%	22.28	26.84
Honda Motor Adr	HMC	AUTO	$4,514.05	2.02	11.50%	14.33	18.83
Beazer Homes USA	BZH	HOMEBILD	$116.93	2.20	17.50%	10.22	13.84
Harris Corp	HRS	ELECTRNX	$62.91	1.62	15.00%	22.49	26.09
Horton DR	DHI	HOMEBILD	$265.60	2.14	17.50%	10.47	13.84
Rare Hospitality	RARE	RESTRNT	$50.68	2.19	15.50%	19.60	22.77
Exelon Corp	EXC	UTILEAST	$4,153.18	1.77	10.50%	9.93	12.99
Manor Care	HCR	MEDSERV	$323.75	1.94	19.50%	29.60	32.42
Borgwarner	BWA	AUTO-OEM	$196.46	1.06	8.50%	13.70	16.29
Union Pacific	UNP	RAILROAD	$2,060.02	1.56	10.00%	15.44	17.93
Mandalay Resort Group	MBG	HOTELGAM	$410.25	2.13	17.50%	21.13	23.59
Albertson's Inc	ABS	GROCERY	$2,200.98	1.72	7.50%	12.81	14.95
Johnson Controls	JCI	AUTO-OEM	$1,167.42	2.47	11.00%	14.80	16.29
Lear Corp	LEA	AUTO-OEM	$759.97	1.53	15.50%	14.87	16.29

Good Companies with Reasonable Pricing (*Continued*)

Company Name	Ticker Symbol	Industry	EVA	Price-to-Book	Projected Growth Rate	Current PE	Industry Average PE
Toro Co	TTC	APPLIANC	$96.60	2.11	13.00%	14.31	15.58
Teleflex Inc	TFX	DIVERSIF	$198.77	2.21	10.50%	15.28	16.43
AnnTaylor Stores	ANN	RETAILSP	$71.85	1.72	16.00%	26.74	27.63
La-Z-Boy Inc	LZB	FURNITUR	$101.50	1.82	10.50%	17.25	17.97
Raytheon Co	RTN	DEFENSE	$1,175.28	1.04	21.00%	23.98	24.40

7

GROW, BABY, GROW!: THE GROWTH STORY

IMELDA'S GROWING PORTFOLIO

Imelda was a conservative investor whose investment in the Vanguard 500 Index fund grew steadily from year to year, but she was jealous of Martha, her neighbor. Martha's portfolio doubled last year and Martha lorded it over Imelda. "Your portfolio is so boring," she would say. "How do you expect to get rich with it?" Finally, Imelda asked Martha for some advice and Martha told her the secret of her success. She suggested that Imelda buy growth stocks. When Imelda protested that these stocks seemed highly priced, Martha told her not to worry. Earnings would grow next year and the high price-earnings ratio would help, not hurt. Finally convinced, Imelda invested her money in the biggest growth companies she could find.

Unfortunately for Imelda, the next year was an awful year for the market, with the market dropping 20%. Imelda's portfolio did much worse. Some of her companies did report higher earnings, but not enough to keep markets happy, and their stock prices tumbled. Other companies went from making money to losing money, as the economy slowed. Imelda lost more than half her portfolio and her only consolation was that Martha did even worse. Chastened, Imelda sold her growth stocks and put her money back into the index fund.

Moral: Growth often comes with a hefty price tag.

Growth stocks are exciting, and investors who seek to make extraordinary returns are drawn to them for that reason. If you succeed at picking the right growth companies to buy, your payoffs can be huge. An investor who bought Microsoft and Cisco when they were small growth companies would have seen her investment grow 50-fold over a decade. Does it follow then that a strategy of investing in stocks with high growth rates will deliver high returns? As you will see in this chapter, succeeding at growth investing is very difficult to do for several reasons. The first is that growth can often be a mirage, since very few growth companies consistently deliver growth. The second is that not all growth is created equal; while some growth is value creating, some growth is value destroying. Finally, even the most attractive growth in the world may not be worth it if you pay too much for it.

CORE OF THE STORY

The sales pitch for growth stocks is easiest to make in buoyant markets when investors believe that growth is not only likely but also inevitable. In such optimistic times, investors are willing to listen to growth stories, and there are at least three themes they will hear:

- *If you want big payoffs, buy growth stocks.* If you want cash flows today, buy bonds. The allure of equity is that companies can grow over time, doubling or tripling revenues and earnings. While you may not receive an immediate payoff in the form of dividends from such growth, you will share in the success as the value of your stockholding increases. For the high returns that can make your small portfolio into a large one and you from a poor to a wealthy individual, you should be buying growth companies.
- *If you buy the right growth companies, there is no additional risk.* Anticipating your concerns that growth companies are riskier than mature companies, propo-

nents of growth stocks will argue that there is no additional risk if you pick the right growth companies to put your money in. After all, there are companies like Coca-Cola, Microsoft and Wal-Mart that seem to be have found the key to delivering consistent growth. If you can find common patterns or themes across these companies, you can look for them in the younger growth companies of today.

■ *Buying growth stocks is more tax efficient.* Historically, price appreciation has been taxed at much lower rates than were dividends. Since the bulk of the returns on high growth stocks take the form of price appreciation, not only can you delay paying until you sell your stock taxes, but when you do, you will pay less.

If you are not risk averse and seek high returns, you will be drawn to growth stocks as investments, in the hope of hitting the equivalent of a jackpot in your portfolio. A more moderate version of this story works for those who worry about paying too much up front for growth stocks. If you buy growth stocks at a reasonable price, what you receive as value from the higher growth will more than cover what you paid for the stock. This strategy, often titled GARP (growth at a reasonable price) underlies the strategies of many growth investing icons like Peter Lynch.

THE THEORY: GROWTH AND VALUE

A company that is expected to have high growth in earnings in the future should generally be worth more than a firm without this growth. Holding everything else constant, increasing growth increases value. But everything else cannot be held constant. To grow faster, you generally have to reinvest more into your business, and it is this requirement that creates a distinction between what can be termed "value creating growth" and "value destroying growth." Distinguishing between the two is central to a good growth investing strategy.

GROWTH IN A DISCOUNTED CASH FLOW VALUATION

While no one will contest the proposition that growth is valuable, it is possible to pay too much for growth. In this section, you will first look at the fundamental determinants of growth and then extend this discussion to look at the value of growth in both a discounted cash flow model and in relative valuation.

Determinants of Growth. When you are attempting to estimate the expected growth in earnings for a firm, you tend to look at how the firm performed in the past (historical growth in earnings) and what analysts following the firm estimate for expected growth in earnings in the future. With both historical and analyst estimates, growth is a variable that affects value but is divorced from the operating details of the firm. The soundest way of incorporating growth into value is to make it a function of how much a firm reinvests for future growth and the quality of its reinvestment. As noted in the last chapter, the expected growth in operating earnings for a firm is the product of the reinvestment rate (the proportion of after-tax operating income that is reinvested into new assets, long term as well as short term) and the return on capital the firm makes on its investments.

Expected Growth Rate in Operating Income =
Reinvestment Rate × Return on Capital

This formulation can be extended fairly simply to growth in earnings per share or net income by using equity measures of how much firms reinvest and how well they do it. For instance, you could look at the proportion of net income, rather than operating income, that is invested back into the business and the return made on just the equity investment in the project. The former is called the retention rate; the latter is the return on equity.

Expected Growth Rate in Equity Income =
Retention Ratio × Return on Equity

Why link growth to these fundamentals? Doing so is useful at two levels. The first level is in bringing home the point that growth is never costless. To grow faster, you have to reinvest more, which leaves less available to return as dividends or stock buybacks. The second is that it allows you to draw the line between the type of growth that creates value and the type of growth that can destroy value.

The Value of Growth in a Discounted Cash Flow Model. To keep the analysis simple, start with the simple perpetual growth model that was used in the earlier chapters. Assume that you have a firm that is expected to have $100 million in net income next year, a return on equity of 10% and a cost of equity of 10%. Assume further that you expect earnings to grow 3% a year forever. To assign a value to equity, you first need to estimate how much this company will have to reinvest to be able to maintain its 3% growth rate:

Retention Ratio = Expected Growth Rate in Equity Earnings /
Return on Equity
= 3% / 10% = 30%

In other words, this company will be able to pay out 70% of its earnings each year. The value of the equity can then be written as:

Value of Equity = Net Income × Payout Ratio /
(Cost of Equity − Expected Growth Rate)
= 100 × 0.70 / (.10 − .03) = $1,000 million

A useful follow-up question to ask is what would happen to the value of the equity of this company if the earnings were not expected to grow at all in perpetuity (i.e., earnings were expected to be $100 million each year forever). First, consider the retention ratio that you would need to maintain a 0% growth rate:

$$\text{Retention Ratio} = 0\% / 10\% = 0\%$$

Since this firm can afford to pay out 100% of its earnings as dividends, you can value the equity in the firm as follows:

$$\text{Value of Equity} = \text{Net Income} \times \text{Payout Ratio} /$$
$$(\text{Cost of Equity} - \text{Expected Growth Rate})$$
$$= 100 \times 1.00 / .10 = \$1,000 \text{ million}$$

In other words, the growth in this firm does not add to the value of the equity in the firm.

If growth increases earnings, why is it not affecting value? The mystery is easily solved if you consider the relationship between the return on equity and the cost of equity. If, as in this case, a firm's return on equity is equal to its cost of equity, what it gains from growth (in terms of higher earnings in the future) will be exactly offset by what it pays to get that growth (in terms of reinvestment needed to sustain that growth).

When will growth create value? Assume, in the preceding example, that the firm had a return on equity of 15% instead of 10% (while maintaining a cost of equity of 10%), and that it was able to grow its earnings 3% a year in perpetuity. The retention ratio and equity value are computed below:

$$\text{Retention Ratio} = 3\% / 15\% = 20\%$$
$$\text{Value of Equity} = 100 \times .80 / (.10 - .03) = \$1,143 \text{ million}$$

Here, growth increases the value of equity by $143 million but only because the firm earns more than its cost of equity.

In the final example, assume that the firm earns a return on equity of 6% on its investments and earnings grow 3% a year in perpetuity:

$$\text{Retention Ratio} = 3\% / 6\% = 50\%$$
$$\text{Value of Equity} = 100 \times .50 / (.10 - .03) = \$714 \text{ million}$$

Here growth reduces the value of equity by $286 million because the firm earns less than its cost of equity on its investments.

The key ingredient in analyzing whether growth increases or decreases value is the quality of a firm's investments, where quality is measured by the return made on those investments relative to the cost of funding them. In general, firms that earn a return on equity (capital) that is greater than their cost of equity (capital) will generate value for their investors. In contrast, firms that earn a return on equity (capital) that is less than their cost of equity (capital) will destroy value, and at an increasing rate as growth accelerates. All too often, investors miss this link because they focus on the growth in proverbial bottom line, which is accounting earnings, and pay little attention to how efficiently the growth is being generated. Not surprisingly, companies that report high earnings growth see their stock prices rise over time. At some point though, there will be a reckoning; and when it occurs, it will leave disappointed investors in its wake.

THE VALUE OF GROWTH IN A RELATIVE VALUATION

Many investors prefer to use multiples such as the price-earnings or price-to-book ratio to assess firms, rather than use discounted cash flow models. The price-earnings ratio for a high growth firm can also be related to fundamentals, and the conclusions parallel those you reached in the last section. If you hold all else constant, a company with a higher expected growth rate in earnings should trade at a higher PE ratio than a company with a lower growth rate in earnings. But if you do not hold all else constant, the relationship between PE and growth becomes more complicated.

- If you compare two companies with similar growth rates and risk profiles but with different returns on equity, you should expect the company with the higher return on equity to trade at a much higher multiple of earnings.

This follows directly from the discussion in the last section of the relationship between the efficiency with which firms generate growth and its effect on value. Firms with higher returns on equity are generating growth far more efficiently (by reinvesting less for the same growth) than firms with lower returns on equity.

■ If you compare two companies with similar growth and returns on equity, but with different exposures to risk, you should expect the company with the greater exposure to risk to trade at a lower multiple of earnings. This is because the higher risk leads to higher discount rates, which in turn reduce the value of future growth.

The interrelationship between growth, return on equity and risk suggests that investors should be cautious about using rules of thumb for value. For instance, a widely used rule of thumb is that a stock that trades at a PE ratio less than its expected growth rate is undervalued. While this may be true for an average-risk stock, it will not hold for a high-risk stock (which should trade at a much lower PE ratio).

LOOKING AT THE EVIDENCE

Are growth companies better or worse investments than mature companies? This question has been answered in a variety of ways. For instance, researchers have looked at whether investing in stocks with high PE ratios generates high returns; these stocks often tend to be high growth companies. Others have adopted a more nuanced approach, whereby they examine whether stocks with high earnings growth that are reasonably priced do better than the market.

HIGH PE STRATEGY

The easiest growth strategy, albeit the riskiest, is to buy the stocks with the highest PE ratios on the market, on the assumption that these are growth companies in which the growth will deliver the excess returns in the future.

The Overall Evidence. The overall evidence on buying stocks with high PE ratios is grim. As noted in Chapter 3, when you look at stocks, a strategy of buying low PE ratio stocks seems to outperform one of buying high PE ratio stocks by significant margins. Figure 7.1 presents the difference in annual returns from buying low PE stock and high PE stock portfolios from 1952 to 2001. Note that these stocks were picked on the basis of their PE ratios at the beginning of each year and the returns represent the returns over the following year.

The returns are computed with two different assumptions. In the equally weighted approach, an equal amount was invested in each stock in each portfolio; in the value-weighted approach, the investments were proportional to the market values of the firms. On both an equally weighted and a value-weighted basis, high PE stocks have underperformed low PE ratio stocks. In fact, it is this consistent underperformance of

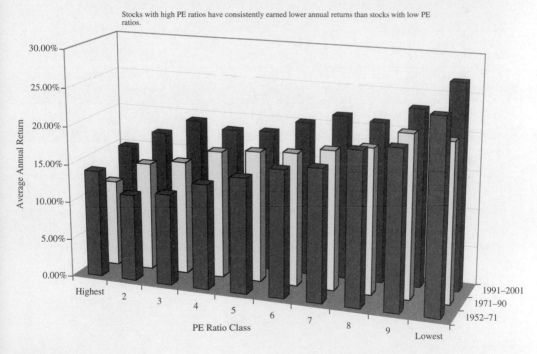

FIGURE 7.1

Returns on PE Ratio Classes: 1952–2001

Data from Fama//French. The stocks were categorized into classes by their PE ratios at the beginning of each year, and the returns were measured over the year.

high PE stocks that has led to the value investing bias that you often see in both academic and practitioner research.

The Growth Investors' Case. Given this sorry performance, what, you might wonder, attracts investors to this strategy? The answer lies in cycles. There have been extended periods during which high PE stocks seem to outperform low PE stocks. For instance, growth investing seems to do much better when the earnings growth in the market is low, and value investing tends to do much better when earnings growth is high. In Figure 7.2, you can see the difference between a low PE and a high PE portfolio and the growth in earnings in each period.

The performance of growth stocks versus value stocks is measured by looking at the difference between the returns earned on a portfolio of stocks in the 10% percent in terms of PE (growth stocks) and a portfolio of stocks in the lowest 10%

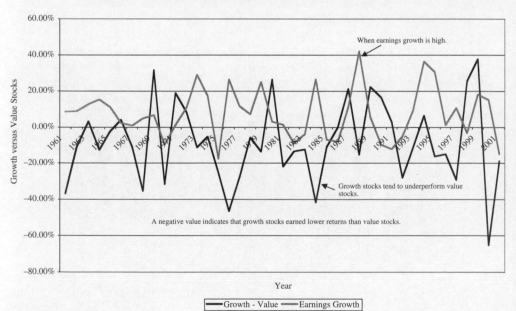

FIGURE 7.2

Relative Performance of Growth and Value vs. Earnings Growth

Data from Fama/French. The difference in annual returns between stocks with the highest PE ratios (growth stocks) and stocks with lowest PE ratios (value stocks) is reported in the figure.

(value stocks). Thus, a positive value indicates that high PE stocks outperformed low PE stocks in that year. Growth investing does best in years when earnings growth is low. This may be because growth stocks are more desirable in these periods since they are scarcer; if earnings growth is low for the market, there will be fewer companies with high expected earnings growth. By the same token, when all companies are reporting high earnings growth, investors seem to be unwilling to pay a premium for growth.

Growth investing also seems to do much better when long-term interest rates are close to or lower than short-term interest rates (downward-sloping yield curve), and value investing does much better when long-term interest rates are higher than short-term rates (upward-sloping yield curve). Figure 7.3 presents the relationship between the slope of the yield curve and the performance of growth investing.

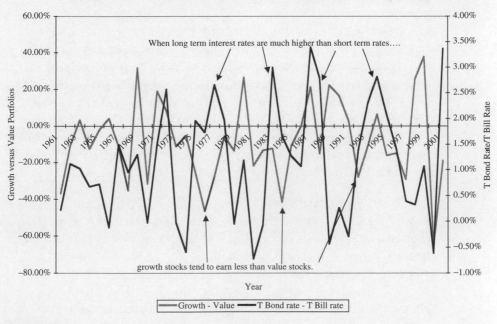

FIGURE 7.3

Relative Performance of Growth Stocks and Value vs. Yield Curve

Data from Fama/French. The difference in annual returns between stocks with the highest PE ratios (growth stocks) and stocks with lowest PE ratios (value stocks) is plotted against the difference between long term and short term rates.

The most interesting evidence on growth investing, however, lies in the percent of active money managers who beat their respective indices. When measured against their respective indices, active growth investors seem to beat growth indices more often than active value investors beat value indices. In a paper on mutual funds in 1995, Burt Malkiel provides additional evidence on this phenomenon.[1] He notes that between 1981 and 1995, the average actively managed value fund outperformed the average actively managed growth fund by only 16 basis points a year, while the value index outperformed a growth index by 47 basis points a year. He attributes the 32 basis point difference to the contribution of active growth managers relative to value managers.

GROWTH AT A REASONABLE PRICE (GARP) STRATEGIES

Many growth investors would blanch at the strategy of buying high PE stocks. Their mission, they would argue, is to buy high growth stocks for which growth is undervalued. To find these stocks, they have developed a number of strategies whereby you consider both expected growth and the current pricing of the stock. You will consider two of these strategies in this section: buying stocks with a PE less than the expected growth rate or buying stocks with a low ratio of PE to growth (called a PEG ratio).

PE Less Than Growth Rate. The simplest GARP strategy is to buy stocks that trade at a PE ratio less than the expected growth rate. Thus, a stock that has a PE ratio of 12 and an expected growth rate of 8% would be viewed as overvalued, whereas a stock with a PE of 40 and an expected growth rate of 50% would be viewed as undervalued. While this strategy clearly has the benefit of simplicity, it can be dangerous for several reasons.

■ *Interest rate effect:* Since growth creates earnings in the future, the value of growth is a present value. In other words, the expected future earnings will be discounted back to the present by investors who want to assess its value. The value created by any given growth rate will be greater when interest rates are low (which makes the present values higher) than when interest rates are high. Thus, the stock with a PE of 40 and an expected growth rate of 50% when interest rates are 7% may find itself with a PE of 60 if interest rates drop to 5% but growth remains unchanged. It is not surprising, therefore, that portfolio managers who use this strategy not only find far more attractive stocks when interest rates are high but also find many emerging market stocks (where interest rates tend to be higher) to be bargains.

The effect on interest rates on the relationship between PE and growth can be best illustrated by looking at the percent of firms that trade at less than their expected growth rate as a function of the treasury bond rate. In 1981, when treasury bond rates hit 12%, more than 65% of firms traded at PE ratios less than their expected growth rates. In 1991, when rates had dropped to about 8%, the percent of stocks trading at less than the expected growth rate also dropped to about 45%. By the end of the nineties, with the treasury bond rate dropping to 5%, the percent of stocks that traded at less than the expected growth rate had dropped to about 25%.

■ *Growth rate estimates:* When this strategy is used for a large number of stocks, you have no choice but to use the growth rate estimates of others. In some cases, the consensus growth rates estimated by all analysts following a firm are obtained from a data service and used. When you do this, you have to wonder both about the differences in the quality of the growth estimates across different analysts and the comparability. Given that these estimated growth rates are at most for five years, you may penalize companies that have expected growth for much longer periods by focusing just on the five-year rate.

It is also possible that in low interest rate scenarios, very few stocks pass this screen and that you will end up with little to invest in.

PEG Ratios.   An alternative approach that seems to offer more flexibility than just comparing the PE ratio to expected growth rates is to look at the ratio of the PE ratio to expected growth. This ratio is called the PEG ratio and is widely used by analysts and portfolio managers following growth companies.

Defining the PEG Ratio.   The PEG ratio is defined as the price-earnings ratio divided by the expected growth rate in earnings per share:

$$PEG\ Ratio = \frac{PE\ Ratio}{Expected\ Growth\ Rate}$$

For instance, a firm with a PE ratio of 40 and a growth rate of 50% is estimated to have a PEG ratio of 0.80. Some analysts argue that only stocks with PEG ratios less than 1 are desirable, but this strategy is equivalent to the strategy of comparing the PE to the expected growth rate.

Consistency requires that the growth rate used in this estimate be the growth rate in earnings per share. Given the many definitions of the PE ratio, which one should you use to estimate the PEG ratio? The answer depends upon the base on which the expected growth rate is computed. If the expected growth rate in earnings per share is based upon earnings in the most recent year (current earnings), the PE ratio that should be used is the current PE ratio. If based upon trailing earnings, the PE ratio used should be the trailing PE ratio. The forward PE ratio should generally not be used in this computation, since it may result in a double counting of growth.[2] Building upon the theme of uniformity, the PEG ratio should be estimated using the same growth estimates for all firms in the sample. You should not, for instance, use five-year growth rates for some firms and one-year growth rates for others. One way of ensuring uniformity is to use the same source for earnings growth estimates for all the firms in the group. For instance, both I/B/E/S and Zacks are information services that provide consensus estimates from analysts of earnings per share growth over the next five years for most U.S. firms.

Using the PEG Ratio. How do analysts use PEG ratios? A stock with a low PEG ratio is considered cheap because you are paying less for the growth. It is viewed as a growth-neutral measure that can be used to compare stocks with different expected growth rates. In a study concluded in 1998, Morgan Stanley found that a strategy of buying stocks with low PEG ratios yielded returns that were significantly higher than what they would have made on the S&P 500. They came to this conclusion by looking at the 1000 largest stocks on the U.S. and Canadian exchanges each year from January 1986

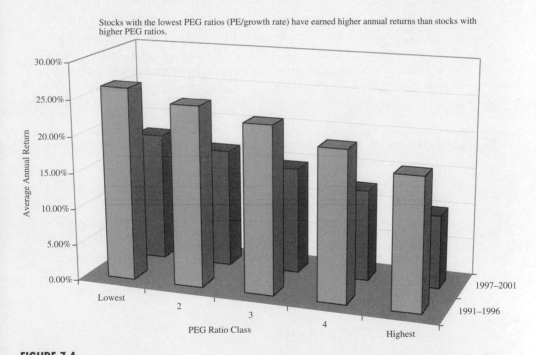

Stocks with the lowest PEG ratios (PE/growth rate) have earned higher annual returns than stocks with higher PEG ratios.

FIGURE 7.4

PEG Ratios and Annual Returns

Data from Value Line. Stocks were categorized by PEG ratios at the start of each year (PE divided by expected growth rate in earnings over the next five years).

through March 1998 and categorizing them into deciles according to the PEG ratio. They found that the 100 stocks with the lowest PEG ratios earned an annual return of 18.7% during the period, much higher than the market return of about 16.8% over the period. While no mention was made of risk adjustment, Morgan Stanley argued that the return difference was larger than could be justified by any risk adjustment.

This study was updated to examine how this strategy would have done from 1991 to 2001 by creating five portfolios at the end of each year based upon the PEG ratio and examining the returns in the following year. Figure 7.4 summarizes the average annual returns on PEG ratio classes in 1991–1996 and 1997–2001.

A strategy of investing in low PEG ratio stocks would have generated an average return about 3% higher than the average returns on a high PEG ratio portfolio, before adjusting for risk, during both time periods. Before you decide to adopt this strategy, though, this analysis found that low PEG ratio stocks are, on average, about 20% riskier than high PEG ratio stocks. In fact, adjusting the average returns on these portfolios for risk eliminates all the excess returns.

CRUNCHING THE NUMBERS

How different are growth rates across the market and what is a high growth rate? To answer these questions, you will need to look at the entire market and examine both past growth in earnings and expected future earnings growth rates. A legitimate follow-up question to this would be to wonder how the market prices grow; you can answer this question by comparing the PE ratios for companies with different expected growth rates.

ACROSS THE MARKET

In a market as large and diverse as the United States, it should come as no surprise that there are large differences in earnings growth across companies. This is true whether you

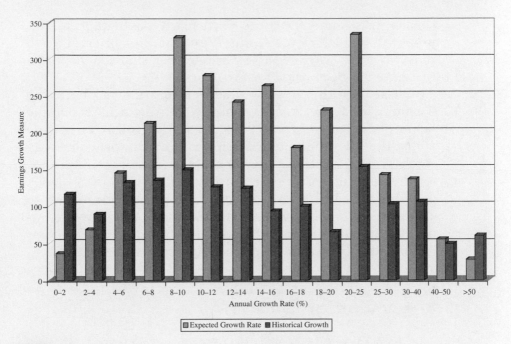

FIGURE 7.5
Earnings Growth: Past and Future

Data from Value Line. Past earnings growth is growth in earnings per share over previous five years.
Expected earnings growth is from analyst estimates.

look at past growth in earnings (historical growth) or at expected future growth. In Figure 7.5, you can see the distribution of earnings growth across U.S. companies for both past and future growth in earnings per share in early 2002.

The expected earnings growth rates are obtained from I/B/E/S, a data service that reports on analyst forecasts, and represents the projected annual growth rate in earnings per share over the next five years. The median projected earnings growth rate is about 15%, but there are firms with projected growth rates in excess of 50%. The past growth rate is the growth in earnings per share from 1997 to 2001, and the median for this growth rate is about 12%. There is a large number of firms for which you cannot compute one or more of these growth rates. For instance, you cannot obtain projected growth rates for firms that are not tracked by analysts;

smaller, less liquid firms are particularly susceptible to this problem. Similarly, you cannot estimate historical growth rates for firms with negative earnings per share or for firms that have not been listed for five years.

These growth rates do change over time as both the economy and the market change. During the economic boom period of the late 1990s, earnings growth rates rose across the spectrum, but the rise was greatest for technology stocks. A stock with expected earnings growth of 25% a year for the next five years may not have made the cut as a high growth stock during this period. In early 2003, after three years of economic stagnation and in much more subdued financial markets, a stock with earnings growth of 15% a year for the next five years would have qualified as a high growth stock.

THE VALUE OF GROWTH

Given the differences in earnings growth across U.S. companies chronicled in the last section, how does the market value these differences? Even if you accept the conventional wisdom that higher growth companies have higher prices for any given level of current earnings, you are still faced with the question of how much higher. To answer this question, we categorized companies into six classes according to projected earnings growth over the next five years; then we estimated the average price earnings ratios—current and trailing—for firms in each class in early 2002. The results are reported in Figure 7.6. The market clearly values expected earnings growth, since high growth companies have substantially higher PE ratios than low growth companies.

Why do these pricing differences matter? If you adopt a strategy of buying high earnings growth companies, you are likely to be paying very high multiples of earnings when you buy them. Even if the earnings growth comes to fruition, it is not clear that you will come out ahead as an investor, because of the rich pricing.

As noted in the last section, you can look for companies that trade at low PE ratios, relative to their expected growth

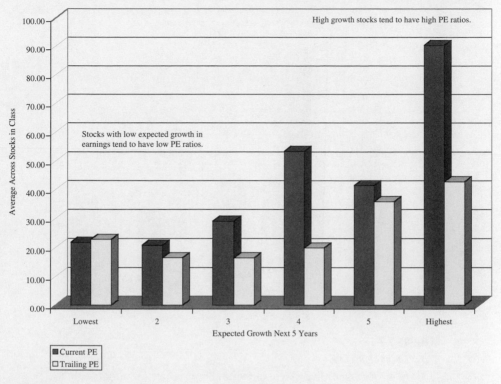

FIGURE 7.6
PE Ratios and Projected Growth: U.S. Stocks in October 2002

Data from Value Line. The expected growth rate in earnings per share is for the next five years and is from analyst estimates. The PE ratio is a current PE.

rate. This low PEG ratio can be viewed as "growth at a reasonable price." In Figure 7.7, the average PEG ratios are reported for the six growth classes used to analyze PE ratios in Figure 7.6. Unlike PE ratios, higher growth companies do not have higher PEG ratios. In fact, there is a tendency for PEG ratios to become lower as expected growth increases and not higher. This is because the price does not increase proportionately as growth increases; as the growth rate doubles from 10% to 20%, the PE increases but it does not double. However, it is the lowest growth stocks where this bias in PEG ratios is most visible; note that PEG ratios are more than twice as high as they are for the highest growth companies.

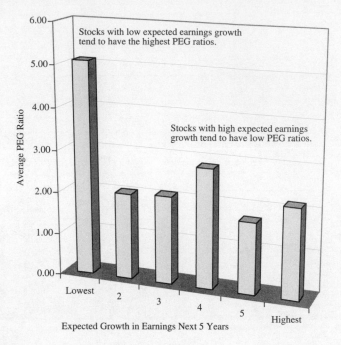

FIGURE 7.7
PEG Ratios by Growth Class

Data from Value Line. Stocks were categorized by expected earnings growth over next five years into five classes. The average PEG ratios of firms in each class is reported.

A HIGH GROWTH PORTFOLIO

As Figure 7.6 makes clear, investing in a portfolio of companies with high earnings growth can expose you to the serious danger of overpaying. To avoid this problem, we create a portfolio of high growth companies, using two cutoff criteria:

- Expected growth in earnings per share over next five years greater than 15%: This will eliminate any firms with negative earnings and also firms that are not tracked by analysts.
- PEG ratios less than 0.5: By restricting the PEG ratio, you reduce the likelihood of overpaying for stocks.

The resulting portfolio of 98 companies is listed in Table 7.1. The portfolio is surprisingly diverse and includes companies

TABLE 7.1 High Growth Firms with Low PEG Ratios: United States in October 2002

COMPANY NAME	TICKER SYMBOL	INDUSTRY	COMPANY NAME	TICKER SYMBOL	INDUSTRY
Optical Communication Prods	OCPI	Telequip	AmeriCredit Corp	ACF	Financl
Petroleum Geo ADR	PGO	Oilfield	ClearOne Communications Inc	CLRO	Telequip
Mail-Well Inc	MWL	Office	TTM Technologies Inc	TTMI	Electrnx
Carrizo Oil & Gas	CRZO	Oilprod	First Cash Inc	FCFS	Financl
SRI/Surgical Express Inc	STRC	Medsuppl	Wet Seal 'A'	WTSLA	Retailsp
Houston Expl Co	THX	Oilprod	Flowserve Corp	FLS	Machine
Comtech Telecomm.	CMTL	Telequip	Charlotte Russe Holding Inc	CHIC	Retailsp
United Rentals	URI	Machine	Newpark Resources	NR	Oilfield
Ryland Group	RYL	Homebild	QLT Inc	QLT.TO	Drug
HEALTHSOUTH Corp	HRC	Medserv	Sunrise Asst. Living	SRZ	Medserv
Brigham Exploration Co	BEXP	Oilprod	Smart & Final	SMF	Grocery
Skechers U.S.A.	SKX	Shoe	CryoLife Inc	CRY	Medsuppl
Rockford Corporation	ROFO	Electrnx	ECtel Limited	ECTX	Teleserv
Metro One Telecom	MTON	Industry	Gulfmark Offshore	GMRK	Maritime
Centex Corp	CTX	Homebild	Ace Cash Express Inc	AACE	Financl
Acclaim Entertainment	AKLM	Ent Tech	Hanover Compressor	HC	Oilfield
Nash Finch Co	NAFC	Foodwhol	Steelcloud Co	SCLD	Computer
Tweeter Home	TWTR	Retailsp	Grey Wolf Inc	GW	Oilfield
Quaker Fabric	QFAB	Textile	MEDAMICUS INC	MEDM	Medsuppl
Radiologix Inc	RGX	Medserv	AsiaInfo Holdings Inc	ASIA	Internet
Gadzooks Inc	GADZ	Retailsp	Amedisys Inc	AMED	Medserv
D & K Healthcare Resources	DKWD	Drugstor	Sanchez Computer Assoc	SCAI	Software
MSC.Software	MNS	Software	TRC Cos	TRR	Environm
Lennar Corp	LEN	Homebild	Administaff Inc	ASF	Human
Entegris Inc	ENTG	Semicond	Nautilus Group Inc	NLS	Retailsp
Varian Semiconductor Equip	VSEA	Semicond	Performance Tech Inc	PTIX	Teleserv
TTI Team Telecom Intl	TTIL	Telefgn	Advent Software Inc	ADVS	Software
Seitel Inc	SEI	Infoser	Rubio's Restaurants Inc	RUBO	Restrnt
XETA Corp	XETA	Telequip	U.S. Energy Sys Inc	USEY	Utileast

(continued)

TABLE 7.1 High Growth Firms with Low PEG Ratios: United States in October 2002 (*Continued*)

Company Name	Ticker Symbol	Industry	Company Name	Ticker Symbol	Industry
Global Power Equipment Group	GEG	Machine	NVIDIA Corp	NVDA	Semicond
Norstan Inc	NRRD	Teleserv	Superior Energy Svcs	SPN	Oilfield
Innotrac Corp	INOC	Indusrv	Famous Dave's of America	DAVE	Restrnt
Orthodontic Centers	OCA	Medserv	First Horizon Pharmaceutical	FHRX	Drug
Shaw Group	SGR	Metalfab	Integra LifeSciences Corp	IART	Medsuppl
Sportsman Guide Inc	SGDE	Retailsp	Culp Inc	CFI	Textile
Green Mountain Pwr	GMP	Utileast	Fischer Imaging Corp	FIMGE	Medsuppl
NVR Inc	NVR	Homebild	Sierra Pacific Res.	SRP	Utilwest
Microsemi Corporation	MSCC	Electrnx	Edge Petroleum	EPEX	Oilprod
Universal Electronics	UEIC	Electrnx	Tripos Inc	TRPS	Software
Micromuse Inc	MUSE	Software	National-Oilwell Inc	NOI	Oilfield
Sonic Automotive	SAH	Retailsp	University of Phoenix Online	UOPX	Educ
Somera Communications Inc	SMRA	Telequip	PAREXEL Int'l	PRXL	Drug
Ohio Casualty	OCAS	Insprpty	Century Casinos Inc	CNTY	Hotelgam
Meridian Resource Corp	TMR	Oilinteg	Cholestech Corp.	CTEC	Medsuppl
LTX Corp	LTXX	Instrmnt	Lam Research	LRCX	Semi-eqp
Fleming Cos	FLM	Foodwhol	Warrantech Corp.	WTEC	Indusrv
EXFO Electro-Optical Engr	EXFO	Teleserv	McDermott Int'l	MDR	Diversif
Atlantic Coast Airlines	ACAI	Airtrans	DaVita Inc.	DVA	Medserv
Mobile Mini Inc	MINI	Metalfab	Labor Ready Inc	LRW	Human

from 31 different businesses. The key question, though, is whether there are hidden problems that you might be confronted with in this portfolio.

MORE TO THE STORY

There are three potential dangers in growth investing strategies. The first is that finding companies whose growth in earnings will be high in future periods may be difficult to do. Neither past growth nor analyst estimates of growth seem to be reliable forecasters of expected growth in earnings. The second problem relates to a point made at the beginning of the chapter: Growth can destroy value if it is generated by investment in projects with low returns. Third, you often find that high growth companies are also exposed to high risk; the benefits of growth may very well be wiped out by the presence of high risk.

IDENTIFYING GROWTH COMPANIES

You generally look at past growth in earnings or analyst estimates of growth in earnings in the future when you are trying to identify companies that will have high growth in earnings in the future. Unfortunately, both measures have their limitations when it comes to this task.

Past and Future Growth in Earnings. Is the growth rate in the past a good indicator of growth in the future? Not necessarily. Past growth rates are useful in forecasting future growth, but there are two problems.

- Past growth rates are extremely volatile and are not very good predictors of future growth. In an examination of earnings growth at U.S. companies in the prior decade in 1960, Little coined the term "Higgledy Piggledy Growth" because he found little evidence that firms that grew fast in one period continued to grow fast in the next period.[3]

In the process of examining the relationship between growth rates in earnings in consecutive periods of different length, he frequently found negative correlations between growth rates in the two periods and the average correlation across the two periods was close to zero (0.02).[4] If past growth in earnings is not a reliable indicator of future growth at many firms, it becomes even less so at smaller firms. The growth rates at smaller firms tend to be even more volatile than growth rates at other firms in the market. The correlation between growth rates in earnings in consecutive periods (five year, three year and one year) for firms in the United States, categorized by market value, is reported in Figure 7.8.

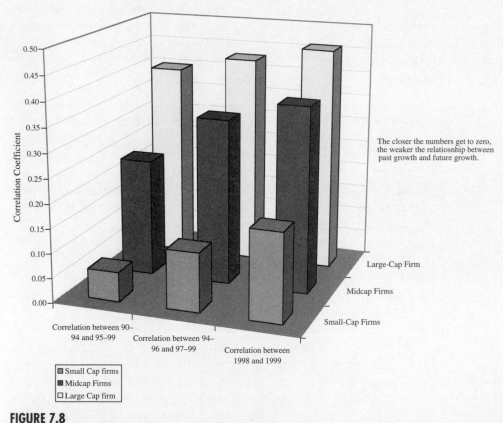

FIGURE 7.8

Correlations in Earnings Growth by Market Capitalization

Data from Compustat. The correlation is computed between earnings in consecutive periods.

While the correlations tend to be higher across the board for 1-year growth rates than for 3-year or 5-year growth rates in earnings, they are also consistently lower for smaller firms than they are for the rest of the market. This would suggest that you should be more cautious about using past growth in earnings as a forecast of future growth at these firms.

■ The second problem is that earnings growth rates at firms tend to revert to the average for the market. In other words, companies that are growing fast will see their growth rates decline toward the market average, whereas below-average-growth companies will see their growth rates increase. This tendency is chronicled by Dreman and Lufkin, who tracked companies in the highest and lowest earnings growth classes for five years after the portfolios are formed. While the highest earnings growth companies have an average growth rate that is 20% higher than the average growth rate for the lowest earnings growth companies in the year the portfolio is formed, the difference is close to zero five years later.

If past earnings growth is not a reliable indicator of future earnings growth, what are the alternatives? One is to use analyst forecasts of growth, which are considered in the next section, but this is an option only available for firms that are tracked by analysts. The other alternative is to use past revenue growth as a measure of growth rather than earnings growth. In general, revenue growth tends to be more persistent and predictable than earnings growth. This is because accounting choices have a far smaller effect on revenues than they do on earnings. Figure 7.9 compares the correlations in revenue and earnings growth over one-year, three-year and five-year periods at U.S. firms.

Revenue growth is consistently more correlated over time than over earnings growth. The implication is that historical growth in revenues is a far more useful number when it comes to forecasting future growth than is historical growth in earnings.

Consider the portfolio of high growth companies that was constructed in the last section. While this portfolio was

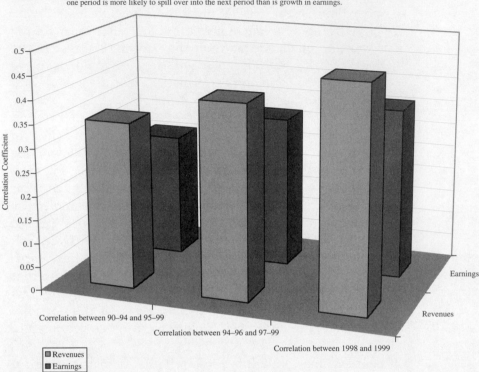

Revenues tend to be more highly correlated over time than are earnings. In other words, high growth in revenues in one period is more likely to spill over into the next period than is growth in earnings.

FIGURE 7.9
Correlation in Revenues and Earnings

Data from Compustat. The correlations are computed only for those firms that have enough historical data on earnings and revenues.

constructed using analyst forecasts of growth in earnings, you could consider an additional test. If you accept the notion that companies with high revenue growth in the past are more likely to sustain growth in earnings in the future, you could screen the portfolio to eliminate firms that have had low revenue growth in the past. Using a cutoff of 10% for revenue growth over in the last five years, you would eliminate 24 firms out of the portfolio of 98 firms.

Analyst Estimates of Growth. Value is ultimately driven by future growth and not by past growth. It seems reasonable to argue, therefore, that you would be better served investing in stocks whose expected growth in earnings is high. Here, you do run into a practical problem. In a market as large as the United States, you cannot estimate expected growth rates for each firm in the market. Instead, you have to rely on analyst estimates of expected growth. That information, though, is freely accessible now to most investors and you could buy stocks with high expected growth rates in earnings. But will such a strategy generate excess returns?

Consider what you would need for this strategy to be successful. First, analysts have to be fairly proficient at forecasting long-term earnings growth. Second, the market price should not already reflect or overprice this growth. If it does, your portfolio of high growth companies will not generate excess returns. On both conditions, the evidence works against the strategy. When it comes to forecasting growth, analysts have a tendency to overestimate growth, and the mistakes they make are highest for long-term forecasts. In fact, some studies find that using historical earnings growth can match or even outperform analyst estimates when it comes to long-term growth. As for pricing growth, markets historically have been more likely to overprice growth than underprice it, especially during periods of high earnings growth for the market.

There is one potential screen that you could use to capture the uncertainty analysts feel about expected growth. The data services that track analyst forecasts report not only the average of analyst estimates of forecasted growth for a given company but also the degree of disagreement among analysts. It should stand to reason that the average growth rate will be much less reliable for firms for which analysts disagree more about future growth than for firms for which there is a high degree of consensus.

SCREENING FOR RISK

Not all growth stocks are risky, but growth stocks do tend to be more volatile and risky than stock in mature companies. This should not be surprising, since you are investing on expectations of the future with growth companies, whereas you are basing your analysis of mature companies on investments already made. The practical consequence for investors is that a portfolio of high growth companies can expose them to significant risk.

You can see the contrast between high growth and stable companies when you contrast how the portfolio of high growth companies constructed in the last section measures up against the rest of the market. Figure 7.10 presents the difference on two measures of risk—standard deviation in stock prices and beta over the previous three years—between the two groups of companies.

High growth companies are much riskier on both measures of risk. Their stock prices tend to be much more volatile and they have significantly higher betas.

You could screen the high growth portfolio to eliminate companies that have unduly high exposures to risk. If you eliminate firms that have standard deviations in stock prices

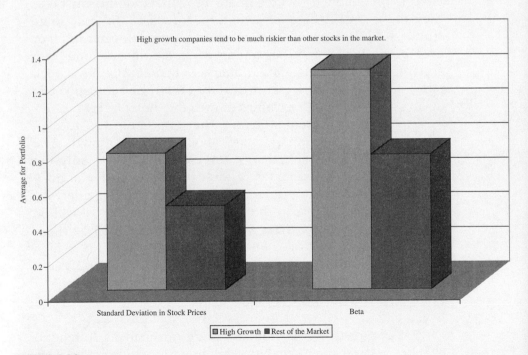

FIGURE 7.10

Risk Differences: High Growth vs. Rest of the Market

Data from Value Line. The beta and standard deviation for three years of returns is computed for the firm in the portfolio and for the rest of the market.

that exceed 80% or betas that are greater than 1.25, you would reduce the portfolio from 74 firms (after the screen of past revenue growth greater than 10%) to 23 firms. The 23 firms are listed in Table 7.2 below:

TABLE 7.2 Firms That Pass Revenue Growth and Risk Screens

Company Name	Ticker Symbol	Industry	Beta	Standard Deviation	Growth Revenue
Sierra Pacific Res	SRP	Utilwest	0.61	47.99	13.00%
Ryland Group	RYL	Homebild	0.93	45.4	13.50%
TRC Cos	TRR	Environm	1.15	61.85	14.00%
Centex Corp	CTX	Homebild	1.01	42.05	14.00%
Newpark Resources	NR	Oilfield	0.73	54.37	14.50%
Gulfmark Offshore	GMRK	Martime	0.95	65.34	15.50%
Mail-Well Inc	MWL	Office	1.44	70.75	16.50%
SRI/Surgical Express Inc	STRC	Medsuppl	−0.15	57.92	17.50%
Comtech Telecomm.	CMTL	Telequip	0.96	72.59	18.50%
D & K Healthcare Resources	DKWD	Drugstor	1.16	79.37	19.00%
Wet Seal "A"	WTSLA	Retailsp	1.03	78.87	19.50%
Gadzooks Inc	GADZ	Retailsp	0.81	65.15	19.50%
Ace Cash Express Inc	AACE	Financl	0.32	35.22	21.00%
Lennar Corp	LEN	Homebild	0.71	38.1	24.50%
Shaw Group	SGR	Metafab	1.44	69.2	25.00%
Meridian Resource Corp	TMR	Oilinteg	0.94	70.82	25.50%
Houston Expl Co	THX	Oilprod	0.62	48.53	27.00%
Cholestech Corp	CTEC	Medsuppl	1	75.77	29.00%
NVR Inc	NVR	Homebild	0.59	49.11	34.00%
DaVita Inc	DVA	Medserv	0.78	70.12	34.00%
Labor Ready Inc	LRW	Human	−1.65	62.62	41.50%
QLT Inc	QLT.TO	Drud	1.21	72.38	52.50%
Famous Dave's of America	DAVE	Restrnt	1.14	61.3	54.00%

POOR-QUALITY GROWTH

Recall that higher growth can sometimes destroy rather than create value if the growth is generated by investing in assets that earn returns less than the costs of equity. A prudent investor should therefore consider not just the level of expected growth but also the quality of this growth.

The simplest measure of the quality of growth is the difference between the return on equity and the cost of equity. Other things remaining equal, you can argue that firms that earn higher returns on equity have higher-quality growth than

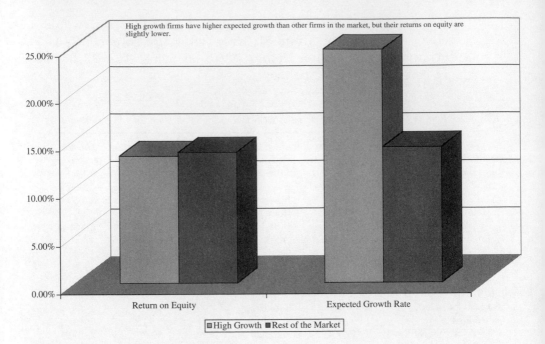

High growth firms have higher expected growth than other firms in the market, but their returns on equity are slightly lower.

FIGURE 7.11
Quality of Growth: High Growth vs. Rest of Market
Data from Compustat. The expected growth rate in earnings per share for the next five years is from analyst forecasts, and the return on equity is the net income divided by the book value of equity.

companies with lower returns on equity. In Figure 7.11, the average return on equity earned by firms in the high growth portfolio in the most recent year is contrasted with the average return on equity earned by the rest of the market.

On average, the high growth firms have a slightly lower return on equity than the rest of the market, which is surprising given the large advantage they have on expected growth rates. This suggests that there are firms in the high growth portfolio with low or negative returns on equity. If you added a condition that firms in the high growth portfolio would need to earn at least a 10% return on equity to be good investments, the portfolio of 23 firms listed in Table 7.2 shrinks to the 12 companies listed in Table 7.3.

TABLE 7.3 Firms That Pass Revenue Growth, Risk and Quality Growth Screens

Company Name	Ticker Symbol	ROE	Projected Growth Rate	Current PE	Sales Growth 5-Year	Beta 3-Year	Std Dev 3-Year
Ryland Group	RYL	27.93%	15.50%	7.21	13.5	0.93	45.4
Centex Corp	CTX	18.65%	17.00%	7.02	14	1.01	42.05
TRC Cos	TRR	14.03%	25.00%	12.37	14	1.15	61.85
Gulfmark Offshore	GMRK	20.39%	25.00%	7.09	15.5	0.95	65.34
D & K Healthcare Resources	DKWD	10.81%	18.43%	5.86	19	1.16	79.37
Ace Cash Express Inc	AACE	15.28%	25.00%	8.31	21	0.32	35.22
Lennar Corp	LEN	26.96%	18.50%	8.54	24.5	0.71	38.1
Shaw Group	SGR	14.42%	20.00%	8.90	25	1.44	69.2
Houston Expl Co	THX	12.33%	15.00%	7.49	27	0.62	48.53
Cholestech Corp	CTEC	15.53%	40.00%	14.52	29	1	75.77
DaVita Inc	DVA	21.74%	52.00%	15.90	34	0.78	70.12

LESSONS FOR INVESTORS

A strategy of investing in high growth companies, based solely upon past earnings growth or analyst projections of growth, can be dangerous for several reasons. You will need to screen this portfolio to make sure that you are not overpaying for the growth, that the growth can be sustained, that the risk exposure is not excessive and that it is high-quality growth. To accomplish these objectives, we screened the universe of U.S. companies with the following criteria:

- *Growth screens:* Only companies with projected earnings growth greater than 15% over the next five years were considered for the portfolio. This does eliminate smaller firms that are not followed by analysts, but expected future growth is too critical an input for this strategy to be based solely on past earnings growth.
- *Pricing screens:* Only companies with PE ratios less than the expected earnings growth (PEG less than 1) were considered for this portfolio. While this is not as strict a screen as the one used earlier in this chapter, it conforms to a widely used standard for pricing (i.e., that stocks trading at PE ratios less than expected growth rates are underpriced).
- *Sustainability of growth:* While there is no simple test for sustainability, the evidence seems to indicate that companies with high revenue growth in the past are more likely to sustain this growth in the future. Consequently, only firms with revenue growth of more than 10% a year over the last five years were considered.
- *Risk exposure:* To keep the risk in the portfolio under reasonable bounds, only firms with betas less than 1.25 and standard deviations in stock prices less than 80% were considered for the analysis.
- *High-quality growth:* Only firms with returns on equity that exceeded 15% in the most recent financial year were considered for the final portfolio. This is stricter

than the standard used in the last section, but high-quality growth is an important factor in the ultimate success of this strategy.

The portfolio of 27 stocks that made it through these screens in January 2003 is listed in the appendix to this chapter.

CONCLUSION

Every investor dreams about buying a young growth company and riding the growth to huge returns. There is no denying that growth can add value to a company, but it is not always true that higher growth translates into higher value. The value of a company will increase as expected growth increases, but only if that growth is generated by investment in assets that earn high returns on equity.

Even if a company's growth is expected to be value generating, its stock may not be a good investment if the market has overpriced growth. In other words, even the best growth company can be a bad investment if you pay too high a price and if the actual growth does not measure up to your high expectations. The essence of successful growth investing is to buy high growth companies at reasonable prices. In fact, a prudent growth investor will consider not only the magnitude of expected growth but also the sustainability of this growth rate—there is a tendency for high growth rates to converge toward normal levels over time—and the quality of this growth. Since growth companies tend to be risky, you will also need to control for risk in designing your portfolio.

ENDNOTES

1. Malkiel, B. G., 1995, *Returns from Investing in Equity Mutual Funds 1971 to 1991,* Journal of Finance, v50, 549–572.

2. If the forward earnings are high because of high growth in the next year and this high growth results in a high growth rate for the next five years, you will understate your PEG ratio.

3. Little, I. M. D., 1962, *Higgledy Piggledy Growth*, Institute of Statistics, Oxford.

4. A correlation of 1 would indicate that companies with high earnings growth in the last period can be guaranteed to have earnings growth in the next period. A zero correlation indicates no relationship, whereas a negative correlation suggests that high earnings growth is more likely to be followed by low earnings growth.

Appendix

High Growth Companies with Sustainable, High-Quality Growth, Low Risk and Low Pricing

Company Name	Ticker Symbol	Stock Price	Current P/E Ratio	Beta	Std Dev 3-Year	Proj EPS Growth Rate	Return on Common Equity	Sales Growth 5-Year
AutoZone Inc	AZO	70.65	15.1	0.95	39.43	18	62.12	24.5
Barr Labs	BRL	65.09	16.6	0.95	46.9	19	31.55	20.5
Bio-Rad Labs "A"	BIO	38.7	13.58	0.85	52.12	25.5	15.56	12
Biovail Corp	BVF	26.41	13.34	1.35	54.86	23.5	17.13	46.5
Block (H&R)	HRB	40.2	13.01	1.1	33.48	15.5	31.72	24
Cardinal Health	CAH	59.19	18.5	0.9	28.13	19	18.98	12
Catalina Marketing	POS	18.5	15.68	1.05	39.32	16	24.27	25
CEC Entertainment	CEC	30.7	11.9	0.85	40.47	16	18.96	13
Centex Corp	CTX	50.2	6.04	1.2	41.03	17	18.05	14
Darden Restaurants	DRI	20.45	13.91	0.8	40.93	16	20.92	11
DaVita Inc	DVA	24.67	12.21	0.95	69.9	59.5	19.47	34
Enzon Inc	ENZN	16.72	13.38	1.75	62.27	41	19.28	15
Express Scripts "A"	ESRX	48.04	16.57	1.05	58.35	26.5	15.03	57
GTECH Holdings	GTK	27.86	11.1	0.85	39.63	18	41.81	11
Harrah's Entertain	HET	39.6	12.65	1.05	32.54	19	17.13	15
Health Mgmt. Assoc	HMA	17.9	16.27	0.95	44.11	17.5	15.55	22
Lennar Corp	LEN	51.6	6.44	1.3	38.39	18.5	25.18	24.5
Lincare Holdings	LNCR	31.62	16.47	0.75	50.33	21.5	19.6	21.5
Lowe's Cos	LOW	37.5	19.95	1.25	40.22	22	15.33	17.5
Manitowoc Co	MTW	25.5	11.18	1.2	44.52	15.5	18.52	22
NVR Inc	NVR	326.5	8.55	1.2	46.76	21	67.82	34
Oxford Health Plans	OHP	36.45	9.8	1.25	42.81	19	63.38	13
Ryland Group	RYL	33.35	5.21	1.35	45.55	15.5	24.24	13.5
Sonic Corp	SONC	20.49	16.01	0.8	31.72	18	20.67	19
UnitedHealth Group	UNH	83.5	17.77	0.75	25.52	23.5	23.46	30
Universal Health Sv. "B"	UHS	45.1	15.34	0.75	41.17	19	16.21	19
WellPoint Health Ntwks	WLP	71.16	14.67	0.8	29.66	21.5	19.44	30.5

8

THE WORST IS BEHIND YOU: THE CONTRARIAN STORY

THE LAST RATIONAL INVESTOR

Jack was a loner with little faith in human nature. He was convinced that the rest of the world was irrational and becoming increasingly so, and he felt that herd behavior was the rule rather than the exception. As he read about a selloff on a blue chip company after an earnings report that fell short of expectations caused the stock to drop to $8 from its 52-week high of $45, he told himself that the stock could not go down much further. After all, the company had been around 50 years and had once been considered a market bellwether. He called his broker and bought 1000 shares at $8, convinced that it was only a matter of time before it bounced back. A few weeks later he checked the price again and the stock was down to $5, and he bought 1000 shares more, believing even more strongly that a rebound was just around the corner. Two months later, the stock had hit $2, and without a hint of self-doubt, Jack bought 1000 shares more and waited for his payoff. Four days later, the company announced that its CEO had resigned and that the stock had been delisted. The only consolation for Jack was that the stock price had finally hit zero and would not go down any further.

Moral: The crowd is more often right than wrong.

uessing when a stock has hit bottom is the source of much talk on Wall Street and it is often the basis for investment strategies. Contrarian investors are often willing to buy a stock after a sustained price decline on the expectation of a rebound. Their belief is that a stock that has dropped 80% to 90% from its peak is much more likely to be a bargain to investors. In this chapter, you will explore the underpinnings of this strategy and any potential limitations. As you will see, bottom fishing can be lucrative but it can also be dangerous, and only investors with the fortitude to withstand reversals succeed with it.

CORE OF THE STORY

By their very nature, contrarians come in all forms. Some draw on investor psychology to make their judgments and others rely on their instincts. They all agree that the stocks that have gone down the most over the recent past are often the best investments. At the risk of oversimplifying the arguments used by contrarians, here are two:

- *It is always darkest before dawn.* The best time to buy a stock is not when good news comes out about it but after a spate of bad news has pushed the price down, making it a bargain. The story rests on the assumption that the average investor tends to overreact to news—good as well as bad—and that investors who are a little less driven by emotion (presumably you and I, as contrarians) can take advantage of this irrationality. The story sells well, at least in the abstract, to those who have the least faith in human rationality. The assumption that investors overreact ties in neatly with the widely held view that crowds are driven by emotion and can be swayed by peer pressure to irrational acts. This view is reinforced in financial markets by the bubbles in prices—from the South Sea Bubble in the 1600s to dot-com companies in the 1990s—that show up at regular intervals.

■ *Lower-priced stocks are cheaper.* There is another and less rational factor behind the contrarian story. Stocks that have gone down a lot often trade at low prices, and there is a feeling among some investors that a lower-priced stock is cheaper than one that is highly priced. Thus, a stock that has dropped from $30 to $3 looks cheaper on an absolute basis to many investors and penny stocks (stocks that trade at well below a dollar) are absolute bargains. The danger, of course, is that the value of this stock (which is what you should be comparing the price to) might have dropped from $35 to $1 during the same period.

THEORETICAL ROOTS: THE CONTRARIAN STORY

To understand the contrarian impulse, you first need to establish a link between prices and information. As new information comes out about a company, its stock price will undoubtedly move, but by how much and what would constitute an overreaction? This section begins by answering these questions. It then considers an alternative view, which is that prices are not predictable and follow a random walk; this would represent a rejection of the notion that markets overreact to new information. The section closes with an examination of the psychological underpinnings of contrarian investing. In other words, what is it about human behavior that leads to overreaction in the first place?

INFORMATION AND PRICE

Any debate about whether markets overreact to new information has to begin with a discussion of the relationship between prices and information. After all, in every market, new information will cause stock prices to move; unexpected good news will generally push up stock prices, whereas unexpected bad news will cause prices to drop. If markets make mistakes in their assessments, the prices will be different from the true values of the underlying assets.

If you define market efficiency in terms of how much the price of an asset deviates from its true value, the smaller and less persistent the deviations are, the more efficient a market is. Market efficiency does not require that the market price be equal to true value at every instant. All it requires is that errors in the market price be unbiased, that is, prices can be greater than or less than true value, as long as these deviations are random. Another way of assessing market efficiency is to look at how quickly and how well markets react to new information. The value of an asset should change when new information that affects any of the inputs into value—the cash flows, the growth or the risk—reaches the market. In an efficient market, the price of the asset will adjust instantaneously and, on average, correctly to the new information. Figure 8.1 illustrates the impact of unexpectedly good news on the stock price in an efficient market.

The key, though, is that it is not good news per se that causes the price to increase but unexpectedly good news. In other words, a company that reports a 20% growth in earnings may see its stock price go down if investors expected it to report a 30% growth in earnings, whereas a company that reports a 10% drop in earnings may see its stock price go up if investors expected earnings to drop by 20%.

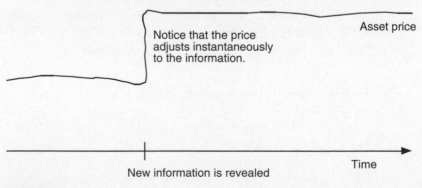

FIGURE 8.1
Price Adjustment in an Efficient Market

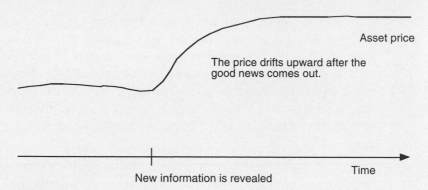

FIGURE 8.2
A Slow-Learning Market

The adjustment will be slower if investors are slow in assessing the impact of the information on value. In Figure 8.2, the price of an asset adjusting slowly to good news is shown. The gradual increase in stock prices (called a price drift) that you observe after the information arrives is indicative of a slow-learning market.

In contrast, the market could adjust instantaneously to the new information but overestimate the effect of the information on value. Then, the price of the asset will increase by more than it should, given the effect of the good news on value, or drop by more than it should, with bad news. Figure 8.3 shows the drift in prices in the opposite direction, after the initial reaction.

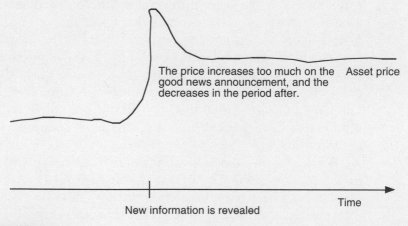

FIGURE 8.3
An Overreacting Market

Contrarian investors buy into this last view of the world. They believe that investors are more likely to overreact than to underreact and that large price movements in one direction will be followed by price movements in the other. Hence, they hold the conviction that you should buy stocks that have been knocked down the most in the market, since these are the stocks for which prices are most likely to increase in the future.

THE RANDOM-WALK WORLD

For four decades, academics have argued that investment strategies that are based upon the presumption that markets overreact or underreact are designed to fail because market prices follow a "random walk." In fact, Burton Malkiel's influential tome on investing, which outlines this argument most persuasively, is called *A Random Walk Down Wall Street*.

To understand the argument for a random walk, you have to begin with the presumption that investors at any point estimate the value of an asset based upon expectations of the future and that these expectations are both *unbiased* and *rational,* given the information that investors have at that point. Under these conditions, the price of the asset changes only as new information comes out about it. If the market price at any point is an unbiased estimate of value, the next piece of information that comes out about the asset should be just as likely to contain good news as bad.[1] It therefore follows that the next price change is just as likely to be positive as it is likely to be negative. The implication, of course, is that each price change will be independent of the previous one and that knowing an asset's price history will not help form better predictions of future price changes. Figure 8.4 summarizes the assumptions.

While the random walk is not magic, there are two prerequisites for it to hold. The first is that investors are rational and form unbiased expectations of the future, based upon all of the information that is available to them at the time. If expectations are consistently set too low or set too high—in other

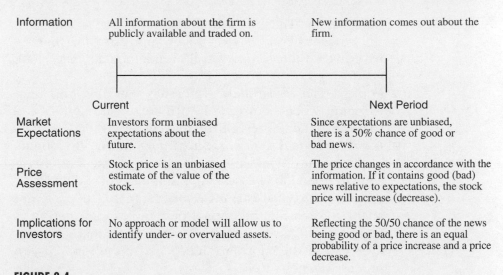

Information	All information about the firm is publicly available and traded on.	New information comes out about the firm.
	Current	Next Period
Market Expectations	Investors form unbiased expectations about the future.	Since expectations are unbiased, there is a 50% chance of good or bad news.
Price Assessment	Stock price is an unbiased estimate of the value of the stock.	The price changes in accordance with the information. If it contains good (bad) news relative to expectations, the stock price will increase (decrease).
Implications for Investors	No approach or model will allow us to identify under- or overvalued assets.	Reflecting the 50/50 chance of the news being good or bad, there is an equal probability of a price increase and a price decrease.

FIGURE 8.4
Information and Price Changes in a Rational Market

words, investors are too optimistic or too pessimistic—information will no longer have an equal chance of containing good or bad news, and prices will not follow a random walk. The second is that price changes are caused by new information. If investors can cause prices to change by just trading, even in the absence of information, you can have price changes in the same direction rather than a random walk.

THE BASIS FOR CONTRARIAN INVESTING

Why would markets overreact to new information? If it happens consistently, the roots have to lie in human psychology. There are three reasons generally provided by students of human behavior:

- *Overweighting of most recent information:* Researchers in experimental psychology suggest that people tend to overweight recent information and underweight prior data in revising their beliefs when confronted with new information. Thus, a firm that reports bad earnings in the current period is excessively punished for that report even though its overall fundamentals may look good.

- *Panic:* Other researchers argue that a few investors tend to panic when confronted with new information and that they take the rest of the market with them.
- *Inability to deal with complex information:* Proponents of this point of view argue that while markets do a reasonably good job of assessing the impact of simple information (decreased earnings, for instance), they are not adept at assessing the impact of complex information (a major restructuring). In the latter case, markets may overreact to the information because of their inability to process the news well.

If markets overreact, it follows that large price movements in one direction will be followed by large price movements in the opposite direction. In addition, the more extreme the initial price movement, the greater will be the subsequent adjustment. If markets overreact, the road to investment success seems clear. You buy assets when others are most bearish about the future and selling, and sell assets when other investors are most optimistic and buying. If your assumption about market overreaction is correct, you should make money as markets correct themselves over time.

LOOKING AT THE EVIDENCE

The debate about whether markets overreact to new information or follow a random walk will never be resolved with theoretical arguments. Both sides are entrenched in their views and are unlikely to be swayed by arguments from the other side. You can, however, look at the empirical evidence to see which hypothesis is more justified by the evidence. In this section, you will look at two sets of studies that may shed light on this question. The first group examines whether price changes in one period are related to price changes in previous periods and indirectly answer the question of whether markets reverse themselves over time. The second group tries to directly answer the question by examining whether investing in stocks that have gone down the most over a recent period is a worthwhile strategy.

SERIAL CORRELATION

If today is a big up day for a stock, what does this tell you about tomorrow? There are three different points of view. The first is that the momentum from today will carry into tomorrow and that tomorrow is more likely to be an up day than a down day. The second is that there will be the proverbial profit taking as investors cash in their profits and that the resulting correction will make it more likely that tomorrow will be a down day. The third is that each day you begin anew, with new information and new worries, and that what happened today has no implications for what will happen tomorrow.

Statistically, the serial correlation measures the relationship between price changes in consecutive periods, whether hourly, daily or weekly, and is a measure of how much the price change in any period depends upon the price change over the previous period. A serial correlation of zero would therefore imply that price changes in consecutive periods are uncorrelated with each other and can thus be viewed as a rejection of the hypothesis that investors can learn about future price changes from past ones. A serial correlation that is positive and statistically significant could be viewed as evidence of price momentum in markets, and it would suggest that returns in a period are more likely to be positive (negative) if the prior period's returns were positive (negative). A serial correlation that is negative and statistically significant could be evidence of price reversals, and it would be consistent with a market in which positive returns are more likely to follow negative returns, and vice versa. In other words, it would be consistent with the contrarian investing strategy described in this chapter.

From the viewpoint of investment strategy, serial correlations can sometimes be exploited to earn excess returns. A positive serial correlation would be exploited by a strategy of buying after stock prices go up and selling after stock prices go down. A negative serial correlation would suggest a strategy of buying after stock prices go down and selling after stock prices go up. Since these strategies generate transactions costs, the correlations have to be large enough to allow investors to generate profits to cover these costs. It is therefore entirely possible that there be serial correlation in returns without any opportunity to earn excess returns for most investors.

The earliest studies of serial correlation all looked at large U.S. stocks and concluded that the serial correlation in stock prices was small.[2] One of the first, in 1965, found that 8 of the 30 stocks listed in the Dow had negative serial correlations and that most of the serial correlations were close to zero. Other research confirms these findings—of very low correlation, positive or negative—not only for smaller stocks in the United States, but also for other markets. While these correlations may be statistically different from zero, it is unlikely that there is enough correlation in short-period returns to generate excess returns after you adjust for transactions costs.

While most of the earlier analyses of price behavior focused on shorter return intervals, more attention has been paid to price movements over longer periods (six months to five years) in recent years. Here, there is an interesting dichotomy in the results. When long term is defined as months rather than years, there seems to be a tendency toward positive serial correlation: stocks that have gone up in the last six months tend to continue to go up for the next six months, whereas stocks that have gone down in the last six months tend to continue to go down. The momentum effect is just as strong in the European markets, though it seems to be weaker in emerging markets.[3] What could cause this momentum? One potential explanation is that mutual funds are more likely to buy past winners and dump past losers, thus generating the price momentum.[4] Thus, there is no evidence to back up contrarian investing strategies when you look at shorter time horizons from a few days to a few months.

However, when long term is defined in terms of years, there is substantial negative correlation in returns, suggesting that markets reverse themselves over very long periods. Fama and French examined five-year returns on stocks from 1941 to 1985 and present evidence of this phenomenon.[5] They found that serial correlation is more negative in five-year returns than in one-year returns, and is much more negative for smaller stocks rather than larger stocks. Figure 8.5 summarizes one-year and five-year serial correlation by size class for stocks on the New York Stock Exchange.

With the smallest stocks, there is very strong evidence that extended periods of positive returns are followed by extended periods of negative returns, and vice versa. This phenomenon has also been examined in other markets, and the findings have been similar. There is evidence that stocks reverse themselves over long periods.

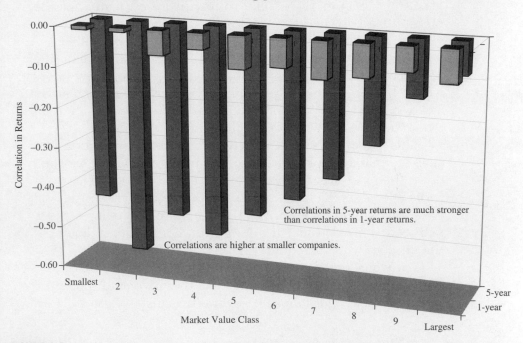

FIGURE 8.5

One-Year and Five-Year Correlations: Market Value Class, 1941–1985

Data from Fama/French. These are the average correlations in consecutive periods for firms in each market value class (from smallest to largest).

What are the overall implications for contrarian investing? The first and most important one is that you need to be a long-term investor to have any chance of contrarian investing working for you. The second is that, in terms of market capitalization, contrarian investing is more likely to pay off for smaller companies than larger companies.

LOSER STOCKS

How would a strategy of buying the stocks that have gone down the most over the last few years perform? To isolate the effect of price reversals on the extreme portfolios, a study constructed a winner portfolio of 35 stocks that had gone up the most over the prior year and a loser portfolio of 35 stocks that had gone down the most over the prior year, at the end of each year from 1933 to 1978.[6] The returns were estimated for the 60 months following the creation of the portfolios. Figure 8.6 graphs the returns on both the loser and winner portfolios.

This analysis suggests that an investor who bought the 35 biggest losers over the previous year and held for five years would have generated a cumulative return of approximately an excess return of 30% over the market and about 40% relative to an investor who bought the winner portfolio.

This evidence is consistent with market overreaction and suggests that a simple strategy of buying stocks that have gone down the most over the last year or years may yield excess returns over the long term. Since the strategy relies entirely on past prices, you could argue that this strategy shares more with charting—consider it a long-term contrarian indicator—than it does with value investing.

Many academics as well as practitioners suggest that these findings may be interesting but that they overstate potential returns on loser portfolios for several reasons:

- There is evidence that loser portfolios are more likely to contain low-priced stocks (selling for less than $5), which generate higher transactions costs, and are also more likely to offer heavily skewed returns, that is, the excess returns come from a few stocks making

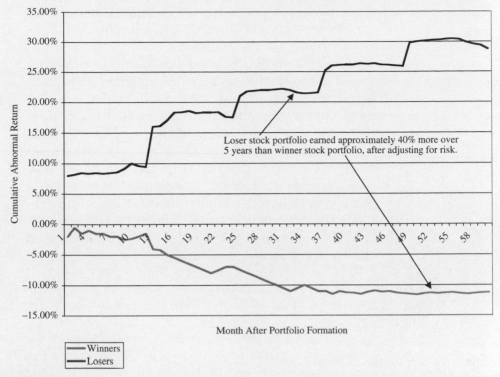

FIGURE 8.6

Cumulative Abnormal Returns: Winners vs. Losers

Data from a study by DeBondt and Thaler. The portfolios represent the 35 best-performing stocks (winners) and the 35 worst-performing stocks (losers); the returns represent the cumulated return on both portfolios over the next 60 months.

> phenomenal returns rather than from consistent performance.

- Studies also seem to find loser portfolios created every December earn significantly higher returns than portfolios created every June. This suggests an interaction between this strategy and tax-loss selling by investors. Since stocks that have gone down the most are likely to be sold toward the end of each tax year (which ends in December for most individuals) by investors, their prices may be pushed down by the tax-loss selling.
- There seems to be a size effect when it comes to the differential returns. When you do not control for firm size, the loser stocks outperform the winner stocks, but when

you match losers and winners of comparable market value, the only month in which the loser stocks outperform the winner stocks is January.[7]

■ The final point to be made relates to the time horizon. As noted in the section on serial correlation, while there may be evidence of price reversals in long periods (three to five years), there is evidence of price momentum—losing stocks are more likely to keep losing and winning stocks to keep winning—if you consider shorter periods (six months to a year). An analysis[8] referenced earlier in support of price momentum identified how important time horizon is for a loser stock strategy by tracking the difference between winner and loser portfolios by the number of months that the portfolios were held.[9] The findings are summarized in Figure 8.7.

There are two interesting findings in this graph. The first is that the winner portfolio actually outperforms the loser port-

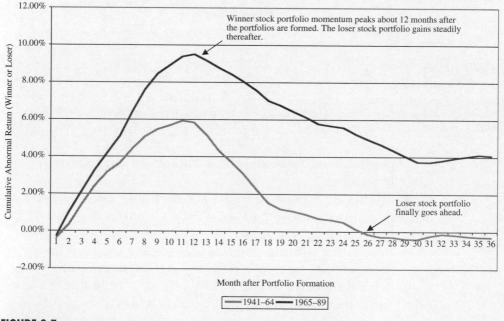

FIGURE 8.7

Differential Returns: Winner vs. Loser Potfolios

Data from a study by Jegadeesh and Titman. The cumulative difference in returns between winner and loser portfolios is tracked month by month for each period.

folio in the first 12 months after the portfolios are created. The second is that while loser stocks start gaining ground on winning stocks after 12 months, it took them 28 months in the 1941–1964 time period to get ahead of them and the loser portfolio does not start outperforming the winner portfolio even with a 36-month time horizon in the 1965–1989 time period. The payoff to buying losing companies depends very heavily on whether you have the capacity to hold these stocks for a long time.

CRUNCHING THE NUMBERS

How much does a stock have to go down for it to be categorized as a "loser stock"? The answer will vary, depending upon the period for which you look at the market. In a period of rising stock prices, a 40% drop in the stock price may qualify a stock to be a "loser." However, in a period where the entire market is down 15% or 20%, a drop of 80% or more may be necessary for a stock to drop to the bottom of the scale. In this section, you will look at the distribution of returns across stocks in the market as well as significant differences in returns across sectors.

ACROSS THE MARKET

To identify stocks that are the worst performers in the market in any period, you have to make two judgments. The first relates to the length of the period that you will use to compute returns. The worst performers over the last year may not be the worst performers over the last six months or the last five years. The second factor that will affect your choices is what you define as the market. The worst performers in the S&P 500 may not even make the list if you were looking at the worst performers across all equity markets in the United States. In Figure 8.8, the distribution of annualized returns across all listed stocks in the United States is presented for four different periods: January through October 2002 (9 months);

October 2001 to October 2002 (1 year); October 1999 to October 2002 (3 years); and October 1997 to October 2002 (5 years).

Note that the overall stock market had negative returns over each of the periods and that the distribution reflects this. More stocks have negative than positive returns, and this tendency is accented when you look at the shorter periods (9 month, 1 year) because markets did far worse during these shorter periods.

The other interesting point is the magnitude of the negative returns earned by some stocks. It should be enduring testimony about the riskiness of stocks that some stocks lost 90% or more of their value in nine months (as did about 200 stocks between October 2001 and October 2002). One reason the number of stocks that have negative returns of this magnitude drop off with the longer periods is that stocks that lose more than 90% of their value year after year generally cease to trade.

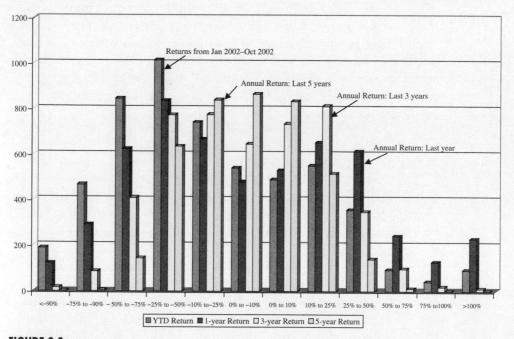

FIGURE 8.8

Distribution of Historical Returns

Data from Value Line. The number of stocks with annual returns that fall into each return class is graphed.

The Sector Effect

As markets move up and down, entire sectors can go up and down by much more or less than the market. This is sometimes because of fundamentals—individual sectors can do much better or worse than the overall economy—and sometimes because of investor psychology; keep in mind the rush to new economy companies in the late 1990s and away from them in early 2001. Why might this matter? If you have a strategy of buying stocks that have gone down the most over a period and some sectors do far worse than others, your portfolio, for better or worse, will be overrepresented with stocks from those sectors.

As with individual stocks, the best and worst sectors shift, depending upon the period that you look at returns. In Table 8.1, the sectors that did the best and worst during the 12-month period from October 2001 to October 2002 are listed.

TABLE 8.1   Best- and Worst-Performing Sectors: Oct. 2001–Oct. 2002

Industry Name	1-Year Return	Industry Name	1-Year Return
Household Products	22.86	Power	−73.07
Recreation	23.79	Wireless Networking	−48.25
Auto Parts	25.35	Cable TV	−45.51
Thrift	25.79	Telecom. Equipment	−40.62
Trucking/Transp. Leasing	26.26	Semiconductor Cap Eq	−40.24
Homebuilding	28.91	Drug	−35.47
Hotel/Gaming	29.96	Telecom. Services	−32.55
Furn./Home Furnishings	35.37	E-Commerce	−28.67
Retail Building Supply	37.13	Biotechnology	−26.25
Precious Metals	157.10	Electrical Equipment	−23.01

The best performing sector was precious metals, which was borne upward by the increase in gold prices during the period. The contrast between the ten best and worst performing sector returns is striking, with the best performing sectors all showing returns greater than 20% while stocks in the worst performing sectors dropped by more than 20% over the same period.

If you extend the period to five years from October 1997 to October 2002, the worst-performing sectors are technology and telecommunication, in which you would have lost on average more than 18% a year each year for the five years. It is worth noting that these were the high-flying sectors of the market boom of the 1990s and would have undoubtedly ranked at the top if you had considered a previous five-year period. Table 8.2 lists the best- and worst-performing sectors from October 1997 to October 2002.

TABLE 8.2   Best- and Worst-Performing Sectors: Oct. 1997–Oct . 2002

INDUSTRY NAME	TOTAL RETURN 5-YEAR	INDUSTRY NAME	TOTAL RETURN 5-YEAR
Canadian Energy	3.82	Wireless Networking	−27.44
Bank (Canadian)	4.59	Internet	−22.47
Thrift	4.64	Telecom. Services	−22.30
Bank	4.78	Telecom. Equipment	−22.03
Bank (Midwest)	5.27	Computer & Peripherals	−21.30
Electric Utility (East)	6.64	Coal	−20.91
Pharmacy Services	7.05	Steel (Integrated)	−19.63
Tobacco	7.27	Computer Software & Svcs	−19.51
Retail Building Supply	8.29	Semiconductor	−19.38
Water Utility	15.05	Healthcare Info Systems	−18.30

If you were a contrarian, constructing a portfolio of loser stocks in October 2002, you should not be surprised to see technology and telecommunication companies dominating the list.

A PORTFOLIO OF LOSERS

To construct a portfolio of loser stocks, you first need to choose a period over which you will estimate returns. While you can make a case for returns over longer periods, much of the empirical research is built around returns over one year. In keeping with this, the 300 worst-performing stocks in the United States between October 2001 and October 2002 were selected. In a preview of a potential problem with this strategy, 166 of these stocks traded at prices less than a dollar. Since the transactions costs of buying these stocks is likely to be very high, only the 134 stocks that traded for more than a dollar were included in the portfolio; they are summarized in Table 8.3. As anticipated, the sectors that were identified as the worst performing sectors in Table 8.2 are overrepresented in this portfolio.

MORE TO THE STORY

While loser stocks seem to earn above-average returns if held for long periods, there are clear dangers with this investment strategy. The first is that the proliferation of low-priced stocks in the portfolio results in high transactions costs for investors. The second is that loser stocks may be exposed to more risk, both in terms of price volatility and in terms of high financial leverage—loser stocks tends to have higher debt ratios. The third is that negative returns usually happen for a reason. If that reason, whether it be poor management or a loss of market share, is not fixed, there may be no catalyst for prices to increase in the future.

TRANSACTIONS COSTS

The first and perhaps biggest problem with a strategy of investing in loser stocks is that many of these stocks trade at low prices. The transactions costs associated with buying and selling these stocks is high for at least three reasons:

- The bid-ask spread in these stocks is high, relative to the stock price. Thus, a bid-ask spread of 50 cents would be only 1% of the price for a $50 stock but would be 20% of a stock trading at $2.50.
- The commissions and other fixed trading costs also rise as a percent of the investment as the stock price drops. The brokerage commissions will be substantially higher

TABLE 8.3 Loser Stocks (October 2001 to October 2002)

Company	Symbol	Company	Symbol	Company	Symbol
VerticalNet Inc	VERT	Actuate Corporation	ACTU	Metris Cos	MXT
Nucentrix Broadband Networks	NCNX	Mail-Well Inc	MWL	Concurrent Computer	CCUR
Genzyme Molecular Oncology	GZMO	MIIX Group Inc	MHU	Medarex Inc	MEDX
Golf Trust of America	GTA	Harmonic Inc	HLIT	CuraGen Corp	CRGN
Bell Canada Intl	BCICF	EntreMed Inc	ENMD	Sprint PCS Group	PCS
Antenna TV S A	ANTV	Biomira Inc	BRA.TO	Nanometrics Inc	NANO
Beta Oil and Gas Inc	BETA	Broadwing Inc	BRW	ClearOne Communications Inc	CLRO
Data Systems & Software	DSSI	EMCORE Corp	EMKR	SmartForce ADR	SKIL
Biotime Inc	BTX	Optical Cable Corp	OCCF	CryoLife Inc	CRY
Nortel Networks	NT	SuperGen Inc	SUPG	Alcatel ADR	ALA
Childtime Learning Ctrs	CTIM	Global Thermoelectric Inc	GLE.TO	Stellent Inc	STEL
Digital Lightwave	DIGL	Corning Inc	GLW	Aquila Inc	ILA
Openwave Systems	OPWV	Beverly Enterprises	BEV	Providian Fin'l	PVN
Medwave Inc	MDWV	MIPS Technologies Inc	MIPS	Emisphere Tech Inc	EMIS
Tumbleweed Communications	TMWD	Artesyn Technologies Inc	ATSN	RSA Security	RSAS
Conexant Systems	CNXT	WHX Corp	WHX	ABIOMED Inc	ABMD
Cygnus Inc	CYGN	Rite Aid Corp	RAD	Powerwave Techn	PWAV
Vitesse Semiconductor	VTSS	Alpha Hospitality Corp	ALHY	ILEX Oncology	ILXO
Classica Group Inc	TCGI	Calpine Corp	CPN	HEALTHSOUTH Corp	HRC
3DO Co	THDO	Sanmina-SCI Corp	SANM	Championship Auto Racing	MPH
Ventiv Health Inc	VTIV	Novadigm Inc	NVDM	Magnum Hunter Resources	MHR
AES Corp	AES	ANADIGICS Inc	ANAD	Biopure Corp	BPUR
ACT Teleconferencing	ACTT	Bioject Medical Tech	BJCT	Cell Therapeutic	CTIC
Corvas Intl Inc	CVAS	BroadVision Inc	BVSN	PerkinElmer Inc	PKI

Company	Symbol	Company	Symbol	Company	Symbol
Student Advantage Inc	STAD	Aphton Corp	APHT	TriQuint Semic	TQNT
Amer. Tower "A"	AMT	Solectron Corp	SLR	AMR Corp	AMR
Atlas Air Inc	CGO	Iona Tech PLC ADR	IONA	Med-Design Corp	MEDC
Miller Exploration	MEXPD	Titan Pharm Inc	TTP	Administaff Inc	ASF
Williams Cos	WMB	Quantum Corporation	DSS	National Service Ind	NSI
KeyTronicEMS Co	KTCC	UAL Corp	UAL	PDI Inc	PDII
Sapient Corp	SAPE	Tesoro Petroleum	TSO	Fleming Cos	FLM
Electroglas Inc	EGLS	Zarlink Semiconductor Inc	ZL	DVI Inc.	DVI
CNET Networks	CNET	Pharmacyclics	PCYC	Cubist Pharm Inc	CBST
SatCon Technology	SATC	GlobespanVirata Inc	GSPN	Microsemi Corp	MSCC
KANA Software Inc	KANA	Covansys Corp	CVNS	Amdocs Ltd	DOX
InterVoice Inc	INTV	Crown Castle Int'l	CCI	AmeriCredit Corp	ACF
Genome Therapeutics Inc	GENE	Starbase Corp	SBAS	Neose Technologies	NTEC
Hollywood Mediacorp	HOLL	Collins & Aikman Corp	CKC	Footstar Inc	FTS
Pegasus Communications	PGTV	Hemispherx Biopharma Inc	HEB	El Paso Corp	EP
Atmel Corp	ATML	Western Wireless "A"	WWCA	ImClone Systems	IMCL
DuraSwitch Inds Inc	DSWT	Quanta Services	PWR	Sepracor Inc	SEPR
SIPEX Corp	SIPX	Kulicke & Soffa	KLIC	VeriSign Inc	VRSN
Elan Corp. ADR	ELN	Amkor Technology	AMKR	Allmerica Financial	AFC
Factory 2-U Stores Inc	FTUS	Gemstar-TV Guide	GMSTE	EPCOS AG	EPC
Razorfish Inc	RAZF	CyberOptics	CYBE	Polycom Inc	PLCM
DMC Stratex Networks Inc	STXN	Lumenis Ltd	LUME	Genesis Microchip Inc	GNSS
SpectRx Inc	SPRX	Vical Inc	VICL	CSG Systems Int'l	CSGS
Dusa Pharmaceuticals	DUSA	PLX Technology Inc	PLXT	Electronic Data Sys	EDS
Visible Genetics Inc	VGIN	Commerce One Inc	CMRC	Power Corp	POW.TO

if you buy 10,000 shares at $2 per share than if you buy 1,000 shares at $20 per share.

- As stock prices drop, institutional investors tend to flee, reducing volatility and trading volume and increasing the transactions costs further.

Though the portfolio of stocks in Table 8.3 was constrained to include only stocks that trade at more than a dollar, the average price of stocks in that portfolio is only $3.36, whereas the average stock price in the rest of the market is more than $26. In addition, the market capitalization of loser stocks is much lower at $388 million than the average market capitalization of stocks in the rest of the market, which is about $1.7 billion. The combination of low stock prices and small market capitalizations will push up transactions costs when you are constructing this portfolio. Figure 8.9 provides a measure of the magnitude of the trading costs you face

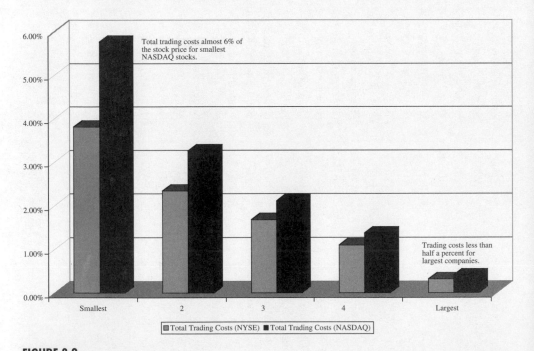

FIGURE 8.9

Total Trading Costs by Market Capitalization

Data from a study by Kothare and Laux. These costs include brokerage commissions, price impact and the bid-ask spread.

with small market capitalization companies as opposed to large ones.

The total trading costs, including the bid-ask spread and commission costs, can amount to more than 5% of the stock price for companies in the smallest market capitalization class. The costs will undoubtedly be even larger if these are low-priced stocks.[10]

What should the minimum price be for inclusion in this portfolio? If you adopt a cutoff of $5 for the stock price, only 26 of the 147 companies in the portfolio survive. They are listed in Table 8.4.

TABLE 8.4 Loser Stocks Trading at More Than $5 per Share

COMPANY NAME	TICKER SYMBOL	INDUSTRY	STOCK PRICE
DVI Inc	DVI	Medserv	$6.30
Power Corp	POW.TO	Financl	$36.85
Footstar Inc	FTS	Retailsp	$7.56
Electronic Data Sys	EDS	Software	$13.72
National Service Ind	NSI	Diversif	$5.75
Fleming Cos	FLM	Foodwhol	$6.14
Sepracor Inc	SEPR	Drug	$7.81
Neose Technologies	NTEC	Biotech	$7.52
ImClone Systems	IMCL	Drug	$7.79
Allmerica Financial	AFC	Insprpty	$8.14
CSG Systems Int'l	CSGS	Indusrv	$11.39
El Paso Corp	EP	Gasdivrs	$7.61
AMR Corp	AMR	Airtrans	$5.15
PDI Inc	PDII	Indusrv	$5.91
Administaff Inc	ASF	Human	$5.42
PerkinElmer Inc	PKI	Instrmnt	$5.00
EPCOS AG	EPC	Electrnx	$9.28
Polycom Inc	PLCM	Telequip	$9.85
Amdocs Ltd	DOX	Indusrv	$6.93
Cubist Pharm Inc	CBST	Drug	$6.83
TriQuint Semic	TQNT	Semicond	$5.07
Genesis Microchip Inc	GNSS	Electrnx	$9.87
Microsemi Corporation	MSCC	Electrnx	$6.85
VeriSign Inc	VRSN	Internet	$7.91
AmeriCredit Corp	ACF	Financl	$6.98
Med-Design Corp	MEDC	Medsuppl	$5.23

VOLATILITY AND DEFAULT RISK

Stocks that have dropped substantially over the last year are often riskier than other stocks. One reason is that at lower stock prices, volatility increases.[11] The second is that sudden and precipitous declines in stock prices often increase financial leverage and default risk.[12]

In Figure 8.10 you can see the contrast on three measures of risk—beta, standard deviation in stock prices and debt to capital ratios—between the firms in the loser portfolio and the rest of the market.

On all three measures on risk, but especially on the price-based measures (beta and standard deviation), loser stocks are far riskier than stocks in the rest of the market.

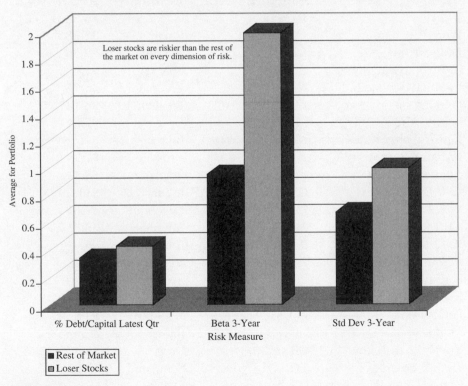

FIGURE 8.10

Loser Stocks vs. Rest of the Market: Risk Measures

Data from Value Line. The average beta and standard deviation over the previous three years and the book debt to capital ratio is presented for loser stocks and the rest of the market.

You could screen the 26 stocks that made it through the price screen ($5 or higher) for excessive risk. In fact, if you do include constraints for stocks with annual standard deviations that exceed 80% (which would eliminate firms in the top 25% in terms of this measure), betas that exceed 1.25 and market debt-to-capital ratios less than 80%, only three firms remain. They are listed in Table 8.5.

TABLE 8.5 Loser Stocks with Price Greater than $5 and Reasonable Risk Exposure

COMPANY NAME	STOCK PRICE	STANDARD DEVIATION	BETA	DEBT/ CAPITAL
Power Corp.	$36.85	50.07%	0.64	16.43%
Electronic Data Sys.	$13.72	55.03%	1.24	41.81%
Footstar Inc.	$7.56	50.53%	0.10	47.95%

The dramatic drop-off in the number of stocks in the portfolio when you impose minimum price limits and risk constraints suggests that a loser stock strategy may be difficult to put into practice even for believers in its contrarian roots.

CATALYSTS FOR IMPROVEMENT

The final and perhaps most difficult factor to consider when buying loser stocks is whether the underlying problems that caused the negative returns have been remedied. While you may not be able to probe the internal workings of each of the firms that you consider for your portfolio, you can look for actions that improve the odds for success:

- *Change in management:* You could, for instance, check to see if the management of the firm has changed recently. Presumably, a new management team will be more inclined to admit to mistakes made in the past and to fix them.
- *Restructuring actions:* You could also screen for recent restructuring decisions made by the firm, including divestitures and acquisitions that change the business mix.

- *Activist investors:* Managers at firms in trouble often need pressure brought on them by activist investors; pension funds and individual investors often take positions in troubled companies and push for change. The presence of one or more of such investors at a firm can be viewed as a promising sign.
- *Survival:* To fix problems that may be long term and structural, firms need time as their ally. They are more likely to get this time if the threat of financial default does not hang over their heads. Restricting your holdings to companies that have manageable debt loads, in addition to acting as a risk screen, also increases the odds of survival.
- *Trends in profitability:* While the long-term trends in profitability for loser stocks are likely to be negative, you may be able to find positive signs in short-term trends. You could, for instance, invest only in companies that have reported positive earnings in the last quarter. While one quarter does not make for a turnaround, it may signal that the company has put some of its troubles behind it.

LESSONS FOR INVESTORS

Buying stocks just because they have gone down in the recent past may look like a winning strategy on paper, but there are significant associated risks. If you are a prudent investor, with a long time horizon and a contrarian investment philosophy, you should want to buy loser stocks with controllable transactions costs and limited exposure to risk. To achieve these goals, you could consider screening all U.S. stocks for the following:

- *Past returns:* Only stocks in the bottom quartile in terms of returns over the last year will be considered for this portfolio. This is a much more relaxed screen than the one used earlier in the chapter (where the 500 stocks with the most negative returns out of 7000 were picked). However, it will then allow for stricter screens for risk and transactions costs.

■ *Transactions costs:* To reduce the overall transactions costs on the portfolio, only stocks that trade at prices greater than $5 are considered.

■ *Risk:* Stocks with standard deviations greater than 80%, betas greater than 1.25 or debt-to-capital ratios that exceed 50% are eliminated from the sample. The first two operate purely as risk screens, and the last one screens for both risk and survival.

■ *Catalyst for improvement:* Only stocks that report positive earnings in the most recent quarter and increased earnings over the previous period are considered for the overall portfolio. The rationale is that stocks that are making money are not only less risky but also have more freedom to make the changes that need to be made to become healthy companies.

The resulting portfolio of 20 stocks, obtained by screening all U.S. companies in January 2003, is listed in the appendix to this chapter.

CONCLUSION

Many contrarian investors believe that buying stocks that have done badly in the recent past is a good strategy. This strategy is predicated on the belief that investors overreact to new information and push down stock prices too much after bad news (a bad earnings announcement, a cut in dividends) and up too much after good news. The empirical evidence seems to bear out this belief. Studies show that stocks that have gone down the most over a recent period generate high returns if held for long periods. However, these stocks also tend to trade at low prices and transactions costs are high with this strategy. These stocks are also riskier than average.

If you want to succeed with this strategy, you have to begin with a long time horizon and a strong stomach for volatility. You will have to construct your portfolio with care to reduce your exposure to both transaction costs and risk. You will often find yourself losing before you begin winning. Even then, this is not a foolproof or a riskless strategy.

ENDNOTES

1. If the probability of good news is greater than the probability of bad news, the price should increase before the news comes out. Technically, it is that the expected value of the next information release is zero.

2. Alexander, S. S., 1964, "Price Movements in Speculative Markets: Trends or Random Walks," in *The Random Character of Stock Market Prices*, MIT Press; Cootner, P. H., 1962, *Stock Prices: Random versus Systematic Changes*, Industrial Management Review, v3, 24–45; and Fama, E. F., 1965, *The Behavior of Stock Market Prices*, Journal of Business, v38, 34–105. All three studies estimated serial correlation in stock prices. Given the difficulty of obtaining data, they worked with small samples over short periods.

3. Rouwenhorst, G. K., 1998, *International Momentum Strategies*, Journal of Finance, v53, 267–284. Rouwenhorst studied 12 European markets and found evidence of momentum in each market. In 1999, he presented evidence of momentum in emerging markets.

   Bekaert, G., C. B. Erb, C. R. Harvey and T. E. Viskanta, 1997, *What Matters for Emerging Market Equity Investments*, Emerging Markets Quarterly (Summer 1997), 17–46. This study finds that momentum investing is not consistently profitable in emerging markets.

4. Grinblatt, M., S. Titman and R. Wermers, 1995, *Momentum Investment Strategies, Portfolio Performance, and Herding: A Study of Mutual Fund Behavior*, American Economic Review, v85, 1088–1105.

5. Fama, E. F., and K. R. French, 1992, *The Cross-Section of Expected Returns*, Journal of Finance, v47, 427–466.

6. DeBondt, W. F. M., and R. Thaler, 1985, *Does the Stock Market Overreact?*, Journal of Finance, v40, 793–805.

7. Zarowin, P., 1990, *Size, Seasonality and Stock Market Overreaction*, Journal of Financial and Quantitative Analysis, v25, 113–125.

8. Jegadeesh, N., and S. Titman, 1993, *Returns to Buying Winners and Selling Losers: Implications for Stock Market Efficiency*, Journal of Finance, 48(1), 65–91.

9. The definition of winner and loser portfolios is slightly different in this study, relative to the one graphed in Figure 8.6. The portfolios were based upon returns over the six months before the creation of the portfolios.

10. Kothare, M., and P. A. Laux, 1995, *Trading Costs and the Trading Systems for NASDAQ Stocks*, Financial Analysts Journal, March/April, v51, 42–53.

11. A stock trading at $2 a share will generally have higher percent volatility in prices and returns than a stock trading at $20 a share. There is no theoretical reason for this, but it remains an empirical reality.

12. Consider a company with $1 billion in debt and $1 billion in equity. If the value of equity drops by 80%, you will generally see this company's debt ratio increase from 50% to a much higher value, since the debt value will not drop as much as equity. In fact, if the debt value does not change, the debt ratio will become 83.33%.

Appendix

Loser Stocks Trading at More Than $5 and with Limited Exposure to Risk and Default

Company Name	Ticker Symbol	Industry Name	Stock Price	Total Return 1-Year	Beta 3-Year	Std Dev 3-Year	EPS Latest Qtr	Market Debt-to-Capital
Almost Family Inc	AFAM	Medical Services	6.56	−55.23%	0.07	56.66%	0.12	46.85%
Ambassadors Intl Inc	AMIE	Industrial Services	9.18	−57.17%	0.4	52.76%	0.02	0.22%
BJ's Wholesale Club	BJ	Retail Store	15.52	−58.50%	0.73	37.70%	0.38	8.40%
CAE Inc	CAE.TO	Aerospace/Defense	5.18	−55.19%	1.21	60.03%	0.11	40.56%
Convergys Corp	CVG	Industrial Services	12.59	−59.59%	1.12	46.25%	0.34	5.06%
Crawford & Co "B"	CRD/B	Financial Svcs (Div)	5.05	−55.55%	0.32	56.68%	0.11	21.48%
Cytyc Corp	CYTC	Medical Supplies	10.81	−60.92%	0.95	66.52%	0.11	0.00%
Enzon Inc	ENZN	Drug	17.8	−70.29%	1.01	60.11%	0.29	33.46%
Fab Industries	FIT	Textile	8.9	−55.22%	0.22	49.33%	0.19	0.71%
Footstar Inc	FTS	Retail (Special Lines)	9.42	−77.76%	−0.05	51.38%	0.69	42.70%
Kendle Intl Inc	KNDL	Medical Services	8.52	−56.35%	0.52	65.58%	0.16	12.71%
Ohio Art Co	OAR	Recreation	17	−55.96%	0.19	59.26%	1.18	31.05%
On Assignment	ASGN	Human Resources	7.5	−62.91%	1.17	61.87%	0.14	0.00%
QLT Inc	QLT.TO	Drug	12.33	−66.91%	1.11	71.34%	0.13	0.00%
SRI/Surgical Express Inc	STRC	Medical Supplies	5.02	−64.56%	−0.33	65.68%	0.05	40.78%
Tenet Healthcare	THC	Medical Services	18.22	−58.11%	−0.38	46.65%	0.68	30.45%
THQ Inc	THQI	Entertainment Tech	12.2	−58.99%	0.68	67.04%	0.12	0.00%
TRC Cos	TRR	Environmental	13.99	−60.61%	0.67	66.06%	0.26	11.72%
Vans Inc	VANS	Shoe	5.06	−55.42%	0.52	51.73%	0.3	7.64%
Veritas DGC Inc	VTS	Oilfield Svcs/Equip	7.65	−57.30%	1.21	64.72%	0.05	34.93%

9

THE NEXT BIG THING: NEW BUSINESSES AND YOUNG COMPANIES

IN SEARCH OF BARGAINS

Gus prided himself on finding bargains. He had bypassed realtors and found a cheap apartment to rent in New York City by contacting land-lords directly. He filled it with antiques that he found in small furniture stores at bargain prices. He ate only in restaurants that had never been reviewed by *The New York Times*, based upon word of mouth and his own research. Heartened by his success at finding bargains, Gus de-cided to apply the same strategy to his investments. He began by look-ing for stocks in small companies that were not followed by equity research analysts at any of the major investment banks. He expanded his search to look at companies that were planning initial public offer-ings and requesting shares in them; lacking the time to do analysis, he chose a dozen at random. He even considered investing some of his money in a friend's new venture that sounded promising.

Even as he made his investments, he noticed that he paid much more than the listed price; his broker mentioned something about a large bid-ask spread. In the weeks after he bought the stocks, he also noted that there were days when these stocks never traded and the prices re-mained static. He also noticed the stock prices moved a great deal when news announcements were made and that prices were more likely to drop than go up. When he tried to sell some of the stocks on which he had made money, he found himself getting less in proceeds than he expected. Gus decided that his strategy, which worked so well with apartments, furniture and restaurants, did not work as well with stocks and he was not sure why. He blamed his broker.

Moral: A bargain can sometimes be very expensive.

Chapter 7 looked at a strategy of investing in publicly traded companies with good growth prospects. While the payoff to picking the right growth companies can be high, it is difficult to acquire these companies at reasonable prices once they are recognized as high growth companies. Some investors believe that the best investment opportunities are in small companies that are not followed by analysts or in firms before they become publicly traded. They argue that investing in young firms and in new business, either when they are private businesses or when they first go public, is the best way to generate high returns. In this chapter, the potential payoff (and costs) associated with these strategies is explored.

CORE OF THE STORY

It is the dream of every investor to find undiscovered gems to invest in—small companies with great business models that other investors have either not found yet or are ignoring. Some investors attempt to put this into practice by looking for bargains among small companies that are lightly held by institutional investors and not followed by analysts. Other investors try to beat the market by buying stocks when or shortly after they go public, arguing that these are the stocks that will be the growth stocks of the future. Still other investors with more resources under their control make their investments in promising private companies in the form of venture capital or private equity investments, hoping to ride their success to wealth.

While investors in small publicly traded companies, initial public offerings and private businesses may adopt very different strategies and have different views of the markets, they do share some common beliefs.

- *Firms that are lightly or not followed by institutions and analysts are most likely to be misvalued.* As firms become larger, they attract institutional investors and analysts. While these investors and analysts are not infallible, they are adept at digging up information about the firms they follow and invest in, making it less likely that these firms will be dramatically misvalued. By focusing your attention on firms for which there are no public investors (private firms and initial public offerings) or on firms for which there are relatively few large investors, you hope to increase the payoff to good research. Stated in terms of market efficiency, you believe that you are more likely to find pockets of inefficiency in these parts of the market.

■ *Good independent research can help you separate the winners from the losers.* Even if you buy in to the notion that stocks that are lightly followed are more likely to be misvalued, you need to be able to separate the stocks that are undervalued from those that are overvalued. By collecting information on and researching lightly followed firms—private companies for private equity investments, firms just before initial public offerings and lightly followed publicly traded firms—you can gain advantages over other investors and increase your exposure to the up side while limiting downside risk.

In other words, these strategies all share the belief that the best bargains are most likely to be found off the beaten path.

THEORETICAL ROOTS: RISK AND POTENTIAL GROWTH

Is there a theoretical basis for believing that an investment strategy focused on private firms, initial public offerings, or smaller, less followed companies will generate high returns? You could legitimately argue that these firms are likely to be riskier than larger, more established firms and that you should expect to earn higher returns over long periods. This, by itself, would not be justification enough for such a strategy since you would have to show not just high returns but excess returns, that is, the returns should be higher than would be expected given the higher risk.

ADDITIONAL RISK

What are the sources of additional risk of investing in private or small, publicly traded companies? First, you will generally have far less information available about these companies at the time of your investment than you would with larger companies. Second, a greater portion of the value of these firms will come from future growth and a smaller portion from existing assets; the former is inherently more uncertain. Third, investments in private or smaller, publicly traded companies are likely to be less liquid than investments in large, publicly traded companies. Getting in and out of these investments is therefore a much more expensive proposition.

Information Risk. The first and biggest risk in this investment strategy is the paucity and unreliability of information on the companies you invest in. There is far less information provided by private firms than by publicly traded ones; there are no SEC requirements or filing with private businesses. Notwithstanding the limitations of the accounting standards that cover publicly traded firms, they generate numbers that are comparable across companies. Private companies, on the other hand, use very different accounting standards, making it difficult to make comparisons. When investing, you also draw on private information—information generated by others following a firm. This information will not be available for private firms, will be available only in bits and pieces for smaller publicly traded companies, and will be widely available on larger publicly traded firms.

Does the fact that there is less information available on private or small firms make them riskier, and does it follow then that you should expect to make higher returns when investing in them? While the answer may seem to be obviously yes, there is a surprising amount of disagreement among theorists on this issue. Many theorists concede that there is more uncertainty associated with investing in smaller and private firms, but they also then go on to posit that much of this risk can be diversified away in a portfolio. They argue that a portfolio of small or private companies will be far less risky than the individual companies that go into that portfolio. In their view, diversified investors would therefore not view these investments as riskier and the expected returns will reflect this judgment.

There are two levels at which you can contest this sanguine view of risk. The first is that investors in private companies or small companies may not be able to diversify easily. For instance, private equity and venture capital investments tend to be concentrated in a few sectors at any given time. The second is that information risk may not be diversifiable even for investors who have the capacity to diversify. This is because the news that is not revealed about companies is more likely to be bad news than good news; firms, after all, have the incentive to let the world know when they are doing better than expected. Consequently, even in large portfolios of private or small companies, surprises are more likely to contain bad news than good.

Growth Risk.   You invest in younger and smaller companies expecting them to grow faster in the future. While you may base your decisions on substantial research, growth is inherently unpredictable. Of every 100 growth companies that are started, relatively few reach the public market, and among those that reach the public market, even fewer live up to their promise and deliver high growth for extended periods. In other words, you may invest in 999 companies before you invest in a Microsoft (if you ever do).

While you cannot pick the companies that will win this growth game with any precision, you can demand a higher return when investing in companies with greater growth potential as opposed to companies that derive most of their value from existing assets. You can consider the additional return that you demand for the former a risk premium for the unpredictability of growth.

Marketability and Liquidity.   All too often, you buy a stock and you have buyer's remorse. If the stock is publicly traded and liquid, you will bear a relatively small cost if you turn around and sell a minute after you buy. First, you will have to pay the trading commissions on both sides of the trade, but in these days of discount brokerage houses, this will be in the tens of dollars rather than the hundreds. Second, you will have to bear the cost of the bid-ask spread; even if the stock price has not changed in the minute since you bought the stock, you will receive less when you sell the stock (the bid price) than you paid when you bought the stock (the ask price). For a large publicly traded stock, this too will be small as a percent of the price.

If the stock is small and lightly traded, the cost of changing your mind increases. The commission may not be much higher, but the difference between the bid price and the ask price will be a higher percent of the stock price. Furthermore, you can affect prices as you trade, pushing prices up as you buy and down as you sell.

With a private company, these costs get larger still. Since there is no ready market for your stake in the company, you will often have to seek out an interested buyer who will often pay you far less than what you paid for the stake because of the illiquidity of the investment. The middlemen in this process also take far more of your money for arranging the transaction than do middlemen in the publicly traded asset markets.

How do you reflect this illiquidity risk in your investment strategy? With publicly traded stocks, you will be willing to pay far less for illiquid stocks than liquid stocks, pushing up their expected returns. After all, you need to be compensated for your expected transactions costs. With private companies, it is even more explicit. It is common practice among those who value private companies to apply what is called an "illiquidity discount," ranging from 20% to 30%, to the estimated value. Thus, a private company that is valued at $10 million may fetch only $7 to $8 million when put up for a sale.

POTENTIAL FOR EXCESS RETURN

The discussion in the last section suggests that investments in private or small, illiquid companies should have higher expected returns than investments in larger, more liquid companies. Does this make the former better investments? Not necessarily, since the argument for the higher returns is based upon the presumption that these stocks are more risky. For investing in smaller or private companies to be a good investment strategy, you would need to present arguments that the expected returns will be even higher than those called for by the higher risk. Several reasons are offered for why this may happen:

1. *Bigger payoff to information collection and analysis with neglected stocks:* You can argue that the payoff to collecting and analyzing information will be greatest for firms for which there is less information and analysis in the public domain. In other words, you are more likely to find bargains among these stocks.

2. *Absence of institutional investors:* This reinforces the first point. Since institutional investors often have more resources at their command (analysts, information databases, etc.), you can categorize them as informed investors. To the extent that you are more likely to lose when you trade with someone who has more information than you do, you have a better chance of success in trading in smaller, less followed stocks or in private companies.

3. *Investor fear of the unknown:* There may also be an element of irrationality driving the pricing of smaller companies. Investors are more likely to stay with the known and the familiar (usually bigger companies that are widely held) and away from smaller, less followed investments. During periods of market turmoil, this may lead to a flight away from the latter, driving prices down well below what you would view as fair.

If you conclude for any or all of the reasons above that you can earn much higher returns than justified by the risk you are taking when investing in smaller companies, the next step becomes examining whether the evidence supports such a strategy.

LOOKING AT THE EVIDENCE

In this section, you will examine the evidence that has accumulated over the last few decades on the efficacy or otherwise of investment strategies oriented around younger and smaller companies. In the first section, the returns from investing in smaller, publicly traded companies are compared to the returns of investing in larger, publicly traded firms. In the second section, the payoff to investing in stocks as they go public is examined, both around the offering date and after the offering. In the third section, you will look at whether investing in private companies (in the form of venture capital or private equity) generates high returns.

SMALL COMPANIES

Thousands of publicly traded stocks are listed on the major exchanges, and they vary widely in terms of size. There are firms like GE and Microsoft whose values run into the hundreds of billions at one extreme, but there are also publicly traded firms whose values are measured in the tens of millions at the other end. In fact, there are unlisted publicly trade companies whose values can be measured in millions. Would a strategy of investing in the smallest publicly traded companies work? Studies have consistently found that smaller firms (in terms of market value of equity) earn higher returns than larger firms of equivalent risk. Figure 9.1 summarizes annual returns for stocks in ten market value classes, for the period from 1927 to 2001.[1] The portfolios were reconstructed at the end of each year, based upon the market values of stock at that point, and held for the subsequent year. The returns are computed both on value-weighted (where the amount invested in each company is proportional to its market capitalization) and equally weighted (where the same amount is invested in each company in a portfolio) portfolios.

If you look at value-weighted portfolios, the smallest stocks earned an annual return of about 20% over the period as contrasted with the largest stocks, which earned an annual

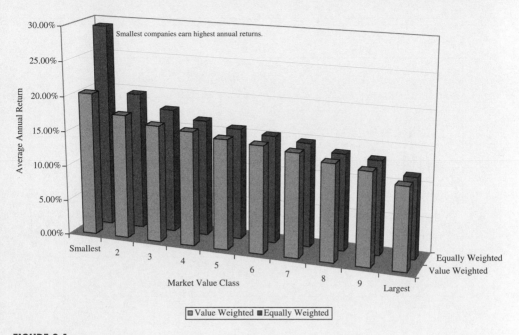

FIGURE 9.1
Annual Returns by Market Value Class: 1927–2001

Data from Fama/French. Firms were categorized at the beginning of each year into ten classes according to market capitalization. The returns were computed over the year on each portfolio.

return of 11.74%. If you use an equally weighted portfolio, the small firm premium is much larger, an indication that the premium is being earned by the smallest stocks. In other words, to capture this premium, you would have to invest in the very smallest companies in the market. Nevertheless, these results are impressive and provide a rationale for the portfolio managers who focus on buying small-cap stocks.

On average, have small capitalization (small-cap) stocks outperformed large capitalization (large-cap) stocks over this period? Absolutely, but, success from this strategy is by no means guaranteed in every period. While small-cap stocks have done better than large-cap stocks in more periods than not, there have been extended periods where small-cap stocks have underperformed large-cap stocks. Figure 9.2 graphs the premium earned by small-cap stocks over large-cap stocks each year from 1927 to 2001.

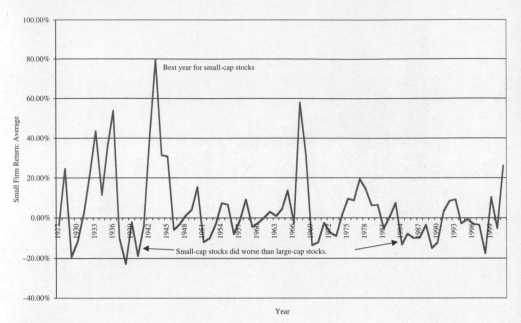

FIGURE 9.2
Small-Firm Premium Over Time: 1927–2001

Data from Fama/French. This is the difference between the annual returns on the smallest stocks (bottom 10%) and the largest market cap stocks (top 10%).

Note that the premium is negative in a significant number of years—small stocks earned lower returns than large stocks in those years. In fact, during the 1980s, large market cap stocks outperformed small-cap stocks by a significant amount, creating a debate about whether this was a long-term shift in the small stock premium or just a temporary dip. On the one side, Jeremy Siegel argues in his book on the long-term performance of stocks that the small stock premium can be almost entirely attributed to the performance of small stocks in the late 1970s.[2] Since this was a decade with high inflation, could the small stock premium have something to do with inflation? On the other side are small-cap portfolio managers, arguing that the events of the 1980s were an aberration and that the small stock premium would return. On cue, the small stock premium returned in the 1990s, as can be seen in Figure 9.3.

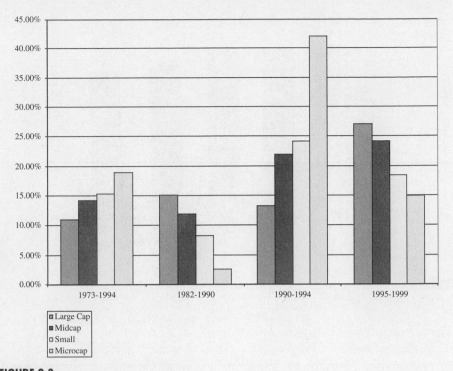

FIGURE 9.3
Small-Cap Effect Over Time
Data from Pradhuman. The categorizations are based upon Merrill Lynch's definition of micro-cap, small-, midcap and large-cap stocks.

A number of researchers have tried to take a closer look at the small-cap effect to see where the premium comes from.[3] The following are some of the conclusions:

■ The small-cap effect is greatest in the microcap companies, that is, the really small companies. In fact, many of these companies have market capitalizations of $250 million or lower. All too often these are also companies that have low-priced and illiquid stocks, not followed by equity research analysts.

■ A significant proportion of the small-cap premium is earned in January.[4] Figure 9.4 contrasts small-cap and large-cap companies in January and for the rest of the year between 1935 and 1986.

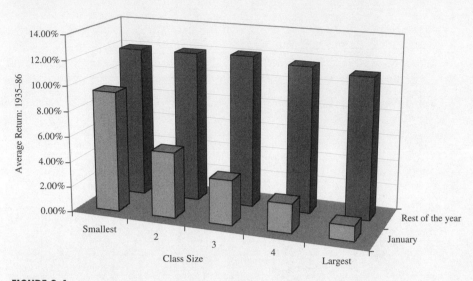

FIGURE 9.4
The Small-Firm Effect in January

Data is from study by Chopra and Ritter. The returns are computed in January and the rest of the year for stocks categorized by market capitalization.

> In fact, you cannot reject the hypothesis that there is no small-cap premium from February to December.

- There is evidence of a small-firm premium in markets outside the United States as well. Studies find small-cap premiums of about 7% from 1955 to 1984 in the United Kingdom,[5] 8.8% in France and a much smaller size effect in Germany,[6] and a premium of 5.1% for Japanese stocks between 1971 and 1988.[7]

- Small-cap stocks seem to do better when short-term interest rates are high relative to long-term rates and when inflation is high. This may account for their superior performance during the 1970s.

Can you attribute the small-cap premium to the fact that smaller companies are not tracked as frequently by equity research analysts as are larger companies? Some researchers have looked at the relationship between annual returns and company following (number of analysts and institutional holdings). They find evidence that returns tend to increase as the number of analysts following a stock decreases and that this effect remains even after they controlled for the fact that small companies are more likely to have fewer analysts.

INITIAL PUBLIC OFFERINGS

In an initial public offering, a private firm makes the transition to being a publicly traded firm by offering shares to the public. In contrast with equity issues by companies that are already publicly traded, for which there is already a market price for the stock that acts as an anchor, an initial public offering has to be priced by an investment banker's perceptions of demand and supply. Some investors believe that they can exploit both the uncertainty in the process and the biases brought to the pricing by investment bankers to make high returns.

Process of an Initial Public Offering. When a private firm becomes publicly traded, the primary benefit it gains is increased access to financial markets and to capital for projects. This access to new capital is a significant gain for high growth businesses, with large and lucrative investment opportunities. A secondary benefit is that the owners of the private firm are able to cash in on their success by attaching a market value to their holdings. These benefits have to be weighed against the potential costs of being publicly traded. The most significant of these costs is the loss of control that may ensue from being a publicly traded firm. Other costs associated with being a publicly traded firm are the information disclosure requirements and the legal requirements.[8]

Assuming that the benefits outweigh the costs, a firm follows four steps to launch an initial public offering. The first is to choose an investment banker to take the firm public, and this choice is usually based upon reputation and marketing skills. In most initial public offerings, this investment banker underwrites the issue and guarantees a specified price for the stock. This investment banker then puts together a group of several banks (called a syndicate) to spread the risk of the offering and to increase marketing reach. The second step is to assess the value of the company and to set issue details. The pricing of the offering is usually based upon comparable firms that are publicly traded[9] and by sounding out potential buyers of the stock and seeing how much they would be willing to pay. The third step is meeting the legal requirements of the Securities and Exchange Commission (SEC) and filing a prospectus that describes the company and what the issuing company plans to do with the issue proceeds. The final step is to allocate the stock to those who apply to buy it at the offering price. If the demand for the stock exceeds the supply (which will happen if the offering price is set too low), the firm will have to ration the shares. If the supply exceeds the demand, the investment banker will have to fulfill the underwriting guarantee and buy the remaining stock at the offering price.

Initial Public Offerings: Pricing and Investment Strategies. How well do investment bankers price initial public offerings (IPOs)? One way to measure this is to compare the price when the stock first starts trading to the offering price. While precise estimates vary from year to year, the average initial public offering seems to be underpriced by 10% to 15%. The underpricing also seems to be greater for smaller public offerings. An examination of the underpricing as a function of the issue proceeds for 1767 IPOs between 1990 and 1994 yielded the results that are presented in Figure 9.5.[10]

The smaller the issue, the greater the underpricing—the smallest offerings often are underpriced by more than 17%, but the underpricing is much smaller for the larger issues.

You can break down initial public offerings on other dimensions to examine the reasons for the underpricing. A survey of the research on initial public offerings[11] provides a comprehensive summary of both the hypotheses on why the underpricing occurs and the empirical evidence on it. A few of the findings are summarized below:

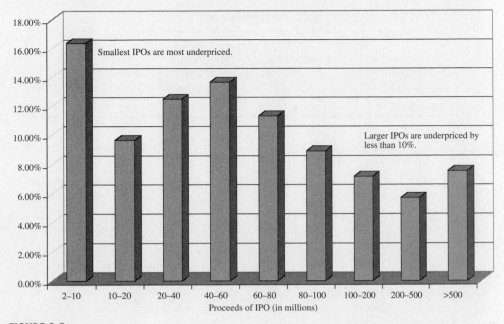

FIGURE 9.5
Average Initial Return and Issue Size
Data from a study by Lee, Lockhead, Ritter and Zhao. The initial return is the return you would have made if you had been able to subscribe at the offer price and sell at the price at the end of the first day of trading.

■ The average initial return is 15.8% across a sample of 13,308 initial public offerings. However, about 15% of all initial public offerings are overpriced. In other words, the stock price drops from the initial offering price on the date of the offering. Thus, investing in IPOs is by no means a riskless or guaranteed profits strategy, even if you receive your requested allotment in every one at the offering price.

■ Initial public offerings for which the offering price is revised upward before the offering are more likely to be underpriced than initial public offerings for which the offering price is revised downward. Table 9.1 contrasts the initial returns and the percent of offerings that were underpriced for both classes from 1991 to 1996.

TABLE 9.1   Average Initial Return: Offering Price Revision

OFFERING PRICE	NUMBER OF IPOs	AVERAGE INITIAL RETURN	% OF OFFERINGS UNDERPRICED
Revised down	708	3.54%	53%
Revised up	642	30.22%	95%

While the evidence that initial public offerings go up on the offering date is strong, it is not clear that these stocks are good investments in the years after. One study[12] tracked returns on 5821 IPOs in the five years after the offerings and contrasted them with returns on nonissuing firms of equivalent risk and size. The results are presented in Figure 9.6.

Note that the IPO firms consistently underperform the nonissuing firms and that the underperformance is greatest in

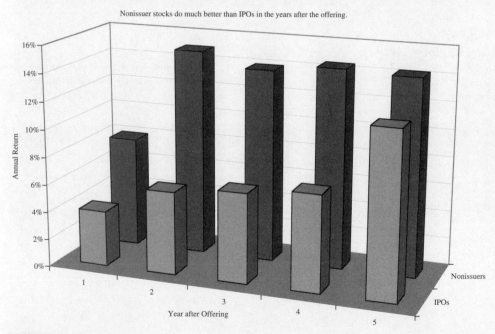

FIGURE 9.6

Postissue Returns: IPOs versus Non-IPOs

Data from Loughran and Ritter. The annual returns in each year after the initial public offering are compared to the returns that would have made by investment in nonissuers.

the first few years after the offering. While this phenomenon is less pronounced for larger initial public offerings, it still persists. What is the significance of this finding? The returns made by investors who buy initial public offerings will depend upon their time horizons; holding these stocks too long may wipe out any gains made around the offering date.

PRIVATE COMPANIES

In venture capital investing, you provide equity financing to small and often risky businesses in return for a share of the ownership of the firm. The size of your ownership share will depend upon two factors. First, at the minimum, you will demand an ownership share based upon how much capital you contribute to the firm relative to total firm value. For instance, if you provide $2 million and the estimated value of the firm is $10 million, you will expect to own at least 20% of the firm. Second, if the business can raise the funds from other sources, its bargaining position will be stronger, and it may be able to reduce your share down to a small premium over the minimum specified above. If a business has no other options available to raise the equity financing, however, its bargaining position is considerably weaker, and the owner of the business will have to give up a disproportionate share of the ownership to get the required funding.

In general, the capacity to raise funds from alternative sources or to go public will increase with the size of the firm and decrease with the uncertainty about its future prospects. Thus, smaller and riskier businesses are more likely to seek venture capital and are also more likely to be asked to give up a greater share of the value of the firm when receiving the venture capital.

Market for Private Equity and Venture Capital. Until a few decades ago, venture capital was provided by a relatively small number of individuals. They tended to specialize in a sector, invest in relatively few firms, and take an active role in the operations of these firms. In recent decades, though, as the market for venture capital has increased, you have seen three categories emerge.

The first are *venture capital funds,* which trace their lineage back to the 1950s. One of the first was American Research and Development; it provided seed money for the founding of Digital Equipment. During the 1960s and 1970s, these funds multiplied and helped start and expand companies, such as Intel and Apple that were then taken public. The second are *leveraged buyout funds,* which developed during the 1980s, using substantial amounts of debt to take over publicly traded firms and make them private firms. The publicity they generated—positive as well as negative—in the form of personalities, books and movies helped shaped the public's view of all acquisitions for a generation.[13] More recently, we have seen the growth of *private equity funds,* which pool the wealth of individual investors and invest in private firms that show promise. This has allowed investors to invest in private businesses without either giving up diversification or taking an active role in managing these firms. Pension funds and institutional investors, attracted by the high returns earned by investments in private firms, have also set aside portions of their overall portfolios to invest in private equity.

Venture capital can prove useful at different stages of a private firm's existence. *Seed-money venture capital, or angel financing,* for instance, is provided to startup firms that want to test a concept or develop a new product, while *startup venture capital* allows firms that have established products and concepts to develop and market them. Additional rounds of venture capital allow private firms that have more established products and markets to expand.

Most private equity funds are structured as private limited partnerships, in which the managers of the fund are the general partners and the investors in the fund—both individual and institutional—are limited partners. The general partners hold on to the power of when and where to invest and are generously compensated, with annual compensation ranging from 1.5% to 2.5% of the total capital invested and significant performance bonuses. Partnerships typically last from 10 to 12 years, and limited partners have to agree to make capital commitments for periods of 5 to 7 years.

Payoff to Venture Capital and Private Equity Investing. Note that the act of seeking and receiving venture capital is voluntary, and both sides enter into the relationship with the hope of gaining from it. The business gains access to funds that would not have been available otherwise; these funds in turn might enable the firm to bridge the gap until it can become a publicly traded firm. The venture capitalist might contribute management and organizational skills to the venture and provide the credibility needed for the business to raise more financing. The venture capitalist also might provide the know-how needed for the firm to eventually make a public offering of its equity. The venture capitalist gains as well. If the venture capitalist picks the right businesses to fund and provides good management skills and advice, there can be large returns on the initial investment. While the venture capitalist may reap returns from the private business itself, the largest payoff occurs when the business goes public and the venture capitalist is able to convert his or her stake into cash at the market price.

How well do venture capital and private equity investors do, relative to the market? There is clearly anecdotal evidence that some private equity investors do very well on individual deals and over time. There are also periods when private equity investing collectively earns extraordinary returns. During the 1990s, for instance, venture capital funds earned an average return of 29.5%, compared to the S&P 500's annual return of 15.1%, but there are three potential problems with this comparison.

The first is that the appropriate comparison would really be to the NASDAQ, which boomed during the 1990s and contained companies much like those in a venture capital portfolio: young technology firms. The second and related point is that these returns (both on the venture capital funds and the NASDAQ) are before they are adjusted for the substantial risk associated with the types of companies in these portfolios. The third is that the returns on the venture capital funds themselves are suspect because they are based upon assessments of value (often made by the venture capitalists) of nontraded investments. In fact, many of these venture capital funds were forced to confront both the risk and self-assessment issues in 2000 and 2001 as many of their investments, especially in new technology businesses, were written down to true value. From September 2000 to September 2001, for instance, venture capital funds lost 32% of their value, private equity funds lost 21%, and buyout funds lost 16% of their value.

When you look at returns on private equity investing over the last two decades what emerges is the sobering evidence that venture capital does yield returns but not of the magnitude that some investors expect. Venture Economics, a data service that tracks the returns on private equity investments, reported short-term and long-term returns on private equity investments as of September 2001 as shown in Table 9.2.

TABLE 9.2 Venture Economics' U.S. Private Equity Performance Index (PEPI) Returns as of September 30, 2001 (in percent)

FUND TYPE	1 YR	3 YR	5 YR	10 YR	20 YR
Early/Seed Venture Capital	− 36.3	81	53.9	33	21.5
Balanced Venture Capital	− 30.9	45.9	33.2	24	16.2
Later Stage Venture Capital	− 25.9	27.8	22.2	24.5	17
All Venture Capital	− 32.4	53.9	37.9	27.4	18.2
All Buyouts	− 16.1	2.9	8.1	12.7	15.6
Mezzanine	3.9	10	10.1	11.8	11.3
All Private Equity	− 21.4	16.5	17.9	18.8	16.9
S&P 500	− 15.3	13.6	14.8	15.6	13.9

On average, private equity and venture capital funds have outperformed the S&P 500, but the difference is surprisingly small. Between 1991 and 2001, for instance, all private equity funds earned an annual average return only 3.2% higher than the S&P 500 over the same period. Given the high risk associated with these investments, that does not seem like a significant excess return.

CRUNCHING THE NUMBERS

The evidence presented in the last section suggests that investing in smaller, less followed companies or in private businesses can generate a payoff for investors. In this section, you will first look at differences in market capitalization and institutional following across publicly traded firms, then at the initial public offerings in a recent quarter, and finally at the portfolios that would emerge if you decided to put these investment strategies into practice.

MARKET CAPITALIZATION

What constitutes a small-cap company? The answer will vary widely depending upon whom you ask and the universe of stocks they invest in. For an investor who restricts his investments to S&P 500 companies, a billion dollar company may be a small company. For an investor who looks at smaller stocks on the NASDAQ, the cutoff will be much lower. It will also shift as the market goes up and down. At the peak of the stock market in 1999, dozens of companies were trading at market capitalizations that exceeded $100 billion. In 2002, after three years of a bear market, only a handful were left.

The best way of assessing the differences that make for small and large companies is to look at the distribution of market capitalizations across the market. Figure 9.7 presents the number of listed firms in the United States that fell into different market capitalization classes at the end of 2002.

Note the extraordinary number of firms (more than 1200) that had market capitalizations that were less than $5 million. This represents the convergence of two phenomena: the large number of small companies that went public in the 1990s and the dramatic fall in value at these companies as the technology bubble burst. In fact, you can safely argue that a large number of the smallest companies will cease to exist as publicly traded entities in the near future. If you adopt commonly used criteria for small cap ($250 million and less, for

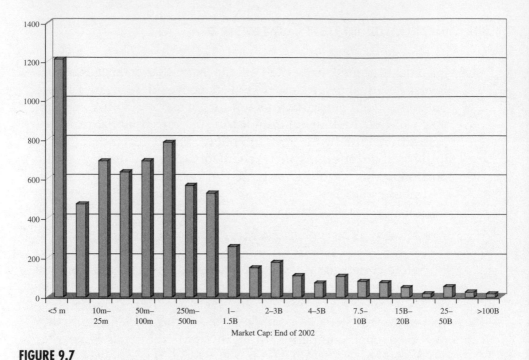

FIGURE 9.7
Market Cap Distribution
Data from Value Line. The number of firms in each market capitalization class is reported.

instance), you would find more than two-thirds of all listed companies being classified as small cap.

If small is difficult to define, lightly followed is even more so. One measure of following is the number of analysts who follow a company. Many of these analysts work for investment banks or for portfolio managers. In Figure 9.8, the distribution of firms, categorized by number of analysts tracking them in early 2003, is provided.

Note again that about 1400 firms have no analysts tracking them and that 1800 are tracked by a lone analyst. Another measure of following is investment by institutional investors—mutual funds and pension funds. Figure 9.9 categorizes companies by the percent of stock held by institutions in early 2003.

While institutions may dominate the holdings of some firms, there is a large number of firms for which institutions hold less than 10% of the outstanding stock.

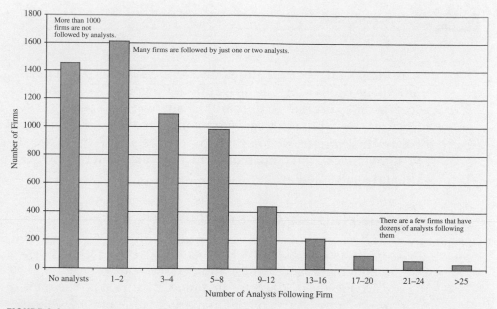

FIGURE 9.8

Number of Analysts Estimating Earnings per Share: U.S. Firms in January 2003

Data from Zacks. These are sell-side analysts tracking each company in January 2003.

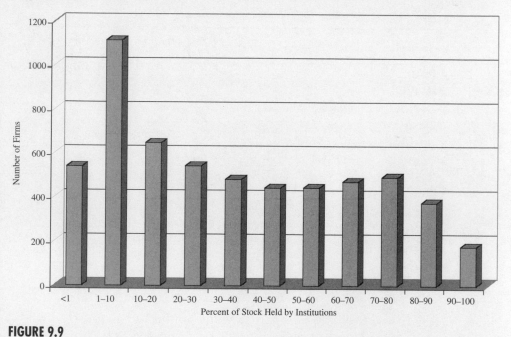

FIGURE 9.9

Institutional Holdings as Percent of Stock

Data from Value Line. This is the percent of stock held by institutional investors. It includes mutual funds and pension funds as a percent of the outstanding stock in a company.

Bringing together all three measures—market capitalization, analyst following and institutional ownership—it should come as no surprise that there is an overlap across these measures. Small-market-cap companies are less likely to be held by institutions or followed by analysts. However, there are some small-cap companies with high institutional ownership and analyst following.

INITIAL PUBLIC OFFERINGS

The number of IPOs varies fairly widely from period to period, depending largely upon market mood and receptivity. In the fourth quarter of 2002, for instance, 21 initial public offerings were made, with a collective market value of $3.7 billion. The breakdown of the sectors to which these 21 companies belonged is provided in Table 9.3.

TABLE 9.3 IPOs by Sector in Fourth Quarter 2002

SECTOR	NUMBER OF IPOs	PERCENT OF OFFERINGS
Insurance	4	19.00%
Banking	3	14.30%
Computer Software & Services	2	9.50%
Leisure	2	9.50%
Health Products & Services	2	9.50%
Computer Hardware	1	4.80%
Real Estate	1	4.80%
Specialty Retail	1	4.80%
Metals & Mining	1	4.80%
Diversified Services	1	4.80%
Energy	1	4.80%
Manufacturing	1	4.80%
Financial Services	1	4.80%

In contrast, 26 companies went public in the fourth quarter of 2001 with a collective market value of $10 billion. At the height of the boom in the stock market in the late 1990s, hundreds of companies were going public every year, with a cumulative market value running into tens of billions of dollars.

How well did the 21 companies that went public in the fourth quarter of 2002 do for investors? Table 9.4 reports the offer price and the price at the end of the quarter for each of these companies and measures the return over the quarter.

TABLE 9.4 Returns for Quarter: IPOs in Fourth Quarter 2002

COMPANY NAME	OFFER PRICE	CLOSE PRICE	RETURN
Dick's Sporting Goods, Inc	$12.00	$19.20	60%
Montpelier RE Holdings Ltd	$20.00	$28.80	44%
Portfolio Recovery Associates, Inc	$13.00	$18.25	40%
VistaCare, Inc	$12.00	$16.01	33%
Chicago Mercantile Exchange Holdings, Inc	$35.00	$43.66	25%
IMPAC Medical Systems, Inc	$15.00	$18.52	23%
Newcastle Investment Corp	$13.00	$15.97	23%
Safety Holdings, Inc	$12.00	$14.38	20%
U.S.I. Holdings Corporation	$10.00	$11.75	18%
Platinum Underwriters Holdings, Ltd	$22.50	$26.35	17%
Taylor Capital Group, Inc	$16.50	$18.60	13%
Commercial Capital Bancorp, Inc	$8.00	$8.87	11%
Natural Resource Partners LP	$20.00	$20.70	4%
Wynn Resorts, Limited	$13.00	$13.11	1%
Constar International, Inc	$12.00	$11.75	– 2%
WellChoice, Inc	$25.00	$23.95	– 4%
Harrington West Financial Group, Inc	$12.00	$11.25	– 6%
Martin Midstream Partners LP	$19.00	$17.75	– 7%
Seagate Technology Holdings	$12.00	$10.73	– 11%
Cosí, Inc	$7.00	$5.56	– 21%
SI International, Inc	$14.00	$10.81	– 23%

It is worth emphasizing that you would not have earned these returns by buying the stock on the first trading day, since the first traded price was very different from the offering price for some of them. Consider, for instance, Table 9.5, which lists the offer price and the price at the end of the first trading day for most of the companies listed in the last table.

TABLE 9.5 First Day Price Movement—IPOs in Fourth Quarter 2002

COMPANY	OFFER PRICE	FIRST DAY CLOSE	RETURN
VistaCare, Inc	$12.00	$15.05	25%
Chicago Mercantile Exchange Holdings, Inc	$35.00	$42.90	23%
Portfolio Recovery Associates, Inc	$13.00	$15.45	19%
IMPAC Medical Systems, Inc	$15.00	$17.72	18%
Montpelier RE Holdings Ltd	$20.00	$23.50	18%
Platinum Underwriters Holdings, Ltd	$22.50	$24.99	11%
Dick's Sporting Goods, Inc	$12.00	$13.15	10%
WellChoice, Inc	$25.00	$27.20	9%
Cosí, Inc	$7.00	$7.60	9%
Safety Holdings, Inc	$12.00	$12.90	8%
Martin Midstream Partners LP	$19.00	$17.70	−7%
Seagate Technology Holdings	$12.00	$11.50	−4%
Newcastle Investment Corp	$13.00	$12.50	−4%
Natural Resource Partners LP	$20.00	$19.40	−3%
Constar International, Inc	$12.00	$11.85	−1%

When underwriters underprice IPOs, as they have Vista-Care, investors may gain from the underpricing but the issuing companies lose out. The difference between the proceeds raised from the offer price and the proceeds that could have been raised if the issue had been priced right is called "money left on the table." Table 9.6 summarizes the cash left on the table at some of the IPOs listed above.

In summary, even in a slow quarter like the one examined, there is evidence that investment bankers continue to underprice initial public offerings and that at least some investors gain from this underpricing.

TABLE 9.6 Cash on Table: IPOs in Fourth Quarter 2002

ISSUING COMPANY	INVESTMENT BANK	OFFER PRICE	OFFER PROCEEDS	TRADED PRICE	TRADED PROCEEDS	CASH ON TABLE
Platinum Underwriters Holdings, Ltd	Goldman, Sachs & Co.	$22.50	$675.90	$25.00	$751.00	$75.10
WellChoice, Inc	Crédit Suisse First Boston	$25.00	$346.50	$28.50	$395.00	$48.50
Montpelier RE Holdings Ltd	Morgan Stanley	$20.00	$190.50	$22.00	$209.50	$19.00
Chicago Mercantile Exchange Holdings	Morgan Stanley	$35.00	$166.30	$39.00	$185.30	$19.00
VistaCare, Inc	Lehman Brothers	$12.00	$72.00	$13.05	$78.30	$6.30
Portfolio Recovery Associates, Inc	William Blair & Company	$13.00	$45.10	$14.75	$51.20	$6.10
Taylor Capital Group, Inc	Keefe, Bruyette & Woods, Inc.	$16.50	$45.80	$17.75	$49.30	$3.50
Cosí, Inc	William Blair & Company	$7.00	$38.90	$7.50	$41.70	$2.80
IMPAC Medical Systems, Inc	Thomas Weisel Partners LLC	$15.00	$32.80	$16.05	$35.10	$2.30
Dick's Sporting Goods, Inc	Merrill Lynch	$12.00	$87.50	$12.25	$89.30	$1.80

PRIVATE EQUITY INVESTMENTS

Obtaining information on individual private equity deals is more difficult than information on initial public offerings. You can get a measure of the overall success of private equity investment by looking at money flows into and out of private equity funds. In 2002, a total of $21.179 billion was invested by venture capitalists in 3011 deals. In contrast, more than $200 billion was invested in 8221 deals in 2000. Table 9.7 summarizes the deal flow in venture capital from 1992 to 2002.

TABLE 9.7 Venture Capital Investments: Number and Dollar Value of Deals

YEAR	COMPANIES	DEALS	INVESTMENT ($MILLIONS)
1992	1065	1415	3594.6
1993	955	1212	3876.3
1994	992	1241	4202.2
1995	1583	1902	7683
1996	2126	2660	11598.2
1997	2612	3251	15548.7
1998	3495	4208	21525.4
1999	4514	5686	55136
2000	6478	8221	106556.5
2001	3878	4712	41296.5
2002	2495	3011	21179

Not surprisingly, venture capital funds flow most to firms in high growth sectors. Table 9.8 breaks deals down by sector in the fourth quarter of 2002.

TABLE 9.8 Venture Capital Investments by Sector in 2002

SECTOR	COMPANIES	DEALS	INVESTMENT ($M)
Software	183	183	869.3
Telecommunications	79	79	561.8
Biotechnology	61	61	474.4
Medical Devices and Equipment	57	57	486.1
Networking and Equipment	48	48	467.7
Industrial/Energy	38	38	140.7

SECTOR	COMPANIES	DEALS	INVESTMENT ($M)
IT Services	33	33	217.7
Media and Entertainment	32	32	142.4
Semiconductors	28	28	242.7
Business Products and Services	27	27	81
Computers and Peripherals	26	26	134
Consumer Products and Services	18	18	68.4
Healthcare Services	17	17	98.2
Financial Services	17	17	52
Retailing/Distribution	16	16	61.6
Electronics/Instrumentation	11	11	53
Other	1	1	2
Total	692	692	4152.9

The vast majority of the deals were in software and technology (both medical and other). The deals were even more skewed toward technology in earlier years.

A PORTFOLIO OF SMALL-CAP, LIGHTLY FOLLOWED STOCKS

Based upon the information provided in the last section, you could go about constructing a portfolio of small-cap, lightly followed stocks by using the following criteria:

- *Market capitalization cutoff:* As you can see from Figure 9.7 on page 284, even a maximum market cap of $10 million would yield more than a thousand firms. Since many firms with small market capitalizations are likely to be in trouble or be offering stock that is difficult to even buy, a minimum market capitalization of $10 million will be required. The maximum market capitalization is set at $50 million to allow other constraints to be built into this portfolio.
- *Analyst following:* Only firms that are not followed by any analysts will be considered for the portfolio. Though

this may seem severe, there are (as Figure 9.8 on page 285 brings forth) enough publicly traded firms that are not followed by any analysts.

- *Institutional ownership:* If the institutional ownership in a firm exceeds 5%, the firm will not be considered for the portfolio. Here again, the fact that small firms tend to have low institutional holdings allows the imposition of this constraint.
- *Stock price minimum:* Since trading stocks that sell for less than a dollar can be prohibitively expensive, only stocks that trade for more than a dollar are considered for this portfolio.

Combining these screens—market cap less than $50 million but greater than $10 million, no analysts following the stock, institutional ownership less than 5% of the stock and a minimum stock price of $1—generates a portfolio of 122 companies. Table 9.9 lists the stocks.

Taking a closer look at this portfolio, you should not be surprised to see no familiar names, since these are not widely followed companies. What is surprising, though, is the diversity of businesses that these firms operate in. Contrary to popular opinion, small companies are not predominantly technology firms but include conventional manufacturing and service companies.

MORE TO THE STORY

Three separate strategies have been presented in this chapter for investing in younger, higher growth companies. The first and perhaps least risky strategy is to invest in small, publicly traded companies that are not widely followed by analysts. The second and potentially riskier strategy is to invest in stocks at the time or just after an initial public offering. The third and riskiest strategy is to invest in young private companies before they go public. Each of these strategies may show promise, but each also comes with potential problems.

TABLE 9.9 Portfolio of Small, Lightly Followed Companies: End of 2002

Company Name	Industry	Company Name	Industry	Company Name	Industry
American Bio Medica Corp	Medserv	Bncorp Inc	Bank	Siebert Finl Corp	Financl
B & H Ocean Carriers	Maritime	Cowlitz Bancorp	Bank	Beta Oil and Gas Inc	Oilprod
Williams Industries Inc	Machine	Canterbury Pk Hldg Corp	Hotelgam	Encore Med Corp	Medsuppl
Capital Title Group Inc	Insdivrs	Codorus Valley Bancorp	Bank	ASTA Funding Inc	Financl
American Ecology Corp	Environm	National Sec Group Inc	Inslife	Quotesmith.com Inc	Indusrv
Educational Development	Publish	Chad Therapeutics	Medsuppl	Credo Pete Corp	Oilprod
Merrill Merchants Bancshares I	Bank	Big Foot Finl	Financl	Creative Host Svcs	Foodwhol
Wellco Enterprises Inc	Shoe	Elamix S.A.De C.V. CL I	Electronx	Cardiotech Intl Inc	Medserv
Citizens First Finl	Thrift	Tag-It Pacific	Apparel	Amerigon Inc "A"	Auto-oem
First Regional Bancorp	Bank	Carmel Container Sys Ltd	Package	Boston Life Sciences Inc	Drug
Tofutti Brands	Foodproc	Halifax Corp	Software	Computer Motion	Medsuppl
Britton & Koontz Capital	Bank	1st Fedl Bancorp Ohio	Bank	Penn Octane Corp	Gasdistr
BF Enterprises	Homebild	Abigail Adams Natl Bncrp	Bank	Global Payment Tech	Financl
Midsouth Bancorp	Bank	Barnwell Industries	Oilprod	Fountain Power Boat	Recreate
Jameson Inns Inc	Hotelgam	ML Macadamia Orchards LP	Foodproc	Canada Southern Petroleum Ltd	Canenrgy
COMMUNITY FINL CORP VA	Bank	Antenna TV S A	Entrtain	Merisel Inc	Retailsp
Guaranty Bancshares Inc Tex	Bank	Poore Brothers	Fodproc	Magic Software Enterprises	Software
Peoples-Sidney Finl	Thrift	Int'l Remote Imaging	Medsuppl	Netsmart Technologies	Software
Falmouth Bancorp	Bank	Aristotle Corp NEW	Apparel	Century Casinos Inc	Hotelgam
United Finl Corp Minn	Thrift	Boston Biomedica	Instrmnt	Immtech Intl Inc	Drug
RGC Resources Inc	Gasdistr	Amcon Distributing Co	Foodwhol	Insightful Corp	Software

(continued)

TABLE 9.9 Portfolio of Small, Lightly Followed Companies: End of 2002 (*Continued*)

COMPANY NAME	INDUSTRY	COMPANY NAME	INDUSTRY	COMPANY NAME	INDUSTRY
Chester Bancorp	Bank	Catalyst Semiconductor Inc	Semicond	Net Guru Inc	Software
Goodrich Petro Corp	Oilprod	Impreso.com	Paper	I-Flow Corp	Medserv
Capital Environmental Resource	Environm	Crystal Systems	Chemspec	Dyntek Inc	Software
Elmer's Restaurants Inc	Restrnt	Valley Forge Scientific Corp	Medsuppl	Jacada Ltd	Software
Dwyer Group Inc	Diversif	C2 Inc	Trucking	NEON Systems Inc	Software
Nicholas Financial Inc	Financl	Innovo Group	Retailsp	Optibase Ltd	Computer
Lifeway Foods	Foodproc	Ameritrans Cap Corp	Financl	Mannatech Inc	Drug
Annapolis Natl Bancorp Inc	Bank	Leather Factory Inc	Houseprd	Cryo-Cell Intl Inc	Medserv
Laser-Pacific Media Corp	Recreate	Double Eagle Pet & Min	Oilprod	DPAC Technologies Corp	Computer
Community Bk Shs Ind Inc	Bank	Food Technology Service Inc	Medsuppl	Pacific Internet Limited	Internet
Birmingham Utilities Inc	Water	Navarre Corp	Software	Datatec Sys Inc	Teleserv
Dynamic Materials	Building	Cohesant Technologies Inc	Chemdiv	Dialysis Corp Amer	Medserv
Energy West Inc	Gasdistr	Palatin Technologies Inc	Medserv	FOCUS ENHANCEMENTS	Software
Golden Enterprises	Foodproc	CECO Environmental	Environm	Logility Inc	Software
American First Apt Inv L P	Fund-Inc	Micronetics Wireless	Electrnx	Certicom Corp	Software
Gallery Of History Inc	Retailsp	Vita Food Prods	Foodproc	New York Health Care	Hlthsys
Sussex Bancorp	Bank	American Technology	Electrnx	Ross Systems Inc	Software
VSE Corp	Indusrv	Rotonics Mfg Inc	Package	Extended Systems	Wireless
Covista Communications Inc	Teleserv	XATA Corp	Electrnx		
Pizza Inn Inc	Foodwhol	TFC Enterprises	Financl		
Transgene SA	Drug	TRANS INDS INC	Electrnx		

SMALL AND LIGHTLY
FOLLOWED STOCKS

The persistence of the small stock premium has led many to argue that what looks like a premium in studies comes from the failure to allow for transactions costs and to adequately measure risk in firms. There is truth in these arguments, though it is unclear whether the small stock premium would disappear even if they were considered.

Costs of Transactions. The transactions costs of investing in small stocks are significantly higher than the transactions costs of investing in larger stocks. The bid-ask spread as a percent of the stock price is higher for smaller companies. In addition the price impact from trading is also higher for small-cap stocks because they are less liquid; you will tend to drive the price up as you buy and down as you sell, especially with larger orders. Can the difference in transactions costs overwhelm the small-cap premium? The answer has to depend upon both the size of your portfolio and your time horizon. With short time horizons, the transactions costs can wipe out any perceived excess returns associated with small-cap companies. With longer time horizons, though, you can spread the costs over your holding period and the excess returns may persist. A larger portfolio can help you reduce some transactions costs (brokerage and commission costs) but may increase other transactions costs (price impact).

In a telling illustration of the difficulties associated with replicating the small-firm premiums that are observed in the research in real time, Figure 9.10 compares the returns on a hypothetical small-firm portfolio (CRSP Small Stocks) with the actual returns on a small-firm mutual fund (DFA Small Stock Fund), which passively invests in the same small stocks.

Note that the returns on the DFA fund consistently lag the returns on the hypothetical portfolio by about 2%, reflecting the transactions and execution costs faced by the fund.

Consider now the lightly followed, small-cap portfolio in Table 9.9. While only stocks with a price of more than a dollar

Every year, the returns on the DFA fund have lagged the returns on the paper portfolio (CRSP small stocks).

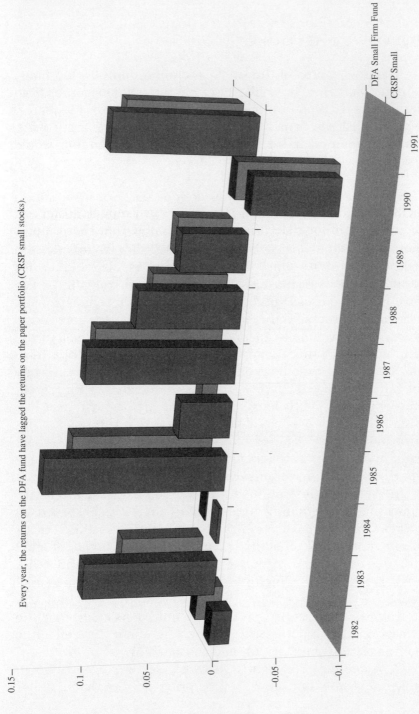

FIGURE 9.10

Returns on CRSP Small Stocks vs. DFA Small Stock Fund

Data from Morningstar and CRSP. The returns in each year from the DFA mutual fund and from the hypothetical small stock portfolio of CRSP are reported.

296

were considered for this portfolio, there is a large number of low-priced stocks in the portfolio. In Figure 9.11, the stocks in the portfolio are broken down by the level of the stock price.

About two-thirds of the stocks in the portfolio trade at less than $5 a share, a level at which transactions costs tend to mount. In fact, if you invested only in stocks that trade above $10, you would reduce the number of stocks in the portfolio by about 80%.

Failure to Consider Liquidity and Estimation Risk. Many of the studies that uncover a small-cap premium measure the risk of stocks by using conventional risk and return models to measure and control for risk. It is entirely possible that these models underestimate the true risk of small stocks. Thus, the small-firm premium may really reflect the failure of risk and return models in finance. The additional risk associated with

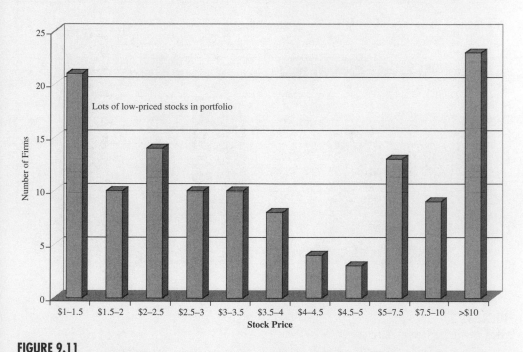

FIGURE 9.11
Stock Prices in Small-Cap Portfolio

Data from Value Line. The number of small-cap stocks that fall into each price class is reported.

small stocks may come from several sources. First, the estimation risk associated with estimates of risk parameters for small firms is much greater than the estimation risk associated with risk parameters for larger firms. The small-firm premium may be a reward for this additional estimation risk.[14] Second, there may be much greater liquidity risk associated with investing in small companies. This risk (which is also partially responsible for the higher transactions costs noted in the previous section) is not captured in conventional risk and return models.

One measure of the liquidity of stocks is the trading volume on the stocks. On this measure, you can see that lightly followed, small-cap stocks are much less liquid than the rest of the market. In Figure 9.12, the trading volume over three months, six months and a year is compared for the stocks in the small-cap portfolio with the trading volume in the rest of the market.

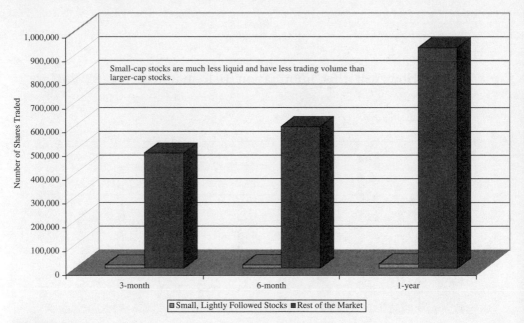

FIGURE 9.12

Trading Volume: Small-Cap vs. Rest of the Market

Data from Value Line. This is the average trading volume, in number of shares traded, for small firms and the rest of the market.

Clearly, there is far less trading volume, both in terms of number of shares outstanding and dollar trading volume. Even small orders can cause the price of the stock to move, reducing any potential returns.

Assume that you decide to screen the small-cap portfolio for minimal trading and invest only in those firms for which the annual trading volume exceeds the number of shares outstanding in the firm. With this screen, you would reduce the size of your portfolio by about 50%. In fact, combining this screen with a requirement that stock prices exceed $5 would reduce the number of stocks in this portfolio from 122 firms to 25 firms.

Exposure to Information Risk. A strategy of investing in smaller firms that are less followed by analysts and not widely held by institutions can expose you to information risk. You will be far more dependent on the firm you are investing in to provide you with information, and you will not have the luxury of analysts investigating the firm's weaknesses and providing you with advance warnings of coming surprises.

How will this information risk manifest itself? You are more likely to see larger price reactions to earnings and dividend announcements made by smaller, less followed firms than by firms that are widely followed. This is clearly visible in Figure 9.13, in which the percentage price change (up or down) in reaction to quarterly earnings announcements in 2001 is graphed for the firms in the small-cap, lightly followed portfolio listed in Table 9.9 and compared to the same measure for firms in the S&P 500.

Two points need to be made about this graph. First, these figures represent the size of the price changes. In other words, this graph indicates that you are more likely to see big price moves on earnings reports for smaller, less followed firms but it does not tell you in which direction; stocks are more likely to both go up a lot and go down a lot for these firms. Second, the percentage changes in prices may be skewed upward for the smaller firms because the stock prices at these firms are also lower.

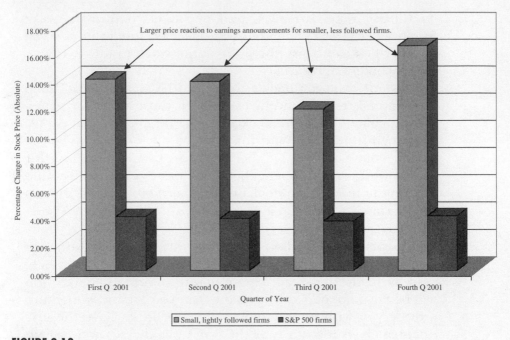

FIGURE 9.13
Price Reaction to Earnings Announcements

Data from Compustat and CRSP. This is the absolute change (either an increase or a decrease) in stock price, stated in percent terms, on the day of the earnings announcement.

How would you screen for this risk? You could go through the tedious task of looking at the stock price reaction to earnings reports in the past for each firm in the sample and only investing in stocks for which the price reaction is muted. A less technical but less burdensome way of reducing your risk exposure is to invest only in companies with stable and growing earnings, on the assumption that you are less likely to be surprised with these firms.

INITIAL PUBLIC OFFERINGS

A strategy of investing in initial public offerings looks promising if you look at the average returns that you can earn from investing in initial public offerings at the offer price. There are, however, two catches. The first is that the allotment process is skewed toward overpriced offerings and away from underpriced offerings; you will get all the shares you ask for in the former and far fewer than you wanted in the latter. The second is that the market for initial public offerings goes through hot and cold phases—lots of IPOs in some years followed by very few in others. If you are dependent upon IPOs for the bulk of your portfolio, you will find yourself with slim pickings in the latter periods.

Allotment Process.   If initial public offerings, on average, are underpriced, an obvious investment strategy is to subscribe a large number of initial public offerings and to construct a portfolio based upon allotments of these offerings. There is, however, a bias in the allotment process that may prevent this portfolio from earning the excess returns you see in the research. When you subscribe to initial public offerings, the number of shares that you are allotted will depend upon whether and by how much the offering is underpriced. If it is significantly underpriced, you will get only a fraction of the shares that you requested. On the other hand, if the offering is correctly priced or overpriced, you will get all of the shares that you requested. Thus, your portfolio will have fewer shares than you want in underpriced initial public offerings and more shares than you want in overpriced offerings. You can see this if you consider the 21 companies that made initial public offerings in the last quarter of 2002. If you had applied for $10,000 worth of shares in each of these companies, you would have received your entire allotment in the five companies for which the offering price was greater than the market price. In the remaining companies, you would have received less than your requested number of shares, with the lowest allotment being in companies like VistaCare that were most undervalued.

There are two ways in which you can win this allotment game. The first is to be the beneficiary of a biased allotment system, whereby the investment bank gives you more than your share of your requested shares in underpriced offerings. While this is illegal in the United States,[15] it is legal in many other countries in the world. The second and more legitimate way is to develop an analytical system that allows you to separate underpriced from overpriced offerings, using public information contained in the prospectus and other SEC filings. You would then request shares in only those offerings that you have identified as underpriced. If you are reasonably accurate, you should end up with a portfolio that more closely resembles (or even beats) the hypothetical portfolios created across all initial public offerings.

The IPO Cycle. Initial public offerings ebb and flow with the overall market. There are periods when the market is flooded with initial public offerings and periods when there are almost no offerings. Contrast, for instance, the salad days of the late 1990s, when firms went public at an extraordinary pace, to 2001, when the number slowed to a trickle. In addition, the initial public offerings during any period tend to share a common sector focus. For instance, the bulk of the initial public offerings during 1999 were of young technology firms. This does create two problems for investment strategies that focus exclusively on initial public offerings. The first is that your portfolio will not be diversified in periods of plenty, and will be overweighted in whichever sector is in favor at that time. The second is that there will be extended periods during which you will find nothing to invest in, because there are few or no initial public offerings.

One comprehensive examination[16] of IPOs summarizes the number of offerings made each year from 1960 to 1996 and the average initial returns on those offerings. The results are presented in Figure 9.14.

Note that the number of offerings drops to almost zero in the early 1970s and the returns to the offerings drops as well. A portfolio manager who focused only on initial public offerings would have gone out of business in that period.

The number of offerings in the fourth quarter of 2002 illustrates the IPO cycle. The 21 companies that went public in that quarter represent a dramatic drop-off from the 178 companies that went public in the fourth quarter in 1999. The shift in sector focus is also significant. While 75% of the offerings in the fourth quarter of 1999 were technology companies,

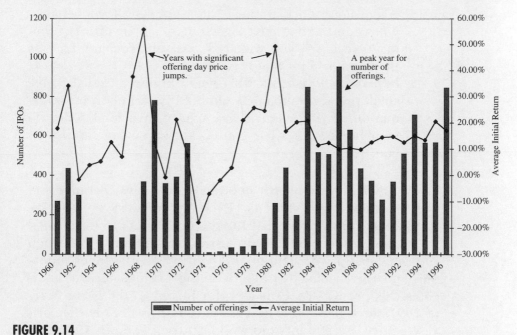

FIGURE 9.14
Number of IPOs and Average Initial Return
Data from Ritter. The number of offerings each year and the return on the first offering day are reported.

only one technology company made an initial public offering in the fourth quarter of 2002.

PRIVATE COMPANIES

Many of the problems associated with the small-firm strategy that were listed earlier in this section are magnified when you are investing in private companies:

- *Transactions costs and liquidity:* The transactions costs associated with private equity investments can be substantial. Not only do you have to do due diligence on your potential equity investments, meeting managers and gauging their plans, but you also bear a substantial cost when you exit these investments. If you change your mind and want to get out of an investment you made recently, you will find yourself receiving far less than you paid for that investment.

■ *Information risk:* As with small publicly traded firms, small private companies can hold back important information. If you, as a private equity investor, do not do your homework, what you do not know can easily hurt you.

Another point is worth making about private equity and venture capital investments. Even the modest average returns that you saw reported for the entire sector are pushed up by the presence of a few investments that make very high returns. Most private equity and venture capital investments fail, and the median (rather than the average return) indicates this propensity. Consider, for instance, the glory years of 1997 through 1999. The conventional wisdom is that private equity investments did well in those years. In 1999, the weighted-average internal rate of return on private equity investments was 119%, but the median return in that year was 2.9%. The median trailed the average badly in 1997 and 1998 as well.

As the stock market declined between 2000 and 2002, private equity and venture capital opportunities also dropped off. This can be partially explained by the weaker economy that prevailed during those years. However, it also illustrates the dependence of private equity investors on a vibrant stock market to exit their investments—the highest returns in private equity come from companies that can be taken public.

LESSONS FOR INVESTORS

The problems that you face when you invest in smaller, lightly followed companies, initial public offerings and private equity investments are often similar, though they may vary in degree. While you cannot ever insulate a portfolio of such companies from risk, you can try to screen for obvious problems.

If you are constructing a portfolio of smaller, lightly followed companies, these are some of the screens to consider:

- *Small but not too small:* If you want to invest in small companies but want to avoid tiny companies that may be delisted, you should specify both a maximum market capitalization and a minimum market capitalization. For instance, you could invest in companies with a market capitalization below $100 million but above $10 million. As your portfolio becomes larger, you may need to revise these screens, increasing both the maximum and minimum market capitalization to meet your needs.

- *Liquidity and transactions costs:* The simplest test for liquidity is the stock price level (a minimum price of $5 is a good standard) and trading volume (annual volume that exceeds shares outstanding). An alternative measure of liquidity is the *float*—the shares that are actually available for trading as a percent of the outstanding stock. You could restrict yourself only to stocks with sufficient float for you to be able to trade easily.

- *Pricing screens:* If the argument for investing in small companies is that they are more likely to be misvalued than larger, heavily followed companies, you want to screen further to make sure that you end up with the most undervalued companies rather than the most overvalued. One simple way of putting this in practice is to invest only in companies that trade at low PE ratios; you could, for instance, require stocks to trade at PE ratios less than 10.

The portfolio of 18 companies that met all of these criteria— market capitalization more than $10 million but less than $100 million, a stock price of at least $5, annual trading volume that exceeds the number of shares outstanding, and PE ratios less than 10—is listed in the appendix to this chapter.

If you are considering investing in initial public offerings, you should try to do at least the following:

- *Play the allotment game well.* The key to winning the IPO game is getting more shares in underpriced IPOs and less shares (or no shares) in overpriced IPOs. Assuming that you will not be given preferential allotments by investment banks, this will require that you not only read the prospectuses filed by these companies but that you try to do preliminary valuations of the companies.
- *Consider mixing this strategy with another more diverse one.* Since a strategy of investing in IPOs can lead to years of plenty followed by years with few or no offerings, and since even in good years, offerings tend to be concentrated in a few sectors, you may want to combine this strategy with another, more diverse one. For instance, you could invest 75% of your portfolio in small, lightly followed, publicly traded companies and 25% in initial public offerings.
- *Be disciplined.* The evidence on IPOs suggests that any price runup that occurs after initial public offering dissipates if you hold the stock too long. In fact, these stocks do not generate high returns if you hold them for extended periods (more than a year) after the initial public offerings.

If you are interested in private equity or venture capital, you have to begin with the recognition that you cannot do this directly as an individual investor. You will have to choose a private equity fund that will accept your investment—most private equity funds have substantial minimum investment constraints. In choosing a private equity fund, you should consider past performance—a good track record would indicate that the fund picks the right firms to invest in—and risk; high-risk funds can quickly go from success to peril. Finally, you should expect to pay far more in management fees and expenses and have restrictions imposed on your investment.

CONCLUSION

The allure of investing in hidden gems—businesses that other investors have not discovered or have ignored—underlies all of the investment strategies described in this chapter. The strategy of investing in smaller, less followed companies is the strategy that is most accessible to individual investors. By putting your money in companies with small-market capitalization that are lightly held by institutions and not followed by analysts, you may be able to generate higher returns. Whether these higher returns are just compensation for the higher risk of these stocks—they are less liquid and information may not be as freely available—or excess returns is the key question that investors have to answer while following this strategy. Your odds of success improve if you can focus on stocks with lower transactions costs and more stable earnings that are priced attractively.

A more risky strategy is investing in companies as they go public by bidding for shares in these companies at the initial public offerings. While the empirical evidence suggests that these stocks are generally underpriced (by about 10% to 15%), this strategy has three problems. The first is that you are likely to get all the shares you request in companies that are overpriced and less than your requested number in underpriced companies. Thus, your final portfolio will earn lower returns than the empirical evidence suggests. The second problem is that a strategy of investing in only IPOs will have to be short term (almost all of the price jump occurs on the first day of trading and can dissipate if you hold the stock too long) and results in portfolios that are overweighted in the hot IPO sectors (technology in 1999, for instance). Finally, the number of IPOs in a year reflects the market mood, dropping off significantly in bear markets and rising in bull markets. As an investor, you may very well find nothing to invest in when confronted with a cold market and too many offerings to look through in hot markets.

The riskiest strategy discussed in this chapter is investing in businesses before they go public and then nurturing them to the point when they can be acquired or go public, at which point you cash out on your investment. This is what private equity and venture capital investors do. Since this strategy requires screening (you have to look at private businesses to decide which ones to invest in) and active monitoring (to ensure that your investment in the business is not being wasted), it is beyond the reach of most individual investors. There are private equity and venture capital funds that do have the resources to screen and monitor investments, but they meet with varied success. Relatively few funds generate high returns, and it is not clear that even these funds can sustain their success.

ENDNOTES

1. These annual returns were obtained from the annual returns data set maintained by Ken French and Gene Fama on market value classes.

2. Siegel, J., 1998, *Stocks for the Long Run*, McGraw Hill, New York.

3. Pradhuman, S., 2000, *Small Cap Dynamics*, Bloomberg Press.

4. Chopra, N., and J. Ritter, 1989, *Portfolio Rebalancing and the Turn-of-the-year Effect*, Journal of Finance, v44, 149–166.

5. Dimson, E., and P. R. Marsh, 1986, *Event Studies and the Size Effect: The Case of UK Press Recommendations*, Journal of Financial Economics, v17, 113–142.

6. Fama, E. F., and K. R. French, 1998, *Value versus Growth: The International Evidence*, Journal of Finance, v53, 1975–1999.

7. Chan, L. K., Y. Hamao, and J. Lakonishok, 1991, *Fundamentals and Stock Returns in Japan*, Journal of Finance, v46, 1739–1789.

8. The costs are twofold. One is the cost of producing and publicizing the information itself. The other is the loss of control over how much information to reveal to the market and when to reveal it.

9. One common approach is to use the average multiple of earnings or revenues that comparable firms trade at in the market to price the initial public offering's shares.

10. Lee, I., S. Lockhead, J. R. Ritter and Q. Zhao, 1996, *The Costs of Raising Capital*, Journal of Financial Research, v19, 59–74.

11. Ritter, J. R., 1998, *Initial Public Offerings*, Contemporary Finance Digest, v2, 5–31.

12. Loughran, T., and J. R. Ritter, 1995, *The New Issues Puzzle*, Journal of Finance, v50, 23–51.

13. Movies like *Wall Street* and *Other People's Money* and books like *Barbarians at the Gate* were based upon raiders who did leveraged buyouts for a living.

14. The problem with this argument is that it does not allow for the fact that estimation risk cuts both ways—some betas will be underestimated and some will be overestimated—and should be diversifiable.

15. Notwithstanding restrictions on this practice, investment banks in the 1990s used allotments in initial public offerings as a lead-in to other business with clients. Thus, large portfolio managers often were given more than their fair share of initial public offerings that were in demand.

16. Ritter, J. R., 1998, *Initial Public Offerings*, Contemporary Finance Digest, v2, 5–31.

Appendix

Small-Cap Companies That Are Lightly Followed: January 2003

Company Name	Ticker Symbol	Industry Name	Stock Price	P/E Trailing 12 Mo	Market Cap $ (Mil)	% Institutional Holdings	Volume
American Community Bancshares	ACBA	Bank	$8.30	10.80	$25.00	1.06	1200
ASTA Funding Inc	ASFI	Financial Svcs. (Div)	$14.91	6.60	$64.10	3.06	3800
B & H Ocean Carriers	BHO	Maritime	$7.11	2.90	$29.10	0.32	100
BFC Financial Corp	BFCFA	Financial Svcs. (Div)	$5.25	4.90	$44.80	0.86	1100
Britton & Koontz Capital	BKBK	Bank	$14.61	9.50	$30.40	4.59	100
Community Bancorp Inc	CMBC	Bank	$9.20	12.00	$34.40	1.73	5600
Crescent Banking Co	CSNT	Bank	$16.90	4.00	$37.60	2.59	400
ECB Bancorp Inc	ECBE	Bank	$19.51	12.00	$38.80	0.72	1300
F.M.S. Financial	FMCO	Thrift	$12.73	10.80	$85.60	1.39	200
Hungarian Tel & Cable Corp	HTC	Telecom. Services	$7.90	8.00	$89.70	0.62	2700
Monarch Cement Co	MCEM	Cement & Aggregates	$18.15	9.30	$75.50	3.73	400
NORTECH SYST	NSYS	Electronics	$6.85	7.50	$18.60	3.56	9700
Pelican Financial Inc	PFI	Bank	$5.72	2.40	$25.50	3.98	100
RGC Resources Inc	RGCO	Natural Gas (Distrib)	$19.49	11.90	$38.00	3.06	900
Security Cap Corp	SCC	Retail (Special Lines)	$6.50	11.30	$46.40	0.1	2400
Thousand Trails Inc	TRV	Recreation	$9.20	5.70	$63.20	4.3	800
Washington Savings Bank FSB	WSB	Thrift	$8.93	11.90	$40.10	4.09	2300
WVS Financial Corp	WVFC	Thrift	$15.94	9.50	$41.70	1.24	500

10 MERGERS AND RETURNS: THE ACQUISITIVE COMPANY

THE HARE AND THE TORTOISE REVISITED

Peter was an impatient man. His portfolio was full of solid stocks that grew slowly but steadily every year and delivered decent returns, but Peter was not satisfied. As he scanned the journal for news about the stocks he owned, he noticed that the companies that made the news every day were the ones that grew through acquisitions. Led by CEOs who were larger than life, these companies grew at exponential rates by gobbling up their competition and embarking into new and different businesses. Reading about these acquisitions, Peter was struck by how much analysts liked these companies and their dynamic strategies. Tired of the staid management of the companies in which he owned stock, Peter sold off all his existing investments and invested heavily in the acquisitive companies that made the news.

For a few months, his strategy looked like it was paying off. The companies continued to post striking growth rates in revenues and earnings, and their stock prices outpaced the market as analysts continued to reward them with strong buy recommendations. The troubles began with a news story about an accounting restatement at one of the companies; its acquisitions, it turned out, had not been properly accounted for, and the earnings of the company from previous years were adjusted downwards. Not surprisingly, its stock price fell, but it was the ripple effect on the other companies that hurt Peter's portfolio. Many of the other companies in his portfolio had used the same accounting techniques as the company in trouble, and rumors of accounting troubles filled the air. As the stock prices in these companies plummeted, the CEOs went from heroes to villains, and the analysts who until very recently had been so optimistic about these companies turned on them with a vengeance. Peter, sadder and wiser from the experience, sold his stocks and put his money back into boring companies.

Moral: Slow and steady beats growth in haste.

G rowth does not come easily to companies. For a firm to grow rapidly, it has to not only find a large number of new investments but these investments have to pay off quickly. Firms that are in a hurry to grow do not want to wait for this payoff to occur. Instead, they try to grow by acquiring other companies. Since they can fund these acquisitions by issuing new stock, there is no real limit (other than what the market will bear) on how many acquisitions these firms can make or how quickly they can grow, especially in buoyant markets. Small companies adopting this strategy can very quickly become large companies, and in the process, may make their investors wealthy.

Acquisitions are large news events and get substantial coverage in the financial press. The announcements of acquisitions cause price convulsions, and it is not surprising that there are investment strategies based upon acquisitions. Some investors bet on acquiring companies, hoping to ride the growth that comes from acquisitions and other related benefits (synergy, for instance) to high returns. Other investors try to make money by investing in target companies either before or after acquisitions are announced. In this chapter, you will look at the potential for both strategies and some of the dangers involved.

CORE OF THE STORY

Different arguments are made for investing in acquiring companies and target companies. Consider first the arguments that are made for investing in acquisitive companies.

- *Invest in small companies that have found a way to speed growth.* Through the last four decades and especially in the last one, companies like WorldCom, Tyco and Cisco adopted strategies that were built around acquisitions to accelerate growth. WorldCom, a small telecom company, showed that size does not have to be an impediment when it acquired MCI, which was several times its size in the late 1990s. Tyco acquired companies in different businesses, rapidly expanding its business mix and changing its character as a company during the same period. Most famously, Cisco went from being a small company in the early 1990s to briefly being the largest market cap company in the world in 1999, with a market capitalization close to $500 billion. Investors in all three companies earned extraordinary returns during the period on the money that they had invested in these companies.

■ *High growth is cheap (at least in your accounting statements).* To understand why investors were attracted to acquisitive companies, you have to begin by first recognizing that most investors like to see growth in earnings and most do not care whether that growth comes from internal investments or from acquisitions. You have to follow this up by understanding how acquisitions are accounted for in accounting statements. If accounting rules allow firms to show the benefits of the growth from acquisitions in the form of higher revenues and earnings, but hide (at least partially) the costs of the acquisitions, it should come as no surprise that acquisitive companies can look very good on a number of accounting dimensions. Earnings and revenues will grow rapidly while little additional investment is made in capital (at least as measured in the financial statements). For several decades in the United States, firms were allowed to use "pooling" to account for acquisitions if they qualified on a number of dimensions.[1] If an acquisition qualified for pooling treatment, only the book value of the assets of the company that was acquired was shown in the balance sheet and not the market value represented by the acquisition price. Thus if $10 billion was paid for a company with a book value of $1 billion, the new assets would show up with a value of $1 billion (the book value) on the balance sheet but the extra $9 billion that was paid would essentially disappear into the footnotes.

- *The CEO is a genius.* One common feature that you often find in acquisitive companies is a high-profile CEO, with a gift for self-promotion–Bernie Ebbers at World-Com, Dennis Kozlowski at Tyco and Jack Welch at GE come to mind. This provides the second rationale that is often presented to investors for buying these companies. These CEOs, you will be told, are geniuses at the acquisitions game, often able to acquire companies at low prices and turn them around to deliver high values.

What about investing in target companies? After all, the real price surge that you see on acquisitions is in the companies that are acquired rather than in the acquiring firms. Not surprisingly, investment strategies built around target firms claim to have found a way to identify these firms before the announcements:

- *Private sources:* The most common sales pitch, of course, is that private (and reliable) sources have provided information on an upcoming acquisition. If the sales pitch is true, it is almost certainly illegal, since any persons who have this information (employees at the companies or the investment bankers involved in the deal) would be classified as insiders by the SEC. If it is not true, you are just chasing another rumor in the market.
- *Analytical models:* Some investors argue that you can use analytical devices or metrics to identify potential takeover targets. These metrics can range from sudden increases in trading volume (indicating that someone is accumulating large numbers of shares in the company) to fundamentals (low PE ratios and poor management). While not every potential target will be taken over, you can still generate high returns even if a small proportion of the firms you invest in get taken over.

Other investors settle for a less ambitious strategy of investing in companies after they have become targets in acquisitions, hoping to make money as the transaction price is finalized or from a bidding war (between two acquirers).

THEORETICAL ROOTS: ACQUISITIONS AND VALUE

If an acquisition creates value, it is possible that both the acquiring and acquired firm stockholders can walk away with more money in their pockets after the transaction. Even if an acquisition can create value, though, the division of value between stockholders of the acquiring and acquired firms will critically depend on the acquisition price. If an acquiring company pays too much for a target firm, relative to value created in the acquisition, its stock price will go down, but target company stockholders will gain proportionately.

ACQUISITIONS AND VALUE CREATION

Can a firm create value by acquiring other firms? While taking a skeptical view of this proposition, you can, at least in theory, see ways in which acquisitions and mergers can increase value. A company can acquire companies that are undervalued by the market and take advantage of market mistakes, thus playing the role of a canny portfolio manager. A merger can work by creating synergy, a rationale much used and misused in acquisitions. Finally, a firm can also create value by buying poorly managed, poorly run firms and turning them around. In this section, each of these value-creating motivations is described.

Acquire Undervalued Firms.   If markets make mistakes in pricing companies, an acquirer can conceivably buy a company at a bargain price, relative to its value. The acquirer can then gain the difference between the value and the purchase price. For this strategy to work, however, three basic components need to come together:

1. *A capacity to find firms that trade at less than their true value:* This capacity would require either access to better information than is available to other

investors in the market or better analytical tools than those used by other market participants.

2. *Access to the funds that will be needed to complete the acquisition:* Knowing a firm is undervalued does not necessarily imply having capital easily available to carry out the acquisition. Access to capital depends upon the size of the acquirer—large firms will have more access to capital markets and to internal funds than smaller firms or individuals—and upon the acquirer's track record: a history of success at identifying and acquiring undervalued firms will make subsequent acquisitions easier.

3. *Skill in execution:* If the acquirer, in the process of the acquisition, drives the stock price up to and beyond the estimated value, there will be no value gain from the acquisition. To illustrate, assume that the estimated value for a firm is $100 million, and that the current market price is $75 million. In acquiring this firm, the acquirer will have to pay a premium. If that premium exceeds 33% of the market price, the price exceeds the estimated value, and the acquisition will not create any value for the acquirer.

While the strategy of buying undervalued firms has a great deal of intuitive appeal, it is daunting, especially when acquiring publicly traded firms in reasonably efficient markets, when the premiums paid on market prices can very quickly eliminate the valuation surplus. The odds are better in less efficient markets or in the acquisition of private businesses.

Create Operating or Financial Synergy. The reason most commonly given as an explanation for the significant premiums paid in most acquisitions is synergy. Synergy is the potential additional value from combining two firms. Synergies can either come from operations or they can be financial.

Operating synergies are those synergies that allow firms to increase their operating income, to increase growth or to do both. You would categorize operating synergies into four types:

- *Economies of scale* that may arise from the merger, allowing the combined firm to become more cost efficient and profitable. These are most likely to occur when two firms in the same business merge to create a larger firm.
- *Greater pricing power* from reduced competition and higher market share, which should result in higher margins and operating income. For this to occur, the competition has to be weak and fragmented relative to the firm created in the merger.
- *Combination of different functional strengths,* as would be the case when a firm with strong marketing skills acquires a firm with a good product line. This presumes that the combined firm will retain both strengths and that the strengths will carry over into the new business.
- *Higher growth in new or existing markets,* arising from the combination of the two firms. For instance, this would be case when a U.S. consumer products firm acquires an emerging market firm, with an established distribution network and brand-name recognition, and uses these strengths to increase sales of its products.

Operating synergies can increase profit margins and expected growth, and through these can increase the value of the firms involved in the merger or acquisition.

With financial synergies, the payoff can take the form of either higher cash flows or a lower cost of capital. Included are the following:

- A combination of a firm with excess cash, or *cash slack,* (and limited project opportunities) and a firm with high-return projects (and insufficient cash to fund them) can yield a payoff in terms of higher value for the combined firm. The increase in value comes from the investments that will be taken with the excess cash that otherwise would not have been taken. This synergy is likely to show up most often when large firms acquire smaller firms or when publicly traded firms acquire private businesses.
- *Debt capacity* can increase because when two firms combine, their earnings and cash flows may become

more stable and predictable. This, in turn, allows them to borrow more than they could have as individual entities, which creates a tax benefit for the combined firm. This tax benefit can either be shown as higher cash flows or take the form of a lower cost of capital for the combined firm.

■ *Tax benefits* can arise either from the acquisition taking advantage of tax laws or from the use of losses to shelter income. Thus, a profitable firm that acquires a money-losing firm may be able to use the losses of the latter to reduce its tax burden.

Clearly, there is potential for synergy in many mergers. The more important issues are whether that synergy can be valued and, if so, how to value it.

Take Over Poorly Managed Firms and Change Management. Some firms are not managed well, and other acquirers often believe they can run these firms better than the current managers. Acquiring poorly managed firms and removing existing managers, or at least changing existing management policies and practices, should make these firms more valuable, allowing the acquirer to claim the increase in value. This value increase is often termed the *value of control*.

While this story can be used to justify large premiums over the market price, the potential for its success rests on the following:

■ The poor performance of the firm being acquired should be attributable to the existing management of the firm, rather than to market or industry factors that are not under management control.

■ The acquisition has to be followed by a change in management practices, and the change has to increase value. Actions that increase value increase cash flows from existing assets increase expected growth rates or reduce the cost of capital.

■ The market price of the acquisition should reflect the status quo, that is, the current management of the firm and their poor business practices. If the market price already has the control premium built into it, there is little potential for the acquirer to earn the premium.

In the last two decades, corporate control has been increasingly cited as a reason for hostile acquisitions.

ACQUISITIONS AND VALUE DIVISION

Acquisitions can be friendly or hostile events. In a friendly acquisition, the managers of the target firm welcome the acquisition and, in some cases, seek it out. In a hostile acquisition, the target firm's management does not want to be acquired. The acquiring firm offers a price higher than the target firm's market price before the acquisition and invites stockholders in the target firm to tender their shares for the price.

In either friendly or hostile acquisitions, the difference between the acquisition price and the market price before the acquisition is called the *acquisition premium*. The *acquisition price,* in the context of mergers, is the price that will be paid by the acquiring firm for each of the target firm's shares. This price is usually based upon negotiations between the acquiring firm and the target firm's managers. In a tender offer, it is the price at which the acquiring firm receives enough shares to gain control of the target firm. This price may be higher than the initial price offered by the acquirer if other firms are bidding for the same target firm or if an insufficient number of stockholders tender at that initial price. For instance, in 1991, AT&T initially offered to buy NCR for $80 per share, a premium of $25 over the stock price at the time of the offer. AT&T ultimately paid $110 per share to complete the acquisition. One final comparison can be made, and that is between the price paid on the acquisition and the accounting book value of the equity in the firm being acquired. This difference will be recorded as goodwill on the acquiring firm's books and written off in subsequent years.[2] Figure 10.1 breaks down the acquisition price into these component parts.

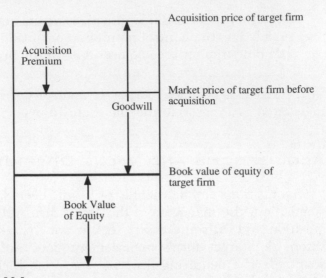

Acquisition price of target firm

Acquisition Premium

Goodwill

Market price of target firm before acquisition

Book value of equity of target firm

Book Value of Equity

FIGURE 10.1
Breaking Down the Acquisition Price

The difference between the market value and the book value is usually categorized as goodwill. In some cases, though, the acquirer is allowed to write up the book value of the target firm at the time of acquisition.

As a stockholder in an acquiring firm, your ultimate gain or loss on an acquisition will be based not upon whether the acquisition creates value or not, but upon how much is paid for the acquired firm. The easiest way to see this is to think of an acquisition as a large project. If a company invests $100 million in a project and gets back only $90 million in value from the investment, its value will decrease by $10 million. If a company acquires another company and pays more than it will get back in cash flows (inclusive of synergy, control and other benefits listed in the last section), its value will also drop by the amount of the overpayment.

Consider an example. Company A, with a market value of $30 million, decides to buy company B with a market value of $20 million, and it believes that it can generate $5 million in value from synergy. If company A can acquire company B for less than $25 million, the stockholders of both companies will gain from the acquisition. If the acquisition price is $25 million, the stockholders of company A will neither gain nor lose and company B's stockholders will gain the entire value of the synergy. If company A pays more than $25 million for company B, the stock price in company A will drop by the amount of the overpayment and company B's stockholders will gain proportionately.

LOOKING AT THE EVIDENCE

In this section, you will begin with an analysis of how the announcement of an acquisition affects the market price of the target and acquiring firms on the day of the acquisition, and follow up by looking at the post-acquisition performance (operating and stock price) of acquiring firms.

ACQUISITION DATE

The big price movements associated with acquisitions occur around the date the acquisition is announced and not when it is actually consummated, which may occur several months later. While much of the attention in acquisitions is focused on the target firms, what happens to the acquiring firm is just as interesting, if not more so.

Target Firms. The evidence indicates that the stockholders of target firms are the clear winners in takeovers—they earn significant returns[3] not only around the announcement of the acquisitions, but also in the weeks leading up to it. In 1983, a review of 13 studies that look at returns around takeover announcements revealed an average return of 30% to target stockholders in successful tender offers and 20% to target stockholders in successful mergers.[4] An examination in 1988 of 663 tender offers made between 1962 and 1985 noted that premiums averaged 19% in the 1960s, 35% in the 1970s, and 30% between 1980 and 1985.[5] Figure 10.2 illustrates the price behavior of a typical target firm in an acquisition, in the 10 days before, the day of, and the 10 days after an acquisition announcement.[6]

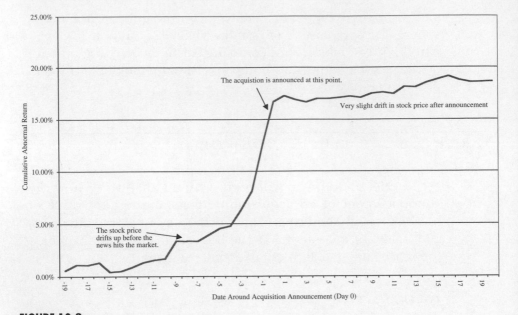

FIGURE 10.2

Cumulative Excess Return to Target Company Stock

Data from Dennis and McConnell. The returns on the target firm stock is cumulated around the date of acquisition.

Note that about half the premium associated with the acquisition is already incorporated in the price by the time the acquisition is announced. This suggests that news about the acquisition is leaked to some investors before it reaches the market, and these investors trade ahead of the announcement. On the acquisition date, there is an additional jump in the stock price but little evidence of prices drifting up thereafter.

If you categorize acquisitions by how the acquiring firm pays for them, you find that the stock prices of target firms tend to do much better on the announcement of cash-based acquisitions (for which the acquirer uses cash only to pay for the acquired company's stock) than of stock-based acquisitions. The premiums in hostile acquisitions are larger than the premiums on friendly mergers, and the premium on tender offers is slightly higher than the premium on mergers. Figure 10.3 illustrates the magnitude of the differences.[7]

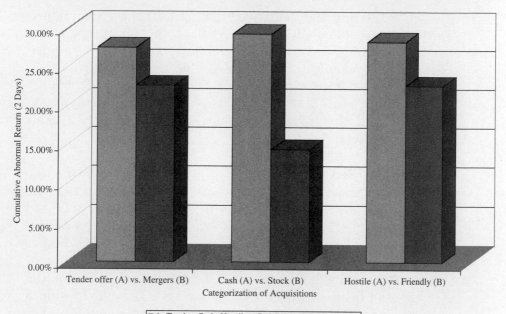

FIGURE 10.3

Target Firm Premiums in Acquisitions

Data from Huang and Walkling. These are the cumulated returns for target firm stockholders in different types of acquisitions.

No matter how you categorize acquisitions, stockholders in target firms have little reason to complain since they walk away with healthy price gains.

Bidding Firms. The effect of takeover announcements on bidder firm stock prices is not as clear-cut as it is for target firms. The survey of mergers in 1983 reported that stock prices increase about 4% for bidding firms around tender offers and found no evidence of price movement around mergers.[8] An examination of tender offers from 1962 to 1985 notes a decline in returns to bidding firm stockholders from 4.4% in the 1960s to 2% in the 1970s to –1% in the 1980s.[9] Other research indicates that the stock prices of bidding firms drop in about half of all acquisitions around the announcement of takeovers, suggesting that investors are skeptical about the perceived value of these takeovers in a significant number of cases.

Considering the evidence, it is quite clear that bidding firm stockholders often do not share the enthusiasm that managers in these firms have about mergers and acquisitions. While managers would argue that this is because stockholders are not privy to the information that is available only to insiders, you will see later in this chapter that many mergers fail and that stockholders are perhaps more prescient than managers.

Does the Market Value Synergy? Synergy is a stated motive in many mergers and acquisitions. An examination of the motives behind 77 acquisitions in 1985 and 1986 reported that operating synergy was the primary motive in one-third of these takeovers.[10] A number of studies examine whether synergy exists and, if it does, how much it is worth. If synergy is perceived to exist in a takeover, the value of the combined firm should be greater than the sum of the values of the bidding and target firms operating independently. For example, assume that acquiring company A is trading at a total value of $150 million before an acquisition, and target company B, trading at a total value of $100 million. If these companies merge and there is synergy, the value of the combined company after the merger should be greater than $250 million. Thus, if the combined company trades at a value of $275 million, the synergy in this merger is valued at $25 million.

Examinations of stock returns around merger announcements generally conclude that the value of the combined firm does increase in most takeovers and that the increase is significant. A 1988 study of 236 interfirm tender offers between 1963 and 1984 reported that the combined value of the target and bidder firms increased 7.48% ($117 million in 1984 dollars), on average, on the announcement of the merger.[11] This result has to be interpreted with caution, however, since the increase in the value of the combined firm after a merger is also consistent with a number of other hypotheses explaining acquisitions, including undervaluation and a change in corporate control. It is thus a weak test of the synergy hypothesis.

FROM ANNOUNCEMENT TO ACTION

Note that the studies presented above all look at the date on which an acquisition is announced and not at the actual transaction date, which may be several weeks or even months later. Clearly, several things can change between the two dates. In some acquisitions a new bidder shows up and a bidding war commences, pushing the price of the target company well above the initial offering price. Some acquisitions fail, either because the target firms fight off bidders, using legal and financial devices, or because the acquiring firm develops cold feet and withdraws its bid. Finally, in other acquisitions, the bidding firm is forced to raise its price because it has difficulty accumulating a controlling stake at the stated price.

Multiple Bidders. When a firm acquires multiple bidders, it is almost always good news for the target company's stockholders and bad news for the bidding company's stockholders. The premiums paid for target firms are generally much higher when there are multiple bidders and there is evidence that the stock of the bidding firm that wins the bidding war is more likely to go down than up when it succeeds. However, the bidding firm that fails in an acquisition bid is also often punished. One analysis of failed mergers reports significant drops in stock prices (of approximately 8%) for bidder firms that lose out to a rival bidder and no price reaction when no rival bidder exists.[12]

Failed Bids. Bids can fail either because the target firm in a hostile acquisition manages to fight off the acquisition or because the bidding firm changes its mind. In both cases, the stock of the bidding firm suffers on the announcement of the failure. The target firm stock price will also fall in both cases, but not to the levels before the acquisition attempt was made. Investors seem to reassess the value of firms when they become targets of acquisitions, on the assumption that the bidding firm has some information that the rest of the market does not or that there will be other bidders down the road. An examination of the effects of takeover failures on target firm stockholders concluded that while the initial reaction to the announcement of the failure is negative, albeit small, a substantial number of target firms are taken over within 60 days of the failure of the first takeover, earning significant excess returns (50% to 66%).

Merger or Risk Arbitrage. Some investors, mostly institutional, believe that they can make money by buying stocks in target companies after a hostile acquisition is announced. As noted in the last section, the stock price of a target company jumps on the announcement of a takeover. However, it trades at a discount, usually to the price offered by the acquiring company. The difference between the post-announcement price and the offer price is called the arbitrage spread, and there are investors who try to profit from this spread in a strategy called merger or risk arbitrage. If the merger succeeds, the investor captures the arbitrage spreads, but if it fails, he or she could realize a substantial loss. In a more sophisticated variant in stock mergers (in which shares of the acquiring company are exchanged for shares in the target company), the arbitrageur will sell short the acquiring firm's stock in addition to buying the target firm's stock.

The strategy is clearly mislabeled as risk arbitrage since there are no guaranteed profits (which is what arbitrage requires) and it is not quite clear why the prefix "risk" is attached to it. Notwithstanding this quarrel with terminology, you can examine whether risk arbitrage delivers the kinds of returns you often hear about anecdotally, and if it does, is it compensation for risk (that the merger may not go through) or is it an excess return? A sample of 4750 mergers and acquisitions was used to answer this question.[13] This analysis concludes that there are excess returns associated with buying target companies after acquisition announcements of about 9.25% annually, but that you lose about two-thirds of these excess returns if you factor in transactions costs and the price impact that you have when you trade (especially on the less liquid companies).

While the overall strategy returns look attractive, the results also point to one unappealing aspect of this strategy. The strategy earns moderate positive returns much of the time, but earns large negative returns when it fails. Does this make it a bad strategy? Not at all, but it points to the dangers of risk arbitrage when it is restricted to a few big-name takeover stocks (as it often is). An investor who adopts this strategy is generally just one big failure away from going under. If he or she borrows money to pursue this strategy, the risks are magnified.

AFTER THE ACQUISITION

There is substantial research examining the extent to which mergers and acquisitions succeed or fail after the deals are made. The general conclusion is that mergers often fail to deliver on their promises of efficiency and synergy, and even those that do deliver seldom create value for the acquirers' stockholders.

The existence of synergy generally implies that the combined firm will become more profitable or grow at a faster rate after the merger than will the firms operating separately. A test of synergy is to evaluate whether after takeovers merged firms improve their performance (profitability and growth) *relative to their competitors*. McKinsey and Co. examined 58 acquisition programs between 1972 and 1983 for evidence on two questions: (1) Did the return on the amount invested in the acquisitions exceed the cost of capital? (2) Did the acquisitions help the parent companies outperform the competition? They concluded that 28 of the 58 programs failed both tests, and 6 failed at least one test. In a follow-up study of 115 mergers in the U.K. and the United States in the 1990s, McKinsey concluded that 60% of the transactions earned returns on capital less than the cost of capital and that only 23% earned excess returns.[14] In 1999, KPMG examined 700 of the most expensive deals between 1996 and 1998 and concluded that only 17% created value for the combined firm, 30% were value neutral and 53% destroyed value.[15]

An examination of the eight largest bank mergers in 1995 concluded that only two (Chase/Chemical, First Chicago/NBD) subsequently outperformed the bank-stock index.[16] The largest, Wells Fargo's acquisition of First Interstate, was a significant failure. In an incisive book on the topic in 1996 titled *The Synergy Trap*, Sirower took a detailed look at the promises and failures of synergy and drew the gloomy conclusion that synergy is often promised but seldom delivered.[17]

The most damaging piece of evidence on the outcome of acquisitions is the large number of acquisitions that are reversed within fairly short time periods. An analysis[18] in 1990 noted that 20.2% of the acquisitions made between 1982 and 1986 were divested by 1988. A study published in1992 found that 44% of the mergers studied were reversed, largely because the acquirer paid too much or because the operations of the two firms did not mesh.[19] Studies that have tracked acquisitions for longer periods (ten years or more) have found the divestiture rate of acquisitions rises to almost 50%, suggesting that few firms enjoy the promised benefits from acquisitions. The bottom line on synergy is that it exists in relatively few mergers and that it often does not measure up to expectations.

CRUNCHING THE NUMBERS

Acquisitions come in such different forms that it is difficult to profile a typical acquisition. In the first part of this section, you will begin by looking across acquisitions to see if you can find common patterns to successes and failures. In the second part, you will try to construct a portfolio of acquiring companies as well as a portfolio of potential target companies.

ACQUIRING AND ACQUIRED FIRMS

Is there a typical acquiring company? On the other side of the transaction, is there a typical target firm? If you want to construct an investment strategy that revolves around acquisitions, you have to attempt to at least answer these questions.

Acquiring Firms. Are there common characteristics shared by acquiring firms and especially by successful acquiring firms? If you look at a small sample of acquisitions or even all the acquisitions done during the course of a year, you will be hard pressed to find any commonalities across acquirers. Researchers, however, have looked at hundreds of acquisitions over long periods, and they have identified some common features shared by successful acquirers over time:

■ Firms that acquire firms of *similar size* (often called mergers of equals) seem to have a lower probability of succeeding than firms that focus on acquiring much smaller firms.[20] Thus, the odds of success would be greater for GE, which acquired dozens of small companies each year during the 1990s, than with the merger of AOL and Time Warner, two companies with very large market capitalizations.

■ Firms that are motivated by *cost savings* when doing acquisitions seem to have a better chance of succeeding than firms that are motivated by growth hopes or expectations. This is especially so when the cost savings are concrete and planned for at the time of the acquisition. Some of the most successful mergers of the 1990s involved banks that merged to save money and gain economies of scale.

■ Acquisition programs that focus on buying *small private businesses* for consolidations have had more success than acquisition programs that concentrate on acquiring publicly traded firms. Firms like Service Industries (funeral homes), Blockbuster Video (video rental stores) and Browning Ferris (waste disposal businesses) all grew by acquiring small private firms.

On the issue of synergy, the KPMG evaluation[21] of the 700 largest deals from 1996 to 1998 concludes the following:

■ Firms that evaluate synergy carefully before an acquisition are 28% more likely to succeed than firms that do not.

■ Cost-saving synergies associated with reducing the number of employees are more likely to be realized than new product development or R&D synergies. For instance, only a quarter to a third of firms succeeded on the latter, whereas 66% of firms were able to reduce headcount after mergers.

Some research finds improvements in operating efficiency after mergers, especially hostile ones.[22] An examination in 1992 concluded that the median post-acquisition cash flow returns improve for firms involved in mergers, though 25% of merged firms lag industry averages after transactions.[23] In 1999, another study examined 197 transactions between 1982 and 1987 and categorized the firms according to replacement of the management (123 firms) at the time of the transaction, and the motive for the transaction.[24] The conclusions:

- On average, in the five years after the transaction, merged firms earned 2.1% more than the industry average.
- Almost all this excess return occurred in cases in which the CEO of the target firm was replaced within one year of the merger. These firms earned 3.1% more than the industry average, whereas firms in which the CEO of the target firm continued in place did not do better than the industry.

In addition, a few studies examine whether acquiring related businesses (i.e., synergy-driven acquisitions) provides better returns than acquiring unrelated business (i.e., conglomerate mergers) and come to conflicting conclusions with no consensus.[25] An examination of 260 stock swap transactions categorized the mergers as either a conglomerate or "same industry" transactions.[26] They found no evidence of wealth benefits for either stockholders or bondholders in conglomerate transactions. However, they did find significant net gains for both stockholders and bondholders in the case of mergers of related firms.

Target Firms. Looking at the stock price reaction of target firms both immediately before and immediately after the acquisition announcement, it is quite clear that the money to be made in acquisitions comes from investing in firms before they become targets rather than after. Absent inside information, is this doable? There may be a way, and the answer lies in looking at firms that typically become target firms. Since the motivations in hostile and friendly acquisitions are very different, it should come as no surprise that the typical target firm in a hostile acquisition is very different from the typical target firm in a friendly takeover. The typical target firm in a hostile takeover has the following characteristics:[27]

1. It has *underperformed other stocks in its industry* and the overall market, in terms of returns to its stockholders in the years preceding the takeover.
2. It has been *less profitable than firms in its industry* in the years preceding the takeover.
3. It has a *much lower stock holding* by insiders than do firms in its peer groups.

A comparison of target firms in hostile and friendly takeovers illustrates their differences. Bhide's findings are summarized in Figure 10.4.

As you can see, target firms in hostile takeovers have earned a 2.2% lower return on equity, on average, than other firms in their industry; they have earned returns for their

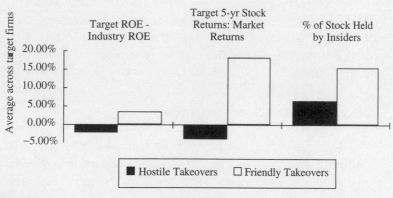

FIGURE 10.4

Target Characteristics: Hostile vs. Friendly Takeovers

Data from Bhide. This study compared the characteristics of target firms in friendly takeovers to those in hostile takeovers in the year of the takeover.

stockholders that are 4% lower than the market; and only 6.5% of their stock is held by insiders.

There is also evidence that these firms make significant changes in the way they operate after hostile takeovers. The study cited above examined the consequences of hostile takeovers and noted the following changes:

1. Many of the hostile takeovers were followed by an increase in debt, which resulted in a downgrading of the debt. The debt was quickly reduced with proceeds from the sale of assets, however.
2. There was no significant change in the amount of capital investment in these firms.
3. Almost 60% of the takeovers were followed by significant divestitures, in which half or more of the firm was divested. The overwhelming majority of the divestitures were units in business areas unrelated to the company's core business (i.e., they constituted reversal of corporate diversification done in earlier time periods).
4. There were significant management changes in 17 of the 19 hostile takeovers, with the replacement of the entire corporate management team in seven of the takeovers.

Thus, contrary to popular view,[28] most hostile takeovers are not followed by the acquirer stripping the assets of the target firm and leading it to ruin. Instead, target firms refocus on their core businesses and often improve their operating performance.

CREATING PORTFOLIOS

As an investor, you may find the evidence on successful acquiring and typical target firms interesting but not particularly relevant since they all represent mergers from the past. How, you may wonder, can you make money from an acquisition that occurred a decade ago? You cannot, but you can use the evidence to construct a portfolio of potential acquirers and target firms today.

Portfolio of Acquiring Firms. To construct a portfolio of acquiring firms, you have to look at history and examine the sources of growth for individual firms. For instance, Table 10.1 reports on the most acquisitive companies in the United States between 2000 and 2002, based upon the dollar value of the acquisitions.

Note the wide range of industries from which the acquisitive companies are drawn and the number of deals made by some of them. GE, for instance, bought 71 companies in this two-year period, though they tended to be smaller on average than the 8 companies bought by Comcast during the same time period.

There is clearly a bias toward larger firms introduced when you rank firms by the dollar value of acquisitions. To get a true sense of how much each of these acquiring companies relies on acquisitions for growth, you would also have to scale the value of the acquisitions by the value of the acquirers. For example, the $2.4 billion spent by Microsoft on acquisitions was less than 1% of overall market value, while AT&T's acquisition spending of $5.6 billion is about 20% of its market value. You could construct a portfolio of acquiring firms, based upon how much acquisitions represent as a fraction of firm value. That portfolio would look very different from the one in Table 10.1 and would include smaller companies.

Portfolio of Potential Targets. If you consider the evidence on typical target firms in acquisitions, you could develop a set of screens that incorporate the variables mentioned above. You could, for instance, invest in smaller companies (in market capitalization terms), with low insider holdings, depressed valuations (low price-to-book ratios or low price-earnings ratios) and low returns on equity (relative to their sectors).

To put these screens into practice, potential target firms were categorized as firms with the following characteristics:

■ *Small companies:* Since it is easier to acquire smaller companies than larger ones, only firms with market capitalization less than $500 million are considered for this portfolio.

TABLE 10.1 Most Acquisitive Companies — United States, 2000–2002

Company	Industry	Total Acquisitions	Total Value ($ Million)
Comcast Corp	Broadcasting	8	47,680.80
Citigroup Inc	Banking & finance	18	21,350.50
General Electric Co	Aerospace, aircraft & defense, banking & finance	71	19,725.00
Tyco International Ltd	Electrical equipment	19	16,882.20
Johnson & Johnson	Toiletries & cosmetics	11	14,062.00
Nestlé SA	Food processing	8	11,266.80
AOL Time Warner Inc	Computer services, leisure & entertainment	13	8,984.20
AT&T Corp	Communications	9	5,616.20
Schlumberger Ltd	Energy services	9	5,242.90
Berkshire Hathaway Inc	Insurance	13	4,776.00
J.P. Morgan Chase & Co	Banking & finance	12	4,442.40
Cendant Corp	Miscellaneous services	33	3,797.80
BB&T Corp	Banking & finance	23	3,098.70
Solectron Corp	Electronics	12	2,496.40
Calpine Corp	Electric, gas, water & sanitary services	9	2,494.80
Microsoft Corp	Computer software, supplies & services	8	2,402.20
Intel Corp	Electronics	11	1,943.10
VeriSign Inc	Computer software, supplies & services	8	1,647.90
Interpublic Group of Cos	Miscellaneous services	12	1,605.30
NRG Energy Inc	Electric, gas, water & sanitary services	10	1,510.70
SPX Corp	Fabricated metal products	10	1,447.90
Baxter International Inc	Drugs, medical supplies & equipment	8	1,185.20
Danaher Corp	Industrial & farm equipment & machinery	11	1,075.40

Source: www.mergerstat.com

TABLE 10.2 Potential Takeover Targets

Company	Industry	Stock Price	P/E Trailing 12 Mo	Market Cap $ (Mil)	% Insider Holdings
AMN Healthcare	Human Resources	11.22	9.6	456.6	3.6
Blair Corp	Retail (Special Lines)	24	9.7	186.2	8.69
Chesapeake Corp	Packaging & Container	16.13	10.2	228.2	5.6
Cone Mills	Textile	2.01	6.4	48.2	9.3
Crompton Corp	Chemical (Specialty)	4.03	8.1	443.6	7.6
Culp Inc	Textile	4.45	6	54.5	4.5
Enesco Group	Retail (Special Lines)	6.91	11.8	90.3	3.8
Information Resources	Information Services	1.32	11.7	41.4	7.1
Int'l Multifoods	Food Processing	19.2	11.6	334.5	5.8
Intermet Corp	Auto Parts	3.58	10.2	91	3.1
Myers Inds	Diversified Co.	9.57	11	264.5	2.7
SEMCO Energy	Natural Gas (Distrib.)	4.12	7.5	74.3	1.3
ShopKo Stores	Retail Store	10.85	6.7	292.2	3.5
Standard Register	Office Equip/Supplies	14.84	10.6	372.9	2.7
Wellman Inc	Chemical (Specialty)	9.59	10.8	284.5	6.7

- *Low insider holdings:* Only firms with insider holdings less than 10% of the outstanding stock are included in the portfolio. In addition, firms with different voting class shares were removed since they are less likely to be targeted for hostile acquisitions.
- *Cheap stocks:* Only stocks that trade at a trailing PE ratio less than 12 are considered cheap and worthy of inclusion in the portfolio.
- *Poor project returns:* Only firms that have returns on equity that are 5 percentage points lower than the industry average are included in the portfolio.

The resulting portfolio of 15 firms is listed in Table 10.2.

There are clearly no guarantees that any or all of these firms will become targets of hostile takeovers, but the portfolio will generate high returns even if only two or three of the firms become takeover targets.

MORE TO THE STORY

Assuming that you decide to create a strategy of investing in companies right after acquisitions, what are some of the factors that may undercut your chances of success? The factors to consider will clearly vary in accordance with the investment strategy you adopt. If you buy acquisitive firms, you will have to worry about both financial overreach (paying too much for acquisitions) and operational overreach (where you expand too quickly into new businesses, putting existing businesses at risk). If you buy potential target firms, you have to allow for the fact that they may never be taken over and that you will be saddled with a portfolio of poorly performing stocks.

INVESTING IN ACQUIRING FIRMS

Consider investing in a portfolio of acquisitive firms. Even if you are careful about picking firms that seem to have succeeded with their acquisition strategies, there is a number of possible risks in the strategy.

Overpaying on Acquisitions. Past success at acquisitions does not preclude future failures. In fact, a firm that grows successfully through acquisitions will find that its very success often lays the groundwork for future failure.

Take, for instance, a firm like Cisco that in the early 1990s established a clear record of success from its acquisition strategy. Starting in 1991, when it had revenues of $183 million, earnings of $43 million and a market capitalization of about $4 billion, Cisco acquired small companies with promising technologies and turned these technologies into great products and earnings growth in short periods. Each year that it succeeded it became a larger firm, both in terms of revenues and market capitalization. To sustain its growth rate, it had to increase both the scale and the number of acquisitions it made each year. By 1999, Cisco had $12.15 billion in revenues and a market capitalization in excess of $400 billion, and finding enough acquisition to make a dent in its growth rate had become much more difficult to do.

The danger to investors is not that this happens but that a firm that has had past success at acquisitions will continue its push toward more acquisitions even in the face of difficulty finding good target firms. In the process, it may well abandon the discipline that made it successful in the first place. You could look at almost every acquisitive firm that has failed and point (at least in hindsight) to the moment when this occurred.

Over time, there is evidence that acquisitive companies have proven to be poor investments, lagging the market in stock returns. Figure 10.5 contrasts the returns in 2000 and 2001 that investors would have earned on the 15 most acquisitive companies in the S&P 100, based upon acquisitions made between 1998 and 2001 (100 largest market cap firms in the United States) with the returns they would have earned on companies that made only one acquisition and companies did not make any acquisitions.

Investors in the most acquisitive firms would have lagged the market and investors in firms that did no acquisitions by more than 10% a year between 2001 and 2002.

How would you screen acquisitive firms to eliminate those that are most likely to overpay? There are several statistics

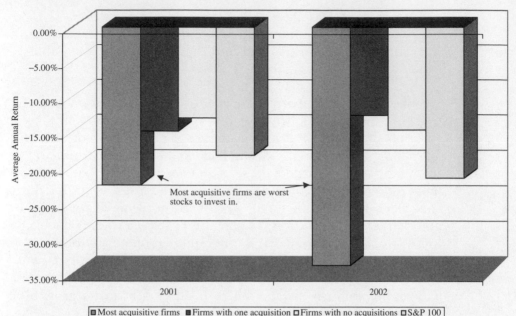

Most acquisitive firms are worst stocks to invest in.

☒ Most acquisitive firms ■ Firms with one acquisition ☐ Firms with no acquisitions ☐ S&P 100

FIGURE 10.5
Returns on Acquisitive Firms

Data from Compustat. The most acquisitive firms that made the most acquisitions (in numbers) in the S&P 500 between 1998 and 2001.

that you can look at. One is the average premium paid by acquiring firms for their acquisitions; firms that pay larger premiums are more likely to have overpaid. A second statistic is the average size of the acquired firms relative to the acquiring firms; again, research indicates that you are more likely to overpay on large acquisitions than on smaller ones. The third statistic to look at is the market reaction to the acquisition announcement; an increase in the acquirer's market price on the acquisition announcement is a much better signal of future success than is a decrease.

Accounting Complexity. Accounting for acquisitions is much more complicated than accounting for internal investments. To begin with, you have more choices in how you record the transaction. Until 1999, you could structure an acquisition as either a purchase or a pooling, with dramatically different consequences for accounting statements. With a purchase transaction, you show the price of the company that you acquire in your balance sheet but you also create a new asset (goodwill) to record the difference between what you pay for the company and the book value of its assets. With pooling, you do not record the purchase price and instead show only the book value of the assets of the company that you acquire as part of your assets. In 2001, the practice of pooling was finally eliminated, but firms still have to deal with goodwill after a transaction. In fact, the accounting standards now require firms to revisit their past acquisitions and write off portions of goodwill if they believe that they overpaid. AOL Time Warner wrote off $100 billion to reflect the reduction in value of AOL's assets between the time of the merger in 1999 and the write-off in 2001.

The most significant evidence that acquisitive firms are more likely to be exposed to accounting problems comes from looking at history. It tells us that of the ten most acquisitive firms of the 1990s, serious accounting problems were unearthed at seven: Enron, WorldCom, Tyco, Lucent, Cendant, AOL Time Warner and Conseco. In fact, the perception was that some of these firms not only bent the accounting rules but broke them. As an investor, you have to allow for the possibility that acquisitive companies will have financial statements that are more difficult to analyze than those of companies that do not do acquisitions. In addition, you may find yourself having difficulty with the most fundamental questions that you need answered about any firm, such as how much capital is invested in the firm, what returns the firm is making on its investments, and how much of the firm's earnings are being reinvested into the business.

Debt and Dilution. There are two ways in which acquisitive firms pay for acquisitions, and both can have negative consequences for investors. One way is to issue new stock to fund the acquisition, increasing the number of shares outstanding and reducing earnings per share at least in the near term. The other way is to borrow the money to raise the necessary funds, which can increase default risk and overburden the

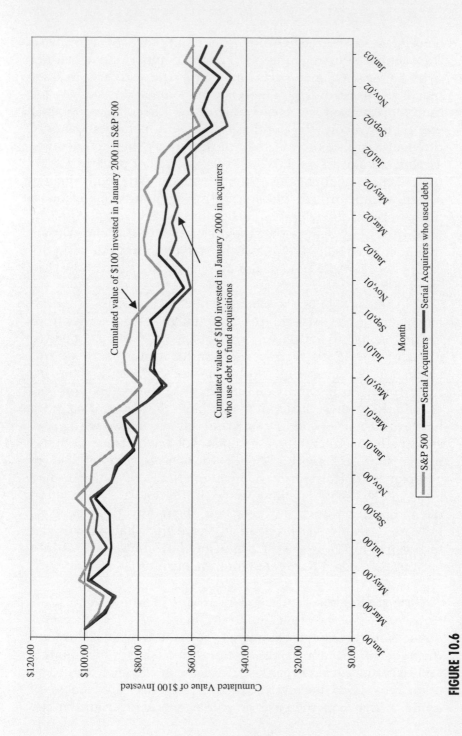

FIGURE 10.6

Acquirers with Debt vs. Rest of the Market

Data from CRSP. The cumulated value of $100 invested in stocks with dividends reinvested is reported for each of the three portfolios.

company with interest and principal payments. In fact, Figure 10.6 indicates that the stock performance of serial acquirers who borrow to fund their acquisitions is even worse than the stock performance of serial acquirers who use stock or cash, and that both groups lag the overall market.

While the conclusions you can draw are constrained by the fact that you are looking at a short and very volatile time period, when the market declines you should clearly be cautious about acquisition strategies based upon debt. One way you can measure this dependence is to look at a firm's debt ratio relative to its peer group. A combination of overdependence on debt and large acquisitions should show up as high financial leverage.

Lack of Focus. Acquisitive firms are more likely to go into businesses unrelated to their primary business than are nonacquisitive firms. After all, it takes considerable work and expertise for a steel company to enter the software business on its own, but it can acquire a software company and accomplish the same objective quickly. It should come as no surprise that conglomerates are usually created through a series of acquisitions rather than with internal investments in a dozen different business areas. As an investor, though, this temptation to stray into other businesses can be dangerous to you. Studies generally find that conglomerates trade at a discount, relative to the value of their component parts, which is attributed by some researchers to lack of management focus and by some to waste. Whatever the reason for the discount, you may want to invest only with acquisitive companies that stay within their area of business expertise.

INVESTING IN TARGET FIRMS

If you had a mechanism for perfectly identifying target firms before they become targets in acquisitions, you would be able to reap incredible rewards. You would probably also have some very curious agents from the SEC quizzing you about your uncommon success. After all, the only way in which investors have been able to do this historically with any consistency is by having access to inside information. If you are staying on the right side of the law and screening stocks for potential takeover targets, your success rate will be much lower and herein lies the risk to this strategy.

Entrenched Management.   One of the indicators that you use to find potential target firms is poor management. That is why you look for firms that have made poor investments (low returns on equity) and whose stock has underperformed the market and the sector. You buy stock in these firms hoping that the management will change, but what if it does not? You could end up with a portfolio of companies with incompetent management who continue to destroy value while you hold the stock.

Consider the 15 firms listed in Table 10.2 as potential takeover targets. Looking at the past history of these firms, it is quite clear that the factors that make them potential targets have been in place for a number of years. Furthermore, the CEOs of 10 of these firms have been in their positions for five years or more. It is difficult to conceive of a quantitative screen that can find firms whose managers are not entrenched. You could use a "length of tenure" screen (by which you avoid firms whose CEOs have been in place for more than five years) or a qualitative screen (by which you only invest in firms with boards of directors that are responsive to stockholders). In either case, you will still be left with considerable uncertainty about future success at changing management.

Market Mood.   Mergers and acquisitions often track the market, rising in buoyant markets and falling in bear markets. Figure 10.7 graphs the ebb and flow of merger activity between 1968 and 2002.

If you invest in a portfolio of potential target firms, you could very well be blindsided by a shift in market mood that makes rarer both hostile and friendly acquisitions. Another characteristic of acquisition activity is that it tends to be concentrated in a few sectors in each period—telecommunication and technology mergers dominated in the late 1990s—and the sectors shift from period to period.

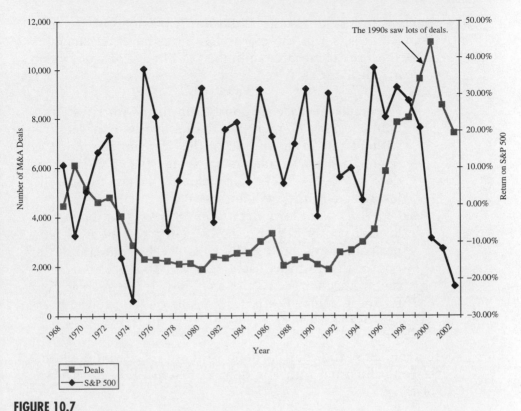

FIGURE 10.7

M&A Activity and Stock Returns

Data from Mergerstat. These data points represent the number of deals made each year.

What are the implications for a strategy of investing in potential acquisitions? The first is that such a strategy is partially based upon your market timing skills (or luck). Even if your portfolio of potential takeover targets is well constructed, the number of firms that actually get taken over may not measure up to expectations if the market mood turns sour. The second is that you have to factor in a sector focus in your portfolio. In other words, you should try to invest far more of your portfolio in stocks in the sectors in which consolidation and mergers are occurring the most.

Risk.   If you buy firms that are poorly managed and poorly run, your upside comes when someone offers to take over the firm and run it better. But there is a downside. These poorly managed firms can also go bankrupt. A portfolio of potential takeover targets will therefore also often have considerable risk exposure. There are a number of dimensions on which you can consider risk:

■ *Financial leverage:* A poorly run firm with substantial debt is clearly more at risk than a poorly managed firm without this debt. In fact, of the 15 firms identified as potential takeover targets in Table 10.2, 7 firms have debt in excess of 50% of total capital. If these firms begin losing money, they will not survive.

■ *Beta and standard deviation:* Stocks that have performed poorly in the past, both in terms of stock and project returns, are usually volatile. The standard deviation of the 15 firms listed in Table 10.2 is about twice the average for the rest of the market; the average beta for these companies is 1.43, again well above the average for the market.

To avoid exposing your portfolio to these risks, you could invest only in firms with low debt ratios and less stock price volatility.

LESSONS FOR INVESTORS

Investment strategies based upon acquisitions may sometimes generate high returns, but they come with risks. If you invest in acquisitive companies, hoping to ride growth in revenues and earnings to higher stock prices, you should consider screening for the following characteristics in acquisitive firms:

■ *Start with acquirers who stay focused and disciplined.* Acquisitive firms that attempt to stay within their core businesses or play to their key strengths when making acquisitions should be considered better candidates for your portfolio. These firms will also need to maintain that discipline even in the face of pressure from the outside.

■ *Be sure they don't overpay for target firms.* The key determinant of whether you as an investor gain from acquisitions is the acquisition price. An acquisitive firm that does a good job of valuing synergy and control should then follow up by ensuring that it gets at least a share of these perceived benefits for its stockholders. Acquisitive firms that enter into bidding wars intent to win at any cost usually do, but their stockholders pay the price.

■ *Be sure they prudently fund their acquisitions.* Acquisitive firms that fund acquisitions without pushing their debt ratios above acceptable levels or viewing their own stock as free currency are likely to be better investments in the long term.

■ *Avoid accounting complexity.* Acquisitive firms that try to present the most information they can about acquisitions and that do not play accounting games are much better investments in the long term.

If you adopt these screens, you will find that the best stocks for your portfolio will not be the serial acquirers who make the news with their big deals but the smaller acquirers who do not make the news. Notwithstanding these screens, you constantly have to monitor the firms you invest in to ensure that they (and their chief executives) are not overreaching.

If you believe that you have a better chance of success by investing in potential takeover targets, the last section suggests possible screens.

■ *Start with poorly managed companies.* Your odds of success are greatest with companies where managers not only do a poor job in terms of where they invest resources (return on equity more than 4% below the peer group ROE) but also generate subpar returns for their investors (stock returns over last year lag peer group returns by more than 5%).

■ *Avoid entrenched managers.* Shift your portfolio toward those companies where insiders hold relatively little stock (insider holdings less than 10%), there are no anti-takeover amendments on the books and where the CEO has not consolidated his or her hold on power.

■ *Reduce exposure to risk.* To reduce your exposure to risk, steer away from companies with too much debt (debt-to-capital ratios that exceed 50%) or high stock price volatility (annualized standard deviation in stock prices exceeds 80%).

Combining these screens, a portfolio of 17 stocks was generated in March 2003. The appendix lists the stocks in the portfolio.

CONCLUSION

Acquisitions make the news for obvious reasons. They cause stock prices to move dramatically, and it is not surprising that investors are attracted to companies involved in acquisitions. Some investors are drawn to acquiring firms, attracted by the rapid growth in earnings and revenues posted by these firms. If there is a lesson to be learned from history, it is that serial acquirers generally do not make good investments. All too often, they overpay for target firms, expand into businesses they do not understand and overreach by borrowing too much to fund their growth. While they are often able to cover their weaknesses in their financial statements, their problems ultimately catch up with them.

The largest payoff in acquisitions is to those who hold stock in target firms at the time the acquisitions are announced. To earn these returns, though, you have to buy these firms before they become acquisition targets; buying shares after an acquisition is announced is a risky strategy with limited returns. Looking at the typical target firms in past acquisitions, you can develop a set of screens for identifying potential target firms in future acquisitions. They tend to be poorly managed, have low insider ownership and earn poor returns both for their stockholders and on projects.

ENDNOTES

1. One requirement to qualify for pooling was that an acquisition had to be financed entirely with stock. Another is that the acquirer faces restrictions on selling the assets of the acquired firm in the year after the acquisition.

2. With the new accounting laws, the amortization of goodwill is based upon accounting estimates of the value of the acquired assets. If the accountants believe that the value has been sufficiently impaired, the acquiring company can be forced to write off goodwill early.

3. The excess returns around takeover announcements to target firms are so large that using different risk and return models seems to have no effect on the overall conclusions.

4. Jensen, M. C., and R. S. Ruback, 1983, *The Market for Corporate Control*, Journal of Financial Economics, v11, 5–50.

5. Jarrell, G. A., J. A. Brickley and J. M. Netter, 1988, *The Market for Corporate Control: The Empirical Evidence Since 1980*, Journal of Economic Perspectives, v2, 49–68.

6. Dennis, D. K., and J. J. McConnell, 1986, *Corporate Mergers and Security Returns*, Journal of Financial Economics, v16, 143–188.

7. Huang and Walkling (1987), *Acquisition Announcements and Abnormal Returns*, Journal of Financial Economics, v19, 329–350.

8. Jensen, M. C., and R. S. Ruback, 1983, *The Market for Corporate Control*, Journal of Financial Economics, v11, 5–50.

9. Jarrell, G. A., J. A. Brickley and J. M. Netter, 1988, *The Market for Corporate Control: The Empirical Evidence Since 1980*, Journal of Economic Perspectives, v2, 49–68.

10. Bhide, A., 1989, *The Causes and Consequences of Hostile Takeovers*, Journal of Applied Corporate Finance, v2, 36–59.

11. Bradley, M., A. Desai and E. H. Kim, 1988, *Synergistic Gains from Corporate Acquisitions and Their Division between the Stockholders of Target and Acquiring Firms*, Journal of Financial Economics, v21, 3–40.

12. Bradley, M., A. Desai and E. H. Kim, 1983, *The Rationale behind Interfirm Tender Offers*, Journal of Financial Economics, v11, 183–206.

13. Mitchell, M., and T. Pulvino, 2001, *Characteristics of Risk in Risk Arbitrage*, Journal of Finance, v56, 2135–2175.

14. This study was referenced in an article titled "Merger Mayhem" that appeared in *Barrons* on April 20, 1998.

15. KPMG measured the success at creating value by comparing the postdeal stock price performance of the combined firm to the performance of the relevant industry segment for a year after the deal was completed.

16. This study was done by Keefe, Bruyette and Woods, an investment bank. It was referenced in an article titled "Merger Mayhem" in *Barrons,* April 20, 1998.

17. Sirower, M. L., 1996, *The Synergy Trap*, Simon & Schuster.

18. Mitchell, M. L., and K. Lehn, 1990, *Do Bad Bidders Make Good Targets?*, Journal of Applied Corporate Finance, v3, 60–69.

19. Kaplan, S., and M. S. Weisbach, 1992, *The Success of Acquisitions: The Evidence from Divestitures*, Journal of Finance, v47, 107–138.

20. This might well reflect the fact that failures of mergers of equals are much more visible than failures of the small firm/large firm combinations.

21. KPMG, 1999, *Unlocking Shareholder Value: The Keys to Success*, KPMG Global Research Report.

22. A study by Healy, Palepu and Ruback (1989) looked at the postmerger performance of 50 large mergers from 1979 to 1983 and concluded that merged firms improved their operating performance (defined as EBITDA/sales) relative to their industries.

23. Healy, P. M., K. G. Palepu and R. S. Ruback, 1992, *Does Corporate Performance Improve after Mergers?*, Journal of Financial Economics, v31, 135–176.

24. Parrino, J. D., and R. S. Harris, *Takeovers, Management Replacement and Post-Acquisition Operating Performance: Some Evidence from the 1980s,* Journal of Applied Corporate Finance, v11, 88–97.

25. See Michel, A., and I. Shaked, 1984, *Does Business Diversification Affect Performance?*, Financial Management, v13, 5–14 and Dubofsky, P., and P. R. Varadarajan, 1987, *Diversification and Measures of Performance: Additional Empirical Evidence*, Academy of Management Journal, 597–608. These studies find that diversification-driven mergers do better than synergy-driven mergers in terms of risk-adjusted returns. Varadarajan, P. R., and V. Ramanujam, 1987, *Diversification and Performance: A reexamination using a new two-dimensional conceptualization of diversity in firms*, Academy of Management Journal, v30, 369–380, find evidence to the contrary.

26. Nail, L. A., W. L. Megginson and C. Maquieira, 1998, *Wealth Creation versus Wealth Redistributions in Pure Stock-for-Stock Mergers*, Journal of Financial Economics, v48, 3–33.

27. Bhide, A., 1989, *The Causes and Consequences of Hostile Takeovers*, Journal of Applied Corporate Finance, v2, 36–59.

28. Even if it is not the popular view, it is the populist view that has found credence in Hollywood, in movies like *Wall Street*, *Barbarians at the Gate* and *Other People's Money*.

APPENDIX:
POTENTIAL TAKEOVER TARGETS AMONG U.S. COMPANIES: MARCH 2003

COMPANY	TICKER SYMBOL	INDUSTRY	STOCK PRICE	P/E TRAILING 12 MO	MARKET CAP $ (MIL)	% INSIDER HOLDINGS	% DEBT/ CAPITAL LATEST QTR	STD DEV 3-YEAR	RETURN ON COMMON EQUITY	INDUSTRY AVERAGE
Universal Corp	UVV	Tobacco	37.09	8.7	949.7	1.8	46	34.87	18.14%	35.85%
ICN Pharmaceuticals	ICN	Drug	8.82	9.9	709.1	8.3	38.1	64.3	10.5%	24.29%
Saks Inc	SKS	Retail Store	7.87	11.1	984.4	9.8	38.9	60.78	1.04%	13.11%
Libbey Inc	LBY	Household Products	25	10.5	379.3	6.3	44.3	32.18	23.82%	35.46%
Conmed Corp	CNMD	Medical Supplies	16.01	11.8	429.9	8.5	39.8	48.3	8.6%	19.63%
Wellman Inc	WLM	Chemical (Specialty)	9.59	10.8	284.5	6.7	25.3	47.4	1.36%	10.30%
Blair Corp	BL	Retail (Special Lines)	24	9.7	186.2	8.69	0.2	38.07	2.24%	10.71%
Information Resources	IRIC	Information Services	1.32	11.7	41.4	7.1	2.8	77.16	2.71%	11.14%

(continued)

Potential Takeover Targets Among U.S. Companies: October 2002 *(Continued)*

Company	Ticker Symbol	Industry	Stock Price	P/E Trailing 12 Mo	Market Cap $ (Mil)	% Insider Holdings	% Debt/ Capital Latest Qtr	Std Dev 3-Year	Return on Common Equity	Industry Average
Hughes Supply	HUG	Retail Building Supply	24.8	9.1	509.9	6.6	40.1	48.19	7.41%	15.80%
Building Materials	BMHC	Retail Building Supply	14.25	7.7	174.7	5.9	39.8	40.15	8.78%	15.80%
Myers Inds	MYE	Diversified Co.	9.57	11	264.5	2.7	47.9	44.4	6.98%	12.51%
Cambrex Corp	CBM	Chemical (Diversified)	23.7	10.8	550.5	13.5	41.8	36.48	12.96%	17.95%
Phillips-Van Heusen	PVH	Apparel	11.97	11	329.5	4.09	46.3	39.56	9.06%	13.93%
Standard Register	SR	Office Equip/ Supplies	14.84	10.6	372.9	2.7	38.5	44.69	6.66%	11.53%
Armor Holdings	AH	Aerospace/ Defense	9.92	11.6	287.8	13.7	3.4	48.6	5.96%	10.78%
IHOP Corp	IHP	Restaurant	23.72	11.2	449.7	9.5	39.8	30.93	12.89%	17.36%
AnnTaylor Stores	ANN	Retail (Special Lines)	19.34	11.1	791.3	3.5	14.7	55.64	6.43%	10.71%

11

A Sure Thing: No Risk and Sure Profits

Linda loved getting something for nothing. She shamelessly took advantage of misprinted coupons at grocery stores and freebies at vacation resorts. She wondered whether there was a way she could apply her skills to improving her portfolio performance. Her friend Brian, who was a broker, suggested that there might be a way to take no risk and make high returns in the stock market. Lots of foreign stocks, he argued, had listings in the United States and some of them traded at much higher prices in the U.S. markets than they did in their local markets. Using his connections, he said he could buy shares cheap in the local market while borrowing the more expensive shares listed in the U.S. market and selling them. A profit was guaranteed, he argued, since the two shares were in the same company.

Linda went along with the plan. Brian bought the shares in an Indonesian company on the Jakarta stock exchange and borrowed and sold shares in the same company in the U.S. market at a price that was 20% higher. He told Linda that the borrowed shares would have to be returned in two months but that the price difference would narrow by then, thus giving her a sure profit. Linda watched the share prices in both the Indonesian and the U.S. market in the days after. When the price difference did not narrow initially, she was not worried. When the price difference was still 20% a month after the trade, she sought out Brian but he reassured her that all was well. Doing her own research, she discovered that the U.S. listing was called an ADR and had always traded at a premium on the local listing, and that an ADR could not be exchanged for a local share. When the difference in prices reached 25%, she told Brian to settle the account to limit her losses, and decided that she her odds were much better with her local grocery store than in the stock market.

Moral: If you see easy money to be made in the stock market, you have not looked hard enough.

Despite being told repeatedly that there are no free lunches, investors never stop looking for them. If you can invest without taking risk and earn more than you could make on government bonds, you have the equivalent of a free lunch in investing. There are both institutional and individual investors who search for these elusive opportunities hoping to find them and mine them for certain profits. These riskless investments that earn more than the riskless rate represent arbitrage opportunities. In this chapter, you will look at arbitrage opportunities in their pure form first, and also in the form in which you are most likely to encounter them: where there is some residual risk. You will also examine why arbitrage opportunities, even when they present themselves, are so difficult to exploit for certain profits.

CORE OF THE STORY

No money down, no risk and unlimited profit! Would you need to be sold on such an opportunity, if it did exist? It would sell itself. Any skeptical investor, though, would view such a sales pitch with derision, having undoubtedly been burned by similar ones in the past. Such an investor would also want to know why such an opportunity would exist in the first place. For an arbitrage sales pitch to succeed, it has to be accompanied by a reason for its existence. Here are a few:

- *No one else knows about it (yet).* This is the pitch to the truly gullible. Every great investment opportunity has to be discovered by someone and that someone conveniently happens to be you. Why the person who discovered this opportunity would share this news with anyone and why you should be the lucky recipient of this largess may not be explained to you, but as with any con game, you are made to feel special.
- *It takes special skill to find it and you can acquire it (cheap).* This is the sales pitch for the investor who

wants to pay something, but not very much, for that "free" lunch. If you acquire the special skill (which may be a book, software or mantra offered by the purveyor) for a price, you will be able to establish a clear advantage over other investors in the market.

- *It will last only a short time (and you have to make up your mind quickly).* It is true that markets sometimes make mistakes and that these mistakes can lead to arbitrage opportunities for those who happen to be in the right place at the right time. On this investment, that happens to be you if you act immediately.
- *It will work only for investors with specific characteristics (and you have them).* This is perhaps the most effective of the sales pitches because it has the best chance of being true. If you are different from other investors (you have lower transactions costs or a different tax rate), you may very well find that what looks like the right price to others offers riskless profits for you.

THEORETICAL ROOTS OF ARBITRAGE

To understand arbitrage, you begin by distinguishing between three types of arbitrage:

- *Pure arbitrage:* Two identical assets have different market prices at the same time, but those prices will converge at a given future time. This type of arbitrage is most likely to occur in derivatives markets—options and futures—and in some parts of the bond market.
- *Near arbitrage:* Assets have identical or almost identical cash flows but trade at different prices, with no guarantee that their prices will converge and with significant constraints on investors forcing them to do so.
- *Speculative arbitrage:* This is really not arbitrage. Investors take advantage of what they see as mispriced or similar (though not identical) assets, buying the cheaper

one and selling the more expensive one. If the investors are right, the price difference should narrow over time, yielding profits. As you will see, the peril of this strategy is the initial assessment of mispricing is usually based on a view of the world that may not be justified.

PURE ARBITRAGE

The requirement that you have two assets with identical cash flows and different market prices makes pure arbitrage elusive. First, identical assets are not common in the real world, especially if you are an equity investor. No two companies are exactly alike, and their stocks are therefore not perfect substitutes. Second, assuming two identical assets exist, you have to wonder why financial markets would allow pricing differences to persist. If in addition, you add the constraint that there is a point at which the market prices converge, it is not surprising that pure arbitrage is likely to occur very infrequently, and even if it does occur, it is likely to be small and fleeting. The conditions that would cause it to occur include the following:

- *Restrictions on the flow of market information to investors in the market:* You may find the same asset trading at different prices in two different markets if investors in one market cannot observe the price in the other market, and vice versa. While this may seem outlandish in these days of CNBC and online trading, it is worth remembering that until a decade or so ago, even in the United States, only a few investors, mostly institutional, had access to real-time trading prices and transactions information. In fact, there are still markets in the world where there is little or no transparency about trading and prices.
- *Restrictions on trading:* To eliminate the mispricing, you have to be able to trade. If you are prevented from doing so by market restrictions, you may very well see the mispricing continue. For example, you may need to

be able to borrow shares from other investors and sell them (short selling of stocks) to create some arbitrage positions but short sales are restricted or prohibited in many markets.

Futures Arbitrage.   A futures contract is a contract to buy a specified asset at a fixed price at a future time period. There are two parties to every futures contract: the seller of the contract, who agrees to deliver the asset at the specified time in the future; and the buyer of the contract, who agrees to pay a fixed price and take delivery of the asset. Consider, for instance, a one-year futures contract on gold, priced at $425 an ounce. If you buy this contract, you are guaranteed delivery of 100 ounces of gold at $425 an ounce one year from now. If your objective is to be in possession of 100 ounces of gold in one year, you could also accomplish this objective by borrowing money today, buying 100 ounces of gold at the current price (in the spot market), and storing the gold for one year. The second approach (borrowing money and storing gold) will create two additional costs to you as an investor:

a. *Interest costs:* Since you have to borrow the money now, you have to pay interest for the period of the borrowing (one year in this case).
b. *Storage costs:* If a storage cost is associated with storing the commodity until the expiration of the futures contract, this cost has to be reflected in the strategy as well. In some cases, there may be a benefit to having physical ownership of the commodity. This benefit is called the convenience yield and will reduce the futures price. The net storage cost is defined to be the difference between the total storage cost and the convenience yield.

Since the two strategies deliver the same end result—ownership of 100 ounces of gold at the end of one year at a cost that you know today—they should cost the same. If they do not, you could potentially generate a riskless profit.

Consider a simple example. Assume that the current spot price of gold is $400 an ounce and that the one-year futures contract on gold continues to be priced at $425 an ounce. You can buy the futures contract and guarantee that you will be able to buy the gold at $425 an ounce a year from now. Alternatively, you can borrow $400 today, buy an ounce of gold, and store it for a year. If you do the latter, you will have to pay interest expenses on your borrowing and the storage cost of gold. If you assume that the annualized riskless interest rate on borrowings is 5% and that the storage cost is $2 an ounce for a year, this strategy will result in a cost of $422 an ounce:

$$\text{Cost of futures contract} = \$425$$

$$\text{Cost of borrowing, buying and storing gold} = \$400\,(1.05) + \$2 = \$422$$

Since these strategies are equivalent in terms of final results (you will take delivery of one ounce of gold a year from now), you can construct an arbitrage position:

Arbitrage position: Borrow $400, buy one ounce of gold and store gold
Sell a futures contract for $425

At the end of the year, you will deliver the gold to the buyer of the futures contract and receive $425. You will then use the proceeds to pay off the loan with interest ($420) and the storage costs ($2), leaving you with an arbitrage profit of $3 an ounce. To prevent arbitrage, the futures contract will have to trade at $422 an ounce.

This arbitrage is based upon several assumptions. First, investors are assumed to borrow and lend at the same rate, which is the riskless rate. Second, when the futures contract is underpriced, it is assumed that the buyer of the futures contract (the arbitrageur) can sell short on the commodity and that he can recover, from the owner of the commodity, the storage costs that are saved as a consequence. To the extent that these assumptions are unrealistic, the bounds on prices within which arbitrage is not feasible expand.

Options Arbitrage. As derivative securities, options differ from futures in a very important respect. They represent rights rather than obligations—calls give you the right to buy and puts give you the right to sell an underlying asset at a fixed price (called an exercise price). Consequently, a key feature of options is that buyers of options will exercise the options only if it is in their best interests to do so and thus they cannot lose more than what they paid for the options. As an example, let's assume that you pay $4 to buy a six-month call option on Microsoft with an exercise price of $50. In effect, you have the right to buy a share of Microsoft at $50 anytime over the next six months. Clearly, you will exercise this right only if Microsoft's stock price exceeds $50; the gross profit you will make on exercise will be the difference between the stock price and the exercise price. If Microsoft's stock price drops below $50, you will not exercise your option and you will lose what you paid for the option. With a put with the same exercise price, you get a right to sell a share of Microsoft at $50 and you will exercise only if the stock price drops below $50.

The easiest arbitrage opportunities in the option market exist when options violate simple pricing bounds. No option, for instance, should sell for less than its exercise value.

With a call option: Value of Call > Value of Underlying Asset − Strike Price
With a put option: Value of Put > Strike Price − Value of Underlying Asset

For instance, a call option with a strike price of $50 on a stock that is currently trading at $60 should never sell for less than $10. If it did, you could make an immediate profit by buying the call for less than $10 and exercising right away to make $10.

In fact, you can tighten these bounds for call options, if you are willing to trade on both the underlying asset and the option and hold your position through the option's expiration. The bounds then become:

With a call option: Value of Call > Value of Underlying
                        Asset – Present Value of Strike Price
With a put option: Value of Put > Present Value of Strike
                        Price – Value of Underlying Asset

To see why, consider the call option in the previous example. Assume that you have one year to expiration and that the riskless interest rate is 10%.

$$\text{Present Value of Strike Price} = \$50 \ / \ 1.10 = \$45.45$$
$$\text{Lower Bound on Call Value} = \$60 - \$45.45 = \$14.55$$

The call has to trade for more than $14.55. What would happen if it traded for less, say $12? You would buy the call for $12, sell short a share of stock for $60 and invest the net proceeds of $48 ($60–$12) at the riskless rate of 10%. Consider what happens a year from now:

- *If the stock price is greater than strike price ($50):* You first collect the proceeds from the riskless investment [$48 (1.10) = $52.80], exercise the option (buy the share at $50), and return the share to cover your short sale. You will then get to keep the difference of $2.80.
- *If the stock price is less than strike price ($50):* You collect the proceeds from the riskless investment ($52.80), buy a share in the open market for the prevailing price then (which will be less than $50) and keep the difference.

In other words, you invest nothing today and are guaranteed a positive payoff in the future. You could construct a similar example with puts.

The arbitrage bounds work best for stocks that do not pay dividends and for options that can be exercised only at expiration (European options). Most options in the real world can be exercised before expiration (American options) and are on stocks that pay dividends. Even with these options, though, you should not see short-term options trading that violates these bounds by large margins, partly because exercise is so rare even with listed American options and dividends tend to be small. As options become long term and dividends become larger and more uncertain, you may very well find options that violate these pricing bounds, but you may not be able to profit from them.

One of the key insights that revolutionized option pricing in the early 1970s was that a portfolio created by borrowing money and buying the underlying stock, if structured right, could have exactly the same cash flows as a call. This portfolio is called the replicating portfolio. In fact, Fischer Black and Myron Scholes used the arbitrage argument to derive their option-pricing model by noting that since the replicating portfolio and the traded option have the same cash flows, they would have to sell at the same price.[1] If you can buy listed options at a price that is less than the cost of creating the replicating portfolio, you will buy the listed option, sell the replicating portfolio and essentially make a riskless profit, since the cash flows on the two positions would offset each other. If the replicating portfolio costs less than the option, you will buy the replicating portfolio and sell the option and lock in your profits.

NEAR ARBITRAGE

In near arbitrage, you either have two assets that are very similar but not identical and that are priced differently, or identical assets that are mispriced but with no guaranteed price convergence. No matter how sophisticated your trading strategies may be in these scenarios, your positions will no longer be riskless. Consider three examples:

- *Same security, multiple markets:* In today's global markets, a number of stocks are listed on more than one market. If you can buy the same stock at one price in one market and simultaneously sell it at a higher price in another market, you can lock in a riskless profit. In the real world, even though the same company may be traded in different markets, it trades in different forms. For instance, many non-U.S. companies trade in the United States as American depository receipts (ADRs) while their shares trade on their local markets at the same time. If there are no restrictions on converting ADRs into local shares, then any significant price differences between the two markets should offer profit potential.

- *Closed-end funds:* In a conventional mutual fund, the number of shares increases and decreases as money comes in and leaves the fund, and each share is priced at net asset value—the market value of the securities of the fund divided by the number of shares. Closed-end mutual funds differ from other mutual funds in one very important respect. They have a fixed number of shares that trade in the market like other publicly traded companies, and the market price can be different from the net asset value. In other words, a closed-end fund can trade for far less or far more than the market value of the securities that it holds at that time. If the market price per share of a closed-end fund is less than the net asset value per share, there is potential for profits but it is not clear how you would cash in on these profits.

- *Convertible arbitrage:* A convertible bond has two securities embedded in it: a conventional bond and a conversion option on the company's stock. When companies have convertible bonds or convertible preferred stock outstanding in conjunction with common stock, warrants, preferred stock and conventional bonds, it is entirely possible that you could find one of these securities mispriced relative to the other and be able to construct a near-riskless strategy by combining two or more of the securities in a portfolio.

PSEUDO OR SPECULATIVE ARBITRAGE

The word arbitrage is used much too loosely in investments, and a large number of strategies characterized as arbitrage actually expose investors to significant risk. Consider the following examples:

- *Paired arbitrage:* In classic arbitrage, you buy an asset at one price and sell an exactly identical asset at a different (and higher) price. In paired arbitrage, you buy one stock (say, GM) and sell another stock that you view as very similar (say, Ford), and argue that you are not exposed to risk. Clearly, this strategy is not riskless since no two stocks are exactly identical, and even if they were very similar, there is no reason why their prices have to converge.
- *Merger arbitrage:* In Chapter 10, we looked at the strategy of buying shares in firms involved in an acquisition after the acquisition was announced. This strategy is called merger arbitrage, though it is difficult to see why it is called arbitrage in the first place. The profits are not riskless and the strategy is speculative.

LOOKING AT THE EVIDENCE

It should come as no surprise that relatively few arbitrage opportunities have been uncovered by empirical research over the last few decades. In fact, it may surprise you that any such opportunities exist in the first place. As you will see in this section, the evidence on arbitrage opportunities is ambiguous and can be interpreted differently, depending upon your point of view. Believers in efficient markets look at the evidence and argue that markets cannot be exploited to make any money, because of transactions costs and execution problems. Those who believe that there are times when markets break down argue that the mispricing of assets can be exploited, perhaps not by all investors but by some investors in the market.

PURE ARBITRAGE

One way to test whether arbitrage opportunities exist is to look at how futures and options contracts are priced by the market. This, by itself, is weak evidence of arbitrage because you have to trade at these prices to make the riskless profits. The second test of arbitrage is to examine the returns of investors who claim to do arbitrage and see if they succeed.

Futures and Option Markets. If futures and option arbitrage is so simple, you may ask, how in a reasonably efficient market would arbitrage opportunities even exist? In the commodity futures market, for instance, a study in 1983 found little evidence of arbitrage opportunities and those findings are echoed in more recent studies. In the futures and options markets, evidence shows that arbitrage is indeed feasible but only to a very small subset of investors and for very short periods.[2] Differences in transactions cost seem to explain most of the differences. Large institutional investors, with close to zero transactions costs and instantaneous access to both the underlying asset and futures markets may be able to find and take advantage of arbitrage opportunities, where individual investors would not. In addition, these investors are also more likely to meet the requirements for arbitrage—being able to borrow at rates close to the riskless rate and sell short on the underlying asset.

Note, though, that the returns are small[3] even to these large investors and that arbitrage will not be a reliable source of profits unless you can establish a competitive advantage on one of three dimensions. First, you can try to establish a transactions cost advantage over other investors, which will be difficult to do since you are competing with other large institutional investors. Second, you may be able to develop an information advantage over other investors by having access to information earlier than others. Again, though, much of the information is pricing information and is public. Third, you may find a quirk in the pricing of a particular futures or options contract before others learn about it.

The arbitrage possibilities seem to be greatest when futures or options contracts are first introduced on an asset, since investors take time to understand the details of futures pricing. For instance, it took investors a while to learn how to price stock index and treasury bond futures.[4] Presumably, investors who learned faster than the market were able to take advantage of the mispricing of futures and options contracts in these early periods and make substantial profits.

Fixed Income Arbitrage. Bonds lend themselves to arbitrage more easily than do stocks because they have finite lives and fixed cash flows. This is especially so for government bonds, for which the fixed cash flows are also guaranteed. Consider one very simple example. You could replicate a 10-year treasury bond's cash flows by buying zero-coupon treasuries with expirations matching those of the coupon payment dates on the treasury bond. For instance, if you invest $1 million in a 10-year treasury bond with an 8% coupon rate, you can expect to get cash flows of $40,000 million every six months for the next 10 years and $1 million at the end of the 10th year. You could have obtained exactly the same cash flows by buying zero-coupon treasuries with face values of $40,000, expiring every six months for the next 10 years, and an additional 10-year zero coupon bond with a face value of $1 million. Since the cash flows are identical, you would expect the two positions to trade for the same price. If they do not trade at the same price, you would buy the cheaper position and sell the more expensive one, locking in the profit today and having no cash flow or risk exposure in the future.

With corporate bonds, you have the extra component of default risk. Since no two firms are exactly identical when it comes to default risk, you may be exposed to some risk if you are using corporate bonds issued by different entities. In fact, two bonds issued by the same entity may not be equivalent because of differences in how they are secured and structured. Some arbitrageurs argue that bond ratings are a good proxy for default risk, and that buying one AA-rated bond and selling another AA-rated bond should be riskless, but bond ratings are not perfect proxies for default risk. In fact, you see arbitrage attempted on a wide variety of securities, such as mortgage-backed bonds, with promised cash flows. While you can hedge away much of the cash flow risk, the nature of the cash flow claims will still leave you exposed to some risk. With mortgage-backed bonds, for instance, the unpredictability of prepayments by homeowners has exposed many "riskless" positions to risk.

Is there any evidence that investors can find bonds mis-priced enough to generate arbitrage profits? An assessment of the treasury strips program—a program allowing investors to break up a treasury bond and sell its individual cash flows—notes that there were potential arbitrage opportunities in these markets in the early years of the program but finds little evidence of trading driven by these opportunities.[5] An analysis of the Spanish bond market may shed some light on this question.[6] Examining default-free and option-free bonds in the Spanish market between 1994 and 1998, this study concludes that there were arbitrage opportunities surrounding innovations in financial markets. You would extend these findings to argue that opportunities for arbitrage with bonds are probably greatest when new types of bonds are introduced: mortgage-backed securities in the early 1980s, inflation-indexed treasuries in the late 1990s and the treasury strips program in the late 1980s. As investors become more informed about these bonds and how they should be priced, arbitrage opportunities seem to subside.

NEAR ARBITRAGE

Near arbitrage is more likely to occur than pure arbitrage, and it can take many forms. In this section, you will look at the evidence accumulated over time on near-arbitrage strategies.

Same Security, Multiple Markets. Many large companies such as Royal Dutch, General Electric and Microsoft trade on multiple markets on different continents. Since there are times during the day when trading is occurring on more than one market on the same stock, it is conceivable (though not likely) that you could buy the stock for one price in one market and sell the same stock at the same time for a different (and higher) price in another market. The stock will trade in different currencies, and for this to be a riskless transaction, the trades have to occur at precisely the same time and you have to eliminate any exchange rate risk by instantaneously converting the foreign currency proceeds into the domestic currency. Your trade profits will also have to cover the different transactions costs in the two markets. There are some exceptional cases in which the same stock trades in different markets in one country. An examination of 84 Czech stocks that trade on the two Czech exchanges—the Prague Stock Exchange (PSE) and the Registration Places System (RMS)—finds that prices adjust slowly across the two markets and that arbitrage opportunities exist (at least on paper); the prices in the two markets differ by about 2%.[7] These arbitrage opportunities seem to increase for less liquid stocks. While the authors of the study consider transactions cost, they do not consider the price impact that trading itself would have on these stocks and whether the arbitrage profits would survive the trading.

Many Asian, Latin American and European companies have American depository receipts (ADRs) listed on the U.S. market. Depository receipts are issued or created when investors decide to invest in a non-U.S. company and contact their brokers to make a purchase. These brokers, through their own international offices or through a local broker in the company's home market, purchase the shares in the local market and request that the shares be delivered to the depository bank's custodian in that country. The broker who initiated the transaction will convert the U.S. dollars received from the investor into the corresponding foreign currency and pay the local broker for the shares purchased. On the same day that the shares are delivered to the custodian bank, the custodian notifies the depository bank. Upon such notification, depository receipts are issued and delivered to the initiating broker, who then delivers the depository receipts to the investor. These depository receipts[8] create a claim equivalent to the one the investor would have had if the shares had been bought in the local market and should therefore trade at a price consistent with the local shares. What makes them different and potentially riskier than the stocks with dual listings is that ADRs are not always directly comparable to the common shares traded locally; for example, one ADR on Telmex, the Mexican telecommunications company, is convertible into 20 Telmex shares. In addition, converting an ADR into local shares can be sometimes costly and time consuming. In some cases, there can be differences in voting rights as well.

In spite of these constraints, you would expect the price of an ADR to closely track the price of the shares in the local market, albeit with a currency overlay, since ADRs are denominated in dollars. An examination of the link between ADRs and local share concludes that about 60% to 70% of the variation in ADR prices can be attributed to movements in the underlying share prices and that ADRs overreact to the U.S. market and underreact to exchange rates and the underlying stock.[9] However, investors cannot take advantage of the pricing errors in ADRs because convergence does not occur quickly or in predictable ways. With a longer time horizon or the capacity to convert ADRs into local shares, though, you should be able to take advantage of significant pricing differences.

Closed-End Funds. In both the United States and the United Kingdom, closed-end mutual funds have shared a very strange characteristic. When they are created, the price is usually set at a premium on the net asset value per share. As closed-end funds trade, though, the market price tends to drop below the net asset value and stay there. In any given period in which they have been examined, about 60% to 70% of closed-end funds trade at a discount on the net asset value. Some of these discounts are substantial and exceed 20%.

So what, you might ask? Lots of firms trade at less than the estimated market value of their assets. That might be true, but closed-end funds are unique for two reasons. First, the assets are all traded stocks and the market value is therefore known at any given time and is not an estimate. Second, liquidating a closed-end fund's assets should not be difficult to do, since the assets are traded stocks or bonds. Thus, liquidation should be neither costly nor time consuming. Given these two conditions, you may wonder why you should not buy closed-end funds that trade at a discount and either liquidate them yourself or hope that some one else will liquidate them. Alternatively, you may be able to push a closed-end fund to convert into an open-end fund and see prices converge on net asset value. Figure 11.1 shows the performance of 94 U.K. closed-end funds that were converted to open-end funds.[10]

Note that as you get closer to the open-ending date (day 0), the discount becomes smaller relative to the average closed-end fund. For instance, the discount goes from being on par with the discount on other funds to being about 10% lower than the typical closed-end fund.

So what is the catch? In practice, taking over a closed-end fund while paying less than net asset value for its shares seems to be very difficult to do for several reasons, some related to corporate governance and some related to market liquidity. There have been a few cases of closed-end funds being liquidated, but they remain the exception. What about the strategy of buying discounted funds and hoping that the discount

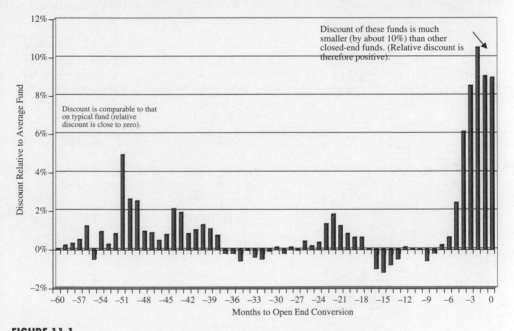

FIGURE 11.1

Relative Discount on Closed-End Funds That Become Open-End Funds

Data from Dimson and Minio-Kozerzki. These are the average relative discounts of closed-end funds that were converted to open-end in the U.K., that is, the difference between the discount on closed-end funds that open end and other closed-end funds. A positive number indicates a smaller discount.

disappears? This strategy is clearly not riskless but it does offer some promise. One of the first studies of this strategy examined closed-end funds from 1940 to 1975 and reported that you could earn an annualized excess return of 4% from buying discounted funds.[11] An analysis in 1986 reports excess returns from a strategy of buying closed-end funds whose discounts had widened and selling funds whose discounts had narrowed—a contrarian strategy applied to closed-end funds. An examination of closed-end funds reported that funds with a discount of 20% or higher earn about 6% more than other closed-end funds.[12] This, as well as research in the U.K., seem to indicate a strong reversion to the average in discounts at closed funds. Figure 11.2, which is from a study of the discounts on

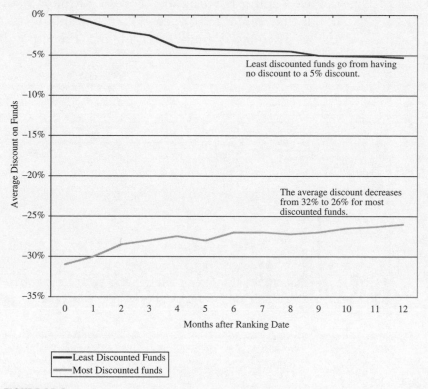

FIGURE 11.2

Discounts on Most Discounted and Least Discounted Funds Over Time

Data from Minio-Paluello. The discounts on the most discounted and least discounted funds are available for 12 months after the funds are selected.

closed-end funds in the U.K., tracks relative discounts on the most discounted and least discounted funds over time.[13]

Note that the discounts on the most discounted funds decrease, whereas the discounts on the least discounted funds increase, and the difference narrows over time.

Convertible Arbitrage. In the simplest form of convertible arbitrage, since the conversion option is a call option on the stock, you could construct its equivalent by combining the underlying stock and the treasury bond (a replicating portfolio). Adding a conventional bond to this should create the equivalent of the convertible bond; this is called a synthetic convertible bond. Once you can do this, you can take advantage of differences between the pricing of the convertible bond and synthetic convertible bond and potentially make arbitrage profits. In the more complex forms, when you have warrants, convertible preferred and other options trading simultaneously on a firm, you could look for options that are mispriced relative to each other, and then buy the cheaper option and sell the more expensive one.

PSEUDO OR SPECULATIVE ARBITRAGE

In Chapter 10, you looked at some of the empirical evidence on merger arbitrage. Summarizing the findings, merger arbitrage does generate healthy returns for investors who use it but it is certainly not riskless. In fact, it is a strategy in which failure can lead to large negative returns while success takes the form of small positive returns. Consider now the evidence on paired arbitrage, in which you find two similar stocks that are mispriced relative to each other and buy (sell) the cheaper (more expensive) one. The conventional practice among those who have used paired arbitrage strategy on Wall Street has been to look for two stocks whose prices have historically moved together, that is, have high correlation over time. This often leads to two stocks in the same sector, such as GM and Ford. Once you have paired the stocks, you compute the spread between them and compare this spread to historic norms. If the spread is too wide, you buy the cheaper stock and sell short the more expensive stock. In many cases, the strategy is self-financing.

For example, assume that Ford has historically traded at a third of GM's price. If Ford is currently trading at $20 and GM is trading at $40, GM is overpriced relative to Ford. You would buy two shares of Ford and sell short one share of GM; this position would be self-financing and would require no investment from you. If you are right and the spread narrows between the shares, you will profit on your paired position.

Can such a simplistic strategy, based entirely upon past prices, make excess returns? In 1999, a study tested a variety of trading rules based upon pairs trading from 1982–1997, using the following process:[14]

- Screening first for only stocks that traded every day, the authors of the study found a matching partner for each stock by looking for the stock that moved most closely with it.[15] Once they had paired all the stocks, they studied the pairs with the smallest squared deviation separating them.
- With each pair, they tracked the normalized prices of each stock and took a position on the pair if the difference exceeded the historical range by two standard deviations, buying the cheaper stock and selling the more expensive one.

Over the 15-year period, the pairs trading strategy did significantly better than a buy-and-hold strategy. Strategies of investing in the top 20 pairs earned an excess return of about 6% over a 6-month period, and while the returns drop off for the pairs below the top 20, they continue to earn excess returns. When the pairs are constructed by industry group (rather than just based upon historical prices), the excess returns persist but they are smaller. Controlling for the bid-ask spread in the strategy reduces the excess returns by about a fifth, but the returns are still significant.

While the overall trading strategy looks promising, there are two points worth emphasizing that should also act as cautionary notes about this strategy. The first is that the study quoted above found that the pairs trading strategy created negative returns in about one out of every six periods, and that the difference between pairs often widened before it narrowed. In other words, it is a risky investment strategy that also requires the capacity to trade instantaneously and at low cost. The second is a quote from a well-known quantitative analyst, David Shaw, who bemoaned the fact that by the late 1990s, the pickings for quantitative strategies (like pairs trading) had become slim because so many investment banks were adopting the strategies. As the novelty has worn off, it seems unlikely that pairs trading will generate the kinds of profits it generated during the 1980s.

CRUNCHING THE NUMBERS

Given the wide range of arbitrage strategies available, your portfolio will look very different depending upon the strategy you pick. In the first part of this section, you will look at one futures market (gold) and one options market (stock index) to see if you can find any obvious candidates for pure arbitrage. In the second part of this section, portfolios of heavily discounted closed-end funds and depository receipts will be constructed and put under the microscope for potential profits.

FUTURES AND OPTIONS ARBITRAGE

Do futures contracts on commodities and financial assets obey the pricing rules preventing arbitrage? Consider, as an illustration, futures contracts on gold, a commodity with small storage costs and a high price. Table 11.1 lists the prices on futures contracts on gold listed on the Chicago Board of Trade on April 4, 2003. At the time, the spot price of gold was $324.9 an ounce; the riskless rates are listed in the table. Assuming that the storage costs are zero, the predicted or theoretical prices are estimated as follows:

Theoretical Price = Spot Price of Gold $(1 + \text{Riskless Rate})^{\text{Time to expiration}}$

TABLE 11.1　Gold Futures Contracts: Actual and Predicted Futures Prices

Month	Actual Futures Price	Time to Maturity	Riskless Rate	Predicted Price	Price difference
Apr 03	325.3	0.08333333	1.25%	325.24	0.02%
May 03	325.6	0.16666667	1.26%	325.58	0.01%
Jun 03	326	0.25	1.27%	325.93	0.02%
Aug 03	326.7	0.41666667	1.27%	326.61	0.03%
Oct 03	327.2	0.58333333	1.28%	327.32	−0.04%
Dec 03	327.7	0.75	1.35%	328.18	−0.15%
Feb 04	328.3	0.91666667	1.38%	329.01	−0.22%
Apr 04	328.8	1.08333333	1.41%	329.87	−0.32%
Jun 04	329.3	1.25	1.43%	330.72	−0.43%
Aug 04	330	1.41666667	1.45%	331.59	−0.48%
Oct 04	331.1	1.58333333	1.48%	332.55	−0.44%
Dec 04	331.9	1.75	1.51%	333.53	−0.49%
Feb 05	332.8	1.91666667	1.52%	334.43	−0.49%
Jun 05	334.6	2.25	1.56%	336.42	−0.54%
Dec 05	337.6	2.75	1.50%	338.48	−0.26%
Jun 06	341.6	3.25	1.58%	341.88	−0.08%
Dec 06	346.2	3.75	1.70%	346.10	0.03%
Jun 07	351.1	4.25	1.84%	351.08	0.01%
Dec 07	355.9	4.75	1.93%	355.78	0.03%

Note that the actual prices are very close (within half of one percent) to the theoretical prices for every one of the futures contracts.

As another exercise, Table 11.2 lists call and put options on the S&P 500 with different exercise prices and their prices on April 4, 2003. The spot price of the index at the time that this table was extracted was $876.04.

There are a number of tests that you can run for simple arbitrage opportunities. Consider, for example, the call and put options due in June 2003. In Table 11.3, the prices of the call and put options are compared to the exercise values of these options.

For example, exercising a call option with an exercise price of $865 will generate an exercise value equal to the difference between the current level of the index ($876.04) and the exer-

TABLE 11.2 S&P 500 Index Options: April 4, 2003

EXERCISE	CALLS			PUTS		
PRICE ($)	APRIL	MAY	JUNE	APRIL	MAY	JUNE
865	23.9	35.8	45.1	15.6	27.5	36.8
870	21	32.9	42.2	17.7	29.6	38.9
875	18.3	30.2	39.5	20	31.9	41.2
880	15.8	27.6	36.9	22.5	34.3	43.6
885	13.6	—	34.4	25.3	—	46.1
890	11.6	23	32	28.3	39.7	48.6

cise price. Exercising a put option with an exercise price of $885 will generate a profit equal to the difference between the exercise price and the current index level. None of the June options trade at less than exercise value. In fact, reverting to Table 11.2, which lists all the traded options on the index, there is not a single option that violates simple arbitrage. While this is a weak test of arbitrage opportunities, you can expand these tests to cover more involved arbitrage opportunities and you will not find any (or at least any that look easy to exploit).

In general, you can scan the futures and options pages every day for weeks without finding obvious arbitrage opportunities. Even if you do find an obvious mispricing, odds are that you are finding a misprint, that you are missing a critical ingredient in your pricing formula, or that you cannot execute

TABLE 11.3 Market Prices versus Exercise Values: June 2003 Options

	CALLS		PUTS	
EXERCISE	MARKET	SIMPLE EXERCISE:	MARKET	SIMPLE EXERCISE:
PRICE ($)	PRICE	S – K	PRICE	K – S
865	$45.10	$11.04	$36.80	$0.00
870	$42.20	$6.04	$38.90	$0.00
875	$39.50	$1.04	$41.20	$0.00
880	$36.90	$0.00	$43.60	$3.96
885	$34.40	$0.00	$46.10	$8.96
890	$32.00	$0.00	$48.60	$13.96

at that price. In other words, pure arbitrage opportunities if they exist in markets are likely to take on more subtle forms and will require more research.

DEPOSITORY RECEIPTS

Hundreds of non-U.S. companies have depository receipts listed on them in the United States. To find evidence of mispricing in this market, Table 11.4 lists the ADR price and the dollar value of the local listing price of the twenty most liquid ADRS on March 4, 2003.

TABLE 11.4 Most Liquid ADRs in the United States: April 4, 2003

Dr Issue	ADR Price	Local Share Price
Nokia Corporation	$14.70	$14.71
Ericsson Lm Telephone Company	$6.99	$6.98
Sap Ag	$19.82	$19.83
Taiwan Semiconductor Manufacturing Co	$7.55	$7.55
Bp Plc	$39.01	$38.95
Royal Dutch Petroleum Co	$42.06	$42.04
Teva Pharmaceutical Industries Ltd	$44.07	$44.07
Vodafone Group Plc	$19.00	$18.99
America Movil Sa De Cv—Series "L"	$14.50	$14.52
Stmicroelectronics NV	$18.64	$18.64
Telefonos De Mexico SA De CV—Series "L"	$30.67	$30.66
Business Objects SA	$18.33	$18.33
Gold Fields Limited	$10.19	$10.19
Tele Norte Leste Participacoes SA	$9.29	$9.30
Astrazeneca Plc	$34.85	$34.86
Hsbc	$52.87	$52.89
United Microelectronics Corporation	$3.27	$3.26
Cemex SA De Cv	$18.25	$18.25
Asml Holding Nv	$6.91	$6.91
Petroleo Brasileiro SA—Preferred	$15.28	$15.26

The prices were obtained from the U.S. and the foreign exchange at the same time, and the local listing price is converted into dollars at the prevailing exchange rate at that time. You can see that the prices are within a cent or two of each other. That should come as no surprise for two reasons. One is that these ADRs can be converted into local shares at relatively low cost. The other is that there is heavy trading in both the local and ADR markets on these shares. Any significant difference between the ADR and the local share price would be almost instantaneously arbitraged.

Some countries impose significant restrictions on converting ADRs into local shares. This is true, for instance, with Indian companies that have ADRs listed in the United States. These ADRs often trade at prices that are very different from the local share price. Table 11.5 summarizes the prices in U.S. dollars of some of the most heavily traded Indian companies in the United States.

TABLE 11.5 ADR and Local Share Prices: Indian Companies

Company	ADR Price	Local Price (Rs)	Local Price	Premium (Discount)	Market Cap in $ (Local Market)
Dr Reddy (Rdy)	$19.60	915.2	$19.35	1.30%	1,629.60
Hdfc Bank (Hdb)	$17.30	240	$15.35	12.70%	1,427.90
Icici Bank (Ibn)	$6.60	136.8	$5.77	14.40%	1,768.60
Infosys Tech (Infy)	$62.90	4,226.80	$44.58	41.10%	5,903.70
Mtnl (Mte)	$4.20	97.5	$4.09	2.60%	1,295.90
Satyam Comp (Say)	$9.10	186	$7.82	16.40%	1,234.00
Silverline Tech (Slt)	$1.50	7.2	$0.30	400.30%	13
Vsnl (Vsl)	$3.40	76.8	$3.25	4.70%	461.5
Wipro (Wit)	$29.50	1,251.50	$26.36	11.90%	6,139.70

Every one of the ADRs trades at a premium on the local share price. For instance, the ADR of Infosys, which is one of India's largest and best-known technology companies, trades at a premium of 41% over the local shares. If you were not restricted in terms of trading, you would buy the local shares on the Bombay stock exchange and sell short the ADRs. You could then convert the local shares into ADRs and deliver them, thus capturing the profits.

CLOSED-END FUNDS

In March 2003, hundreds of closed-end funds were listed in the United States. Figure 11.3 provides the distribution of price to net asset value for all closed-end funds in the United States in June 2002.

Note that almost 70% of the closed-end funds trade at a discount to net asset value and that the median discount is about 5%.

Some of these funds trade at significant discounts; the 20 most heavily discounted funds are listed in Table 11.6.

The closed-end funds range the spectrum but emerging market funds dominate. If you could buy these funds at their discounted market prices and liquidate their assets at market value, you could generate substantial profits. With the Equus

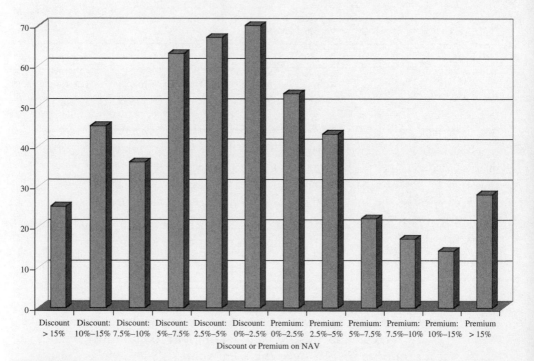

FIGURE 11.3

Discounts/Premiums on Closed-End Funds: June 2002

Data from Morningstar. This is the discount or premium at which the closed-end fund shares trade, relative to the net asset value (NAV).

TABLE 11.6   Most Discounted Closed-End Funds in the United States: March 2003

Ticker name	Discount	Trading Volume	Assets: $Million
Equus II (EQS)	–44.33%	3,881	171
meVC Draper Fisher Jurvetson I (MVC)	–27.77%	36,565	109
Bexil Corporation (BXL)	–25.03%	2,349	9
Indonesia Fund (IF)	–22.28%	28	11
Thai Capital (TF)	–22.20%	473	19
Singapore Fund (SGF)	–20.76%	14,794	66
New Ireland (IRL)	–19.95%	7,517	96
Morgan Funshares (MFUN)	–19.84%	533	6
First Israel (ISL)	–19.64%	5,651	75
New Germany (GF)	–19.27%	39,393	124
Morgan Stanley India Investment Fund (IIF)	–18.61%	32,567	172
Latin America Equity (LAQ)	–17.68%	9,409	89
Latin American Discovery (LDF)	–17.63%	12,821	85
Scudder New Asia (SAF)	–16.80%	11,506	84
Malaysia Fund (MF)	–16.67%	13,049	46
Emerging Mkts Telecommunications (ETF)	–16.61%	12,365	112
Central Securities (CET)	–16.37%	11,511	366
Swiss Helvetia (SWZ)	–16.36%	21,471	287
John Hancock Bank & Thrift (BTO)	–16.29%	189,085	804
Brazil Fund (BZF)	–16.27%	26,316	168

II fund, for instance, you could have bought all the shares in the fund for about $100 million, sold the marketable securities for $171 million, and claimed a profit of $71 million.

MORE TO THE STORY

If you are a skeptical investor, you are probably waiting for the other shoe to drop. After all, investing would be easy if arbitrage opportunities abounded. In this section, you will consider why it is so difficult for investors to find and take advantage of arbitrage opportunities.

PURE ARBITRAGE

The nature of pure arbitrage—two identical assets that are priced differently—makes it likely that it will be short-lived. In other words, in a market in which investors are on the lookout for riskless profits, it is very likely that small pricing differences will be exploited quickly and, in the process, disappear. Consequently, the first two requirements for success at pure arbitrage are access to real-time prices and instantaneous execution. It is also very likely that the pricing differences in pure arbitrage will be very small, often a fraction of a percent.

To make pure arbitrage feasible, therefore, you can add two more conditions. The first is access to borrowing at favorable interest rates, since that approach can magnify the small pricing differences. Note that many of the arbitrage positions require you to be able to borrow at the riskless rate. The second is economies of scale, with transactions amounting to millions of dollars rather than thousands. Institutions that are successful at pure arbitrage often are able to borrow several times their equity investment at or close to the riskless rate to fund arbitrage transactions, using the guaranteed profits on the transaction as collateral.

With these requirements, it is not surprising that individual investors have generally not been able to succeed at pure arbitrage. Even among institutions, pure arbitrage is feasible only to a few, and even to those, it is a transient source of profits in two senses. First, institutions cannot count on the existence of pure arbitrage opportunities in the future, since it requires that markets repeat their errors over time. Second, the very fact that some institutions make profits from arbitrage attracts other institutions into the market, reducing the likelihood of future arbitrage profits. To succeed in the long term with arbitrage, you will need to be constantly on the lookout for new arbitrage opportunities.

NEAR ARBITRAGE

Studies that have looked at closed-end funds, dual-listed stocks and convertibles all seem to conclude that there are pockets of inefficiency that can exploited to make money. However, there is residual risk in all of these strategies, arising sometimes because the assets are not perfectly identical and sometimes because there are no mechanisms for forcing the prices to converge.

Not Perfectly Identical Assets.   In convertible arbitrage, you attempt to create synthetic convertibles by combining stocks and bonds issued by the firm, and you then compare the costs of these synthetic convertibles to the prices of actual convertible bonds. While, in theory, synthetic and actual convertible bonds are identical, significant constraints in the real world can prevent this theory from being actualized. First, many firms that issue convertible bonds do not have straight bonds outstanding, and you have to substitute a straight bond issued by a company with similar default risk. Second, companies can force conversion of convertible bonds, which can wreak havoc on arbitrage positions. Third, convertible bonds have long maturities. Thus, there may be no convergence for long periods, and you have to be able to maintain the arbitrage position over these periods. Fourth, transactions costs and execution problems (associated with trading the different securities) may prevent arbitrage.

What does this imply? You can create what looks like an arbitrage position by buying (selling) the convertible bond and selling (buying) the synthetic convertible bond, but the differences between the bond and its synthetic counterpart may generate unexpected losses. These losses will be exaggerated when you borrow money to fund these positions.

Absence of Convergence Mechanisms.   In the last section, you saw evidence of potential arbitrage opportunities in closed-end funds and some ADRs. Closed-end funds trade at a discount to the market value of the securities that they hold, and there are sometimes significant price differences by real world constraints between ADRs and local shares. In both cases, though, you may find yourself stymied by real-world constraints in your search for arbitrage.

■ With closed-end funds, you will need to buy the fund at the discounted market price, liquidate its marketable securities, and claim the difference as a certain profit. There are problems at each stage. Many closed-end funds are lightly traded and you may very well push the price up to net asset value as you accumulate shares in these funds. Many closed-end funds also are tightly controlled, and gaining control of them may prove difficult. Even assuming that you do accumulate the shares of the closed-end fund at the discounted price and are able to liquidate the assets, you will have to pay capital gains taxes when you sell stocks and these taxes may well wipe out the potential gains. Finally, your transactions costs have to be small enough to leave you with a profit at the end. Note that of the 20 most heavily discounted closed end funds listed in Table 11.6, roughly half were emerging market funds, for which transactions costs are much higher. It should come as no surprise that so few closed-end funds are forced into liquidation.

■ With ADRs, there are two potential roadblocks on the way to your arbitrage profits. Consider, for instance, the Infosys ADR that was highlighted in Table 11.5. To make a profit, you would have to convert the local shares into ADRs and sell short the ADRs. You would be restricted from doing the former, and the ADRs are often very difficult to sell short for long periods. Even if you are able to sell short the ADRs for a few months and you buy the local shares, there is no guarantee that the premium will decrease or disappear over those months, and it may, in fact, increase.

SPECULATIVE ARBITRAGE

The fact that the strategies in this section are classified as speculative arbitrage is not meant to be a negative comment on the strategies. These are promising investment strategies that have a history of delivering excess returns, but they are not risk free. More ominously, it is easy for those who have successfully done pure arbitrage in the past to drift into near arbitrage and then into speculative arbitrage as they have funds to invest. In some cases, their success at pure or near arbitrage may bring in funds that require this shift. As these investors make the shift, though, there are some potential dangers that they have to consider.

Too Much Leverage (Borrowing).   The use of financial leverage has to be scaled to reflect the riskiness of the strategy. With pure arbitrage, you can borrow 100% of what you need to put the strategy into play. In futures arbitrage, for instance, you borrow 100% of the spot price and borrow the commodity. Since there is no risk, the leverage does not create any damage. As you move to near and speculative arbitrage, this leverage has to be reduced. How much it has to be reduced will depend upon both the degree of risk in the strategy and the speed with which you think prices will converge. The more risky a strategy and the less certain you are about convergence, the less debt you should take on.

Price Impact.   Speculative arbitrage strategies work best if you can operate without a market impact. As you get more funds to invest and your strategy becomes more visible to others, you run the risk of driving out the very mispricing that attracted you to the market in the first place. In other words, this strategy will work best for smaller investors who can operate under the radar and not very well for larger investors who draw attention to their strategies when they trade.

Small Upside, Big Downside.   While it may be dangerous to extrapolate from just two strategies, both merger arbitrage and paired trading share a common characteristic. You win most of the time with both strategies but the returns when you win are modest. You lose infrequently, but your losses are large when they occur. These unequal payoffs can create problems for careless investors. For instance, investors can be lulled by a long string of successes into thinking that their strategies are less risky than they truly are. If they then proceed to borrow more money to fund these strategies, they risk dramatic losses.

The Long Term Capital Management Saga.   Investors considering speculative arbitrage as their preferred investment philosophy should pay heed to the experiences of Long Term Capital

Management (LTCM). The firm, which was founded in the early 1990s by ex-Salomon trader, John Merriweather, promised to bring together the best minds in finance to find and take advantage of arbitrage opportunities around the world. Delivering on the first part of the promise, Merriweather lured the best bond traders from Salomon and brought on board two Nobel prize winners: Myron Scholes and Bob Merton. In the first few years of its existence, the firm also lived up to the second part of the promise, earning extraordinary returns for the elite of Wall Street. In those years, LTCM was the envy of the rest of the street as it used low-cost debt to leverage its capital and invest in pure and near arbitrage opportunities. As the funds at their disposal got larger, the firm had to widen its search to include speculative arbitrage investments. By itself, this would not have been fatal but the firm continued to use the same leverage on these riskier investments as it did on its safe investments. It bet on paired trades in Europe and decreasing spreads in country bond markets, arguing that the sheer number of investments it had in its portfolio would create diversification—if it lost on one investment, it would gain on another. In 1997, the strategy unraveled as collapses in one market (Russia) spread into other markets as well. As the portfolio dropped in value, LTCM found itself facing the downside of its size and high leverage. Unable to unwind its large positions without affecting market prices and facing the pressures of lenders, LTCM faced certain bankruptcy. Fearing that LTCM would bring down other investors in the market, the Federal Reserve engineered a bailout of the firm.

What are the lessons that you can learn from the fiasco? Besides the cynical one that it is good to have friends in high places, you could argue that the fall of LTCM teaches the following:

a. Size can be a double-edged sword. While it gives you economies of scale in transactions costs and lowers the cost of funding, it also makes it more difficult for you to unwind positions that you have taken.
b. Leverage can make low-risk positions into high-risk investments, since small moves in the price can translate into large changes in equity.

c. The most brilliant minds in the world and the best analytical tools cannot insulate you from the vagaries of the
market.

In many ways, the rise and fall of Long Term Capital Management should stand as testimony to how even the brightest minds
in investing can sometimes either miss or willfully ignore these
realities. Long Term Capital Management's eventual undoing can
be traced to many causes, but the immediate cause was the
number of speculative arbitrage positions they put in place—
pairs trading, interest rate bets—with tremendous leverage.

LESSONS FOR INVESTORS

This chapter should act as a cautionary note for those investors who believe that they have found the proverbial free
lunch in investing. If you seek pure arbitrage—two identical
assets that you can buy at different prices and lock in the profits—you will generally not find it in liquid markets. In illiquid
markets, you may come across such mispricing but your
transactions costs will have to be small for you to earn arbitrage profits.

Your chances of success are greater if you look for near arbitrage, in which two assets that are almost identical are mispriced. If you choose to pursue these opportunities, you will
improve your odds of success if you do the following:

■ *Identify your differential advantage (if any).* A little in-
trospection may be a valuable first step. You have to
identify the special characteristic you possess that will
allow you to take advantage of arbitrage opportunities
while other investors cannot. If you are an institutional
investor, you may have better and more timely information and lower transactions costs than other investors and use this advantage to earn arbitrage profits.
If you are a smaller individual investor, your advantage
may be that you control the time horizon of your

investment and that you do not have to respond to impatient clients.

- *Be aware of the residual risk.* Near arbitrage is not riskless, and you need to be aware of both the source and the magnitude of the risk that you are exposed to in your strategy. This will allow you to be realistic in the funding and design of your investment strategies.
- *Use leverage prudently.* Since deviations from arbitrage tend to be small, investors often borrow substantial amounts to magnify their profits. There is a tradeoff, though, that you have to keep in mind. As you borrow money, you also magnify your risks. The extent to which you use borrowed money has to reflect the risk associated with your investment strategy; the more risk there is, the less you should borrow. Cookbook arbitrage strategies, whereby you borrow the same amount for all strategies, can be a recipe for disaster.
- *Execute your strategy efficiently.* Arbitrage opportunities tend to be fleeting and you have to execute promptly to take advantage of them. Execution has to be speedy while transactions costs are kept under control, a difficult combination to achieve.

In general, near-arbitrage strategies will not work for very small investors or for very large investors. Small investors will be stymied both by transactions costs and execution problems. Very large investors will quickly affect prices when they trade and eliminate excess returns. If you decide to adopt these strategies, you need to refine your strategies and focus them on those opportunities in which convergence is most likely. For instance, if you decide to try to exploit the discounts of closed-end funds, you should focus on the closed-end funds that are most discounted and concentrate especially on funds that management can be pressured to make open-ended. You should also avoid funds with substantial illiquid or non-traded stocks in their portfolios, since the net asset values of these funds may be significantly overstated.

If you decide to go after speculative arbitrage opportunities, do so with open eyes. Recognize that there is really nothing riskless about these strategies and that they really represent bets that pricing relationships between assets will return to long-term norms. The biggest danger in this strategy is that while you may be right most of the time, you can lose very large amounts when you are wrong. There are two keys to success with speculative arbitrage:

- *Research:* Establishing the long-term normal relationship between assets is important since this is the number at which you assume prices will ultimately converge. This research will require not only access to data over long periods but enough statistical skill to separate facts from noise.
- *Downside protection:* Since one losing position can wipe out the profits generated over several winning positions, your expected returns from this strategy will improve dramatically if you can develop signals that allow you to identify and get out of losing positions early.

The overall message will be a disappointment for those investors who still seek free lunches. It is difficult to find and even more difficult to take advantage of arbitrage opportunities, but that is to be expected in a world in which millions of investors are seeking ways of making money. The good news is that investors who do their homework and work at establishing differential advantages over others can still hope to generate substantial profits from these strategies.

CONCLUSION

Invest no money, take no risk, and make profits. While this sounds like the recipe for a money machine, this is how you can describe pure arbitrage. For pure arbitrage to exist, you need two assets with exactly the same cash flows trading at different prices. Buying the lower-priced asset and selling the higher-priced asset will allow you to lock in the price difference as a certain profit; the cash flows on the two assets exactly offset each other, resulting in a riskless investment. Pure arbitrage opportunities, if they exist, are most likely to be found in futures and options markets and will almost certainly be small and fleeting. Only investors with significant information or execution advantages are likely to be able to take advantage of them.

In near arbitrage, you have two almost identical assets trading at different prices, but significant restrictions prevent the prices of the two from converging. A closed-end fund that trades at a significant discount on the market value of the securities that it owns would be one example. If you could buy the entire fund at the market price and liquidate its securities, you should be able to make a hefty profit. Unfortunately, restrictions on liquidating the fund may reduce you to holding shares in the fund and hoping that the discount gets smaller over time.

Speculative arbitrage, whereby you have similar but not identical assets trading at prices that are not consistent with their historical norms, provides investors with the illusion of a free lunch. In reality, these are risky positions that generate profits (albeit small ones) most of the time but that generate large losses when they fail.

ENDNOTES

1. Black, F., and M. Scholes, 1972, *The Valuation of Option Contracts and a Test of Market Efficiency*, Journal of Finance, v27, 399–417.

2. Garbade, K. D., and W. L. Silber, 1983, *Price Movements and Price Discovery in Futures and Cash Markets*, The Review of Economics and Statistics, v115, 289–297.

3. A study of 835 index arbitrage trades on the S&P 500 futures contracts estimated that the average gross profit from such trades was only 0.30%.

4. With index futures, it took investors a while to understand the effect of uneven dividends on futures prices. With treasury bond futures, the wild-card feature (whereby you are allowed to deliver the cheapest of a menu of bonds) resulted in some early mispricing of futures contracts.

5. Grinblatt, M., and F. A. Longstaff, 2000, *Financial Innovation and the Role of Derivative Securities: An Empirical Analysis of the U.S. Treasury's Strips Program*, Journal of Finance.

6. Alejandro Balbás and Susana López, 2001, *Financial innovation and arbitrage in the Spanish bond market*, Working Paper, Social Science Research Network.

7. Swaicki, J., and J. Hric, 2001, *Arbitrage Opportunities in Parallel Markets: The Case of the Czech Republic*, Working Paper, Social Science Research Network.

8. Depository receipts can be sponsored by the company, in which case they can be used by the company to raise capital, or they can be unsponsored, in which case they are issued by intermediaries (like banks) to meet market demand.

9. Kin, M., A. C. Szakmary and I. Mathur, 2000, *Price Transmission Dynamics between ADRs and Their Underlying Foreign Securities*, Journal of Banking and Finance, v24, 1359–1382.

10. Dimson, E., and C. Minio-Kozerzki, 1998, *Closed-end Funds, A Survey*, Working Paper, London Business School.

11. Thompson, Rex, 1978, *The Information Content of Discounts and Premiums on Closed-End Fund Shares,* Journal of Financial Economics, v6, 151–186.

12. Pontiff, Jeffrey, 1997, *Excess Volatility and Closed-End Funds,* American Economic Review, v87, 155–169.

13. Minio-Paluello, Carolina, 1998, *The UK Closed-End Fund Discount*, PhD thesis, London Business School.

14. Gatev, E. G., W. N. Goetzmann and K. G. Rouwenhorst, 1999, *Pairs Trading, Performance of a Relative Value Arbitrage Rule*, Working Paper, Social Science Research Network.

15. To find this stock, they look for the minimum squared difference between the returns of two stocks. If two stocks move in lock step, this difference will be zero.

12

IT'S ALL UPSIDE: THE MOMENTUM STORY

BIG MO'

Martha believed in getting a good start to each day. She was convinced that a day begun well would only got better, whereas one begun badly would go downhill. She carried this philosophy into her investing as well. She bought only stocks that had gone up significantly in the months before, believing that the stock's surge would act as inducement for other investors to buy it, thus creating a self-fulfilling prophecy. When asked about whether she was worried that the price may have gone up too much, Martha responded that it did not matter to her as long as she could sell to someone else at an even higher price.

Martha noticed that the stocks in her portfolio almost never did as well when she held them as they had before she bought them and that their prices were extraordinarily volatile. She also discovered that even small pieces of bad news sometimes triggered spates of selling in some of her stocks, quickly wiping out any potential gains she may have made in the previous weeks. Much as she wanted to believe that good things led to more good things, the rule did not seem to work for stocks. Disillusioned, she decided that the market was really not a good place to test out her life philosophy.

Moral: You live by the crowd, you will die by it.

G o with the flow. That, in a nutshell, is the momentum story. The underlying theme is that stocks that have gone up in the past are more likely to keep going up than stocks that have gone down in the past. Variations exist, however, in how you measure momentum. Some investors look at the percentage change in stock prices over a period—a week, three months, six months or longer—and buy stocks with the highest percentage increases. Others incorporate trading volume into their investment decisions, arguing that stocks that have gone up on high volume are the best stocks to invest in. Still others build their strategy around earnings announcements, buying stocks after the announcements report better-than-expected earnings and hoping that the resulting price increases spill over into the following days.

In this chapter, you will look at the basis of the momentum story as well as empirical evidence that has accumulated over time on its effectiveness. You will then create a portfolio of stocks with high momentum—price and volume—and consider the potential risks associated with such a strategy.

CORE OF THE STORY

The momentum story has power because it can be a self-fulfilling prophecy. If investors buy into the momentum story and buy stocks that have gone up in the past, these stocks will go up further. The momentum can continue as long as new investors are attracted to the stock, pushing up demand and prices. Thus, the strongest argument for momentum is herd behavior. In general, there are three reasons given for why investors may indulge in this herd behavior and why you should be able to take advantage of it.

■ *Investors learn slowly.* If investors are slow to assess the effects of new information on stock prices, you can see sustained up or down movements in stock prices after news comes out about the stock: up movements after good news and down movements after bad news. The investors who are quickest at assessing the effect of information will profit as investors who are slower at assessing impact gradually come on board.

- *Investors learn by watching other investors.* Some investors learn by watching other investors trade rather than by analyzing fundamentals. If you accept this view of the world, sustained price increases accompanied by high trading volume will attract new investors to a stock.
- *Investors weight the recent past much more than they should.* Psychologists have uncovered fairly strong evidence that human beings tend to weight recent information far more than they should and old information far less than they should. In other words, a positive news announcement by a company can lead to a disproportionately large increase in its stock price as investors react to the announcement.

Momentum stories almost invariably are accompanied by a sense of urgency. You need to get on the momentum bus or it will leave, you are told. Not surprisingly, some investors—individual as well as institutional—climb on, afraid of being left behind.

THEORETICAL ROOTS OF MOMENTUM INVESTING

Momentum investing has relatively little theory backing it up, though, as you will see in the next chapter, it has some empirical support. In this section, you will look at some of the measures used by momentum investors and follow up by looking at what you would need to assume about investor behavior for momentum investing to exist.

MEASURES USED BY MOMENTUM INVESTORS

Momentum investors firmly believe that the trend is your friend and that it is critical that you look past the day-to-day movements in stock prices at the underlying long-term trends.

The simplest measure of trend is a *trend line*. Figure 12.1 contains two trend lines: the graph on the top is for a silver futures contract over the few months of its existence and the graph on the bottom is for cocoa futures over a much longer period.

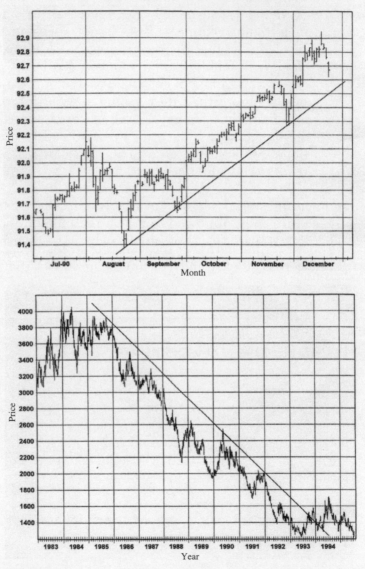

FIGURE 12.1
Trend Lines

In the silver futures contract, you see an uptrend line, drawn by connecting a series of lows in prices, each one higher than the other. On the bottom graph, cocoa prices had been declining over the period in question, and a downtrend line is drawn by connecting a series of lower highs. As momentum investors, you would buy stocks that are going up and staying above the uptrend line. If the price falls below the uptrend line, it is viewed as a sign that the trend has reversed itself. Conversely, if the price rises above a downtrend line, it is considered a bullish sign.

A closely followed momentum measure is called *relative strength,* which is the ratio of the current price to an average over a longer period (say, six months or a year). Stocks that score high on relative strength are therefore stocks that have gone up the most over the period, whereas those that score low are stocks that have gone down. The relative strength can be used either in absolute terms, whereby only stocks that have gone up over the period would be considered good investments. Alternatively, the relative strength can be compared across stocks, and you invest in stocks that show the highest relative strength, that is, that have gone up the most relative to other stocks.

These are but two of dozens of technical indicators that are used by momentum investors. Many indicators, like the trend line and relative strength, are based upon past price patterns, but some incorporate trading volume as well.

MODELS FOR MOMENTUM

Two different models generate momentum in stock prices. The first is an information-based model, in which investors learn slowly and the effects of news percolates slowly into market prices. The second is a model based on trading volume, in which investors learn from watching other investors trade.

Information-Based Model. In an efficient market, the market price of a stock changes instantaneously when new information comes out about it. Rational investors assess the effect of the information on value immediately and the price adjusts to the new value. While investors make mistakes, the mistakes tend to cut both ways, with the price tending to go up too much in some cases and too little in other cases. If this occurs, there will be no patterns in stock prices after information announcements and no information in past prices.

To see how slow learning on the part of markets will translate into price momentum, assume that a firm reports higher earnings than expected. The stock price will rise on the news and continue to increase as investors slowly assess the effects of information on value. This will translate into a price drift upward after the earnings announcement. With bad news, you will see the reverse. The stock price will drop on the news announcement and continue to drop as investors gradually adjust their assessments of value.

The peril with this story is that it requires irrationality on the part of investors. If it is indeed true that markets take time to adjust to new information, you could earn high returns by buying stocks right after good news announcements and making money as the price drifts upward. If enough investors do this, the price will adjust immediately and there will be no price drift after the announcement. Similarly, after bad news, you could sell short on stocks and make money as the price continues to trend down. Again, if enough investors follow your lead, the price will drop after the bad news and there will be no price drift. If you believe in momentum investing you have to come up with a good argument for the persistence of price drifts. With bad news, you can argue that many investors (but not you) are restricted from selling short, which would effectively prevent them from taking advantage of slow-learning markers. With good news, you have to assume that most investors are either blind to obvious investment opportunities or that the transactions costs are so high for these investors that they drown out potential returns from following the strategy.

Trading-Volume Model. Investors learn by watching other investors trade. A sophisticated version of a momentum model builds on this theme. An increase in demand for a stock manifests itself in both higher trading volume and increased prices.

Other investors observe both the price increase and the higher trading volume and conclude that:

a. The investors who are buying the stock have proprietary or inside information that suggests that the stock is underpriced;

b. Continued buying of the stock will sustain the price at least for the short term.

These investors then buy the stock, pushing up its price. This, in turn, attracts new investors into the company, thus creating a cycle of trading generating more trading, and price increases begetting more price increases over time. The reverse will occur with price decreases.

While both the trading volume and information stories have the same end result of price momentum, there are at least two differences. The first is that the trading volume will generate price momentum even in the absence of new information coming out about a stock. Since investors get to observe the act of trading and not the motivation for the trading, an investor with no special information about a company can get momentum going just by buying a large block of stock. Other investors will observe the trade, assume that there is information in the trade, and put in their own buy orders. The cascading effect on prices will end only when investors realize that there was no informational basis for the first trade. The second is that momentum measures that flow from this view of the world will have to incorporate both price and volume momentum. In other words, you should expect to see price increases or decreases continue only if they are accompanied by above-average trading volume.

LOOKING FOR THE EVIDENCE

What is the evidence that markets learn slowly? Three categories of studies are relevant to answering this question. The first set looks at stock prices over time to see if they reveal a tendency to move in the same direction for extended periods of time. The second set looks at how markets react to news about a firm—earnings and dividend announcements, for instance—and how prices adjust to the new information. The final set looks at mutual funds for evidence that mutual funds that have done well in the past continue to do so in the future.

SERIAL CORRELATION IN STOCK PRICE DRIFTS

In Chapter 8, when looking at contrarian investing, you considered the evidence on whether stocks that have gone up are more likely to go down in the future. The evidence that was presented on the correlation between price changes in consecutive periods in that chapter is relevant for momentum investing as well. After all, contrarian and momentum investors take opposite views of the world, and evidence supporting one strategy has to be viewed as rejecting the other.

Serial correlation measures the relationship between price changes in one period and price changes in the next. As noted in Chapter 8, a positive serial correlation would indicate that stocks that have gone up are more likely to continue to go up, whereas a negative serial correlation would indicate that stocks that have gone down are more likely to reverse themselves and go up in the future. Figure 12.2 summarizes these possibilities.

As a momentum investor, you would want price changes to be serially correlated, but are they? The earliest research on serial correlation, cited in Chapter 8, finds little evidence of serial correlation in short-period (daily and weekly) returns. There is some recent research that finds evidence of serial correlation in stock returns over hourly and daily returns, but the correlation is different for high volume and low volume stocks. With high volume stocks, stock prices are more likely to reverse themselves over short periods, that is, to have negative serial correlation. With low volume stocks, stock prices

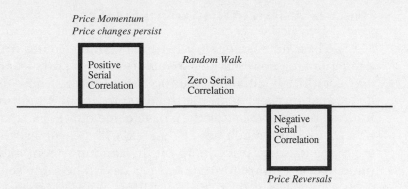

FIGURE 12.2
Serial Correlation and Price Patterns

are more likely to continue to move in the same direction, that is, to have positive serial correlation.[1] None of this work suggests that you can make money from these correlations. You will see more evidence of the interrelationship between price momentum and volume later in this chapter.

When you look at serial correlation in returns over longer periods, there is more evidence for both price momentum and reversal, depending upon how long you make the periods. Jegadeesh and Titman[2] present evidence of price momentum in stock prices over periods of up to eight months: stocks that have gone up in the last six months tend to continue to go up, whereas stocks that have gone down in the last six months tend to continue to go down. If you define long term as years, the contrarians win the argument, and there is clear evidence of price reversals, especially in five-year returns. In other words, stocks that have gone up the most over the last five years are more likely to go down in the next five years.

In summary, the evidence on price runups suggests that momentum strategies can be exceedingly sensitive to how long a period you measure momentum over and how long you plan to hold the stocks you plan to buy. Momentum can be your friend if you hold stocks for a few months, but it can very quickly turn against you if you hold stocks for too long or too short a time.

INFORMATION ANNOUNCEMENTS

The best support for slow-learning markets comes from examinations of how markets react to news reports—earnings and acquisition announcements, for instance. There is evidence that markets continue to adjust to the new information in these reports well after they have come out. For instance, a firm that reports much better than expected earnings will generally see its stock price jump on the announcement and continue to drift upward for the next few days. The same seems to occur to a target firm in an acquisition. While there are alternative explanations for price drifts, one potential explanation is that markets learn slowly and that it takes them a while to assimilate the information. If the initial news was good—a good earnings report or an earnings upgrade from an analyst—you should expect to see prices continue to go up after the news comes out. If the news was bad, you should expect to see the opposite.

Earnings Announcements. When firms make earnings announcements, they convey information to financial markets about their current and future prospects. The magnitude of the information and the size of the market reaction should depend upon how much the earnings report exceeds or falls short of investor expectations. In an efficient market, there should be an instantaneous reaction to the earnings report if it contains surprising information, and prices should increase following positive surprises and decrease following negative surprises.

Since actual earnings are compared to investor expectations, one of the key parts of any examination of earnings reports is the measurement of these expectations. Some of the earlier studies used earnings from the same quarter in the preceding year as a measure of expected earnings, that is, firms that report increases in quarter-to-quarter earnings provide positive surprises and those that report decreases in quarter-to-quarter earnings provide negative surprises. In more recent research, analyst estimates of earnings were used as a measure of expected earnings and were compared to the actual

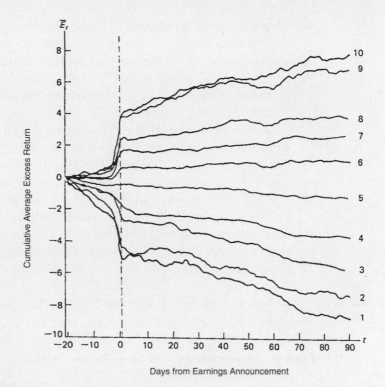

FIGURE 12.3

Price Reaction to Quarterly Earnings Report

Data from Rendleman, Jones, and Latane. Earnings surprises are categorized from biggest negative (1) to biggest positive (10) surprises, and returns are computed around the date of earnings announcement.

earnings. Figure 12.3 graphs price reactions to earnings surprises, classified on the basis of magnitude into different classes from "most negative" earnings reports (Group 1) to "most positive" earnings reports (Group 10).[3]

The evidence contained in this graph is consistent with what has been found in most research on earnings announcements:

    a. The earnings announcement clearly conveys valuable information to financial markets; stock prices go up the most after the most positive announcements (10) and go down the most after the reports that contain the most disappointing earnings (1).

b. There is some evidence of a market reaction in the days immediately before the earnings announcement consistent with the nature of the announcement, that is, prices tend to go up in the days before positive announcements and down on the days before negative announcements. This can be viewed either as evidence of insider trading or information leakage.

c. There is some evidence, albeit weak, of a price drift in the days following an earnings announcement. Thus, a positive report evokes a positive market reaction on the announcement date, and the stock price continues to go up in the days and weeks following the earnings announcement. With negative earnings reports, the stock price drops on the announcement and continues to go down.

While the study quoted above looked at all earnings announcements, other research indicates that the returns associated with earnings surprises are more pronounced with some types of stocks than with others. For instance,

- An examination of value and growth stocks found that the returns in the three days around earnings announcements were much more positive for value stocks (defined as low PE and PBV stocks) than for growth stocks across all earnings announcements, positive as well as negative. This suggests that you are much more likely to get a positive surprise with a value stock than with a growth stock, indicating perhaps that markets tend to be overly optimistic in their expectations for growth companies.[4]
- Earnings announcements made by smaller firms seem to have a larger impact on stock prices on the announcement date, and prices are more likely to drift after the announcement.

Stock Splits. A stock split increases the number of shares outstanding, without changing the current earnings or cash flows of the firm. As a purely cosmetic event, a stock split should not affect the value of the firm or of outstanding equity. Rather, the price per share will go down to reflect the stock split, since there are more shares outstanding. One of the first event studies examined the stock price reaction to 940 stock splits between 1927 and 1959 by looking at stock returns in the 60 months around the actual split date.[5] The result of the study is shown in Figure 12.4.

On average, stock splits tended to follow periods of positive returns; this is not surprising, since splits typically follow price runups. No evidence was found of excess returns around the splits themselves, suggesting that the splits were neutral events. One of the limitations of the study was its use of monthly return rather than daily returns. More recent studies that look at the daily price reaction to stock splits find a mild positive effect: stock prices go up slightly when splits are announced.[6] A look at all two-for-one stock splits between 1975 and 1990 estimated that stock prices increase, on average, 3.38% on the announcement of a stock split and that the announcement effect is much greater for small stocks

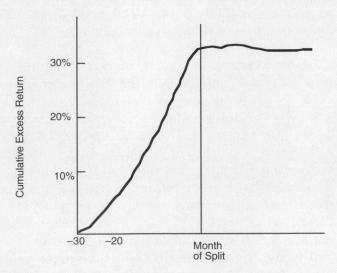

FIGURE 12.4
Market Reaction to Stock Splits

Data from Fama, Fisher, Jensen and Roll. This is the cumulated excess return in the 30 months before and 30 months after stock splits.

(10.04%) than for large stocks (1.01%).[7] Researchers attribute this to a signaling effect, that is, only companies that expect their stock prices to go up in the future will announce stock splits.

In recent years, some research has pointed out that stock splits may have an unintended negative effect on stockholders by raising transactions costs. For instance, the bid-ask spread, which is one component of the transactions costs, is a much larger percentage of the price for a $20 stock than it is for a $40 stock.[8] There is some evidence of an increase in transactions costs and a decline in trading volume following splits.[9] This additional cost has to be weighed against the potential signaling implications of a stock split; investors may view a stock split as a positive signal about future prospects. In an interesting development in the last few years, stocks that have seen their stock prices drop significantly, often to $2 or less, have tried to push their prices back into a reasonable trading range by doing reverse stock splits, by which the number of shares outstanding in the company is reduced. These reverse stock splits are sometimes initiated to prevent being delisted, a distinct possibility if the stock price drops below a dollar, and sometimes to reduce transactions costs.[10]

Dividend Changes. Financial markets examine every action a firm takes for implications for future cash flows and firm value. When firms announce changes in dividend policy, they are conveying information to markets, whether they intend to or not. An increase in dividends is generally viewed as a positive signal, since firms that make these commitments to investors must believe that they have the capacity to generate these cash flows in the future. Decreasing dividends is a negative signal, largely because firms are reluctant to cut dividends. Thus, when a firm cuts or eliminates dividends, markets see it as an indication that this firm is in substantial and long-term financial trouble. Consequently, such actions lead to a drop in stock prices. The empirical evidence, cited in Chapter 2, concerning price reactions to dividend increases and decreases is consistent, at least on average, with this signaling theory. On average, stock prices go up when dividends are increased and go down when dividends are decreased, though the price reaction to the latter seems much more.[11] While the price change on the dividend announcement itself might not offer opportunities for investors (unless they have access to inside information), another study looked at the price drift after dividend changes are announced and found that prices continue to drift up after dividend increases and drift down after dividend decreases for long periods.[12] Investors may be able to take advantage of this drift and augment returns on their portfolios.

THE CONFOUNDING EFFECT OF TRADING VOLUME

Earlier in the chapter, we hypothesized that one reason for momentum may be that investors learn by watching other investors trade. As with prices, there is evidence that trading volume carries information about future stock price changes. An analysis in 1998 showed that low volume stocks earned higher returns than high volume stocks, though the researchers attributed the extra return to a liquidity premium on the former.[13] A more surprising result emerges from a look at the interrelationship between price and trading volume.[14] In particular, the price momentum effect that was documented earlier in the chapter—that stocks that go up are more likely to keep going up and stocks that go down are more likely to keep dropping in the months after—is much more pronounced for high volume stocks. Figure 12.5 classifies stocks according to how well or badly they have done in the last six months (winners, average and loser stocks) and their trading volume (low, average and high) and looks at returns on these stocks in the following six months.

Note that the price momentum effect is strongest for stocks with high trading volume. In other words, a price increase or decrease that is accompanied by strong volume is more likely to continue into the next period. This result has also been confirmed with shorter period returns; with daily returns, increases in stock prices that are accompanied by

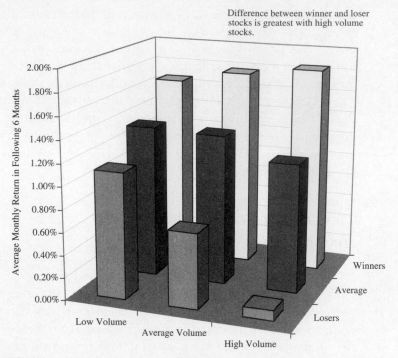

FIGURE 12.5
Volume and Price Interaction: NYSE and AMEX Stocks, 1965–1995

Data from Lee and Swaminathan. The average monthly returns in the six months following the creation of the portfolios is reported.

high trading volume are more likely to carry over into the next trading day.[15]

In summary, the level of trading volume in a stock, changes in volume and volume accompanied by price changes all seem to provide information that investors can use to pick stocks. It is not surprising that trading volume is an integral part of momentum investing.

MOMENTUM IN MUTUAL FUNDS

While there is little evidence that mutual funds that are ranked highly in one period continue to be ranked highly in the next, there is some evidence that has accumulated about the very top ranked mutual funds. A number of studies[16] seem to indicate that mutual funds that earn above-average returns in one period will continue to earn above-average returns in the next period. Burt Malkiel, in his analysis of mutual fund performance over two decades (1970s and 1980s), tested for this "hot hands" phenomenon by looking at the percentage of winners each year who repeated the next year. His results are summarized in Table 12.1.

TABLE 12.1   Repeat Winners by Year: 1971–1990

YEAR	PERCENT OF REPEAT WINNERS	YEAR	PERCENT OF REPEAT WINNERS
1971	64.80%	1980	36.50%
1972	50.00%	1981	62.30%
1973	62.60%	1982	56.60%
1974	52.10%	1983	56.10%
1975	74.40%	1984	53.90%
1976	68.40%	1985	59.50%
1977	70.80%	1986	60.40%
1978	69.70%	1987	39.30%
1979	71.80%	1988	41.00%
1971–79	65.10%	1989	59.60%
		1990	49.40%
		1980–90	51.70%

This table tells a surprising story. The percent of repeat winners clearly is much higher than dictated by chance (50%) in the 1970s. However, the percent of repeat winners during the 1980s looks close to random. Is this because mutual fund rankings became more ubiquitous during the 1980s? Maybe. It is also possible that what you are seeing are the effects of overall market performance. In the 1970s, when the equity markets had a string of negative years, mutual funds that held more cash consistently moved to the top of the rankings. You can also compare the returns you would have earned on a strategy of buying the top funds (looking at the top 10, top 20, top 30 and top 40 funds) from each year and holding it for the next year. The returns are summarized in Figure 12.6.

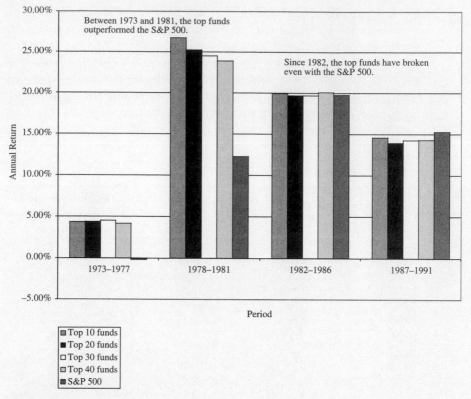

FIGURE 12.6

Returns on Top-Ranked Funds: 1973–1991

Data from Malkiel. The top funds are picked according to performance over the preceding year, and the returns are computed over the following year.

Again, the contrast is striking. While the top funds outperformed the S&P 500 in 1973–1977 and 1978–1981 periods, they matched the index from 1982 to 1986 and underperformed the index from 1987 to 1991.

In summary, there is little evidence, especially in recent years, that investing in the mutual funds that were ranked highest last year in terms of performance will deliver above-average returns. In fact, these funds tend to increase their fees and costs and may be worse investments than some of the lower-ranked funds.

CRUNCHING THE NUMBERS

There are many measures of momentum and most of them are relative. In other words, a stock that goes up 30% during a period in which all stocks increased substantially may not be viewed as having strong momentum, whereas a stock that goes up 5% in a bear market may qualify. You will begin by looking at how different measures of momentum vary across the market and then go about constructing a portfolio of momentum stocks.

MOMENTUM MEASURES

This section examines differences across firms on three sets of momentum measures. The first set includes price momentum measures: price changes and relative price strength. The second set of measures looks at trading volume, and the final set looks at earnings surprises.

Price Momentum.   To get a measure of price momentum over a recent period, consider the returns from price appreciation that you would have made investing in individual stocks in the six-month period from October 2002 to March 2003. Figure 12.7 presents the distribution of stock returns (from price appreciation) over this period.

In this six-month period, the market was up approximately 13%, and more stocks went up than down. These price appreciation returns can be converted into measures of relative price strength for each stock by the following formula:

$$\text{Relative Price Strength} = \frac{(1 + \text{Price Appreciation (\%) on stock over period})}{(1 + \text{Price Appreciation (\%) on market over same time period})}$$

For example, the price appreciation on the market between October 2002 and March 2003 was 14.83%. The relative price strengths of Viacom, which saw its price drop by –3.16% during the period, and Staples, which saw its price go up by 44.56%, are computed below:

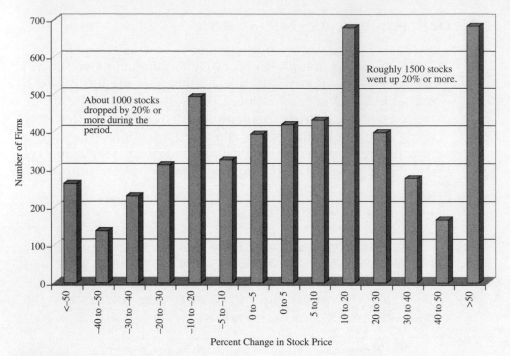

FIGURE 12.7

Price Appreciation (%), October 2002–March 2003

Data from Value Line. This is the percentage price change over the period.

$$\text{Relative Price Strength}_{\text{Viacom}} = (1 - .0316) / (1.1483) = 0.84$$

$$\text{Relative Price Strength}_{\text{Staples}} = (1.4456) / 1.1483 = 1.26$$

Figure 12.8 summarizes the distribution of relative price strength across the market for the six-month period (Oct. 2002–March 2003).

While many firms have price changes that resemble the price change on the market (relative price strength close to 1), a larger number of firms have price changes that are very different from the market and it is these firms that make it into momentum portfolio. There are other measures of relative price strength used by investors, but they share common features. They all look at price increases over a period and scale them for overall market movements.

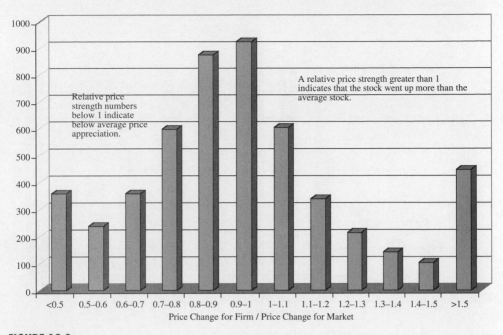

FIGURE 12.8

Relative Price Strength: U.S. Firms from October 2002–March 2003

Data from Value Line. The relative strength measure is obtained by dividing the percentage price change for each stock by the percentage price change for the market.

Trading Volume. If price momentum varies widely across companies, trading volume varies even more widely. Some stocks are extremely liquid and millions of shares are traded every day. Others hardly ever trade, and volume momentum has to take into account the differences in the level of trading volume. You could, for instance, compare the average daily trading volume on a stock in a 6-month period with the average daily trading volume on the same stock in the preceding six months for every stock in the market and compute a percentage change in volume. Figure 12.9 summarizes this distribution.

The trading volume from October 2002 to March 2003 was compared with the volume from April 2002 to September 2002 for every firm. As with price momentum, the changes in trading volume can be scaled to changes in volume in the overall market to come up with a measure of relative volume momentum:

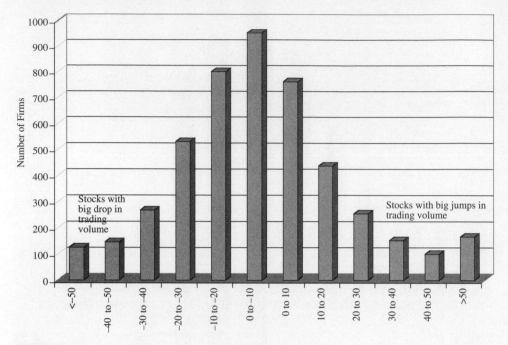

FIGURE 12.9
Percent Change in Trading Volume: Six-Month Periods

Data from Value Line. This is the percent change in trading volume from one six-month period (April 2002–Sept. 2002) to the next (Oct. 2002–March 2002).

$$\text{Relative Volume Momentum} = \frac{(1 + \% \text{ change in volume of trading in the stock})}{(1 + \% \text{ change in volume for the market})}$$

Thus, a stock that registers a 50% trading volume increase in a market in which aggregate trading volume increases by 20% will have a relative volume momentum of 1.25 (1.5/1.2). Figure 12.10 presents the distribution of relative trading volume across the market.

As with relative price strength, while many firms report increases in volume that are close to the increase in volume for the market, a substantial number of firms report significantly higher or lower increases in trading volume than the market.

Earnings Surprises. Earnings announcements, in which firms report the actual earnings per share over the preceding

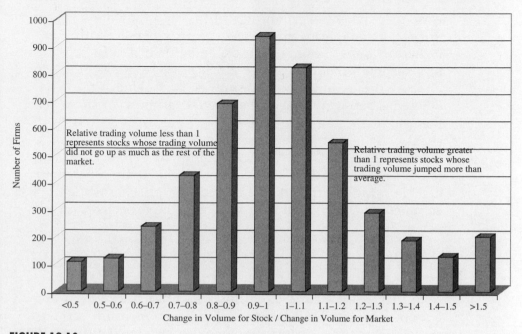

FIGURE 12.10

Relative Trading Volume: U.S. Stocks, October 2002–March 2003

Data from Value Line. Relative trading volume is computed by dividing the percent change in trading volume for the stock by the average percent change for the market.

period, contain important information not only about a firm's performance in that period but also about its expected performance in future periods. To measure how much information is contained in an earnings report, you should compare the earnings reported for a period to the earnings that were expected for the period. For the latter to be obtained, the firm has to be followed by analysts and the earnings estimates of these analysts for the firm have to be compiled. In the last two decades, services like I/B/E/S, Zacks and First Call have provided information on analyst forecasts to investors. In fact, the consensus estimates of earnings per share for most firms are widely disseminated and discussed in the financial press.

Given the resources that analysts can bring to the task of estimating earnings and the access that analysts have to managers at firms, you would expect earnings forecasts to be fairly close to actual earnings for most firms, and they are for most firms. But some firms manage to surprise markets with much higher or lower earnings than expected, and it is these earnings surprises that cause large stock price reactions. You can measure the magnitude of the surprise by looking at the dollar difference between actual and expected earnings per share, but this will bias you toward finding larger surprises at firms with larger earnings per share. A firm that is expected to have earnings per share (EPS) of $2 is more likely to report larger surprises than a firm that is expected to have earnings per share of $0.20. One way to scale the earnings surprise for the level of earnings is to compute it as a percent of the expected earnings per share:

Earnings Surprise (%) = (Actual EPS − Expected EPS) / Expected EPS

Note that this measure of earnings surprise has its own limitations. One is that it becomes difficult to measure earnings surprises for firms that are expected to lose money (negative expected earnings per share) or for firms for which the expected earnings per share is close to zero. Notwithstanding this problem, the distribution of earnings surprises (in % terms) in the first quarter of 2003 is reported in Figure 12.11.

The sample was restricted only to firms that were expected to have positive earnings per share and that had analyst coverage. As a consequence, smaller, less liquid and younger companies (that are more likely to have negative earnings and to not be followed by analysts) are eliminated from the sample. Even with this sample of larger and more liquid firms, a couple of interesting findings emerge:

- Most earnings surprises are small, with actual earnings falling within 10% of expected earnings.
- Some firms report larger earnings surprises, but among these firms, positive surprises are much more common than negative surprises. Firms that are doing badly clearly find ways to get the news out to analysts and lower expectations before the earnings are actually reported.

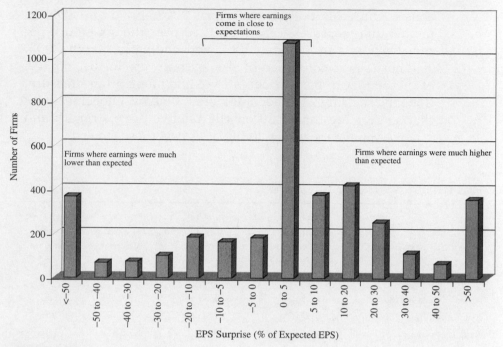

FIGURE 12.11
EPS Surprises in U.S. Market: First Quarter 2003

Data from Zacks. The earnings surprise is the difference between the actual earnings and the actual earnings per share, divided by the expected earnings per share.

CONSTRUCTING A MOMENTUM PORTFOLIO

You can construct two different kinds of momentum portfolios. One portfolio will include stocks with price and volume momentum, using the momentum measures constructed in the last section. The other portfolio will be composed of stocks that have had large positive earnings surprises. In this section, you will construct both portfolios with the intent of putting them under the microscope for potential problems.

Price/Volume Momentum. If you accept the proposition that price momentum carries over into future prices, especially if accompanied by increasing trading volume, you can construct a portfolio of stocks that have both characteristics. In constructing this portfolio in April 2003, price and volume momentum measures were estimated over the six-month period beginning in October 2002 and ending in March 2003. The portfolio is composed of stocks that were in the top 10% of the market in both price and volume momentum measure. Roughly speaking, we accomplished that by choosing firms that score more than 1.50 on the relative price strength and relative volume measures. Table 12.2 lists these stocks.

TABLE 12.2 Stocks with Price and Volume Momentum

COMPANY NAME	RETURN OVER LAST 26 WEEKS	RELATIVE STRENGTH OVER 6 MONTHS	PERCENT CHANGE IN VOLUME	RELATIVE TRADING VOLUME
Aceto Corp	123.59%	1.95	68.55%	1.74
Allen Telecom	107.00%	1.80	68.63%	1.74
Alpha Pro Tech Ltd	82.93%	1.59	46.97%	1.52
Ask Jeeves Inc	707.07%	7.03	68.00%	1.74
Avid Technology	143.75%	2.12	71.84%	1.78
Boots & Coots Intl Well Cntrl	711.11%	7.06	104.35%	2.11
Captiva Software Corp	235.56%	2.92	62.02%	1.68
Castelle	474.07%	5.00	60.11%	1.66
CNB Finl Corp	74.86%	1.52	47.55%	1.53
Concur Technologies Inc	201.70%	2.63	46.55%	1.52
Document Sciences Corp	163.06%	2.29	60.88%	1.66
DOR BioPharma Inc	271.43%	3.23	55.72%	1.61
Double Eagle Pet & Min	90.27%	1.66	56.69%	1.62
E-LOAN Inc	82.64%	1.59	50.80%	1.56
Evolving Sys Inc	927.59%	8.95	52.72%	1.58
FindWhat.com Inc	151.51%	2.19	54.78%	1.60
First Colonial Group	84.71%	1.61	62.01%	1.68
Flamel Technologies SA	181.01%	2.45	65.01%	1.71
Forward Inds Inc	133.33%	2.03	66.81%	1.73
Garmin Ltd	93.03%	1.68	59.95%	1.66
GRIC Communications Inc	87.04%	1.63	70.33%	1.76
Group 1 Software	170.00%	2.35	64.64%	1.70
Hi-Tech Pharm	201.74%	2.63	80.00%	1.86
ID Biomedical Corp	97.83%	1.72	69.79%	1.76
IEC Electrs Corp	350.00%	3.92	86.66%	1.93

ImageX.com Inc	131.82%	2.02	46.97%	1.52
ImagicTV Inc	160.00%	2.26	47.00%	1.52
InterDigital Commun	95.94%	1.71	48.41%	1.54
KVH Inds Inc	113.90%	1.86	47.71%	1.53
Metrologic Instruments Inc	142.77%	2.11	52.63%	1.58
Metropolitan Finl	74.07%	1.52	61.57%	1.67
Movie Star Inc	127.27%	1.98	45.77%	1.51
Netease.com Inc ADS	382.13%	4.20	83.73%	1.90
Network Equip Tech	85.10%	1.61	65.23%	1.71
North Coast Energy Inc	73.75%	1.51	62.04%	1.68
Old Dominion Freight	75.32%	1.53	93.85%	2.01
Pacific Internet Limited	183.82%	2.47	85.74%	1.92
Packeteer Inc	199.11%	2.60	57.81%	1.63
Pan Am Beverages "A"	135.17%	2.05	53.53%	1.59
Perceptron Inc	106.67%	1.80	44.78%	1.50
Premier Bancorp Inc	98.38%	1.73	52.29%	1.58
ProBusiness Services	101.35%	1.75	53.48%	1.59
Pumatech Inc	825.00%	8.05	56.78%	1.62
Rambus Inc	222.35%	2.81	50.76%	1.56
Sanfilippo John B	115.00%	1.87	61.72%	1.67
Sohu.com Inc	514.59%	5.35	62.07%	1.68
Stratasys Inc	204.74%	2.65	48.10%	1.53
Transcend Services Inc	129.59%	2.00	51.50%	1.57
United Security Bancshares Inc	82.76%	1.59	72.60%	1.79
US SEARCH.com	87.34%	1.63	55.27%	1.61
Vital Images Inc	140.39%	2.09	57.25%	1.63
Whitman ED Group	146.02%	2.14	76.02%	1.82
Xybernaut Corp	80.95%	1.58	46.00%	1.51

The 54 stocks represent a wide cross section of industries. This price/volume momentum portfolio would have been very different if you used a different period (three months versus six months, for instance). Thus, you can expect to see variations even among momentum investors on what they hold in their portfolios.

Information Momentum. While there is a variety of information announcements around which you can build a portfolio, earnings announcements stand out because all U.S. firms make them four times a year and the announcements receive considerable media attention. In contrast, relatively few firms make stock split and acquisition announcements. Using the definition of earnings surprise developed in the last section (as a percent of the expected earnings per share), you can construct a portfolio of stocks with the largest recent earnings surprises. The problem, though, is that this will bias you toward a portfolio of stocks with very small earnings. To prevent this from occurring, we use two criteria in constructing this portfolio. The first is that the actual earnings per share have to exceed $0.25; this eliminates firms with very low earnings per share. The second is that the earnings surprise has to exceed 50%; the actual earnings per share have to be more than 50% higher than the predicted earnings per share. The resulting portfolio of 105 firms is presented in Table 12.3.

TABLE 12.3   Firms with EPS Greater than $0.25 and Earnings Surprises Less than 50%

COMPANY	STOCK PRICE	ACTUAL EPS	EXPECTED EPS	EPS SURPRISE
Electr Arts Inc	$57.56	$1.79	$0.33	442.42%
Mobile Mini Inc	$15.24	$0.41	$0.29	41.38%
Advanta Co Cl B	$8.00	$0.43	$0.29	48.28%
Artesian Res	$30.48	$0.45	$0.30	50.00%
Coach Inc	$38.97	$0.68	$0.29	134.48%
Columbia Sports	$38.00	$0.72	$0.29	176.92%
Kellwood	$28.45	$0.38	$0.26	46.15%
Toro Co	$71.60	$0.38	$0.26	46.15%
Lee Entrprs	$32.83	$0.51	$0.34	50.00%
Mettler–Toldeo	$32.70	$0.69	$0.37	86.49%
Avon Prods Inc	$57.57	$0.80	$0.41	95.12%
Education Mgmt	$41.91	$0.70	$0.50	40.00%
Shaw Group Inc	$9.70	$0.42	$0.30	40.00%
Landstar System	$61.22	$0.88	$0.61	44.26%
Ansys Inc	$25.13	$0.43	$0.29	48.28%
Sunrise Assist	$24.95	$0.83	$0.55	50.91%
Odyssey Hlthcr	$23.58	$0.42	$0.27	55.56%
Chicago Merc Ex	$47.12	$1.02	$0.63	61.90%

(continued)

TABLE 12.3 Firms with EPS Greater than $0.25 and Earnings Surprises Less than 50% *(Continued)*

COMPANY	STOCK PRICE	ACTUAL EPS	EXPECTED EPS	EPS SURPRISE
Harland (John H)	$23.83	$0.66	$0.40	65.00%
Certegy Inc	$25.02	$0.46	$0.26	76.92%
Career Edu Group	$50.71	$0.65	$0.35	85.71%
Diebold	$36.14	$0.67	$0.36	86.11%
Bausch & Lomb	$34.45	$0.60	$0.31	93.55%
Meritage Corp	$36.30	$1.72	$0.88	95.45%
Firstenergy CP	$31.04	$1.19	$0.47	153.19%
Raytheon Co	$27.98	$0.64	$0.25	156.00%
Polaris Indus	$49.82	$1.51	$0.54	179.63%
WCI Communities	$10.88	$0.99	$0.25	296.00%
Flir Systems	$47.21	$0.71	$0.50	42.00%
Invacare Corp	$37.42	$0.56	$0.39	43.59%
Viacom Inc Cl B	$40.40	$0.36	$0.25	44.00%
Yum! Brands Inc	$24.73	$0.55	$0.38	44.74%
Omnicom Grp	$59.27	$1.08	$0.71	52.11%
McClatchey Co-A	$52.80	$0.86	$0.56	53.57%
Biovail Corp	$40.10	$0.60	$0.38	57.89%
L-3 Comm Hldgs	$36.48	$0.79	$0.47	68.09%
Intl Bus Mach	$79.01	$1.34	$0.79	69.62%
Coastal Bancorp	$31.80	$1.05	$0.61	72.13%
Knight Ridder	$59.65	$1.16	$0.64	81.25%
Newell Rubbermd	$29.93	$0.49	$0.27	81.48%
SPX Corp	$31.31	$1.37	$0.54	153.70%
Gannett Inc	$72.28	$1.29	$0.92	40.22%
Tribune Co	$46.85	$0.57	$0.38	50.00%
NY Times A	$44.22	$0.69	$0.42	64.29%
Ryland Grp Inc	$48.00	$2.50	$1.24	101.61%
Beckman Coulter	$34.57	$0.90	$0.43	109.30%
Pulte Homes Inc	$53.96	$2.78	$1.22	127.87%
Bunge Ltd	$27.30	$0.98	$0.33	196.97%
Waters Corp	$20.70	$0.41	$0.29	41.38%
Select Ins Group	$24.67	$0.41	$0.28	46.43%
Viacom Inc Cl A	$40.47	$0.37	$0.25	48.00%
America Svc Grp	$12.75	$0.46	$0.28	64.29%
Boeing Co	$27.09	$0.71	$0.42	69.05%

(continued)

TABLE 12.3   Firms with EPS Greater than $0.25 and Earnings Surprises Less than 50% *(Continued)*

COMPANY	STOCK PRICE	ACTUAL EPS	EXPECTED EPS	EPS SURPRISE
Goodrich Corp	$14.17	$0.66	$0.35	88.57%
Lockheed Martin	$44.75	$0.85	$0.42	102.38%
Black and Decker	$36.20	$1.05	$0.43	144.19%
Sears Roebuck	$26.55	$2.11	$0.56	276.79%
Old Dominion Fl	$33.38	$0.57	$0.40	42.50%
Engelhard Corp	$22.45	$0.44	$0.30	46.67%
Marriott Intl-A	$33.01	$0.55	$0.36	52.78%
Fossil Inc	$17.68	$0.48	$0.29	65.52%
Union Pac Corp	$57.50	$1.10	$0.60	83.33%
Radioshack Corp	$23.20	$0.59	$0.32	84.38%
Ingersoll Rand	$40.30	$1.19	$0.61	95.08%
Washington Post	$705.89	$9.83	$3.71	164.96%
Energizer Hldgs	$26.37	$0.91	$0.33	175.76%
Honeywell Intl	$22.00	$0.50	$0.33	51.52%
Estee Lauder	$29.30	$0.44	$0.28	57.14%
Ameristar Casin	$12.57	$0.62	$0.36	72.22%
Coors Adolph B	$48.24	$0.63	$0.30	$110.00%
Safeway Inc	$19.90	$0.80	$0.53	50.94%
Capitol Fedl FN	$30.43	$0.38	$0.25	52.00%
Baxter Intl	$19.26	$0.59	$0.37	59.46%
SBS Commun Inc	$21.05	$0.62	$0.35	77.14%
MDU Resources	$28.00	$0.63	$0.26	142.31%
Roadway Corp	$36.03	$1.48	$0.35	322.86%
Garmin Ltd	$35.16	$0.42	$0.30	40.00%
Startek Inc	$24.35	$0.45	$0.29	$55.17%
Electr Data Sys	$16.27	$0.51	$0.32	59.38%
Hon Inds	$28.80	$0.48	$0.28	71.43%
UTD Defense Ind	$21.80	$0.82	$0.47	74.47%
Standard Pac	$27.95	$1.58	$0.64	146.88%
Bear Stearns	$67.48	$2.00	$1.33	50.38%
Cemex SA Adr	$18.48	$0.54	$0.28	92.86%
Lear Corp	$38.45	$1.76	$0.99	77.78%
G&K Svcs A	$24.69	$0.48	$0.32	50.00%
Ryder Sys	$20.38	$0.58	$0.31	87.10%
Steel Dynamics	$11.90	$0.65	$0.34	91.18%

(continued)

TABLE 12.3 Firms with EPS Greater than $0.25 and Earnings Surprises Less than 50% *(Continued)*

COMPANY	STOCK PRICE	ACTUAL EPS	EXPECTED EPS	EPS SURPRISE
Seagate Tech	$10.83	$0.43	$0.27	59.26%
Ocular Sciences	$14.26	$0.48	$0.28	71.43%
Textron Inc	$28.62	$1.04	$0.51	103.92%
Corrections Crp	$19.40	$1.14	$0.48	137.50%
Northrop Grummn	$81.38	$1.73	$0.62	179.03%
Arkansas Best	$26.58	$0.57	$0.33	72.73%
Mohawk Inds Inc	$51.32	$1.25	$0.61	104.92%
Alliant Engy CP	$16.77	$0.62	$0.34	82.35%
Invision Tech	$22.04	$2.40	$1.62	48.15%
Timberland Co A	$43.48	$0.73	$0.33	121.21%
Hooker Furnitur	$27.00	$0.88	$0.55	60.00%
Landamerica Fin	$41.94	$3.42	$2.27	50.66%
Haverty Furnit	$11.35	$0.36	$0.25	44.00%
Paccar Inc	$53.67	$1.05	$0.61	72.13%
Carmike Cinema	$20.94	$0.89	$0.25	256.00%
Nautilis Group	$10.91	$0.69	$0.44	56.82%
Nucor Corp	$38.91	$0.50	$0.25	100.00%

MORE TO THE STORY

In the last section, portfolios of stocks with price/volume momentum and stocks with large positive earnings surprises were constructed. With the former, you buy the stocks hoping that the price momentum will continue into the future. With the latter, your returns depend on stocks continuing to drift up after large positive earnings announcements. In this section, you will look at the weaknesses of each strategy and possible ways of reducing exposure to these weaknesses.

RISK

When constructing the two portfolios in the last section, we paid no attention to the riskiness of the stocks that went into the portfolios. To the extent that riskier stocks are more likely to show price and volume momentum, you may find your eventual portfolio to be far riskier than the market. Figure 12.12 looks at risk in two dimensions—beta and standard deviation in stock prices—and compares the firms in the high price/volume momentum portfolio with the rest of the market.

The difference in risk levels is striking. The momentum stocks have an average beta almost twice that of the rest of the market (1.91 versus 0.98) and are much more volatile (standard deviation of 100% versus the market average of 60%) than the market. A momentum portfolio thus has to beat the market by a hefty margin to justify the additional risk. Putting a cap of 1.20 on the beta and 80% on the standard deviation reduces the portfolio listed in Table 12.2 from 54 firms to 15 firms.

With the earnings surprise portfolio, the risk can lie in the estimate of expected earnings. Note that the consensus estimate of earnings per share that was used as the predicted earn-

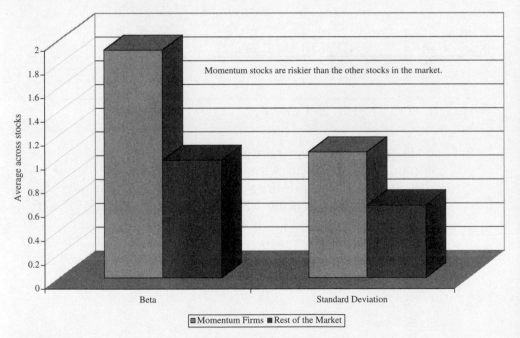

FIGURE 12.12

Risk Comparison: Momentum Stocks vs. Rest of the Market

Data from Value Line. The beta and standard deviation are computed by using three years of data for all stocks.

ings per share represents an average across estimates made by different analysts following the company. There can be disagreement among analysts that is not reflected in the consensus estimate, and the uncertainty that may be generated by this disagreement will have to be factored into the investment strategy. To illustrate, assume that you have two firms that have just reported actual earnings per share of $2 and that the predicted earnings per share for both firms was $1.50. However, assume that there was relatively little disagreement about the predicted earnings per share among analysts following the first firm but a great deal among analysts following the second. A legitimate argument can be made that the earnings surprise for the first firm (with little disagreement among analysts) contains more good news than the earnings surprise for the second (where there is disagreement). Following up, you would be far more likely to invest in the first firm. Figure 12.13 compares

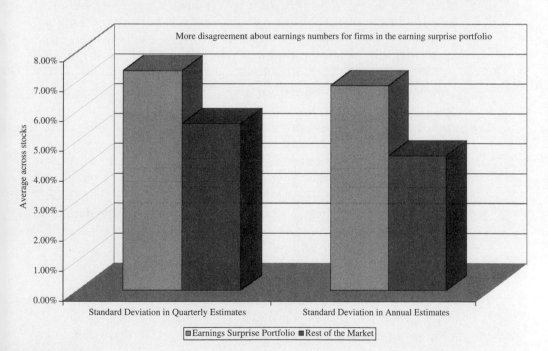

FIGURE 12.13

Disagreement Among Analysts: Surprise Portfolio vs. Market

Data from Zacks. The standard deviation is computed across estimates of earnings per share across analysts following each stock.

the standard deviation in earnings estimates by analysts for companies in the high earnings surprise portfolio with the standard deviation in earnings estimates for companies in the rest of the market; the standard deviation in EPS estimates is divided by the consensus estimate for comparability.

There is clearly more disagreement among analysts regarding earnings estimates for firms in the earnings surprise portfolio than in the rest of the market.

MOMENTUM SHIFTS
(WHEN DO YOU SELL?)

One of the perils of a momentum-based strategy is that the momentum that is your friend for the moment can very quickly become your foe. As you saw in the empirical tests of these strategies, your returns are very sensitive to how long you hold the stock. Holding a stock for too short or too long a period can both work against you, and telling when momentum is shifting is one of the most difficult tasks in investing.

There are signs that, while not infallible, provide early warning of shifting momentum. One is *insider buying and selling;* insiders often are among the first to sell a stock when momentum carries the price too high. Unfortunately, the information on insider buying and selling comes to you several weeks after the trades are made and in some cases, the warning comes too late. Another is *standard valuation metrics* such as price-earnings ratios. Investing in momentum stocks that trade at unsustainable multiples of earnings is clearly a more dangerous strategy than investing in stocks that trade at reasonable values. In Figure 12.14, the average price-earnings, price-to-book and price-to-sales ratios are reported for firms in the momentum portfolio and the rest of the market.

On every measure, the momentum portfolio is more highly priced than the rest of the market. To illustrate, the stocks in the momentum portfolio have an average PE ratio of 63, whereas the rest of the market has an average PE ratio of 16. With price-to-book ratios, the average for the momentum portfolio is 4, whereas the average for the rest of the market is

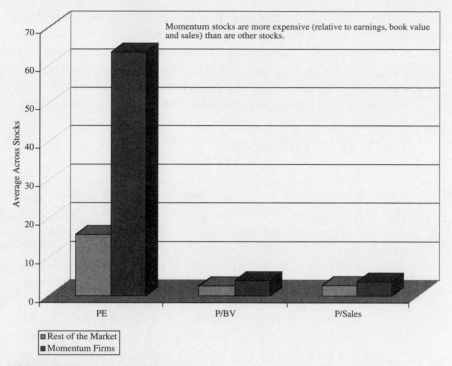

FIGURE 12.14

Valuation Metrics: Momentum Firms vs. Market

Data from Value Line from April 2003. The price-earnings ratio is the current price divided by the earnings per share.

about 2.6. Thus, a momentum portfolio may include a large number of overpriced stocks. Applying a cap of 20 on PE ratios, for instance, reduces the number of the firms in the momentum portfolio from 53 firms to 10 firms.

With the earnings surprise portfolio, the key question that you need to address is whether the positive earnings surprises are created by temporary items (one-time earnings, currency gains) or by improved performance; the latter is much better news. Your need to invest right after an earnings announcement will clash with your desire to examine the details of the earnings announcement, but the payoff to waiting may be substantial. Alternatively, you can use other screens that find stocks for which the earnings surprises and price momentum are likely to be sustained. One tactic is to consider *earnings surprises in previous quarters,* arguing that firms that deliver actual earnings that beat expectations several quarters in a row have more sustainable improvement in earnings than other firms. Considering these statistics for the 105 firms with the most positive earnings surprises in Table 12.3, you find that 25 of these firms also had positive earnings surprises in the previous quarter.

EXECUTION COSTS

By their very nature, momentum- and information-based investment strategies require frequent trading and will generate large transactions costs. The transactions costs include not just the commissions but also the price impact that you can have as you trade. Obviously, this price impact will be minimal if you are an individual investor, but even small trades can affect prices when you are trading illiquid stocks.

With earnings surprise strategies, timing can make the difference between success and failure. If you are able to place a trade immediately after an earnings announcement, you will be able to realize a much bigger gain from the price runup. Unfortunately, the earnings announcement will trigger a wave of buying, and individual investors may be at a disadvantage relative to institutional investors when it comes to execution speed. Options are available to individual investors who want to trade more efficiently, but they will be expensive.

LESSONS FOR INVESTORS

If you decide to pursue a price/volume momentum strategy, you have to be a short-term investor and be willing to trade frequently. While the strategy will always be risky, there are ways in which you can reduce your exposure to its limitations. In general, you should consider doing the following:

- *Have a clear strategy based upon empirical analysis.* Ultimately, the question of whether momentum carries over into future price changes is an empirical question.

While the past is not necessarily prologue, there is evidence of stock price momentum but it is very sensitive to time horizon. Investors therefore have to put their momentum strategies to the test on past data, using specific time horizons to maximize their chances of earning returns.

■ *Develop screens to eliminate "troublesome" stocks.* Momentum stocks tend to be riskier than the rest of the market and often trade at high prices relative to fundamentals. Since there is a good chance of momentum reversing itself with these highly priced stocks, you should eliminate the riskiest, most overpriced stocks from your portfolio.

■ *Execute.* Trading costs can very quickly overwhelm any additional returns from a momentum strategy, and these costs can be exaggerated by the need to trade quickly to take advantage of momentum. Keeping trading costs under control is key to success with this strategy.

■ *Be disciplined.* To earn your promised returns, you have to stay true to your tested strategy. All too often, investors deviate from their strategies when confronted with failure.

Incorporating these factors, a portfolio of momentum stocks was created using the following screens:

■ *Price and volume momentum greater than 1.40:* These screens are not as strict as the screens used in the last section but will allow you to screen for high-risk and overpriced stocks.

■ *Risk criteria—Beta less than 1.20 and standard deviation in stock prices less than 80%:* These screens will eliminate the riskiest stocks in the portfolio. The levels used for the screen represent the 75th percentile of all U.S. stocks, thus ensuring that the stocks in top quartile in terms of risk will be eliminated from the portfolio.

■ *Pricing screens:* Only stocks with PE ratios less than 20 are included in the final portfolio.

The resulting portfolio of seven stocks is listed in Appendix 1.

If you choose to adopt an earnings surprise or information-based investment strategy whereby you plan to buy after good news and sell after bad, your time horizon will be measured in hours rather than weeks. If you want to maximize your returns from this strategy, you should try to do the following:

- *Invest in information and execution.* Since stock prices react to information, you will need to have access to information immediately. Investing in an information system that delivers news to you in time to trade is a necessary prerequisite for the strategy to work.
- *Develop rules that can be used to screen stocks with minimal information.* Investors who use this strategy often have to trade on incomplete information. For instance, you may have to buy stock after a positive earnings report without having access to the details of the earnings reports. Rules that you can use to screen earnings reports for potential problems may help protect against downside risk. For instance, a positive earnings report from a company with a history of earnings revisions and shady accounting practices may be viewed with more skepticism than a report from a company with a better reputation.
- *Constantly track your investment to decide on the optimal holding period.* The momentum from news announcements seems to peak at some point and then reverse itself. You will either have to develop an optimal holding period, based upon looking at past history, and stay consistent, or use technical rules (such as a drop in trading volume) that allow you to detect when the momentum shifts.
- *Factor in transactions costs and tax liabilities.* Trading on news is expensive. Not only will you have to trade often but you may also have to pay more for speedy execution. These costs can accumulate over time and eliminate any profits from the strategy.

Factoring these concerns, we came up with the following to construct an earnings surprise portfolio:

■ *Expected EPS in most recent quarter greater than $0.25:* This eliminates firms with miniscule earnings that are likely to report large earnings surprises. A side benefit is that this screen will also eliminate firms with shares that trade at very low prices and have high transactions costs.

■ *EPS surprise greater than 40%:* The earnings surprise, defined as the difference between actual and predicted earnings per share in the most recent quarter, divided by the predicted earnings per share, has to be larger than 40%. In other words, the actual earnings have to be at least 40% above expectations.

■ *Standard deviation in analyst forecasts less than 5%:* Since earnings surprises should have more impact when there is agreement among analysts about the predicted earnings per share, firms are eliminated from the portfolio when analysts significantly disagreed about predicted earnings.

■ *EPS surprise previous period greater than 0:* Firms that reported a positive earnings surprise in the previous quarter are considered as having more sustainable earnings increases than firms that reported earnings less than anticipated in the last quarter.

■ *Low PE ratio:* Studies indicate that prices are more likely to drift after value companies report earnings surprises. Pursuant to this finding, only companies that trade at PE ratios less than 20 were considered for the portfolio.

The resulting portfolio of 29 stocks is summarized in Appendix 2.

CONCLUSION

Momentum-based strategies appeal to investors because it seems intuitive that stocks that have gone up in the past will continue to go up in the future. There is evidence of price momentum in financial markets, but with a caveat. Stock prices that have gone up in the past—winner stocks—are likely to continue to go up in the near future. The momentum, however, reverses itself after a few months, and stock price reversals are more likely if you hold for longer time periods. With information announcements such as earnings reports and stock splits, the evidence is similarly ambiguous. When firms report good news, stock prices jump on the announcement and continue to go up after the announcement, but only for a few days. As with price momentum, there is a point at which price momentum seems to stall and prices reverse themselves. In both cases, the empirical evidence suggests that price momentum is more likely to be sustained if it is accompanied by an increase in trading volume.

There are two classes of momentum strategies that you can construct. In the first, you buy stocks with both price and volume momentum, that is, stocks that have gone up more than other stocks in the market over a previous period with an accompanying increase in trading volume. These stocks tend to be riskier than other stocks in the market, and your odds of success improve if you can screen these stocks to eliminate stocks overpriced because insiders are selling. In the second, you buy stocks after positive earnings surprises, hoping to gain as the stock prices increase. Here again, you can improve your odds of success if you can separate the firms that have sustainable earnings increases from the firms that do not.

ENDNOTES

1. Conrad, J. S., A. Hameed and C. Niden, 1994, *Volume and Autocovariances in Short-Horizon Individual Security Returns*, Journal of Finance, v49, 1305–1330.

2. Jegadeesh, N., and S. Titman, 1993, *Returns to Buying Winners and Selling Losers: Implications for Market Efficiency*, Journal of Finance, v48, 65–91.

3. Rendleman, R. J., C. P. Jones and H. A. Latene, 1982, *Empirical Anomalies Based on Unexpected Earnings and the Importance of Risk Adjustments*, Journal of Financial Economics, v10, 269–287.

4. LaPorta, R., J. Lakonishok, A. Shleifer and R. Vishny, *Good News for Value Stocks: Further Evidence of Market Inefficiency*, NBER Working Paper.

5. Fama, E., L. Fisher, M. Jensen and R. Roll (1969), *The Adjustment of Stock Price to New Information*, International Economic Review, v10, 1–21.

6. Charest, G., 1978, *Split Information, Stock Returns and Market Efficiency-I*, Journal of Financial Economics, v6, 265–296; Grinblatt, M. S., R. W. Masulis and S. Titman, 1984, *The Valuation Effects of Stock Splits and Stock Dividends*, Journal of Financial Economics, v13, 461–490.

7. Ikenberry, D. L., G. Rankine and E. K. Stice, 1996, *What Do Stock Splits Really Signal?*, Journal of Financial and Quantitative Analysis, v31, 357–375. They report that stocks that split continue to earn excess returns in the two years after the split: 7.93% in the first year and 12.15% in the second year.

8. The bid-ask spread refers to the difference between the price at which a security can be bought (the ask price) or sold (the bid price) at any point.

9. Copeland, T. E., 1979, *Liquidity Changes Following Stock Splits*, Journal of Finance, v34(1), 115–141.

10. While there are no comprehensive studies of reverse stock splits yet, the preliminary evidence indicates that they are viewed by the market as bad news—an indication that the firm doing the split does not believe that its earnings and fundamentals will improve in the near term.

11. Aharony, J., and I. Swary, 1981, *Quarterly Dividends and Earnings Announcements and Stockholders' Returns: An Empirical Analysis*, Journal of Finance, v36, 1–12.

12. Michaely, R., R. H. Thaler and K. L. Womack, 1995, *Price Reactions to Dividend Initiations and Omissions: Overreaction or Drift?* Journal of Finance, v50, 573–608.

13. Datar, V., N. Naik and R. Radcliffe, 1998, *Liquidity and Asset Returns: An Alternative Test*, Journal of Financial Markets, v1, 203–220.

14. Lee, C. M. C., and B. Swaminathan, 1998, *Price Momentum and Trading Volume*, Working Paper, Social Science Research Network.

15. Stickel and Verecchia, 1994, *Evidence That Trading Volume Sustains Stock Price Changes*, Financial Analysts Journal, Nov–Dec, v50, 57–67.

16. See Grinblatt, M., and S. Titman, 1992, *The Persistence of Mutual Fund Performance*, Journal of Finance, v42, 1977–1984; Goetzmann, W. N., and R. Ibbotson, 1994, *Do winners repeat? Patterns in mutual fund performance*, Journal of Portfolio Management, v20, 9–18; and Hendricks, D., J. Patel and R. Zeckhauser, 1995, *Hot Hands in Mutual Funds: Short Run Persistence in Performance, 1974–1987*, Journal of Finance, v48, 93–130.

APPENDIX 1:
STOCKS WITH PRICE AND VOLUME MOMENTUM, LOW RISK AND LOW PE

COMPANY	RETURN OVER 6 MONTHS	RELATIVE PRICE STRENGTH	RELATIVE VOLUME	PE RATIO	BETA	STANDARD DEVIATION
Chronimed Inc	68.35%	1.47	1.46	18.76	0.76	79.83%
Movie Star Inc	127.27%	1.98	1.51	20.40	1.11	70.26%
Aceto Corp	123.59%	1.95	1.74	17.06	0.74	52.04%
North Coast Energy Inc	73.75%	1.51	1.68	8.52	0.56	46.32%
Sanfilippo John B	115.00%	1.87	1.67	11.87	0.71	44.28%
First Colonial Group	84.71%	1.61	1.68	23.89	0.36	32.94%
CNB Finl Corp	74.86%	1.52	1.53	22.20	0.66	25.10%

Appendix 2:
Stocks with Positive Earnings Surprises
and Consensus on Expected Earnings

Company	Stock Price	Actual EPS	Expected EPS	EPS Surprise	Previous EPS Surprise	Std Deviation in Forecasts	PE
Shaw Group Inc	9.7	0.42	0.3	40.00%	1.45%	2.00%	3.87
Coastal Bancorp	31.8	1.05	0.61	72.13%	11.48%	3.00%	4.97
Firstenergy Cp	31.04	1.19	0.47	153.19%	19.70%	2.00%	4.98
Ryland Grp Inc	48	2.5	1.24	101.61%	12.58%	4.00%	5.64
Harland(John H)	23.83	0.66	0.4	65.00%	3.92%	2.00%	5.96
Sunrise Assist	24.95	0.83	0.55	50.91%	1.61%	2.00%	6.27
Meritage Corp	36.3	1.72	0.88	95.45%	14.49%	2.00%	6.41
America Svc Grp	12.75	0.46	0.28	64.29%	46.43%	5.00%	6.58
Bunge Ltd	27.3	0.98	0.33	196.97%	12.94%	4.00%	6.93
Pulte Homes Inc	53.96	2.78	1.22	127.87%	1.67%	4.00%	6.96
Polaris Indus	49.82	1.51	0.54	179.63%	0.64%	2.00%	7.02
Black & Decker	36.2	1.05	0.43	144.19%	14.46%	5.00%	7.49
Yum! Brands Inc	24.73	0.55	0.38	44.74%	2.08%	3.00%	7.64
Bausch & Lomb	34.45	0.6	0.31	93.55%	9.09%	2.00%	8.31
Toro Co	71.6	0.38	0.26	46.15%	14.81%	1.00%	9.19
Newell Rubbermd	29.93	0.49	0.27	81.48%	2.22%	3.00%	11.37
Mcclatchy Co-A	52.8	0.86	0.56	53.57%	2.90%	3.00%	11.70
Diebold	36.14	0.67	0.36	86.11%	1.69%	2.00%	11.83
Intl Bus Mach	79.01	1.34	0.79	69.62%	3.13%	3.00%	11.87
Columbia Sports	38	0.72	0.26	176.92%	5.19%	0.00%	12.32
Lee Entrprs	32.83	0.51	0.34	50.00%	2.38%	1.00%	13.73
Gannett Inc	72.28	1.29	0.92	40.22%	1.02%	4.00%	13.97
Select Ins Grp	24.67	0.41	0.28	46.43%	2.70%	5.00%	14.67
Landstar System	61.22	0.88	0.61	44.26%	1.22%	2.00%	15.94
Biovail Corp	40.1	0.6	0.38	57.89%	2.17%	3.00%	16.40
Tribune Co	46.85	0.57	0.38	50.00%	21.05%	4.00%	16.68
Flir Systems	47.21	0.71	0.5	42.00%	17.65%	3.00%	16.77
Education Mgmt	41.91	0.7	0.5	40.00%	14.29%	2.00%	19.39
Avon Prods Inc	57.57	0.8	0.41	95.12%	2.13%	1.00%	19.78

13 FOLLOW THE EXPERTS

Stanley had been searching for enlightenment all his life. He tried new religions and new diets with equal enthusiasm, convinced that all he had to do to was follow the right advice to become happy. When he started investing, he watched CNBC and read books by financial experts on how to get rich. He was sure that only they had the key to success in investing and that all he had to do was imitate them. When the portfolio manager of one of America's largest mutual funds listed his top ten stocks to buy in Barron's, Stanley followed along and bought every single one. After all, this portfolio manager had access not only to the best minds and the best data on Wall Street but also to the managers of these companies. In the months that followed, Stanley was deeply disappointed. While a couple of stocks on the list did reasonably well, his portfolio badly underperformed the market. Trying to figure out what had gone wrong, Stanley looked for any news he could find about the portfolio manager whose advice he had followed and found a news item that he had been fired because the mutual fund he had run for a decade had done so badly. Stanley sold all his stocks and bought a book on surviving financial crises by an expert on bankruptcy.

Moral: Smart people don't always pick good stocks.

T here are investors who seem to know more than others and claim to do much better on their investments than the rest of the market. If you could follow these "expert" investors and copy their investment decisions, you may be able to piggyback on their successes. It is this belief that leads investors to read investment newsletters and to watch television shows on the stock market. It is also this belief that allows investment experts—equity research analysts, investment advisors and portfolio managers—to have as much influence as they do in financial markets. In this chapter, you will examine whether these experts do better on their investments than the rest of the market and whether following the advice they provide pays off in higher returns.

CORE OF THE STORY

Every discipline has its experts and the investing world has more than its share. Some investors like Warren Buffett and Peter Lynch earn their expert status by generating high returns on their portfolios over many years. Others become experts because of the positions they hold—market strategists for investment banks and equity research analysts, for example. Still others become experts because of what they know—insiders at companies and those close to decision makers. Finally, there are those that anoint themselves as experts in aspects of investing with nothing specific to back them up and because of their sales prowess, pull it off; they write books about successful investing and offer newsletters you can subscribe to. Why are novice investors so attracted to expert advice? A number of beliefs underlie this attraction:

- *Experts know more about markets and hence are less likely to make mistakes.* Investing can be daunting, especially in today's markets, where choices abound and investments become increasingly complex. Investors worry about putting their pension funds and savings at risk by picking the wrong investment at the wrong time and assume that experts can steer them away from catastrophic mistakes.

■ *Experts can bring more resources (data, models, people) to the stock selection process and hence can pick better investments.* Individual investors are constrained in terms of how much time they can spend on analyzing investments and how many resources they can bring to the process. An equity research analyst at an investment bank or a portfolio manager at a mutual fund can bring more resources and more time to investment analysis, and presumably this pays off as better investment choices.

■ *Experts have better access to private information (buzz, rumor, news) and hence get advance notice of big happenings.* Markets move on information and investors with timely access to good information should be able to use that information to earn higher returns. While individual investors may not be able to talk to the managers of a firm, analysts have access to these highly placed sources. Many investors assume that information is leaked to Wall Street before it gets to Main Street.

THEORETICAL ROOTS: THE VALUE OF EXPERT OPINION

To understand how and why experts may be able to beat the market, you have to begin by examining the process by which market prices are set. While market prices are set by demand and supply, the market price of an asset is an estimate of its value. Investors in the market assess the value according to their expectations for the future. They form these expectations by using the information that is available to them, and this information can arrive in different forms. It can be information about the past price performance of the asset, public information available in annual reports or filings with the SEC, or information available to one or a few investors.

While the steps in this process—receive information, process the information to form expectations and trade on the asset—may be the same for all investors, there are wide variations across investors in how much information they have available and how they process the information. Some investors have access to more information than others. For instance, an equity research analyst whose job it is to evaluate Cisco as an investment will have access to more information about the firm than will a small investor making the same decision. These differences in information are compounded by the different ways in which investors use the information to form expectations. Some investors build complex quantitative models, converting the information into expected earnings and cash flows, and assign value to stocks. Other investors use the same information to make comparisons across stocks. The net effect is that, at any point, investors will disagree on how much an asset is worth. Those who think that it is worth more will be the buyers of the asset, and those who think it is worth less will sell the asset. The market price represents the price at which the market clears, that is when demand (buying) is equal to supply (selling).

The price can and usually will deviate from the value for three reasons. It is these flaws in the pricing process that may provide experts with potential excess returns.

- First, the information available to most investors may be insufficient or incorrect; then, expectations based upon this information will also be wrong. Investors with access to better or more complete information will be able to use their information advantage to earn potential excess returns. This is usually the advantage that insiders at companies have over outside investors in these companies.
- Second, investors may not do a good job of processing the information to arrive at expectations. Investors who are better at processing this information (using better and more complex models) may be able to find mispricing and take advantage of it. This is potentially the value created by analysts and portfolio managers.

■ Third, even if the information is correct and investors, on average, form expectations properly, there might still be investors who are willing to trade at prices that do not reflect these expectations. Thus, an investor who assesses the value of a stock to be $50 might still be willing to buy the stock for $60, because he or she believes that it can be sold to someone else for $75 later. Investors who see this irrationality and are willing to bet on it or against it may be able to make higher returns in the long term. This presumably is what successful investors like Warren Buffett and Peter Lynch bring to the process.

With this framework, you can see a role for experts in the markets. Experts can attain their status by getting information earlier than other investors, processing that information better, or by finding systematic mistakes in how markets price assets. Other investors can learn from them and partake in at least a portion of their success.

LOOKING AT THE EVIDENCE

Do investors who have information that no one else has access to, that is, private information, use this information to profit? While the answer seems obvious (yes), it is very difficult to test to see whether they do because investors who trade on this information will not do so in the open. The reason for this is that the regulatory authorities, at least in the United States, specifically forbid trading in advance of significant information releases. Thus, insiders who follow the law and register their trades with the SEC are not likely to be trading on specific information in the first place. Notwithstanding this selection bias, this section begins by looking at whether insider buying and selling operate as signals of future price movements, since insiders may still have access to general information about the firm that outsiders do not. The second part of the section look at the more difficult question of whether those who trade illegally on private information make excess returns. While this may seem like an impossible test to run, you can at least draw inferences about this trading by looking at trading volume and price movements before major news announcements. In the final section, you will look at whether you can augment your returns by listening to equity research analysts and following their advice.

INSIDERS

The Securities and Exchange Commission (SEC) defines an insider to be an officer or director of the firm or a major stockholder (holding more than 5% of the outstanding stock in the firm). Insiders are barred from trading in advance of specific information on the company and are required to file with the SEC when they buy or sell stock in the company. In this section, you will begin by looking at the relationship between insider trading and subsequent stock price changes, and then consider whether non-insiders can use information on insider trading to earn excess returns themselves.

Insider Trading and Stock Prices. If it is assumed, as seems reasonable, that insiders have better information about the company and consequently better estimates of value than other investors, the decisions by insiders to buy and sell stock should signal future movements in stock prices. Figure 13.1, derived from an early study of insider trading, examines excess returns on two groups of stock, classified on the basis of insider trades.[1] The "buy group" includes stocks for which insider buys exceeded sells by the biggest margin, and the "sell group" includes stocks for which insider sells exceed buys by the biggest margin.

Stocks for which insiders were buying more aggressively did much better in the months after the insider trading than stocks for which insiders were selling. Research done since support this finding,[2] but it is worth noting that insider buying does not always precede price increases; about 4 in 10 stocks that insiders are buying turn out to be poor investments, and

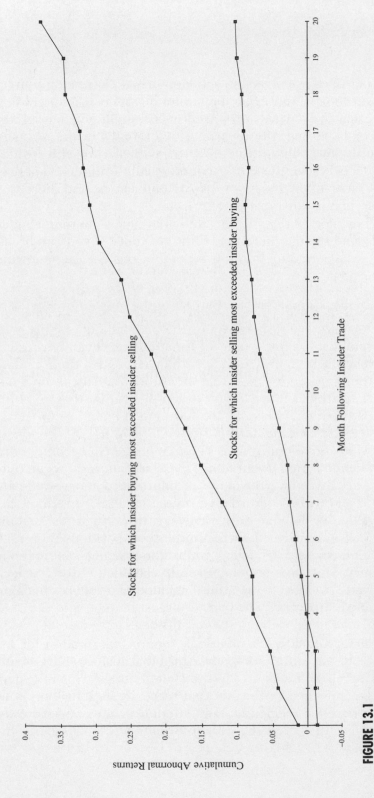

FIGURE 13.1

Cumulative Returns Following Insider Trading: Buy vs. Sell Group

Data from Jaffe. The insider buy (sell) group includes companies for which insider buying (selling) most exceeded insider selling (buying). The returns are cumulated in the 24 months after the portfolios are created.

even on average, the excess returns earned are not very large. A closer look at the price movements around insider trading found that firms with substantial insider selling had stock returns of 14.4% over the subsequent 12 months, which was significantly lower than the 22.2% earned by firms with insider buying.[3] However, the link between insider trading and subsequent returns was greatest for small companies, and there was almost no relationship at larger firms.

While most of the studies cited above focus on total insider buying and selling, there may be value added if you can break down insider trading into more detail. Consider the following propositions:

- *Not all insiders have equal access to information.* Top managers and members of the board should be privy to much more important information and thus their trades should be more revealing than trades by their underlings. A study finds that investors who focus only on large trades made by top executives rather than total insider trading may, in fact, earn much higher returns.[4]
- *As investment alternatives to trading on common stock have multiplied, insiders have also become more sophisticated about using these alternatives.* As an outside investor, you may be able to add more value by tracking these alternative investments. For instance, insider trading in derivative securities (options specifically) to hedge their common stock positions increases immediately following price runups and before poor earnings announcements.[5] In addition, stock prices tend to go down after insiders take these hedging positions.

In summary, insider trading does contain information for insiders, but the information advantage that insiders have is not overwhelming, at least not in the United States. This may partially be explained by the fact that these are legal insiders who cannot trade on upcoming news announcements and partially by the fact that even the best information is not precise. Investors who base their trades on insider buying or selling have to recognize that insiders often are wrong in their assessments of value.

Illegal Insider Trading.   None of the research discussed above answers the question of whether insiders themselves make excess returns. The reporting process, as set up now by the SEC, is biased toward legal and less profitable trades and away from illegal and more profitable trades. Though direct evidence cannot be easily offered for this proposition, insiders trading illegally on private information must make much higher returns than legal insiders. In support of this proposition, three pieces of evidence can be presented.

- The first (and weakest) is anecdotal. When insiders are caught trading illegally, they almost invariably have made a killing on their investments. Clearly, some insiders made significant returns from their privileged positions. The reason that it has to be viewed as weak evidence, though, is because the SEC looks for large profits as one of the indicators of whether it will prosecute. In other words, an insider who trades illegally on information may be breaking the law but is less likely to be prosecuted for the act if he or she loses money.
- Almost all major news announcements made by firms are preceded by a price runup (if it is good news) or a price drop (if it is bad news). Thus, you see that the stock price of a target firm drifts up before the actual takeover announcement and that the stock price of a firm reporting disappointing earnings drops in the days before the earnings report. While this may indicate a very prescient market, it is much more likely that someone with access to the privileged information (either at the firm or the intermediaries helping the firm) is using the information to trade ahead of the news. In fact, the other indicator of insider trading is the surge in trading volume in both the stock itself and derivatives before big news announcements.[6]

■ In addition to having access to information, insiders are often in a position to time the release of relevant information to financial markets. Knowing as they do that they are not allowed to trade ahead of this information, insiders often adjust information disclosure to make it less likely that they will be targeted by the SEC. One analysis[7] finds that insiders sell stock between three and nine quarters before their firms report a break in consecutive earnings increases.[8] This study also finds, for instance, that insider selling increases at growth firms before periods of declining earnings.

Using Insider Trading in Investment Decisions. Tracking what legal insiders are doing has become both easier and more timely. You can look at the filings made by companies on the SEC web site (http://www.sec.gov). The insider trading information is available in forms 3, 4 and 144s. Many of the more popular financial web sites such as Yahoo! Finance report on recent insider transactions on individual companies. If you are willing to pay more, you can subscribe to services that consolidate the information and provide it to you.

As the information on insider trades has become more accessible, it has also become less useful as an investment tool. In addition, the spurt in the use of options in management compensation schemes has introduced a substantial amount of uncertainty in the reporting system, since a large proportion of insider trades now are associated with managers exercising options and then selling a portion of their stock holding for liquidity and diversification reasons. For information on insider trading to pay off, you need to look beyond the total insider trading numbers at the insiders themselves, focusing on large trades by top managers at smaller, less followed firms. Even then, you should not expect miracles, since you are using publicly available information.

The real payoff comes from tracking illegal insider trading by looking at trading volume and bid-ask spreads. The relationship between trading volume and private information may provide an intuitive rationale for the use of some of the volume measures as technical indicators.

ANALYSTS

Analysts clearly hold a privileged position in the market for information, operating at the nexus of private and public information. Using both types of information, analysts make earnings forecasts for the firms that they follow, and issue buy and sell recommendations to their clients, who trade on that basis. In this section, you will consider where there is valuable information in earnings forecasts and recommendations and whether incorporating it into investment decisions leads to higher returns.

Earnings Forecasts. Analysts spend a considerable amount of time and resources forecasting earnings per share both for the next quarter and for the next financial year. Presumably, this is where their access to company management and private information should generate an advantage. Thus, when analysts revise their earnings forecasts upward or downward, they convey information to financial markets, and prices should react. This section examines how markets react to analyst forecast revisions and whether there is potential for investors to take advantage of this reaction.

Information in Analyst Forecasts. There is a simple reason to believe that analyst forecasts of growth should be better than just looking at past earnings growth. Analysts, in addition to using past earnings data, can avail themselves of other information that may be useful in predicting future growth.

1. *Firm-specific information that has been made public since the last earnings report:* Analysts can use information that has come out about the firm since the last earnings report to predict future growth. This information can sometimes lead to significant reevaluation of the firm's expected earnings and cash flows. For instance, information that a firm has a signed a lucrative contract with the federal government or that its management has been replaced should affect your estimates of earnings growth in future periods.

2. *Macroeconomic information that may impact future growth:* The expected growth rates of all firms are affected by economic news on GNP growth, interest rates and inflation. Analysts can update their projections of future growth as new information comes out about the overall economy and about changes in fiscal and monetary policy. Information, for instance, that shows the economy growing at a faster rate than forecast will result in analysts increasing their estimates of expected growth for cyclical firms.

3. *Information revealed by competitors on future prospects:* Analysts can also condition their growth estimates for a firm on information revealed by competitors on pricing policy and future growth. For instance, a report of slowing sales growth at one retail firm can lead to a reassessment of earnings growth for other retail firms.

4. *Private information about the firm:* Analysts sometimes have access to private information about the firms they follow and this information may be relevant in forecasting future growth. This avoids answering the delicate question of when private information becomes illegal inside information. There is no doubt, however, that good private information can lead to significantly better estimates of future growth. In an attempt to restrict this type of information leakage, the SEC issued new regulations preventing firms from selectively revealing information to a few analysts or investors. Outside the United States, however, firms routinely convey private information to analysts following them.

5. *Public information other than earnings:* Models for forecasting earnings that depend entirely upon past earnings data may ignore other publicly available information that is useful in forecasting future earnings. It has been shown, for instance, that other financial variables such as earnings retention, profit margins and asset turnover are useful in predicting future growth. Analysts can incorporate information from these variables into their forecasts.

Quality of Earnings Forecasts.[9]   If firms are followed by a large number of analysts and these analysts are indeed better informed than the rest of the market, the forecasts of growth that emerge from analysts should be better than estimates based upon either past earnings growth or other publicly available information. But is this presumption justified? Are analyst forecasts of growth superior to other estimates?

The general consensus from research that has looked at short-term forecasts (one quarter ahead to four quarters ahead) of earnings is that analysts provide better forecasts of earnings than do models that depend purely upon historical data. The absolute difference between the actual earnings and the forecast for the next quarter, in percentage terms, is smaller for analyst forecasts than it is for forecasts based upon historical data. Summarizing the conclusion on the accuracy of analysts' forecasts:

■ *Analyst estimates are more precise than past growth rates but not by much.* An examination[10] of the relative accuracy of forecasts in the *Earnings Forecaster,* a publication from Standard and Poor's that summarizes forecasts of earnings from more than 50 investment firms, looked at the forecast errors by month of the year and computed the ratio of analyst forecast error to the forecast error from time-series models of earnings, which use only past earnings. It found that the time-series models actually outperform analyst forecasts from April until August, but underperform them from September through January. The authors hypothesize that this is because more firm-specific information is available to analysts during the latter part of the year.

■ *Analysts' advantages deteriorate for longer-term earnings forecasts.* A comparison[11] of consensus analyst forecasts from the Institutions Brokers Estimate System (I/B/E/S) with forecasts, based purely on past earnings, from one quarter ahead to four quarters ahead finds that analyst forecasts outperform the time-series model for one-quarter-ahead and two-quarter-ahead forecasts, do as well as the time-series model for three-quarter-ahead forecasts, and do worse than the time-series model for four-quarter-ahead forecasts. Thus, the advantage gained by analysts from firm-specific information seems to deteriorate as the time horizon for forecasting is extended.

■ *Analysts make surprisingly large mistakes when forecasting earnings.* An examination of analyst forecasts from 1974 to 1991 found that in more than 55% of the forecasts examined, analyst estimates of earnings were off by more than 10% from actual earnings.[12] One potential explanation given for this poor forecasting is that analysts are routinely overoptimistic about future growth. An analysis concludes that a great deal of this forecast error comes from the failure of analysts to consider large macroeconomic shifts.[13] In other words, as Figure 13.2 indicates, analysts tend to overestimate

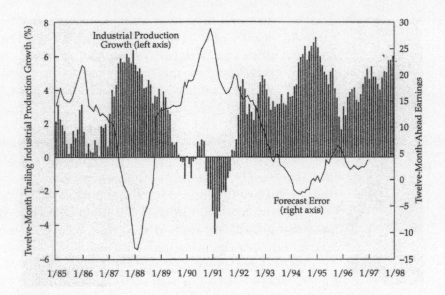

FIGURE 13.2

Earnings Forecasts Errors and Economic Growth

Data from Chopra. Industrial production measures the pace of economic growth, and the earning forecast error is the average forecast error on earnings estimates (relative to actual earnings) across all analysts.

growth at the peak of a recovery and underestimate growth in the midst of a recession.

Note that analysts consistently underestimate earnings during periods of high economic growth and overestimate earnings during periods of low economic growth. A comparison of analyst forecast errors across seven countries suggests, not surprisingly, that analysts are more accurate and less biased in countries that mandate more financial disclosure.[14]

■ *With long term forecasts (5 years), there is little evidence that analyst forecasts add any information.* There is little evidence to suggest that analysts provide superior forecasts of earnings when the forecasts are over three or five years. An early study compared long-term forecasts by five investment management firms in 1962 and 1963 with actual growth over the following three years to conclude that analysts were poor long-term forecasters.[15] This view was contested in a later analysis which found that the consensus prediction of five-year growth in the I/B/E/S was superior to historically oriented growth measures in predicting future growth.[16]

There is an intuitive basis for arguing that analyst predictions of growth rates must be better than models based on time series or other historical data simply because they use more information. The evidence indicates, however, that this superiority in forecasting is surprisingly small for long-term forecasts and that past earnings growth rates play a significant role in determining analyst forecasts.

Market Reaction to Revisions of Earnings Forecast. In the price momentum strategies described in Chapter 12, investors buy stocks that have gone up the most in recent periods, expecting the momentum to carry forward into future periods. You could construct similar strategies on the basis of earnings momentum. While some of these strategies are based purely upon earnings growth rates, most of them are based upon how earnings measure up to analyst expectations. In fact, one strategy is to buy stocks for which analysts are revising earnings forecasts upward, and hope that stock prices follow these earnings revisions.

A number of studies in the United States seem to conclude that it is possible to use forecast revisions made by analysts to earn excess returns. In one of the earliest examinations of this phenomenon, researchers created portfolios of 49 stocks in three sectors, based upon earnings revisions, and reported earning an excess return on 4.7% over the following four months on the stocks with the most positive revisions.[17] A study reported that a portfolio of stocks with the 20 largest upward revisions in earnings on the I/B/E/S database would have earned an annualized return of 14% as opposed to the index return of only 7%.[18] An examination of the excess returns suggests that the high returns are concentrated in the weeks around the revision: 1.27% in the week before the forecast revision and 1.12% in the week after. The study further showed that analysts categorized as leaders (based upon timeliness, impact and accuracy) have a much greater impact on both trading volume and prices.[19] In 2001, the research was extended to earnings forecasts in other countries, with the conclusion that you could have earned excess returns of 4.7% in the U.K, 2% in France and 3.3% in Germany from buying stocks with the most positive revisions.[20]

Earnings estimates and revisions to them are widely publicized; you can track them through services such as Zacks and First Call. These services collate earnings estimates made by analysts and report a consensus estimate of earnings per share, based upon the average value. They also report changes in individual estimates and reflect revisions in the consensus value. Investors can track these earnings revisions and buy stocks with the largest upward revisions.

Analyst Recommendations. The centerpiece of analyst reports are the recommendations that they make on stocks. You would expect stock prices to react to analyst recommendations when they are made, if for no other reason than that some investors follow these recommendations and buy (sell) after favorable (unfavorable) recommendations. In this section, you will consider some key empirical facts about analyst recommendations first and then consider how markets react to them. The section closes with an analysis of whether investors who use these recommendations to make investment decisions can make money from them in the short and the long term.

The Recommendation Game. Three empirical facts about recommendations need to be laid on the table before you start examining how markets react to them.

- If you categorize analyst recommendations into buy, sell and hold, the overwhelming number are buy recommendations. In 2001, for instance, buy recommendations outnumbered sell recommendations 7 to 1, but that was actually a drop from the late 1990s, when sell recommendations were often outnumbered by more than 25 to 1.
- Part of the reason for this imbalance between buy and sell recommendations is that analysts often have many more layers beyond buy, sell and hold. Some investment banks, and investment advisory firms, for instance, have numerical rating systems for stocks whereby stocks are classified from 1 to 5 (as is the case with Value Line), whereas others break buy and sell recommendations into subclasses (strong buy, weak buy). What these systems allow analysts to do is not only rate stocks with more gradations but also send sell signals without ever saying the word. Thus, an analyst downgrading a stock from a strong buy to a weak buy is sending a sell signal on the stock.
- As with earnings forecasts, there is herd behavior when it comes to recommendations. Thus, when one analyst upgrades a stock from a weak buy to a strong buy, there tends to be a rush of other analyst upgrades in the following days.

Market Reaction to Recommendations. How do markets react to recommendations made by analysts? You can examine the stock price response to buy and sell recommendations on the day of the recommendation and in the weeks following. While both buy and sell recommendations affect stock prices, sell recommendations affect prices much more than buy recommendation.[21] This should not be surprising when you remember that buy recommendations vastly outnumber sell recommendations. Interestingly, the price effect of buy recommendations tends to be immediate and there is no evidence of price drifts after the announcement, whereas prices continue to trend down after sell recommendations. Figure 13.3 graphs the findings.

Stock prices increase by about 3% on buy recommendations, whereas they drop by about 4% on sell recommendations at the time of the recommendations (three days around

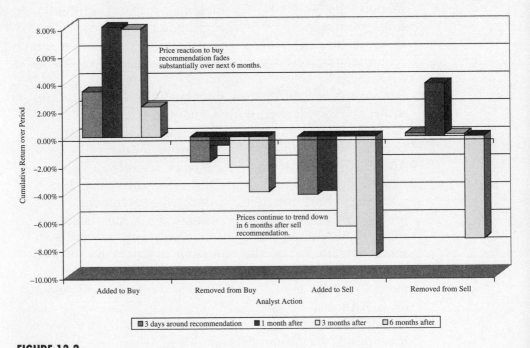

FIGURE 13.3

Price Reaction to Analyst Recommendations

Data from Womack. The stocks are categorized according to changes in recommendations made by analysts following the stock.

reports). In the six months following, prices decline an additional 5% for sell recommendations, while leveling off for buy recommendations.

Can you make money from analyst recommendations? The answer seems to be yes, at least in the short term. Even if no new information were contained in recommendations, the self-fulfilling prophecy created by clients who trade on these recommendations pushes stock prices up after buy recommendations and pushes them down after sell recommendations.[22] If this is the only reason for the stock price reaction, though, the returns are not only likely to be small but could very quickly dissipate, leaving investors with large transactions costs and little to show for them.

INVESTMENT ADVISORS AND OTHER EXPERTS

Insiders and analysts are but two players in a very crowded market place of ideas for investors. Investment advisory newsletters purport to pick the best stocks in the market, investment advisory services such as Value Line and Morningstar offer their own proprietary stock-picking advice (for a modest cost), and ubiquitous talking heads on television, claim to have found an inside track to investment success. Rather than revisit all the research ever done on the success (or lack thereof) of this expert advice, you can summarize the evidence as follows:

■ *There are few examples of long term and consistent stock-picking success among investment advisors and experts.* Investment newsletters that claim to use proprietary stock selection models to pick stocks often have little to back up their claim that they pick better stocks. An analysis of more than 153 active newsletters tracked by the *Hulbert Financial Digest* finds little evidence of stock-picking skill, even before adjusting for transactions costs.[23] Given that many of these newsletters require frequent trading, the returns to an investor who followed their advice would undoubtedly be even worse. There are a few exceptions. A number of studies[24] have found that Value Line, one of the oldest investment advisory services, has had some success in identifying good stocks with its rankings.[25]

■ *Even among those investment advisory services that seem to offer good investment advice (like Value Line), there is a significant "implementation shortfall."* In other words, there is a big gap between the returns on paper and the actual returns that you would earn on a real portfolio. An examination of the Value Line rankings from 1979 to 1991 indicated that while the paper portfolio of the best stocks (timeliness of 1) generated 26.2% in annual returns, an investor who bought the same stocks would have earned only 16.1% a year. In fact, a fund created by Value Line in the 1980s to follow its own advice significantly underperformed the paper portfolio returns.

■ *Investment advisors who find a successful formula for picking stocks seem to have their greatest success when they first begin offering advice.* In the long term, success is self-defeating since imitators can very quickly eliminate the source of the additional returns. Much of Value Line's initial success can be attributed to its pioneering use of earnings momentum (the rate at which the earnings growth rate change) in its timeliness rankings. Once Value Line succeeded, others started using earning momentum in their stock selection strategies, undercutting its effectiveness as a tool.

■ *Much of the investment advice offered by superstar money managers and analysts in the public press is self-serving,* and there is little evidence that investors who read this advice have any success with it. As an example, Barron's, the weekly financial newsmagazine, has a roundtable every year of the most prominent money managers in the country who offer their picks for the best stocks for the coming year. A closer look at these stock picks finds that there is a price runup of about 2% in the two weeks between the recommendation day and the publication day, but no excess returns from the publication date for holding periods from one to three years.[26]

CRUNCHING THE NUMBERS

Before you decide to follow the experts and buy stocks after insiders buy and analysts issue buy recommendations, you should take a look at differences across the market and get a sense of how much stock insiders hold at individual companies, how often they trade, what types of companies are most followed by analysts, and the nature of analyst recommendations. In this section, you will look at cross sectional differences in insider trading and analyst following.

INSIDER TRADING

Using the SEC definition of an insider as a director, manager or employee of the firm, you can compute the percent of stock held in a company by insiders. In companies like Microsoft and Oracle, in which the founders still play a role in management and have substantial holdings, you will find insider holdings to be a high percent of the outstanding stock. In Oracle, for instance, Larry Ellison owned in excess of 20% of the outstanding stock of the company in April 2003. In more mature companies that have been in existence for a while, insider holdings are much smaller. In Figure 13.4, you can see the distribution of insider holdings as a percent of outstanding stock across companies in the United States in April 2003.

Note that there are a few companies where insiders hold 70%, 80% or even 90% of the outstanding stock.

While it is useful to know how much stock in a firm is held by insiders, most investment strategies are based upon changes in insider holdings. But do insiders trade often enough for this to be the basis of an investment strategy? To answer this question, we computed the percent change in insider holdings at 500 U.S. companies in the 12-week period

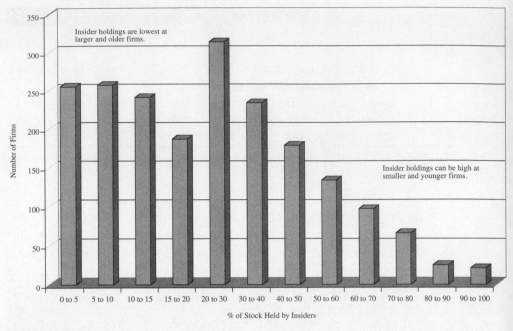

FIGURE 13.4

Insider Holdings at U.S. Firms

Data from Value Line. The SEC definition of insider includes firm employees and directors and holders of more than 5% of the outstanding stock.

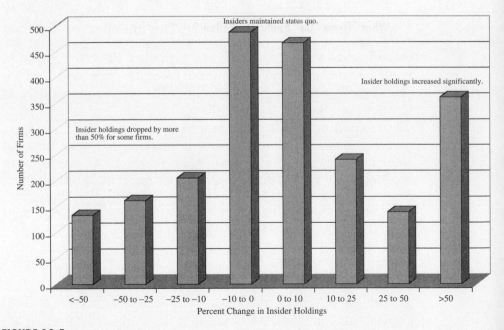

FIGURE 13.5

Change in Insider Holdings: January to March 2003

Data from Value Line. This is the percent change in insider holdings over a 12-month period.

from January to March 2003. The distribution of these changes is graphed in Figure 13.5.[27]

Even over a three-month period, the insider holding changes significantly at least at some firms. For instance, the insider holdings increased by more than 50% in about 350 firms and dropped by more than 50% in about 150 firms between January and March of 2003.

ANALYST RECOMMENDATIONS AND REVISIONS

Hundreds of analysts on Wall Street and elsewhere track U.S. companies, but not all companies attract the same amount of attention. This section begins with a look at differences in analyst-following across companies and continues by examining how often analysts make buy and sell recommendations, how often they change these recommendations, and how frequently they revise earnings estimates.

What Firms Do Analysts Follow? The number of analysts tracking firms varies widely across firms. At one extreme are firms like GE, Cisco and Microsoft that are followed by dozens of analysts. At the other extreme, hundreds of firms are not followed by any analysts. Why are some firms more heavily followed than others? These seem to be some of the determinants:

- *Market capitalization:* The larger the market capitalization of a firm, the more likely it is to be followed by analysts. In fact, this fact was posited as one possible reason for the excess returns earned by small-cap companies over time.
- *Institutional holding:* The greater the percent of a firm's stock that is held by institutions, the more likely it is to be followed by analysts. The open question, though, is whether analysts follow institutions or whether institutions follow analysts. Given that institutional investors are the biggest clients of equity research analysts, the causality probably runs both ways.

■ *Trading volume:* Analysts are more likely to follow liquid stocks. Here again, though, it is worth noting that the presence of analysts and buy (or sell) recommendations on a stock may play a role in increasing trading volume.

Bias in Analyst Recommendations. Analyst recommendations take different forms. While some analysts categorize stocks simply into buy, sell and hold groups, most analysts categorize stocks into more groups; one common variation is to put stocks into strong buy, buy, hold, sell and strong sell groups. The bias toward buy recommendations is well established on the street. There are a couple of ways you can see this bias. You could compute the average recommendation across all analysts following a stock and look at how many stocks fall into each category. In Figure 13.6, this distribution is presented for U.S. stocks in April 2003.[28]

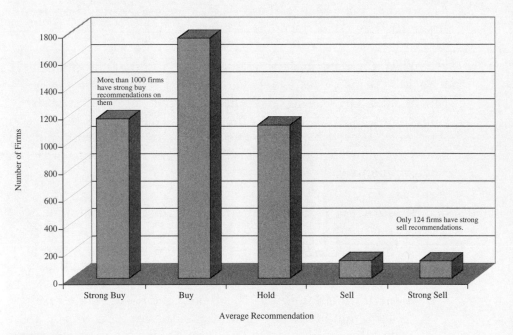

FIGURE 13.6

Average Recommendation: U.S. Stocks in April 2003

Data from Zacks. The recommendations of individual analysts are aggregated and consolidated into a consensus recommendation for each stock.

Of the more than 4000 stocks that were followed by analysts, less than 300 had sell and strong sell recommendations on them. In contrast, almost 3000 firms had buy and strong buy recommendations.

Looking at recommendations across analysts following a stock and categorizing them in percentage terms into buy, hold and sell recommendations is another way that you can see the bias toward buy recommendations. In Figure 13.7, this statistic is reported across 900 firms in the United States in April 2003.

Here again, the contrast between buy and sell recommendations is clearest when you look at the two ends of the distribution. There are almost 900 stocks for which more than 90% of the analysts following the stocks made buy recommendations; in contrast, there were fewer than 20 stocks for which less than 10% of the analysts had buy recommendations on the stock. With sell recommendations, the reverse holds true.

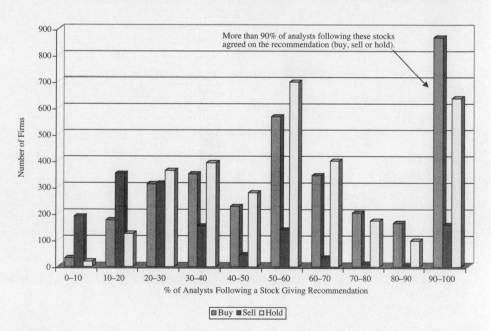

FIGURE 13.7

Recommendation Breakdown for Individual Stocks

Data from Zacks. This graph represents the percentage of analysts following each stock who have buy, sell and hold recommendations on the stock. With each stock, the percentages should add up to 100%.

Analyst Earnings Estimates.   In addition to making recommendations on stocks, analysts estimate earnings per share in advance of earnings reports. As noted in the last section, upward revisions in these earnings estimates may be a potent signal of future price increases.

How often do analysts revise earnings estimates and how big are these revisions? To answer this question, all earnings estimate revisions made in a four-week period in March 2003 were examined. These revisions were being made in advance of the first-quarter earnings reports that would be made in April 2003. Figure 13.8 reports on the percentage change in consensus estimates of earnings per share during this four-week period for all U.S. stocks tracked by analysts.

Looking at Figure 13.8, the first fact is that the changes in earnings forecasts are fairly small for most companies; note

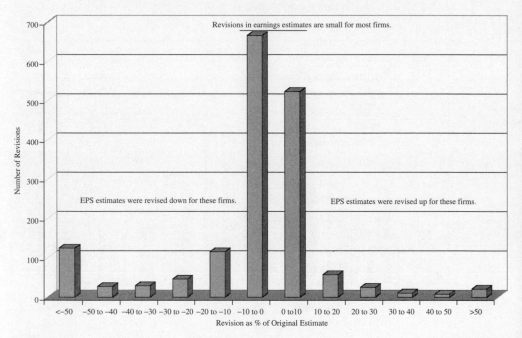

FIGURE 13.8

Revision in Quarterly Earnings Estimate: February 2003 to March 2003

Data from Zacks. These represent the percentage changes in consensus earnings estimates for firms tracked by analysts.

that the consensus earnings estimate is changed by less than 10% (plus or minus) for about 70% of the sample. There are, however, a large number of firms for which the estimate revisions are much more substantial. The earnings estimate increased by more than 50% for more than 100 firms. These are the firms that you presumably would invest in if you followed an earnings momentum strategy.

PORTFOLIO OF "EXPERT" STOCKS

If you were to incorporate all the findings in this chapter into a portfolio, you would want to buy stocks that both insiders and analysts are optimistic about. To create such a portfolio, you would need to screen for at least the following:

- *Positive analyst recommendations:* Notwithstanding that buy recommendations are far more frequent than sell recommendations, only stocks for which more than 80% of the recommendations are buy recommendations are considered for the portfolio. Since stocks with only one or two analysts may qualify too easily for this portfolio, only stocks with more than three buy recommendations were considered. Finally, only stocks that have been upgraded by at least one analyst in the last week are considered, since it is changes in recommendations that seem to carry weight with investors.
- *Recent upward earnings revisions:* It is recent revisions in earnings estimates that matter. In keeping with this objective, only firms for which earnings estimates have been revised upwards in the four weeks before the screening date are considered.
- *Net insider buying:* Only stocks of which insiders were buying more shares than they were selling (in the three months before the screening date) are considered in the sample.

The resulting portfolio of 16 stocks, based upon data available on April 15, 2003, is reported in Table 13.1.

TABLE 13.1 Companies with Insider Buying & Optimistic Analysts

Company Name	Current Price	# Rating Strong Buy or Buy	# Rating Hold	# Rating Strong Sell or Sell	Revision in Earnings Estimate: Last 4 Weeks	Increase in Insider Holdings: Last Quarter
Amgen Inc	$59.54	24	3	0	0.33%	17.48%
Applebees Intl	$28.09	12	6	0	0.14%	47.30%
Biomet	$28.86	13	6	1	0.50%	1.80%
Anheuser Busch	$47.23	9	6	0	0.01%	4.12%
Corinthian Col	$39.66	6	2	0	1.29%	5.54%
Cognizant Tech	$20.16	10	2	1	1.15%	155.60%
Donaldson Co	$39.69	3	2	0	2.42%	3.69%
Ebay Inc	$88.41	9	4	0	3.75%	10.93%
Express Scripts	$54.53	13	3	1	0.15%	139.09%
Hot Topic Inc	$22.77	14	3	0	0.12%	39.57%
Hutchinson Tech	$24.22	4	1	1	0.43%	12.46%
Medtronic	$46.65	18	9	0	0.15%	2.00%
Merrill Lync&Co	$39.75	11	7	0	2.43%	10.13%
Altria Group	$31.70	7	2	1	0.20%	22.95%
Peets Coffe&Tea	$15.65	5	1	0	1.67%	8.66%
Pfizer Inc	$31.36	24	4	0	0.35%	4.24%
Boston Beer Inc	$11.31	3	0	0	160.00%	500.00%
USA Interactive	$27.69	13	1	0	57.26%	0.01%
Williams-Sonoma	$23.05	10	6	0	2.39%	333.33%
Zimmer Holdings	$44.70	12	7	0	0.69%	362.47%

Note that most of these are liquid and widely held stocks. This is largely the result of the requirement that was imposed that only firms with at least three buy recommendations would be considered for the portfolio. The percent changes in insider holdings also have to be considered with caution since many of the bigger increases (in percentage terms) occur in firms with small insider holdings.

MORE TO THE STORY

What can go wrong when you follow the experts? There are many potential problems, but this section focuses on the most important problems with each of the three screens you looked at in the last section: insider trades, estimate revisions and analysts recommendations.

FOLLOWING INSIDERS:
TIMING IS EVERYTHING

If insider trading offers advance warning, albeit a noisy one, of future price movements, can outside investors use this information to make better investment decisions? In other words, when you are looking for stocks to buy, should you consider the magnitude of insider buying and selling on the stock? To answer this question, you first have to recognize that since the SEC does not require an immediate filing of insider trades, investors will find out about insider trading on a stock with a delay of a few weeks or even a few months. In fact, until recently, it was difficult for an investor to access the public filings on insider trading. Since these filings have been put online in recent years, this information on insider trading has become available to more and more investors.

An examination of the excess returns around both the date the insiders report to the SEC and the date that informa-

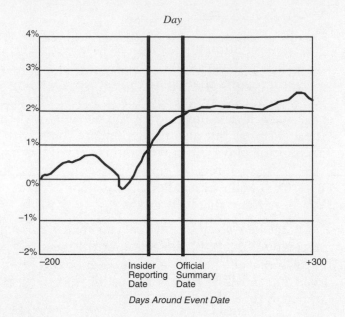

FIGURE 13.9
Abnormal Returns Around Reporting Day/Official Summary Availability Day

The insider reporting date is the date on which the insider files with the SEC. The actual trade may precede this date by a few weeks The official summary date is the date the insider filing is made public.

tion becomes available to investors in the official summary presents an interesting contrast, summarized in Figure 13.9.

Given the opportunity to buy on the date the insider reports to the SEC, investors could have marginal excess returns (of about 1%), but these returns diminish and become close to zero if investors are forced to wait until the official summary date. If you control for transactions costs, there are no excess returns associated with the use of insider trading information.[29]

It is possible that as more and more companies make their filings online, investors will be able to find out about insider trades sooner. It is not clear, though, that will translate into higher returns, since all investors will have access to this data. The key to success when following insiders is timely trading. Investors may well find that imperfect indicators of insider trading such as jumps in trading volume may offer more promise than waiting for the SEC filings to be made public.

EARNINGS REVISIONS

The limitation of an earnings momentum strategy is its dependence on two of the weakest links in financial markets: earnings reports that come from firms and analyst forecasts of these earnings. In recent years, investors have become increasingly aware not only of the capacity of firms to manage their earnings but also to manipulate them with questionable accounting ploys. At the same time, investors have discovered that analysts' forecasts may be biased by their closeness to the firms they follow and their investment banking relationships. To the extent that analysts influence trades made by their clients, they are likely to affect prices when they revise earnings. The more influential they are, the greater the effect they will have on prices, but the question is whether the effect is lasting. If earnings numbers are being manipulated by firms and analysts are biased in their estimates, price changes around earnings estimate revisions are likely to be fleeting.

Trading on earnings estimate revisions is a short-term strategy that yields fairly small excess returns over investment horizons ranging from a few weeks to a few months. The increasing skepticism of markets toward both earnings reports from firms and forecasts by analysts bodes ill for these strategies. While forecast revisions and earnings surprises by themselves are unlikely to generate lucrative portfolios, they can augment other, more long-term, screening strategies. One way you may be able to earn higher returns from this strategy is to identify key analysts who are both independent and influential and then build an investment strategy around forecast revisions made by them, rather than looking at consensus estimates made by all analysts.

ANALYST RECOMMENDATIONS

One of the key issues that equity research analysts were confronted with in the aftermath of the bursting of the dot-com bubble is the extent to which recommendations were perceived to be driven not by views on the stock itself but as cheerleading for investment banking business done by the firms followed by the analysts. A test of this proposition[30] looks at the stock price performance of buy recommendations after initial public offerings and compares recommendations made by analysts who work for the underwriters on these offerings to recommendations from analysts who do not. The findings are summarized in Figure 13.10.

Note that stock prices for recommendations made by nonunderwriters do significantly better than the market, but the stocks recommended by underwriters (in those stocks) tend to do poorly. While this may seem obvious, many investors in the late nineties deliberately overlooked the connections between analysts and the firms that they analyzed and paid a significant price for it.[31]

To incorporate analyst recommendations into an investment strategy, you need to adopt a nuanced approach. You

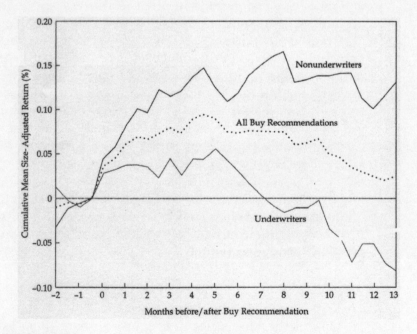

FIGURE 13.10

Performance Comparison for Companies Receiving New Buy Recommendations Within One Year of IPO: 1990–1991

Based on data from Michaely and Womack (1999).

should begin by identifying the analysts who are not only the most influential but also have the most content (private information) in their recommendations. In addition, you may want to screen out analysts whose potential conflicts of interest are too large for the recommendations to be unbiased. How does one go about finding the best analysts following a stock? Do not fall for the hype. The highest-profile analysts are not always the best, and some analysts are notorious for self-promotion. The best sources of information on analysts tend to be outside services without an axe to grind. For instance, the *Wall Street Journal* has a special section on sell-side equity research analysts, in which it evaluates analysts on the quality of their recommendations and ranks them on that basis. A few online services track equity research forecasts and recommendations and report on how close actual earnings numbers were to their forecasts. There are qualitative factors to consider as well. Analysts who have clear, well-thought-out analyses that show a deep understanding of the businesses that they analyze should be given more weight than analysts who make spectacular recommendations based upon facile analysis. Most importantly, good analysts should be just as willing to stand up to the management of companies and disagree with them (and issue sell recommendations).

Once you have identified the analysts that you trust, you should invest according to their recommendations, preferably at the time the recommendations are made.[32] Assuming that you attach credence to the views of these analysts, you should also watch the analysts for signals that they have changed or are changing their minds. Since these signals are often subtle, you can easily miss them.

LESSONS FOR INVESTORS

If you decide to follow the experts, the evidence presented in this chapter provides some pointers on how you can improve your odds of success:

■ *Pick your experts well.* Some insiders are more inside than others, and some analysts are more credible than others. The key to an expert-based strategy is to separate the true experts from the charlatans. In the case of insiders, this may mean tracking some insiders (CEOs and directors) more closely than others. With analysts, you may want to look at their history when it comes to revisions and recommendations. Earnings revisions by analysts who have a history of forecasting earnings accurately should be weighted more than analysts who do not have this reputation.

■ *Screen for bias.* Analysts often have multiple objectives, and a buy recommendation from an analyst may sometimes have more to do with maintaining access and investment banking deals than with whether the stock is a good buy. There are two possible screens for bias. One is to consider only analysts who work for entities that have no business relationship with the companies they analyze. The other is to look at the track record of the analyst. Analysts who have a history of standing up to company management and issuing sell recommendations have more credibility than analysts who always seem to find only good things to say about the companies they analyze.

■ *Look for clues of forthcoming activity.* With both insider trading and analyst recommendations, a large portion of the price runup precedes the actual news (insider filing with the SEC or analyst changing a recommendation). While there are no foolproof early warning systems, you can look at trading volume to get a measure of upcoming news. Trading volume will often jump as a result of insider trading, especially in lightly traded companies.

■ *Track closely.* It goes without saying that you should be in possession of insider trading information or analyst recommendations as soon as feasible. This may require an investment in better information systems. For instance, there are paid services that cull through SEC insider filings as soon they are made and provide quick summaries to clients within a few minutes.

■ *Trade quickly.* Once you find out insiders have been buying a stock or that a top analyst has upgraded a stock, you will need to trade quickly. If you want to do other analyses—check pricing multiples or do a discounted cash flow valuation—you should have done this before the fact. For instance, if you want to buy only stocks that trade at less than 20 times earnings, you should screen for those stocks first and prepare a list of companies that meet this criterion. If there is news about insider buying or analyst upgrades with these stocks, you can immediately add them to your portfolios.

CONCLUSION

There are probably more experts, real and self-proclaimed, in the investment business than in any other. They write columns for the financial press, appear on television and write books on how to get rich quickly. Investors follow their advice, content in the belief that these experts know more than they do and are therefore less likely to make mistakes.

Expert status can come either from access to better information than is available to other investors or to better processing (models, indicators, etc.) of the same information that others possess. Insiders at firms—top managers and directors—should be able to lay claim to the information advantage, and the evidence suggests that they are able to use it to advantage. Stocks with significant insider buying are much more likely to go up than are stocks with substantial insider selling. The time lag between insider trading and reporting makes it more difficult for individual investors to replicate their success. Analysts affect stock prices when they make recommendations on which stocks to buy and which to sell and when they revise estimates of how much these firms will earn in the next quarter. In either case, the bulk of the reaction occurs on the recommendation/revision but there is evidence of a price drift after the announcement. In other words, prices tend to continue to increase in the days or weeks after a buy recommendation or an upward revision in earnings.

Analysts with more investor following and credibility have a bigger price impact than less followed analysts with clear conflicts of interest.

As investors, you should focus on the real experts (inside insiders and unbiased analysts), track their words and actions closely, and trade promptly after you find out their views. If you succeed, you will have a short-term investment strategy with high transactions costs but your returns will cover these costs and leave you with a profit.

ENDNOTES

1. Jaffe, J., 1974, *Special Information and Insider Trading*, Journal of Business, v47, 410–428.

2. See Finnerty, J. E., 1976, *Insiders and Market Efficiency,* Journal of Finance, v31, 1141–1148; Rozeff, M., and M. Zaman, 1988, *Market Efficiency and Insider Trading: New Evidence,* Journal of Business, v61, 25–44; Seyhun, H. N., 1998, *Investment Intelligence from Insider Trading,* MIT Press, Cambridge.

3. Lakonishok, J., and I. Lee, 1998, *Are Insiders' Trades Informative?* Working Paper, Social Sciences Research Network.

4. Bettis, J., D. Vickrey, and Donn Vickrey, 1997, *Mimickers of Corporate Insiders Who Make Large Volume Trades,* Financial Analyst Journal, v53, 57–66.

5. Bettis, J. C., J. M. Bizjak and M. L. Lemmon, 2002, *Insider Trading in Derivative Securities: An Empirical Investigation of Zero Cost Collars and Equity Swaps by Corporate Insiders,* Working Paper, Social Sciences Research Network.

6. It is for this reason that the SEC tracks trading volume. Sudden increases in volume often trigger investigations of insiders at firms.

7. Ke, B., S. Huddart and K. Petroni, 2002, *What Insiders Know About Future Earnings and How They Use It: Evidence from Insider Trades,* Working Paper, Social Sciences Research Network.

8. You generally face legal jeopardy when you sell in the quarter or two before the news announcement.

9. Sell-side analysts work for brokerage houses and investment banks and their research is offered to clients of these firms as a service. In contrast, buy-side analysts work for institutional investors and their research is generally proprietary.

10. Crichfield, T., T. Dyckman and J. Lakonishok, 1978, *An Evaluation of Security Analysts Forecasts,* Accounting Review, v53, 651–668.

11. O'Brien, P., 1988, *Analysts Forecasts as Earnings Expectations,* Journal of Accounting and Economics, v10, 53–83.

12. Dreman, D. N., and M. Berry, 1995, *Analyst Forecasting Errors and Their Implications for Security Analysis,* Financial Analysts Journal, May/June, 30–41.

13. Chopra, V. K., 1998, *Why So Much Error in Analyst Forecasts?,* Financial Analysts Journal, Nov/Dec, 35–42.

14. Higgins, H. N., 1998, *Analyst Forecasting Performance in Seven Countries,* Financial Analysts Journal, May/June, v54, 58–62.

15. Cragg, J. G., and B. G. Malkiel, 1968, *The Consensus and Accuracy of Predictions of the Growth of Corporate Earnings,* Journal of Finance, v23, 67–84.

16. Vander Weide, J. H., and W. T. Carleton, 1988, *Investor Growth Expectations: Analysts vs. History,* Journal of Portfolio Management, v14, 78–83.

17. Givoly. D., and J. Lakonishok, 1984, *The Quality of Analysts' Forecasts of Earnings,* Financial Analysts Journal, v40, 40–47.

18. Hawkins, E. H., S. C. Chamberlin, W. E. Daniel, 1984, *Earnings Expectations and Security Prices,* Financial Analysts Journal, September/October, 20–38.

19. Cooper, R. A., T. E. Day and C. M. Lewis, 1999, *Following the Leader: A Study of Individual Analysts Earnings Forecasts,* Working Paper, Social Science Research Network.

20. Capstaff, J., K. Paudyal and W. Rees, 2000, *Revisions of Earnings Forecasts and Security Returns: Evidence from Three Countries,* Working Paper, Social Science Research Network.

21. Womack, K., 1996, *Do Brokerage Analysts' Recommendations Have Investment Value?* Journal of Finance, v51, 137–167.

22. This can be a significant factor. When the *Wall Street Journal* publishes its Dartboard column, it reports on the stocks being recommended by the analysts its picks. These stocks increase in price by about 4% in the two days after they are picked but reverse themselves in the weeks that follow.

23. Metrick, A., 1999, *Performance Evaluation with Transactions Data: The Stock Selection of Investment Newsletters,* Journal of Finance, v54, 1743–1775. This study examined the returns you would have made as an investor if you followed the investment advice in these newsletters. Metrick used a variety of models to adjust for risk and came to the same conclusion (that you could not have made money following the advice in the newsletters) with every model.

24. One of the earliest was by Fischer Black, titled *Yes, Virginia, There is Hope: Tests of the Value Line Ranking System* (Financial Analysts Journal, v29, 10–14). As an avid believer in efficient markets, Black was surprised to see that following the Value Line rankings would have generated excess returns. A more recent study by Choi in 2000 concluded that while the Value Line rankings make some excess returns, these excess returns do not survive transactions costs. (Choi, J. J., *The Value Line Enigma: The Sum of the Known Parts,* Journal of Financial and Quantitative Analysis, v35).

25. Value Line categorizes firms into five classes in terms of what it calls timeliness, with 1 being best and 5 being worst.

26. Desai, H., and P. C. Jain, 1995, *An Analysis of the Recommendations of the Superstar Money Managers at the Barron's Roundtable,* Journal of Finance, v50, 1257–1273. They examined the 1599 buy recommendations contained in the Barron's roundtable publications from 1968 to 1991.

27. To be clear, if insider holdings increase from 4% of outstanding stock to 5%, it is categorized as a 25% increase in holdings.

28. Consider a stock with five analysts. If three analysts have a strong buy recommendation and two have a buy recommendation, you would assign a score of 1 to each of the strong

buy recommendations and a score of 2 to each of the buy recommendations. The weighted score for this stock would be 1.4.

$$\text{Weighted Score} = (1 * 3 + 2 * 2) / 5 = 1.4$$

This stock would be categorized as a strong buy. If the weighted score had been 1.6, the stock would be categorized as a buy.

29. This is also the conclusion drawn by Seyhun (1986) and Rozeff and Zaman (1988), referenced earlier in the chapter.

30. Michaely, R., and K. L. Womack, *Conflicts of Interests and the Credibility of Underwriter Analysts Recommendation,* Review of Financial Studies, Winter, 635–686.

31. In June 2002, Merrill Lynch agreed to pay $100 million to settle with New York State, after the state uncovered emails sent by Henry Blodgett, Merrill's well-known Internet analyst, that seemed to disparage stocks internally as he was recommending them to outside clients. The fact that many of these stocks were being taken to the market by Merrill added fuel to the fire. Merrill agreed to make public any potential conflicts of interest it may have on the firms followed by its equity research analysts.

32. This might not be your choice to make since analysts reveal their recommendations first to their clients. If you are not a client, you will often learn about the recommendation only after the clients have been given a chance to take positions on the stock.

14

IN THE LONG TERM ...
MYTHS ABOUT MARKETS

IF YOU WAIT LONG ENOUGH...

Sarah was a patient woman. She believed that good things came to those who waited long enough, and she was therefore not upset when she opened up the statements from her broker and discovered that she had lost 20% over the previous year on her pension fund investments. "It is only a paper loss," she told herself, "and stocks always come back in the long term." In fact, she had read somewhere that stocks had never done worse than bonds over any ten-year period in history and that stocks tended to bounce back after bad years. Since she had thirty years left to retirement, she did not worry about her losses.

Sarah's faith in the long term was shaken when she talked to her good friend Kazumi Kawamoto. Kazumi had grown up in Japan and had been saving for retirement in the Japanese stock market. She had accumulated a substantial amount in her portfolio by 1989 and was looking forward to early retirement a decade later. Unfortunately, the market plummeted in the 1990s and her portfolio declined in value by 75% over the next 15 years. Comforted at every stage by brokers who told her that stocks always won in the long term, Kazumi was now confronted with the reality that she would never make her money back and that early retirement was not an option. Realizing that stocks can lose even in the very long term, Sarah moved some of her retirement money into bonds.

Moral: Stocks don't always win in the long term.

The chapters so far have looked at sales pitches that revolve around picking the best stocks in the market, but the most powerful investment myths in investing are about the overall stock market. In this chapter, you will consider a few of these myths and the damage that believing in them can do to investors. The first and most deadly myth is that stocks always beat bonds in the long term. Following this line of reasoning, stocks become riskless to investors with long time horizons. The second myth is that market timing beats stock picking when it comes to stock returns. Buying into this belief, investors spend far more time than they should thinking about which way the market is going to move and too little picking the right stocks for their portfolios. The third myth is that market timing is easy to do and that lots of investors are successful market timers.

CORE OF THE STORY

STOCKS ALWAYS WIN IN THE LONG TERM

Many investment advisors and experts claim that while stocks may be risky in the short term, they are not in the long term. In the long term, they argue, stocks always beat less risky alternatives. As evidence, they point to the history of financial markets in the United States and note that stocks have earned a higher return than corporate or treasury bonds over any 20-year period that you look at since 1926. They then draw the conclusion that if you have a long enough time horizon (conservatively, this would be 20 years), you will always generate a higher ending portfolio value investing in stocks than in alternatives.

It is not just individual but also professional investors who have bought into this sales pitch. Following these pied pipers of equity, younger workers have invested all of their pension fund savings in stocks. After all, a 35 year-old investor will not be accessing her pension fund investment for another 30 years, a time horizon that should make stocks essentially riskless. Companies have reconfigured the contributions they make to pension plans on the assumption that pension plans will be invested predominantly or entirely in equities. By making this assumption of higher equity returns, they are able to lower their contributions and report higher earnings. State and local governments have used the same assumptions to meet budget constraints.

Aggravating the problem is the shifting definition of long term. While a conservative advisor may mean 20 years or longer when he talks about long term, more aggressive investors and advisors reduce this number, arguing that while stocks may not beat bonds over every 5-year or 10-year period in history, they come out ahead so often (again based upon the data from the U.S. equity markets in the 20th century), they are safe. During bull markets, investors are all too willing to listen and invest a disproportionately large amount of their savings, given their ages and risk preferences, in equities. It should come as no surprise that books and articles pushing the dominance of equity as an investment class peaked in 1999 at the height of one of the great bull markets of all time.

THEORETICAL ROOTS: MARKET TIMING

Hindsight is the most powerful weapon in the arsenal of those selling market timing. Consider, they say, how much money you could have made if you had bought into the NASDAQ in 1992 and got out at the end of 1999. The essence of market timing is that it lets you capture upside risk and avoid downside risk. This section looks at two widely made claims about timing equity markets.

MARKET TIMING TRUMPS STOCK SELECTION

In a 1986 article, a group of researchers[1] raised the shackles of many an active portfolio manager by estimating that as much as 93.6% of the variation in quarterly performance at professionally managed portfolios could be explained by asset allocation, that is, the mix of stocks, bonds and cash at these portfolios.[2] A different study in 1992 examined the effect on annual returns of an investor being able to stay out of the market during bad months.[3] It concluded that an investor who would have missed the 50 weakest months of the market between 1946 and 1991 would have seen his or her annual returns almost double, from 11.2% to 19%. In an assessment of the relative importance of asset allocation and security selection of 94 balanced mutual funds and 58 pension funds, all of which had to make both asset allocation and security selection decisions, about 40% of the differences in returns across funds could be explained by asset allocation decisions and 60% by security selection.[4] When it comes to the level of returns, almost all the returns can be explained by the asset allocation decision. Collectively, these studies suggest that the asset allocation decision has important consequences for your returns, and its importance increases with your time horizon.

While how much of actual portfolio returns are due to asset allocation is open to debate, there can be no denying that market timing has a much bigger and speedier payoff than stock selection. It should come as no surprise that investors who have been disappointed with their stock selection skills turn to or at least try market timing in the hope of earning these high returns. Professional money managers are not immune from the allure of market timing either. To the extent that mutual fund managers believe that they can time stock markets, they will adjust how much they hold in cash and stocks. Thus, portfolio managers who believe that the stock market is overvalued and is ripe for a correction will hold a substantial portion of their portfolios in cash.

MARKET TIMING WORKS

There is a widely held belief that lots of indicators can predict future market movements. Some of these indicators are crude but have popular appeal. A common example shows up every January around the time of the Super Bowl. If a team from the old American Football Conference wins the Super Bowl, you will be told, it will be a bad year for the stock market. Other indicators are more sophisticated and follow economic logic. If markets are driven by the economy and interest rates, it seems logical that you should be able to use the level of interest rate or the rate of growth in Gross Domestic Product to forecast what will happen to the market in the following period. Still other indicators are based upon extending measures that work for individual companies. If companies that trade at low multiples of earnings are cheap, then markets that trade at low multiples of earnings, relative to other markets or their own history, must also be cheap. Whatever the indicator, though, the underlying thesis is that it can be used to decide when to go into stocks and when to get out.

Closely linked to these indicators is the assumption that other investors are successful as market timers. This explains the attention that market strategists at investment banks attract when they come out with their periodic views on the right asset allocation mix; the more bullish (bearish) a strategist, the greater (lesser) the allocation to equities. This also explains why the dozens of investment newsletters dedicated to market timing continue to prosper.

Why are so many investors willing to believe that market timing works? It may be because it is so easy to find market-timing indicators that work on past data. If you have a great deal of historical data on stock prices and a powerful enough computer, you could potentially find dozens of indicators (out of the hundreds that you try out) that seem to work. Using the same approach, most market-timing newsletters purport to show that following their investment advice would have generated extraordinary returns on hypothetical portfolios over time. It may also be because professional market timers are masters at self-promotion, telling everyone in the market when they are right and fading into the background when they are wrong.

LOOKING AT THE EVIDENCE

To examine the myths about market timing, you have to look at history. Organized equity markets in the United States have been around for more than a century and it is not surprising that much of the work done on market timing is based upon looking at their performance. This section looks at how stocks have done, relative to alternative investments over very long periods. It follows up by looking at whether the indicators that purport to time markets and the investors who claim to be market timers actually are successful.

DO STOCKS ALWAYS WIN IN THE LONG TERM?

Consider what all investors are told about investing in stocks. If you have a short time horizon, say, a year or less, stocks will generate higher expected returns but they are also far riskier than bonds. The risk implies that stocks can do much worse than bonds during the period. If you have a longer time horizon, stocks supposedly become less risky; you can have a bad year in which stocks do badly but there will be good years in which they more than compensate. Over these longer time horizons, you will be told that stocks almost always do better than less risky alternatives.

This story clearly has some intuitive appeal, but does the evidence back it up? The answer provided by those who tell this story is to point to the equity market returns in the United States over the 20th century. In fact, the most widely used equity market data for the United States comes from a service in Chicago called Ibbotson Associates and covers the U.S. equity market from 1926 to the present. Ibbotson's data suggests that stocks, on average, earn about 6% to 7% more than treasury bonds and bills during this period.

For a closer and more detailed look at equity returns, the period was extended to go back to 1871 and stock returns were examined through the present.[5] Figure 14.1 presents the year-by-year equity returns for the entire period.

While stocks, across the period, have been winners, there have been extended periods of market malaise and very negative returns—the early 1930s and the 1970s—and there are many years of negative stock returns. In fact, stock market

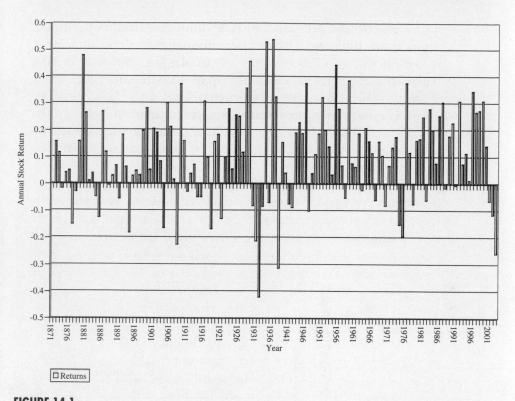

FIGURE 14.1

Stock Returns in the United States: 1871–2002

Data from Professor Shiller's web site. These are the annual returns on stocks from 1871 to 2002.

returns are negative in about one out every four years and are lower than the treasury bill rate one out of every three years.

Proponents of stocks would point out that stocks are risky in the short term but that they are not in the long term. Using 10-year holding periods, the compounded annual returns were computed for every 10-year period beginning in 1871. To allow for the fact that investors could begin investing in any of the intermediate years, overlapping 10-year periods are considered: 1871 to 1881, 1872 to 1882 and so on until 1992 to 2002. There are 121 overlapping 10-year periods between 1871 and 2002. Figure 14.2 presents the distribution of the compounded annual returns you would have earned over 10-year periods investing in stocks and treasury bills.

Over 10-year periods, the risk of stocks is smoothed out. There were only two 10-year periods between 1871 and 2002 in which the annual return is negative. The contrast in risk between stocks and treasury bills is also visible in Figure 14.2. Treasury bill returns are centered around 4% to 5%, with the worst 10-year period generating annual returns of between 0% and 1% and the best 10-year period generating annual returns of between 10% and 11%; the best 10-year periods for stocks deliver annual returns in excess of 15%.

Comparing stock returns to bill returns in each 10-year period allows you to judge the two investment alternatives. In Figure 14.3, the differences in compounded annual returns on stocks and bonds in every 10-year period from 1871 to 2002

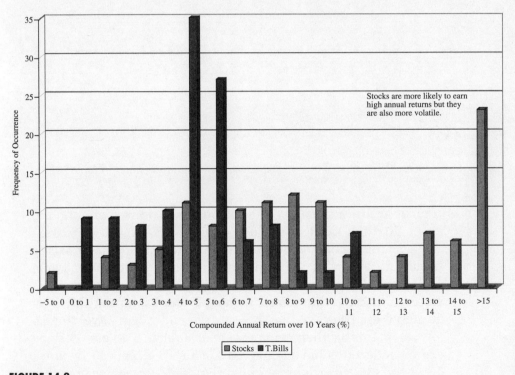

FIGURE 14.2

Annual Returns over 10-year Periods: 1871–2002

Data from Shiller. The number of years in which returns fell into each return class between 1871 and 2002 is reported for both stocks and treasury bills.

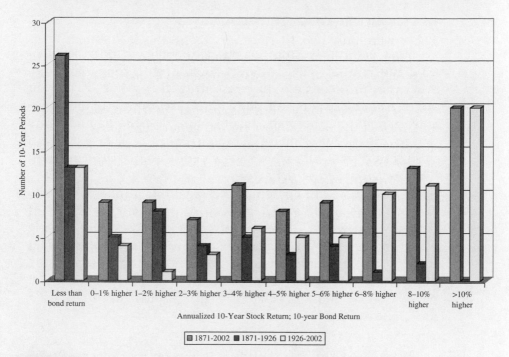

FIGURE 14.3

Stock Returns versus Treasury Bill Returns: Annual Returns over 10-Year Periods

Data from Shiller. This is the difference between the compounded 10-year returns on stocks and the returns on bills computed each year from 1871 and 2002.

are examined to see how often equities deliver higher returns than bills.

There are ninety-five 10-year periods between 1871 and 2002 in which stocks have outperformed bills and twenty-six 10-year periods in which treasury bills have outperformed stocks. Thirteen of these twenty-six periods occur between 1871 and 1926. Since 1945, there has been only one stretch of time[6] during the 1970s in which stocks have underperformed treasuries.

In summary, there is substantial evidence that stocks in the United States have delivered higher returns than treasury bonds or bills over long periods, but there are no guarantees. If you consider the longer history of stock and bill returns, going back to 1871, stocks do worse than bonds even over 10-year periods about 20% of the time.

MARKET TIMING INDICATORS

Most equity investors continue to believe that they can time markets. A substantial portion of the financial press every day is dedicated to presenting the views of market strategists and experts on the future direction of equity markets. In addition, there are dozens of market-timing indicators that investors subscribe to, hoping to gain the elusive edge. In this section, you will review the evidence on market timing indicators and whether they work.

Market timing indicators run the gamut. At one end of the spectrum are nonfinancial indicators such as the winner of the Super Bowl as a forecast of market movements. At the other end are models that apply to entire markets valuation metrics like PE that are used to price individual stocks. In the middle are approaches that track trading volume and price patterns—the tools of chartists—to predict future market movements.

Nonfinancial Indicators. Through the decades, some investors have claimed to foretell the market's future by looking at nonfinancial indicators. Some of these indicators, such as whether the NFC or AFC team wins the Super Bowl are clearly of dubious origin and would fall into a category titled spurious indicators. Other indicators, such as the hemline index, which relates stock prices to the length of hemlines on skirts, fall into the grouping of "feel-good indicators" that measure the overall mood of people in the economy, who after all are both the consumers who act as the engine for the economy and the investors determining prices. Finally, there are the "hype indicators" that measure whether market prices are becoming disconnected from reality.

Spurious Indicators. Millions of investors track what happens to their stocks and to the market every day, and it is not surprising that they find other occurrences that seem to predict what the market will do in the next period. Consider one very widely talked-about indicator: who wins the Super

Bowl.[7] In the 35 years that the Super Bowl has been played, from 1966 to 2001, for 25 years the winner has come from the National Football Conference (or is an old pre-merger NFL team like the Steelers or Colts), and the market has risen in 22 out of the 25 years. In the 10 years that an American Football Conference team has won, the market has fallen seven times. In fact, there are academic researchers who claim that the success rate of 83% (29 out of 35 years) is far too high to be due to chance.[8]

So why not invest in the market after observing who wins the Super Bowl? There are several potential problems. First, it is not true that chance cannot explain this phenomenon. When you have hundreds of potential indicators that you can use to time markets, some will show an unusually high correlation purely by chance. Second, a forecast of market direction (up or down) does not really qualify as market timing, since how much the market goes up clearly does make a difference. Third, you should always be cautious when you can find no economic link between a market-timing indicator and the market. There is no conceivable reason why the winner of the Super Bowl should affect or be correlated with overall economic performance. Indicators such as these may make for amusing anecdotes at parties but can be lethal to your portfolio as market-timing devices.

Feel-Good Indicators. When people feel optimistic about the future, it is not just stock prices that are affected by this optimism. Often, there are social consequences as well, with styles and social mores affected by the fact that investors and consumers feel good about the economy. In the 1920s, you had the Great Gatsby and the go-go years, as people partied and the markets zoomed up. In the 1980s, in another big bull market, you had the storied excesses of Wall Street, documented in books like *Liar's Poker* and movies like *Wall Street.* It is not surprising, therefore, that people have discovered linkages between social indicators and Wall Street. Consider, for instance, a decades-old index, called the hemline index, that finds a correlation between the hemlines on women's skirts and the stock market. This politically incorrect index is based on the notion that shorter dresses and skirts are associated with rising stock prices, whereas longer dresses are predictors of stock market decline. Assuming the index works, you would argue that you are seeing a manifestation of the same phenomenon. As people get more upbeat, fashions do seem to get more daring (with higher hemlines following) and markets also seem to go up. You could undoubtedly construct other indices that have similar correlations. For instance, you should expect to see a high correlation between demand at highly priced restaurants at New York City (or wherever young investment bankers and traders go to celebrate) and the stock market.

The problem with feel-good indicators, in general, is that they tend to be contemporaneous or lagging rather than leading indicators. In other words, the hemlines don't drop before the markets drop but in conjunction with or after a market drop. These indicators are of little use to you as an investor, since your objective is to get out before the market drops and to get in before the market goes up.

Hype Indicators.   It is said that Joseph Kennedy, a well-known speculator in stocks in his own time, knew it was time to get out of the market when he heard his shoeshine boy talking about stocks. In the present time, some people believe that the market peaked when financial channel CNBC's ratings exceeded those of long-running soap operas. In fact, one recent indicator, called the "cocktail party chatter" indicator, tracks three measures: the time elapsed at a party before talk turns to stocks, the average age of the people discussing stocks and the fad component of the chatter. According to the indicator, the less time it takes for the talk to turn to stocks, the lower the average age of the market discussants, and the greater the fad component, the more negative you should be about future stock price movements.

If you consider how a stock market bubble forms, you realize that propagation is critical to bubbles getting bigger. In the media world, this will involve print, television and the Internet and an overflow into day-to-day conversations. Thus, the discussion at the water cooler in a typical business is more likely to be about stocks than about football or other such daily (and more normal) obsessions when markets are buoyant.

While hype indicators, of all nonfinancial indicators, offer the most promise as predictors of the market, they do suffer from several limitations. For instance, defining what constitutes abnormal can be tricky in a world in which standards and tastes are shifting—a high rating for CNBC may indicate too much market hype or may be just reflective of the fact that viewers find financial markets to be both more entertaining and less predictable than a typical soap opera. Even if you decide that there is an abnormally high interest in the market today and you conclude (because of the hype indicators) that stocks are overvalued, there is no guarantee that stocks will not become more overvalued before the correction occurs. In other words, hype indicators may tell you that a market is overvalued, but they don't tell you when the correction will occur.

Technical Indicators.   A number of chart patterns and technical indicators are used by analysts to differentiate between under- and overvalued stocks. Many of these indicators are also used by analysts to determine whether and by how much the entire market is under- or overvalued. In this section, you consider some of these indicators.

Past Prices.   In earlier chapters, you looked at the evidence of negative long-term correlation in stock prices—stocks that have gone up the most in recent periods are more likely to go down in future periods. *The research does not seem to find similar evidence when it comes to the overall market.* If markets have gone up significantly in the most recent years, there is no evidence that market returns in future years will be negative. If you consolidate stock returns from 1871 to 2001 into five-year periods, you find a positive correlation of .2085 between five-year period returns; in other words, positive returns over the last five years are more likely to be followed by positive returns than negative returns in the next five years. Table 14.1 reports the probabilities of an up year and a down year following a series of scenarios, ranging from two down years in a row to two up years in a row and based upon actual stock price data from 1871 to 2001.

TABLE 14.1 Market Performance: 1871–2001

| | | IN FOLLOWING YEAR | |
| | | | |
PRIORS	NUMBER OF OCCURRENCES	% OF TIME STOCK MARKET GOES UP	RETURN ON THE STOCK MARKET
After two down years	19	57.90	2.95%
After one down year	30	60.00	7.76%
After one up year	30	83.33	10.92%
After two up years	51	50.98	2.79%

It is true that markets are more likely to go down after two years of positive performance than under any other scenario, but there is also evidence of price momentum, with the odds of an up year increasing if the previous year was an up year. Does this mean that you should sell all your stocks after two good years? Not necessarily, for two reasons. First, the probabilities of up and down years do change but note that the likelihood of another good year remains more than 50% even after two consecutive good years in the market. Thus, the cost of being out of the market is substantial with this market-timing strategy. Second, the fact that the market is overpriced does not mean that all stocks are overpriced. As a stock picker, you may be able to find undervalued stocks even in an overpriced market.

Another price-based indicator that receives attention at least from the media at the beginning of each calendar year is the *January indicator*. The indicator posits that as January goes, so goes the year—if stocks are up in January, the market will be up for the year, but a bad beginning usually precedes a poor year.[9] According to the venerable Stock Trader's Almanac that is compiled every year by Yale Hirsch, this indicator worked 88% of the time in the 20th century. Note, though, that if you exclude January from the year's returns and compute the returns over the remaining 11 months of the year, the signal becomes much weaker and returns are negative only 50% of the time after a bad start in January. Thus, selling your stocks after stocks have gone down in January may not protect you from poor returns.

Trading Volume.   Some analysts believe that trading volume can be a much better indicator of future market returns than past prices. Volume indicators are widely used to forecast future market movements. In fact, price increases that occur without much trading volume are viewed as less likely to carry over into the next trading period than those that are accompanied by heavy volume. At the same time, very heavy volume can also indicate turning points in markets. For instance, a drop in stocks with very heavy trading volume is called a *selling climax* and may be viewed as a sign that the market has hit bottom. This supposedly removes most of the bearish investors from the mix, opening the market up presumably to more optimistic investors. On the other hand, an increase in stocks accompanied by heavy trading volume may be viewed as a sign that market has topped out. Another widely used indicator looks at the trading volume on puts as a ratio of the trading volume on calls. This ratio, called the *put-call ratio,* is often used as a contrarian indicator. When investors become more bearish, they sell more puts and this (as the contrarian argument goes) is a good sign for the future of the market.

Technical analysts also use *money flow,* which is the difference between the trading volume when stock prices increase (uptick volume) and trading volume when stock prices decrease (downtick volume), as predictor of market movements. An increase in the money flow is viewed as a positive signal for future market movements, whereas a decrease is viewed as a bearish signal. Using daily money flows from July 1997 to June 1998, one study finds that stock prices tend to go up in periods during which money flow increases, which is not surprising.[10] While they find no predictive ability with short period returns—five-day returns are not correlated with money flow in the previous five days—they do find some predictive ability for longer periods. With 40-day returns and money flow over the prior 40 days, for instance, there is a link between high money flow and positive stock returns.

If you extend this analysis to global equity markets, you find that equity markets show momentum; markets that have done well in the recent past are more likely to continue doing well, whereas markets that have done badly remain poor performers.[11] However, the momentum effect is stronger for equity markets that have high trading volume and weaker in markets with low trading volume.

Volatility. In recent years, a number of studies have uncovered a relationship between changes in market volatility and future returns. One study finds that increases in market volatility cause an immediate drop in prices but stock returns increase in subsequent periods.[12] The authors of the study concluded this by assessing daily price volatility from 1897 through 1988 and looking for periods when the volatility has increased or decreased significantly relative to prior periods.[13] The returns both at the time of the volatility change and in the weeks following for both volatility increases and decreases are summarized in Figure 14.4.

Note that volatility increases cause stock prices to drop but that stock prices increase in the following four weeks. With volatility decreases, stock prices increase at the time of the volatility change, and they continue to increase in the weeks after, albeit at a slower pace.

Does this mean that you should buy stocks after an increase in volatility? Not necessarily. The increase in returns in the weeks following a volatility increase may just reflect the reality that stocks are riskier. However, if you believe that a surge in volatility is temporary and that stock volatility will revert to normal levels, a strategy of buying stocks after an increase in equity market volatility may bear fruit.

Other Technical Indicators. A number of nonprice indicators are used by analysts to forecast future market movements. As with stock-specific technical indicators, marketwide indicators are often used in contradictory ways by momentum and contrarian analysts, with an increase in a specific indicator being viewed as bullish by one group and bearish by the other:

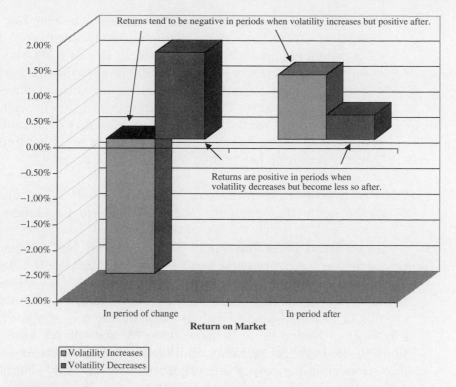

FIGURE 14.4

Returns Around Volatility Changes

Data from Haugen, Talmor and Torous. The returns are computed in the four weeks before and after significant changes in stock market volatility.

- *Price indicators* include many of the pricing patterns that are used by chartists to analyze individual stocks. Just as support and resistance lines and trend lines are used to determine when to move in and out of individual stocks, they can also be used to decide when to move in and out of the stock market.

- *Sentiment indicators* try to measure the mood of the market. One widely used measure is the confidence index, which is defined to be the ratio of the yield on BBB-rated bonds to the yield on AAA-rated bonds. If this ratio increases, investors are becoming more risk averse or at least demanding a higher price for taking on risk, which is negative for stocks. Another indicator that is viewed as bullish for stocks is aggregate insider buying of stocks. When this measure increases, according to its proponents, stocks are more likely to go up.[14] Other sentiment indicators include mutual fund cash positions and the degree of bullishness among investment advisors or newsletters. These are often used as contrarian indicators; an increase in cash in the hands of mutual funds and more bearish market views among mutual funds are viewed as bullish signs for stock prices.[15]

While many of these indicators are used widely, they are mostly backed with anecdotal rather than empirical evidence.

Normal Ranges (Mean Reversion).   Many investors believe that prices tend to revert to what can be called normal levels after extended periods in which they might deviate from these norms. With the equity market, the normal range is defined usually in terms of price-earnings (PE) ratios. Buy if the PE drops below 12 and sell if it rises above 18. You will see variations of this advice in many market timing newsletters. A more academic version of this argument was made by Campbell and Shiller, who looked at PE ratios from 1871 to recent years and concluded that stocks revert to a PE ratio of about 16 times normalized earnings. They defined normalized earnings as the average earnings over the previous 10 years. The implicit belief here is that there is a normal range for PE ratio and that if the PE rises above the top end of the range, stocks are likely to be overvalued, whereas if they fall below the bottom of the range, they are likely to be undervalued. While the approach is straightforward, where does the normal range of PE ratios come from? In most cases, it seems to come from looking at history and attaching a subjective judgment to the upper and lower limits.

Consider Figure 14.5, which presents PE ratios for the S&P 500 going back to 1960.

An attempt was made to draw a normal range for interest rates in the United States, based upon history, though it indicates the subjective judgments that you have to make along

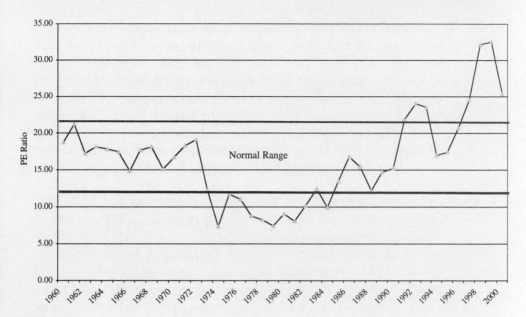

FIGURE 14.5
PE Ratio for S&P 500: 1960–2001

Data from Value Line. The PE ratio is computed for each year for the S&P 500 using the level of the index at the end of each year and the aggregate earnings on the index during the year.

the way. Based upon this band, stocks would be considered as overvalued if they traded at a PE ratio greater than 22 and undervalued if they traded at a PE less than 12.

The limitations of this approach should be obvious. In addition to trusting history to repeat itself, you are making two other assumptions. The first is that you can identify a normal trading range by looking at historical data. As you can see from the graph, you will not get any consensus; someone else looking at this graph might end up with a different band for PE. The second assumption is that the fundamentals have not shifted significantly over time. If interest rates are much lower today than they have been historically, you should expect stocks to trade at much higher PE ratios than they have historically. Under such scenarios, it is dangerous to make investment and market-timing decisions based upon the premise that PE ratios are higher or lower than a normal range.

Market Fundamentals as Indicators. Just as the prices of individual stocks must reflect their cash flows, growth potential, and risk, entire markets (equity, bond and real asset) have to reflect the fundamentals of these assets. If they do not, you can argue that they are misvalued. You can try to time markets by developing simple signals based upon the level of interest rates or the strength of the economy. In this section, you will consider these signals—some old and some new—that have been used by portfolio managers as market-timing tools.

Short-Term Interest Rates. Buy stocks when short-term interest rates (treasury bills) are low and sell them when short-term rates are high, or so goes the conventional wisdom. But is there a basis to this advice? Looking back at history, there is little evidence of any predictive power in the level of rates. Stock prices are just as likely to go up in years when short-term rates are low as they are in years when short-term rates are high. There is, however, some evidence that stocks are more likely to go up if short-term interest rates decline than if they increase. Between 1928 and 2001, for instance, treasury bill rates dropped in 34 years, and stocks earned an average return of approximately 12% in the following years. In the 39 years in which the treasury bill rate increased, stock returns averaged about 10.75% in the following year. This result has been confirmed by research.[16] A closer look at the data does raise cautionary notes about this strategy; the correlation between treasury bill rates and stock market returns was examined in subperiods from 1929 to 2000.[17] This study found that almost all of the predictability of stock market returns comes from 1950 to 1975 and that short-term rates have had almost no predictive power since 1975. It also concludes that short rates have more predictive power with the durable goods sector and with smaller companies than they do with the entire market.

Long-Term Interest Rates. Intuitively, it is the treasury bond rate—the long-term riskless rate—that should have a much stronger impact on stock prices since it offers a direct alternative to investing in stocks for long periods. If you can make 8% by investing in treasury bonds for the next 30 years, why would you settle for less when investing in stocks? Thus, you should expect to see stock prices go up if the treasury bond rate is low and go down, if the rate is high. Figure 14.6 presents a plot of stock returns each year against the T bond rate at the start of the year.

The relationship is murky at best. In 1981, for instance, the treasury bond rate at the start of the year was 14%, but stocks did very well during the year, earning 15%. In 1961, the treasury bond rate at the beginning of the year was 2%, and stocks dropped 11% during the year. There is little evidence of a link between the treasury bond rate at the start of a period and stock returns during that period.

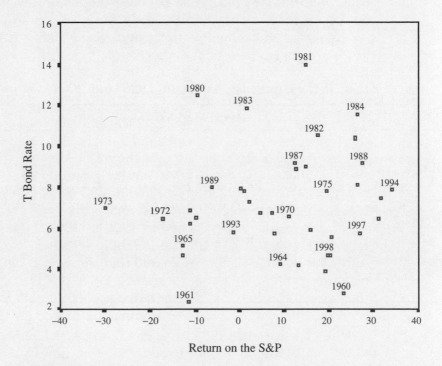

FIGURE 14.6

T Bond Rates and Stock Returns: 1960–2001

Data from Federal Reserve. Each point represents a year, and the stock return in that year is plotted against the treasury bond rate at the start of the year.

This link between treasury bond rates and stock returns may become stronger if you consider how much you can earn as a return on stocks. You could define this return narrowly as the dividend yield (dividends/current stock prices) on the market or use a much broader measure, such as earnings yield, which looks at the overall earnings on the market as a percent of the current level of the index. The earnings yield is the inverse of the price-earnings ratio and is used widely by market strategists as a measure of how equities are priced relative to their earnings. Rather than focus on the level of the treasury bond rate, some market strategists often look at the difference between earnings yields and the treasury bond rate. They believe that it is best to invest in stocks when earnings yields are high relative to the treasury bond rate. To examine this proposition, the difference between the earnings yield and the T bond rate at the end of every year from 1960 to 2000 was estimated and compared to the returns on the S&P 500 in the following year (see Table 14.2).

TABLE 14.2   Earnings Yield, T Bond Rates and Stock Returns: 1960–2001

EARNINGS YIELD— T BOND RATE	NUMBER OF YEARS	STOCK RETURNS			
		AVERAGE	STANDARD DEVIATION	MAXIMUM	MINIMUM
> 2%	8	11.33%	16.89%	31.55%	−11.81%
1% to 2%	5	−0.38%	20.38%	18.89%	−29.72%
0% to 1%	2	19.71%	0.79%	20.26%	19.15%
−1% to 0%	6	11.21%	12.93%	27.25%	−11.36%
−2% to 1%	15	9.81%	17.33%	34.11%	−17.37%
< −2%	5	3.04%	8.40%	12.40%	−10.14%

When the earnings yield exceeds the treasury bond rate by more than 2%, which has occurred in 8 out of the 41 years, the return on the S&P 500 in the following year has averaged 11.33%. However, the returns are almost as good when the earnings yield has lagged the treasury bond rate by 0% to 1%. It is true that the annual returns are only 3.04% in the five years following periods when the earnings yield was lower than the treasury bond rate by more than 2%, but the annual returns were also negative in the five years when the earnings yield exceeded the treasury bond rate by 1%–2%. Thus, there seems to be little historical support for using earnings yield and treasury bond rates to predict future stock market movements.

Business Cycles. As with treasury bonds, there is an intuitive link between the level of stock prices and economic growth. You would expect stocks to do much better in economic booms than during recessions. What makes this relationship tricky, however, is that market movements are based upon predictions of changes in economic activity in the future, rather than levels of activity. In other words, you may see stock prices rising in the depths of a recession if investors expect the economy to begin recovering in the next few months. Alternatively, you may see stock prices drop even in the midst of robust economic growth if the growth does not measure up to expectations. In Figure 14.7, the returns on the S&P 500 index and real GDP growth are graphed, going back to 1960.

There is a positive relationship between GDP growth during a year and stock returns during the year, but there is also a lot of noise in the relationship. For instance, the worst single year of stock returns was 1931, when GDP dropped by about 7%. The best year of stock returns was 1954, but GDP declined slightly that year. The same dichotomy exists during years of positive GDP growth; stock returns dropped in 1941 even though the economy grew strongly that year, but returns in 1995 were very positive as GDP grew about 4% that year. Even if the relationship were strong enough to pass muster, you cannot use it for market timing unless you can forecast real economic growth. The real question then becomes whether you can make forecasts of future stock market movements after observing economic growth in the last year. To examine whether there is any potential payoff to investing after observing economic growth in the prior year, let's look at the relationship between economic growth in a year and

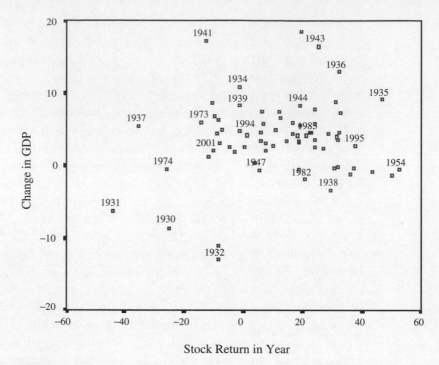

FIGURE 14.7
GDP Growth and Stock Returns

Data from Federal Reserve. Each point represents a year, and the stock return in that year is plotted against GDP growth during the year.

stock returns in the following year, using data from 1929 to 2001, as shown in Table 14.3.

TABLE 14.3 Real Economic Growth as a Predictor of Stock Returns: 1960–2001

		STOCK RETURNS IN NEXT YEAR			
GDP ANNUAL GROWTH	NUMBER OF YEARS	AVERAGE RETURN	STANDARD DEVIATION IN RETURNS	BEST YEAR	WORST YEAR
> 5%	23	10.84%	21.37%	46.74%	−35.34%
3.5%–5%	22	14.60%	16.63%	52.56%	−11.85%
2%–3.5%	6	12.37%	13.95%	26.64%	−8.81%
0%–2%	5	19.43%	23.29%	43.72%	−10.46%
< 0%	16	9.94%	22.68%	49.98%	−43.84%
All years	72	12.42%	19.50%	52.56%	−43.84%

There seems to be no clearly discernible relationship between returns next year and GDP growth this year. It is true that the years with negative GDP growth are followed by the lowest stock returns, but the average stock returns in this scenario are barely higher than the average returns you would have earned if you had bought after the best economic growth years (growth exceeds 5%).

If you can forecast future growth in the economy, it can be useful at two levels. One is in overall market timing, since you will steer more of your funds into stocks before better-than-expected economic growth and away from stocks when you foresee the economy slowing. You can also use the information to overinvest in those sectors that are most sensitive to the economic cycle—automobile and housing stocks, for instance—if you believe that robust economic growth is around the corner.

MARKET TIMERS

While a variety of ways of timing markets have been looked at, a more fundamental question has not been asked: Do those who claim to time markets actually succeed? This section looks at the performance of market timers—portfolio managers, investment newsletters, and market strategists.

Mutual Fund Managers. Most equity mutual funds do not lay claims to market timing, but they do try to time markets at the margin by shifting their assets in and out of cash. You will begin by looking at whether they succeed on average. Some mutual funds claim market timing as their primary skill; these funds are called tactical asset allocation funds. You will look at the track records of these funds and pass judgment on whether their claims hold up.

How do you know that mutual funds try to time markets? While all equity mutual funds need to hold some cash—investments in treasuries and commercial paper—to meet redemption needs and for day-to-day operations, they collectively hold much more cash than is necessary. In fact, the only explanation for the cash balances that you observe at equity mutual funds is that mutual funds use them to signal their views of future market movements: they hold more cash when they are bearish and less cash when they are bullish. In Figure 14.8, the average cash balance at mutual funds is presented for each year from 1980 to 2001, along with the returns on the S&P 500 each year.

Note that the cash balances seem to increase after bad years for the market and decrease after good years, but there is little predictive power in the level of cash holdings. The question of whether mutual funds are successful at market timing has been examined widely in the literature going back four decades.

Other studies have looked at whether mutual funds succeed at shifting their money into higher beta stocks[18] just before equity markets surge and at whether mutual funds earn higher returns in years in which the market does well, but these studies have found little evidence of market timing prowess on the part of mutual funds.[19]

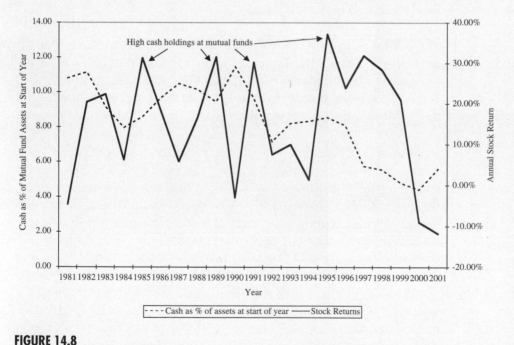

FIGURE 14.8
Mutual Fund Cash Holding and Stock Returns
In each year, the stock return in that year and the cash holdings at mutual funds at the end of the year are shown.

Tactical Asset Allocation Funds and Other Market-Timing Funds. In the aftermath of the crash of 1987, a number of mutual funds sprang up, claiming that they could have saved investors the losses from the crash by steering them out of equity markets before the crash. These funds were called tactical asset allocation funds and made no attempt to pick stocks. Instead, they argued that they could move funds between stocks, treasury bonds and treasury bills in advance of major market movements and allow investors to earn high returns. Since 1987, though, the returns delivered by these funds has fallen well short of their promises. Figure 14.9 compares the returns on a dozen large tactical asset allocation funds over 5-year and 10-year periods (1987–1998) to both the overall market and to fixed mixes: 50% in both stocks and bonds, and 75% stocks/25% bonds. The last two are called

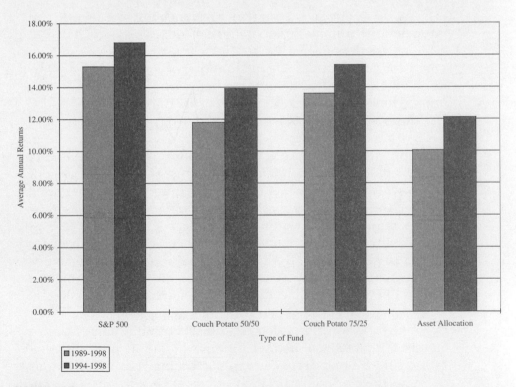

FIGURE 14.9

Performance of Unsophisticated Strategies vs. Asset Allocation Funds

The couch potato strategies represent fixed allocations (50/50 is always 50% stock and 50% bonds). The average across asset allocation funds is compared to the couch potato strategies.

couch potato mixes, reflecting the fact that an investor is making no attempt to time the market.

One critique of this study may be its focus on a few tactical asset allocation funds. In 1998, an examination[20] of a much larger sample—more than 100 asset allocation funds—between 1990 and 1995 also found little evidence of success at market timing at these funds.

Investment Newsletters. There are hundreds of investment newsletters that investors subscribe to for sage advice on investing. Some of these investment newsletters are centered on suggesting individual stocks for investors but some are directed toward timing the market. For a few hundred dollars, you are told, you too can be privy to private signals of market movements.

An analysis[21] of the market timing abilities of investment newsletters examined the stock/cash mixes recommended in 237 newsletters from 1980 to 1992. If investment newsletters are good market timers, you should expect to see the proportion allocated to stocks increase before the stock market goes up. When the returns earned on the mixes recommended in these newsletters is compared to a buy-and-hold strategy, 183 of the 237 newsletters (77%) delivered lower returns than the buy-and-hold strategy. One measure of the ineffectuality of the market-timing recommendations of these investment newsletters lies in the fact that while equity weights increased 58% of the time before market upturns, they also increased by 53% before market downturns. There is some evidence of continuity in performance, but the evidence is much stronger for negative performance than for positive. In other words, investment newsletters that give bad advice on market timing are more likely to continue to give bad advice than newsletters that gave good advice are to continue giving good advice.[22]

The only hopeful evidence on market timing comes from a study of professional market timers who are investment advisors. These timers provide explicit timing recommendations only to their clients, who then adjust their portfolios accordingly, shifting money into stocks if they are bullish and out of stocks if they are bearish. An examination of the timing calls made by 30 professional market timers who were monitored by MoniResearch Corporation, a service that monitors the performance of such advisors, finds some evidence of market-timing ability.[23] Note, though, that the timing calls were both short term and frequent. One market timer had a total of 303 timing signals between 1989 and 1994, and there were, on average, about 15 signals per year across all 30 market timers. Notwithstanding the high transactions costs associated with following these timing signals, following their recommendations would have generated excess returns for investors.[24]

Market Strategists. The market strategists at major investment banks represent perhaps the most visible symbols of market timing. Their prognostications about the market are widely disseminated not only by their investment banks but also by the media. Abby Cohen (Goldman Sachs), Doug Cliggott (Morgan Chase) and Byron Wien (Morgan Stanley) are all widely known. While much of what market strategists say about markets cannot be easily categorized as bullish or bearish—good market strategists are difficult to pin down when it comes to explicit forecasts—they also make specific recommendations, presented in the *Wall Street Journal,* on preferred asset allocation mixes. Table 14.4 lists the asset allocation mixes recommended by major investment banks in June 2002.

TABLE 14.4   Asset Allocation Mixes; Investment Bank Strategists

FIRM	STRATEGIST	STOCKS	BONDS	CASH
A.G. Edwards	Mark Keller	65%	20%	15%
Banc of America	Tom McManus	55%	40%	5%
Bear Stearns & Co	Liz MacKay	65%	30%	5%
CIBC World Markets	Subodh Kumar	75%	20%	2%
Crédit Suisse	Tom Galvin	70%	20%	10%
Goldman Sachs & Co	Abby Joseph Cohen	75%	22%	0%
J.P. Morgan	Douglas Cliggott	50%	25%	25%
Legg Mason	Richard Cripps	60%	40%	0%

(*continued*)

TABLE 14.4 Asset Allocation Mixes; Investment Bank Strategists (*Continued*)

FIRM	STRATEGIST	STOCKS	BONDS	CASH
Lehman Brothers	Jeffrey Applegate	80%	10%	10%
Merrill Lynch & Co	Richard Bernstein	50%	30%	20%
Morgan Stanley	Steve Galbraith	70%	25%	5%
Prudential	Edward Yardeni	70%	30%	0%
Raymond James	Jeffrey Saut	65%	15%	10%
Salomon Smith	John Manley	75%	20%	5%
UBS Warburg	Edward Kerschner	80%	20%	0%
Wachovia	Rod Smyth	75%	15%	0%

How do these allocation mixes yield market predictions? One way is to look at the percent allocated to stocks. More bullish market strategists will recommend that a larger proportion of the portfolio be invested in stocks, whereas bearish strategists will overweight cash and bonds. The other way is to look at changes in holdings recommended by the same strategist from period to period: an increase in the proportion allocated to stocks would indicate more bullishness. On both dimensions, the market-timing skills of strategists are questionable. The *Wall Street Journal,* in addition to reporting the asset allocation mixes of strategists, also compares the returns that would have been generated by following each bank's allocation advice to the returns you would have made by being fully invested in stocks over 1-year, 5-year and 10-year periods. To counter the argument that it is unfair to compare a 100% equity portfolio to a asset allocation mix, the *Journal* also reports on the returns on a robot mix—a fixed allocation across stocks, bonds and bills. Figure 14.10 summarizes the returns on all three, as well as the returns you would have earned by following the strategist who had the best mixes over the period and the one with the worst mixes.

Note that the returns on the robot mix are higher than the average returns generated by following the average market strategists. Of the 16 banks that the *Wall Street Journal* tracks, only five would have generated returns higher than the robot mix over the period and even those would have been well within a statistical margin for error. Finally, even the best

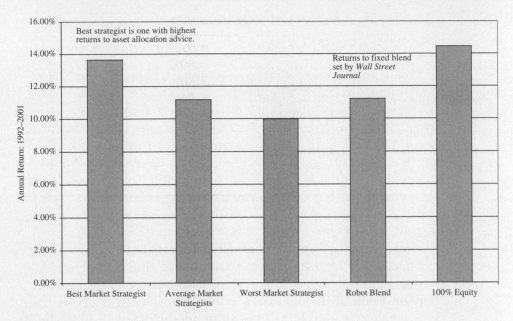

FIGURE 14.10

Annual Return from Market Strategists' Mixes: 1992–2001

Data from *Wall Street Journal.* These are the annual returns you would have made between 1992 and 2001 by following the asset allocation advice offered by market strategists at major investment banks.

strategist's asset mix would have underperformed a strategy of being fully invested in stocks. Overall, the evidence indicates that the market-timing skills of leading market strategies are vastly overstated.

MORE TO THE STORY

The evidence on stock market timing is decidedly mixed. While some timing indicators seem to offer promise in predicting market direction, those who use them do not earn excess returns. How do you explain this contradiction? In this section, you will look at the reasons why an unshakeable faith in equity markets in the long term can be dangerous and why market-timing indicators do not pay off for most investors.

STOCKS ARE NOT RISKLESS
IN THE LONG TERM

In bear markets, you do not have to spend much time convincing investors that investing in stocks is risky, but a prolonged and strong bull market often leads these same investors to the conclusion that equity is not risky, at least in the long term. Earlier in the chapter, you examined some of the evidence, primarily from the U.S. market since 1926, used to sustain this point of view. In this section, you will evaluate the evidence from other equity markets in the world to see if it backs up the evidence in the United States.

Survivor Market Bias. One of the problems with extrapolating the findings from the U.S. equity market in the 20th century is that the United States was perhaps the most successful economy and market in the world in that century. In other words, you have a selection bias. To provide an analogy with individual stocks, this would be the equivalent of picking the top ten companies in the United States, in terms of market capitalization today, and examining whether you would have made money investing in these companies. The answer, not surprisingly, will be yes since these companies acquired their large market capitalization status by being successful over long periods.

To provide some balance, therefore, you have to look at the returns investors in equities would have earned in other (and less successful) equity markets. The most detailed look at these returns estimated the returns you would have earned on 14 equity markets between 1900 and 2001 and compared these returns with those you would have earned investing in bonds.[25] Figure 14.11 presents the risk premiums, that is, the additional returns, earned by investing in equity over treasury bills and bonds over that period in each of the 14 markets.

While equity returns were higher than what you would have earned investing in government bonds or bills in each of the countries examined, there are wide differences across countries. If you had invested in Spain, for instance, you would have earned only 3% over government bills and 2% over government bonds annually basis by investing in equities. In

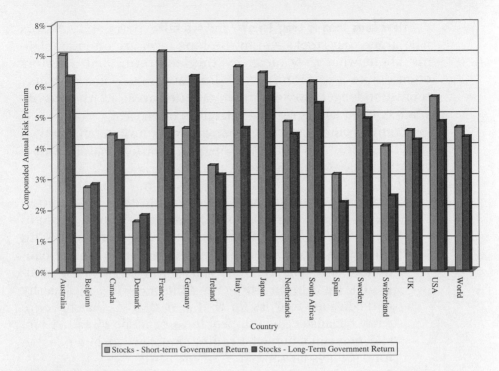

FIGURE 14.11

Equity Risk Premiums: By Country

Data from Dimson et al. The differences in compounded annual returns between stocks and short-term governments/long-term governments are reported for each country.

France, in contrast, the corresponding numbers would have been 7.1% and 4.6%. Looking at 40- or 50-year periods, therefore, it is entirely possible that equity returns can lag bond or bill returns, at least in some equity markets.

Equity investors therefore have to wonder whether the market they are investing in currently will be one of the winner markets (like the United States in the 20th century) or a lagging market (like the Japanese market since 1989). Since there is a probability that every market (including the U.S. equity market today) can be a lagging market over the next few decades, you should be cautious about investing too much in equities in any particular market. You may be able to improve the odds by investing in a global equity fund, but even there, you can be exposed to risk over long periods.

How Long Term Is Long Term? Financial experts and advisors who argue that stocks win in the long term are often ambiguous about what they mean by the long term, and investors often define long term in very different ways—one year may represent long term for an impatient investor, whereas 20 years may be long term to a patient investor.

Equities clearly are not riskless over one year, but are they close to riskless if you have a 20-year time horizon? Not necessarily, for several reasons:

- *Even long time horizons can be shortened by unanticipated events.* For example, consider the advice given to a 35-year old about her pension fund investments. With 30 years left to retirement, she seems like a perfect candidate for a long-term investment strategy. That is predicated, though, on the belief that she will stay healthy and continue to work for that period. If she has to retire early because of health problems or if she loses her job, she may find herself needing to draw on her pension fund savings far sooner.
- *Investors save over time and they save more in up markets and in their later years.* Assume that you are 35 years old and that you have 30 years until retirement. You will be saving over time for your retirement, and your contributions to your pension fund will tend to get larger as you get older (and closer to retirement). In effect, this will reduce the effective time horizon you have on your investments. In addition, you will tend to save more and invest more in stocks in buoyant stock markets and less in depressed markets. Given the history of the market, this will imply that you will be overinvested in stocks when they are overvalued and underinvested when stocks are a good bargain.
- *Even the most optimistic assessment of the historical data on stock returns can only lead to the conclusion that while there is a high probability that stocks will earn higher returns than less risky alternatives over the long term, there is no guarantee.* In fact, a more realistic evaluation of stock market history, in the United

States and elsewhere, suggests that the probability that equities will underperform government bonds over longer periods is too large to be ignored by investors. Even a 5% probability that stocks will underperform bonds over the long term may be sufficient to induce more risk-averse investors to invest more in bonds and less in stocks.

The perils of investing in equities even with a long time horizon are illustrated when you look at the Japanese equity market over the last 15 years. An investor who invested his wealth in the Nikkei in 1989 when the index peaked at close to 40000 would have lost 80% of his investment by 2003 and is extremely unlikely to recover his losses whole in his lifetime.

MARKET TIMING WORKS ONLY INFREQUENTLY

Why do market timers succeed so infrequently if so many market-timing indicators make money, at least on paper? In this section, you will consider some of the dangers involved with trying to time markets and with following the advice of market gurus.

Hindsight Bias. Market timing always seems simple when you look back in time. After the fact, you can always find obvious signals of market reversals—bull markets turning to bear markets, or vice versa. Thus, in 2001, there were investors who looked back at 1999 and bemoaned the fact that they missed getting out of stocks when the market topped at the end of that year. At that time, though, the signs were not so obvious. There were analysts who argued that the market was overvalued and indicators that supported that point of view, but there were just as many analysts, if not more, who saw the market continuing to rise and had supporting models.

In practice, there is almost never a consensus among investors on whether markets have hit bottom or peaked at the time that it occurs. It is an interesting fact that optimism about the future is greatest just as markets top out and the market mood is darkest just as markets turn around. To succeed at market timing, you cannot wait until a bottom has been established before buying or for a market top before selling. If you do, you will miss much of the subsequent payoff.

Timing of Information. If you are considering timing the market by using macroeconomic variables such as inflation or economic growth, you should also take into account the time lag before you will get this information. Consider, for instance, research that shows that stock prices tend to go up after quarters of high GDP growth. An obvious strategy would be to buy stocks after a quarter of high GDP growth and sell after a quarter of negative or low GDP growth. The problem with the strategy is that the information on GDP growth will not be available to you until you are two months into the next quarter.

If you use a market variable such as the level of interest rates to make your market forecasts, you are in better shape since this information should be available to you contemporaneously with the stock market. In building these models, you should be careful to ensure that you are not building a model by which you will have to forecast interest rates in order to forecast the stock market. To test for a link between the level of interest rates and stock market movements, you would look at the relationship between interest rates at the beginning of each year and stock returns over the year. Since you can observe the former before you make your investment decision, you would have the basis for a viable strategy if you find a correlation between the two. If you had run the test between the level of interest rates at the end of each year and stock returns during the year, implementing an investment strategy even if you find a correlation would be problematic since you would have to forecast the level of interest rates first.

Noise in Forecast. As the evidence in the last section should make clear, no market-timing indicator is perfect or even close to perfect. In fact, the best market timers are right perhaps 60% to 65% of the time, and even then, only about market direction and not magnitude. In other words, a specific indicator, be it the returns in January or the level of interest rates, may give you some indication of whether the market is more likely to go up or down over the rest of the year but not by how much.

Both of these characteristics of market timing indicators— the significant proportion of the time they are wrong in calling market direction and their lack of success at forecasting the size of the market movement—restrict the investment strategies that you can use to time markets. Derivatives such as stock index futures and options, which would generate the highest returns, have to be avoided because the risk of being wrong is too large.

Lack of Consistency.   Market timers are the meteors of the investment universe. While they attract a great deal of attention when they shine, they fade quickly. Looking at the high-profile market timers (market gurus) over time, from Jesse Livermore in the early part of this century to Ralph Acampora, Prudential's flamboyant market strategist, in the 1990s, you find a diverse group.[26] Some were chartists, some used fundamentals and some were mysterious about their methods, but they seem to share three common characteristics:

1. *A capacity to see the world in black and white:* Market gurus do not prevaricate. Instead, they make bold statements that seem outrageous when they make them about where the market will be six months or a year from now. Acampora, for instance, made his reputation with his call that the Dow would hit 7000 when it was at 3500.

2. *A correct call on a big market move:* All market timers make their reputation by calling at least one big market move. For Livermore, it was the market crash of 1929 and for Acampora, it was the bull market of the 1990s.

3. *Outside personalities:* Market gurus are born showmen, who use the media of their time as megaphones to publicize not only their market forecasts but the

news of their successes. In fact, part of their success can be attributed to their capacity to make other investors act on their predictions, making these predictions, at least in the near term, self-fulfilling prophecies.

So why do great market gurus stumble? The same factors that contribute to their success seem to underlie their failures. The absolute conviction they have in their market-timing abilities and their success at timing markets seems to feed into more outrageous calls that ultimately destroy their reputations. Joe Granville, one of the market gurus of the late 1970s, for instance, spent all of the eighties recommending that people sell stocks and buy gold and his newsletter was ranked the worst, in terms of performance, for the decade.

Costs in Transactions, Opportunities, and Taxes. If market timing were costless, you could argue that everyone should try to time markets, given the huge returns to getting it right. There are, however, significant costs associated with trying to time markets (and getting it wrong):

- In the process of switching from stocks to cash and back, you may miss the best years of the market. An article titled "The Folly of Stock Market Timing," examined the effects of annually switching from stock to cash and back from 1926 to 1982 and concluded that the potential downside vastly exceeds the potential upside.[27] In an analysis of market timing, Bill Sharpe suggested that unless you can tell a good year from a bad year 7 times out of 10, you should not try market timing.[28] This result is confirmed by Monte Carlo simulations on the Canadian market, which show that you have to be right 70% to 80% of the time to break even from market timing.[29]
- This research does not consider the additional transactions costs that inevitably flow from market-timing strategies, since you will trade far more extensively if you follow them. In its most extreme version, a stock/cash

switching strategy will mean that you will have to liquidate your entire equity portfolio if you decide to switch
into cash and start from scratch again the next time you
want to be in stocks.

■ A market-timing strategy will also increase your potential tax liabilities. To see why, assume that you have a
strategy of selling your stocks after two good years in
the market, based upon the empirical findings that a
bad year is more likely to follow. You will have to pay
capital gains taxes when you sell your stocks, and over
your lifetime as an investor, you will pay far more in
taxes.

LESSONS FOR INVESTORS

Trying to time markets is a much more daunting task than
picking stocks. All investors try to time markets and very few
seem to succeed consistently. If, notwithstanding this history
of failure, you decide to time markets, you should try to do the
following:

1. *Assess your time horizon.* Some market-timing indicators such as those based upon charting patterns and
trading volume try to forecast market movements in
the short term, whereas other techniques such as
using a normalized PE ratio to predict stock prices are
long-term strategies. You need to have a clear sense of
your time horizon before you pick a market-timing
strategy. In making this judgment, you will need to
look not only at your willingness (or lack thereof) to
wait for a payoff but also at how dependent you are on
the cash flows from your portfolio to meet your living
needs; if your job is insecure and your income is
volatile, your time horizon will shrink.

2. *Examine the evidence.* The proponents of every
market-timing strategy will claim that the strategy

works and present you with empirical evidence of the incredible returns you could have made from following it. When you look at the evidence, you should consider all the caveats from the last section, including the following:

a. Is the strategy being fit back into the same data from which it was extracted? You should be suspicious of elaborate trading strategies that seem to have no economic basis or rationale: buy small-cap stocks with price momentum at 3 p.m. every Thursday and sell at 1 p.m. the next day, for instance. Odds are that thousands of strategies were tested out on a large database and this one emerged. A good test will look at returns in a different time period (called a holdout period).

b. Is the strategy realistic? Some strategies look exceptionally good as constructed but may not be viable since the information on which they are based would not have been available at the time you would have had to trade. You may find, for instance, that you can make money (at least on paper) if you buy stocks at the end of every month, when investors put more money into mutual funds than they take out. The problem, though, is that this information will not be available to you until you are well into the next month.

c. Have execution costs and problems been considered? Many short-term market-timing strategies require constant trading. The trading costs and tax liabilities created by this trading will be substantial, and the returns before these costs are considered have to be substantially higher than a buy-and-hold strategy for the strategy to make sense.

3. *Integrate market timing with security selection.* While many investors consider market timing and security selection to be mutually exclusive, they don't have to be. You can and should integrate both into your overall strategy. You can, for instance, use a volume indicator to decide when and whether to get into equities, and

then invest in stocks with low PE ratios because you believe these stocks are more likely to be undervalued.

CONCLUSION

If you can time markets, you can make immense returns, and it is this potential payoff that makes all investors into market timers. Some investors explicitly try to time markets by using technical and fundamental indicators, whereas others integrate their market views into their asset allocation decisions, shifting more money into stocks when they are bullish on stocks. Looking at the evidence, though, there are no market-timing indicators that deliver consistent and solid returns. In fact, there is little proof that the experts at market timing—market strategists, mutual funds and investment newsletters, for example—succeed at the endeavor.

Notwithstanding this depressing evidence, investors will continue to time markets. If you choose to do so, you should pick a market-timing strategy that is consistent with your time horizon, evaluate the evidence on its success carefully, and try to combine it with an effective stock-selection strategy.

ENDNOTES

1. Brinson, G. L., R. Hood, and G. Beebower, 1986, *Determinants of Portfolio Performance,* Financial Analysts Journal, July/August, 39–44.

2. This is a much quoted and misquoted study. A survey by Nutall and Nutall found that of 50 writers who quoted this study, 37 misread it to indicate that 93% of the total return came from asset allocation. (Nuttall, J. A., and J. Nuttall, 1998, *Asset Allocation Claims—Truth or Fiction?,* Working Paper.)

3. Shilling, A. Gary. *Market Timing: Better Than a Buy-and-Hold Strategy,* v48(2) (March–April 1992), 46–50.

4. Ibbotson, R., and Kaplan, P., 2000, *Does asset allocation explain 40, 90, or 100 per cent of performance?*, Financial Analysts Journal, January/February.

5. This analysis was made possible by the excellent data provided on Robert Shiller's web site.

6. Stocks did worse than T bills in terms of annual returns in each of the 10-year periods ending in the late seventies (1974–1980).

7. For those unfamiliar with the Super Bowl, it is played between the winner of the American Football Conference (AFC) and the winners of the National Football Conference (NFC). It is played on the last Sunday in January.

8. Krueger, T., and W. Kennedy, 1991, *An examination of the Superbowl stock market predictor,* Journal of Finance, v45, 691–697.

9. Note that there are narrower versions of the January indicator, using just the first 5 or 10 days of January.

10. Bennett, J. A., and R. W. Sias, 2001, *Can Money Flows Predict Stock Returns?* Financial Analysts Journal, Nov–Dec, v57, 64–77.

11. Chan, K., A. Hameed and W. Tong, 2000, *Profitability of Momentum Strategies in the International Equity Markets,* Journal of Financial and Quantitative Analysis, v35, 153–172.

12. Haugen, R. A., E. Talmor and W. N. Torous, 1991, *The Effect of Volatility Changes on the Level of Stock Prices and Subsequent Expected Returns,* Journal of Finance, v46, 985–1007.

13. Daily price volatility is estimated over four-week windows. If the volatility in any four-week window exceeds (falls below) the volatility in the previous four-week window (at a statistical significance level of 99%), it is categorized as an increase (decrease) in volatility.

14. See Chowdhury, M., J. S. Howe and J. C. Lin, 1993, *The Relation between Aggregate Insider Transactions and Stock Market Returns,* Journal of Financial and Quantitative Analysis, v28, 431–437. They find a positive correlation between aggregate insider buying and market returns but report that a strategy based upon the indicator would not earn enough to cover transactions costs.

15. See Fisher, K., and M. Statman, 2000, *Investor Sentiment and Stock Returns,* Financial Analysts Journal, March/April, v56, 16–33. They examined three sentiment indicators—the views of Wall Street strategists, investment newsletters and individual investors—and concluded that there is indeed evidence supporting a contrarian investment strategy.

16. Ang, A., and G. Bekaert, 2001, *Stock Return Predictability: Is it there?* Working Paper, Columbia Business School. They documented that treasury bill rates dominate other variables as a predictor of short-term stock market movements. Breen, W., L. R. Glosten and R. Jagannathan, 1989, *Economic Significance of Predictable Variations in Stock Index Returns,* Journal of Finance, v44, 1177–1189, evaluated a strategy of switching from stock to cash, and vice versa, depending upon the level of the treasury bill rate. They concluded that such a strategy would have added about 2% in excess returns to an actively managed portfolio.

17. Abhyankar, A., and P. R. Davies, 2002, *Return Predictability, Market Timing and Volatility: Evidence from the Short Rate Revisited,* working paper, Social Sciences Research Network.

18. See Treynor, Jack L., and Kay Mazuy, 1966, *Can mutual funds outguess the market?* Harvard Business Review, v44, 131–136. They argued that if mutual funds have market-timing skills, they should buy high beta stocks just before up movements in the stock market, since these stocks should up go up even more. Their conclusion was that mutual funds did the exact opposite—moved into high beta stocks just before market declines.

19. Henriksson, Roy D., and Robert C. Merton, 1981, *On market timing and investment performance. II. Statistical procedures for evaluating forecasting skills,* Journal of Business, v54, 513–533.

20. Beckers, C., W. Ferson, D. Myers, and M. Schill, 1999, *Conditional Market Timing with Benchmark Investors,* Journal of Financial Economics, v52, 119–148.

21. Graham, John R., and R. Harvey Campbell, 1996, *Market timing ability and volatility implied in investment newsletters' asset allocation recommendations,* Journal of Financial Economics, v42, 397–421.

22. A good market-timing newsletter is likely to repeat its success about 50% of the time. A poor market-timing newsletter has a 70% chance of repeating its poor performance.

23. Chance, D. M., and M. L. Hemler, 2001, *The performance of professional market timers: Daily evidence from executed strategies,* Journal of Financial Economics, v62, 377–411.

24. The study looked at excess returns after transactions costs but before taxes. By its very nature, this strategy is likely to generate large tax bills, since almost all gains will be taxed at the ordinary tax rate.

25. Dimson, E., P. March and M. Staunton, 2002, *Triumph of the Optimists,* Princeton University Press.

26. One of the best books on Livermore is the classic *Reminiscences of a Stock Market Operator* by Edwin LeFevre, John Wiley and Sons.

27. Jeffrey, R., 1984, *The Folly of Stock Market Timing,* Financial Analysts Journal (July/August), 102–110.

28. Sharpe, W. F., 1975, *Are Gains Likely From Market Timing,* Financial Analysts Journal, v31(2) (March/April), 60–69.

29. Chua, J. H., R. S. Woodward, and E. C. To, 1987, *Potential Gains From Stock Market Timing in Canada,* Financial Analysts Journal (September/October), v43(5), 50–56.

15 Ten Lessons for Investors

While the investment stories examined in this book reflect very different investment philosophies and are designed for a wide range of investors, some lessons can be drawn by looking across the stories. In this chapter, you will see a number of propositions about investing that apply across investment strategies. Hopefully, these broad propositions about investing will stand you in good stead when you are subjected to the next big investment story by an overeager salesperson.

Lesson 1: The more things change, the more they stay the same.

Each of the investment stories listed in this book has been around for as long as there have been financial markets. Notwithstanding this reality, investment advisors rediscover these stories at regular intervals and present them as their own. To provide a façade of novelty, they often give these stories new and fancy names (preferably Greek). Calling a strategy of buying low PE stocks the Omega or the Alpha strategy seems to do wonders for its curb appeal to investors. In addition, as more and more data on stocks becomes available to investors, some investors have become more creative in how they use this data to find stocks. In fact, the ease with which they can screen stocks for multiple criteria—low PE, high growth and momentum—has allowed some investors to create composite screens that they can then label as unique.

Proposition 1: Be wary of complex, fancifully named investment strategies that claim to be new and different.

LESSON 2: IF YOU WANT GUARANTEES, DON'T INVEST IN STOCKS.

No matter what the proponents of an investment strategy tell you, no stock strategy can offer guaranteed success. Stocks are volatile and are driven by hundreds of different variables, some related to the overall economy and some arising as a result of information that has come out about the firm. Even the most elaborate and best-planned strategies for making money in stocks can be derailed by unexpected events.

Proposition 2: The only predictable thing about stocks is their unpredictability.

LESSON 3: NO PAIN, NO GAIN.

It is perhaps the oldest lesson in investments that you cannot expect to earn high returns without taking risk, but it is a lesson that is often ignored. Every investment strategy exposes you to risk, and a high return strategy cannot be low risk. If you are an investor who is uncomfortable with large risk exposures, you should avoid any high-risk strategy, no matter how promising it looks on paper. Why are some investors so willing to delude themselves into thinking that they can earn high returns without taking much risk? One reason may be that the risk in some strategies is hidden and shows up sporadically. These strategies succeed most of the time and deliver solid and modest returns when they do, but create large losses when they fail.

Proposition 3: If you cannot see the risk in a high return strategy, you just have not looked hard enough.

LESSON 4: REMEMBER THE FUNDAMENTALS.

The value of a business has always been a function of its capacity to generate cash flows from its assets, to grow these cash flows over time and the uncertainty associated with these cash flows. In every bull market, investors forget the fundamentals that determine value—cash flows, expected growth and risk—and look for new paradigms to explain why stocks are priced they way they are. This was the case in the technology boom of the late 1990s. Faced with stratospheric prices for new economy companies that could not be explained by conventional approaches, investors turned to dubious models, in which growth in revenues substituted for earnings and cash flows did not matter. In the aftermath of every bull market, investors discover the truth that the fundamentals do matter and that companies have to earn money and grow these earnings to be valuable.

Proposition 4: Ignore fundamentals at your peril.

LESSON 5: MOST STOCKS THAT LOOK CHEAP ARE CHEAP FOR A REASON.

In every investment story in this book, a group of companies is identified as cheap. Early in this book, for instance, companies were categorized as cheap because they traded at low multiples of earnings or below book value. At the risk of sounding like professional naysayers, we should note that most of these companies only looked cheap. There was generally at least one good reason, and in many cases more than one, why these stocks traded at low prices. You saw, for instance, that many stocks that traded at below book value did so because of their poor earning power and high risk and that stocks that traded at low PE ratios did so because of anemic growth prospects.

Proposition 5: Cheap companies are not always good bargains.

LESSON 6: EVERYTHING HAS A PRICE.

Investors are constantly on the lookout for characteristics that they believe make the companies they invest in special—superior management, brand name, high earnings growth and a great product all come to mind. Without contesting that these are good characteristics for a firm to possess, you have to still recognize that markets generally do a good job of pricing-in these advantages. Companies with powerful brand names trade at high multiples of earnings, as do companies with higher expected growth. Thus, the question that you have to answer as an investor is not whether having a strong brand name makes a company more valuable, but whether the price attached to the brand name by the market is too high or too low.

Proposition 6: Good companies may not be good investments.

LESSON 7: NUMBERS CAN BE DECEPTIVE.

For those investors who are tired of anecdotal evidence and investment stories, numbers offer comfort because they provide the illusion of objectivity. A study that shows that stocks with high dividends would have earned you 4% more than the market over the last five years is given more weight than a story about how much money you could have made investing in one stock five years ago. While it is sensible to test strategies by using large amounts of data over long periods, a couple of caveats are in order:

- Studies, no matter how detailed and long term, generate probabilistic rather than certain conclusions. For instance, you may conclude after looking at high dividend paying stocks over the last five years that there is a 90% probability that high dividend stocks generate higher returns than do low dividend stocks, but you will not be able to guarantee this outcome.
- Every study also suffers from the problem that markets change over time. No two periods are exactly identical, and it is possible that the next period may deliver surprises that you have never seen before and that these surprises can cause time-tested strategies to fall apart.

Proposition 7: Numbers can lie.

LESSON 8: RESPECT THE MARKET.

Every investment strategy is a bet against the market. You are not only making a wager that you are right and the market is wrong but that the market will see the error of its ways and come around to your way of thinking. Consider, for instance, a strategy of buying stocks that trade at less than book value. You believe that these stocks are undervalued and that the market is making a mistake in pricing these stocks. To make money, not only do you have to be right about this underlying belief but markets have to see and correct their mistakes. In the process, the prices of these stocks will be pushed up and you as an investor will make money.

While you may be justified in your views about market mistakes, it is prudent to begin with a healthy respect for markets. While markets do make large mistakes in pricing stocks and these mistakes draw attention (usually after the fact), they do an extraordinary job for the most part in bringing together investors with diverse views and information about stocks and arriving at consensus prices. When you do uncover what looks like a market mispricing and an investment opportunity, you should begin with the presumption that the market price is right and that you have missed some critical component in your analysis. It is only after you have rejected all the possible alternative explanations for the mispricing that you should consider trying to take advantage of the mispricing.

Proposition 8: Markets are more often right than wrong.

LESSON 9: KNOW YOURSELF.

No investment strategy, no matter how well thought out and designed it is, will work for you as an investor if it does not match your preferences and characteristics. A strategy of buying stocks that pay high and sustainable dividends may be a wonderful strategy for risk-averse investors with long time horizons who do not pay much in taxes but not for investors with shorter time horizons who pay high taxes. Before you decide to adopt any investment strategy, you should consider whether it is the right strategy for you. Once you adopt it, you should pass it through two tests:

a. *The acid test:* If you constantly worry about your portfolio and its movements keep you awake at nights, you should consider it a signal that the strategy that you just adopted is too risky for you.

b. *The patience test:* Many investment strategies are marketed as long term strategies. If you adopt one of these strategies but you frequently find yourself second-guessing yourself and fine-tuning your portfolio, you just may be too impatient to carry this strategy to fruition.

In the long term, not much that is good—either physically or financially—comes out of these mismatches.

> *Proposition 9: There is no one best investment strategy that fits all investors.*

LESSON 10: LUCK OVERWHELMS SKILL (AT LEAST IN THE SHORT TERM).

The most depressing lesson of financial markets is that virtues such as hard work, patience and preparation do not always get rewarded. In the final analysis, whether you make money or not on your portfolio is only partially under your control and luck can play a dominant role. The most successful portfolio managers of last year, all too often, are not the ones with the best investment strategies but those who (by chance) happened to be at the right place at the right time. It is true that the longer you invest, the more likely it is that luck will start to even out and that your true skills will show through; the most successful portfolio managers of the last 10 years are less likely to get there because they were lucky.

As an investor, you should take both success and failure with a grain of salt. Neither is a reflection of your prowess or lack thereof as an investor or the quality of your underlying investment strategy. While you may not able to manufacture good luck, you should be ready to take advantage of it when it presents itself.

Proposition 10: It pays to be lucky.

CONCLUSION

Beating the market is neither easy nor painless. In financial markets, human beings, with all their frailties, collect and process information and make their best judgments on what assets are worth. Not surprisingly, they make mistakes, and even those who believe that markets are efficient will concede this reality. The open question, though, is whether you can take advantage of these mistakes and do better than the average investor. You can, but only if you do your homework, assess the weaknesses of your investment strategies, and attempt to protect yourself against them. If you have a short time horizon, you will also need luck as an ally.

INDEX

8 reasons why you should read the Financial Times for 4 weeks RISK-FREE!

To help you stay current with significant
developments in the world economy ...
and to assist you to make informed business
decisions — the Financial Times brings you:

1 Fast, meaningful overviews of international affairs ... plus daily briefings on major world news.

2 Perceptive coverage of economic, business, financial and political developments with special focus on emerging markets.

3 More international business news than any other publication.

4 Sophisticated financial analysis and commentary on world market activity plus stock quotes from over 30 countries.

5 Reports on international companies and a section on global investing.

6 Specialized pages on management, marketing, advertising and technological innovations from all parts of the world.

7 Highly valued single-topic special reports (over 200 annually) on countries, industries, investment opportunities, technology and more.

8 The Saturday Weekend FT section — a globetrotter's guide to leisure-time activities around the world: the arts, fine dining, travel, sports and more.

FT FINANCIAL TIMES
World business newspaper

The *Financial Times* delivers
a world of business news.

Use the Risk-Free Trial Voucher below!

To stay ahead in today's business world you need to be well-informed on a daily basis. And not just on the national level. You need a news source that closely monitors the entire world of business, and then delivers it in a concise, quick-read format.

With the *Financial Times* you get the major stories from every region of the world. Reports found nowhere else. You get business, management, politics, economics, technology and more.

Now you can try the *Financial Times* for 4 weeks, absolutely risk free. And better yet, if you wish to continue receiving the *Financial Times* you'll get great savings off the regular subscription rate. Just use the voucher below.

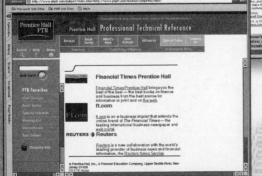